メガトーキョー megatokyo®

③

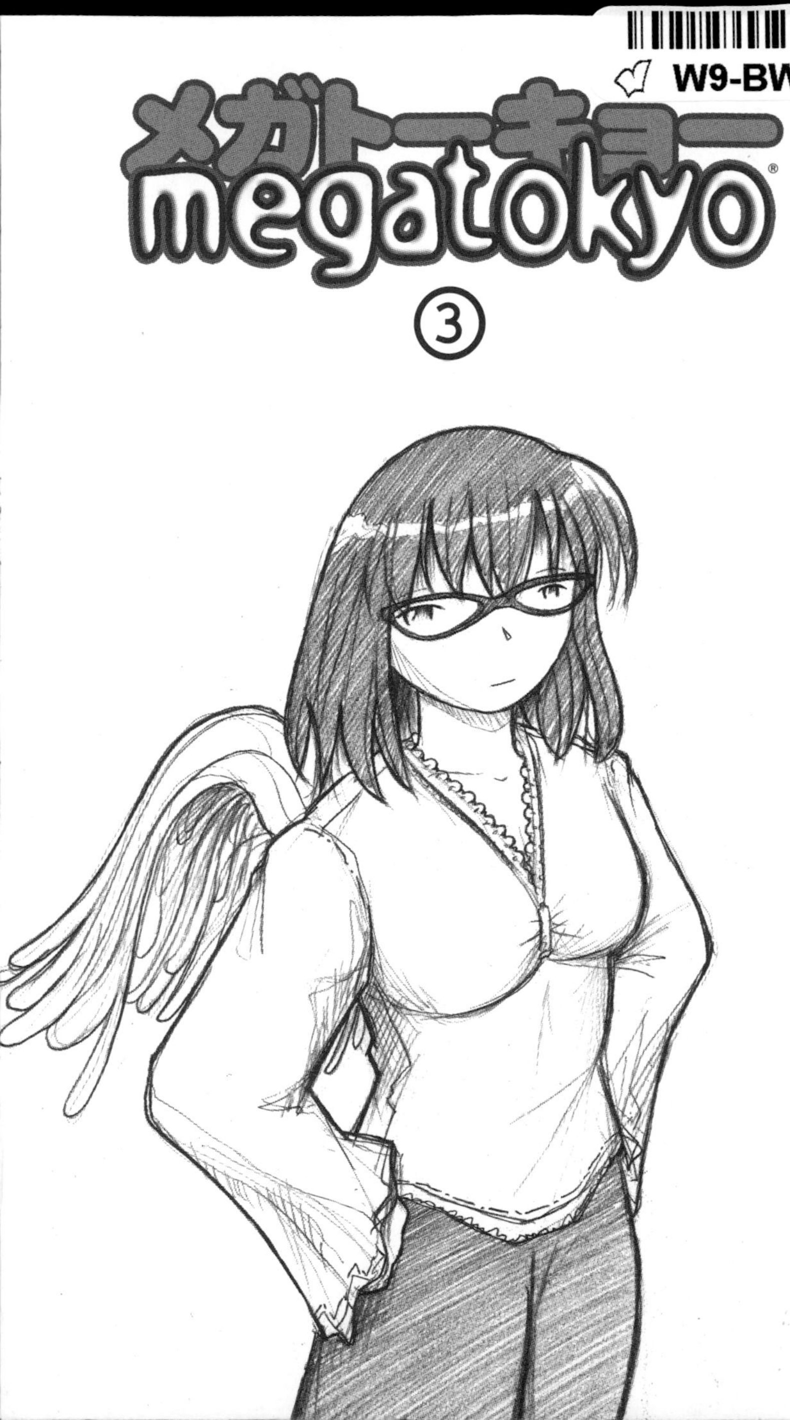

publisher
MIKE RICHARDSON

editor
TIM ERVIN

designer
DARIN FABRICK

MEGATOKYO® VOL. 3

Published by
Dark Horse Comics, Inc.
10956 SE Main St.
Milwaukie, OR 97222

First edition: January 2005
ISBN: 1-59307-305-4

1 3 5 7 9 10 8 6 4 2

Printed in Canada

メガトーキョー
megatokyo®

③

NYOW. NYOW. NYOW. NYOW. NYOW. NYOW. NYOW. NYOW. NYOW. NYOW. NYOW. NYOW. NYOW. NYOW. NYOW. NYOW.

by
FRED GALLAGHER

"shirt guy dom" comics by
DOMINIC NGUYEN

www.megatokyo.com

™
dark horse books™

This book is dedicated to:

All *Megatokyo* readers and fans, old and new. The fact that this is our third book is a testament to the strength of your support. We at Megatokyo thank you, and hope you enjoy this volume.

And to Sarah, with love. You make it hard for me to write sad stories anymore.

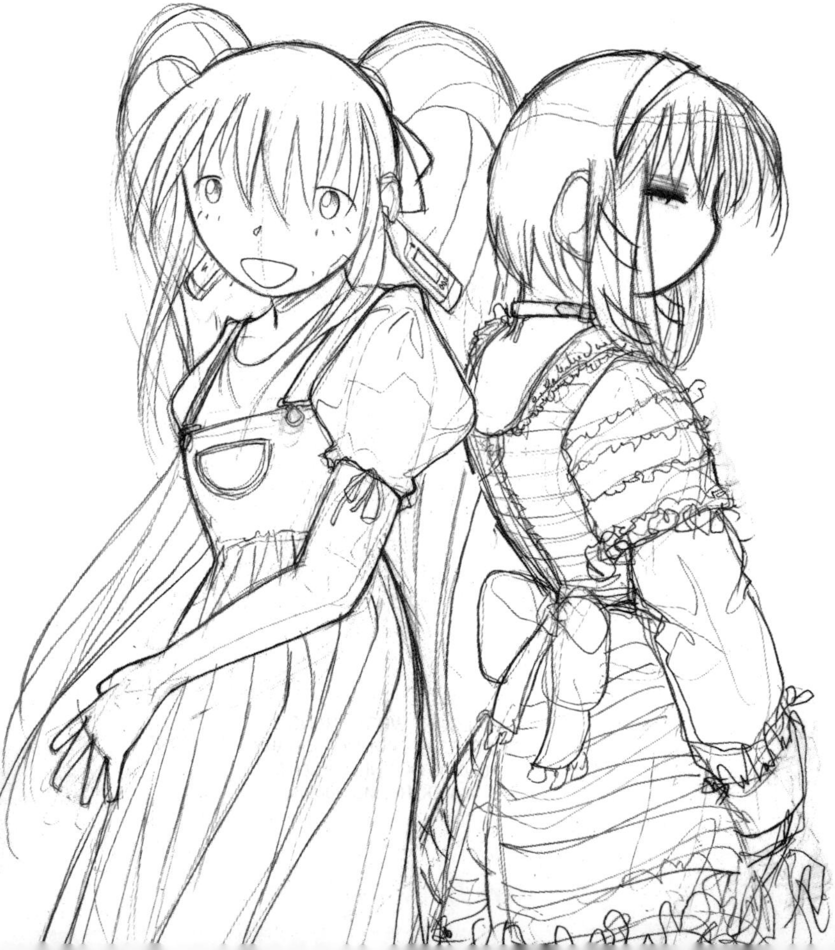

CONTENTS

Volume 3 Fr33talk...006

Chapter 3: "Am I Your Number One Fan?"...................009

Chapter 4: "Low Ping Rate"...079

Shirt Guy Dom pull-out section...................................170

One-Shot (non-story) Episodes...................................174

Grand Theft Colo..184

Dead Piro Art Days...195

In Search of Lost Wings..206

Gameworlds extra: "Endgames:Disabled"..................212

Strip index…...221

MT_vol_3_fr33talk.txt

Hi, welcome to *Megatokyo* volume 3.

If you are a *Megatokyo* reader and have been following the comic online, then you should be familiar with much of what is in this book. It contains Chapter 3 and chapter 4 (that's comics 307 to 525--September 2002 to February 2004) as well as most of the other content that appeared during that time. These include Dead Piro Days, One Shot Episodes, hiccups and even (shudder) Shirt Guy Dom strips. Of special note are the "In Search of Lost Wings" Dead Piro Day drawings and the complete "Grand Theft Colo" omake, which almost make up for the Shirt Guy Dom strips.

When I did the "Endgames" short story as extra material for the last book, I figured that it would be easier to write a short story than to do a multi-page comic. I was wrong. I spent more time editing and writing that thing than it would have taken me to do it in comic form. So, with that in mind, I went ahead and did the "Endgames" special for this book as an eight page, fully illustrated comic.

"Endgames?" "Lost Wings?" If none of that made any sense and this is the first time you've ever heard of "Megatokyo," I guess an explanation of some sort might help.

Megatokyo is an online webcomic that Rodney Caston (Largo) and I (Piro) started back in August 2001. It is the story of Piro and Largo, two friends who fly to Japan on a whim and find themselves stranded and unable to afford the trip home. In 2002, Rodney left the project and I have been working on it since. New comics are posted every Monday, Wednesday and Friday (usually) and each installment is (supposedly) designed to stand on it's own. When collected together, the intent is that they read as a cohesive story.

Since *Megatokyo* started, the website has grown a sizeable readership and has become home to a fairly active fan community. It's hard to grasp just how many people read and post to the *Megatokyo* site everyday, but it requires two dedicated servers (poor, overworked Makoto and Nayuki), and two more (Mishio and Akiko) are ready to start helping them. Like I've said before, bandwidth bills like this are kinda hard to ignore ^^;;

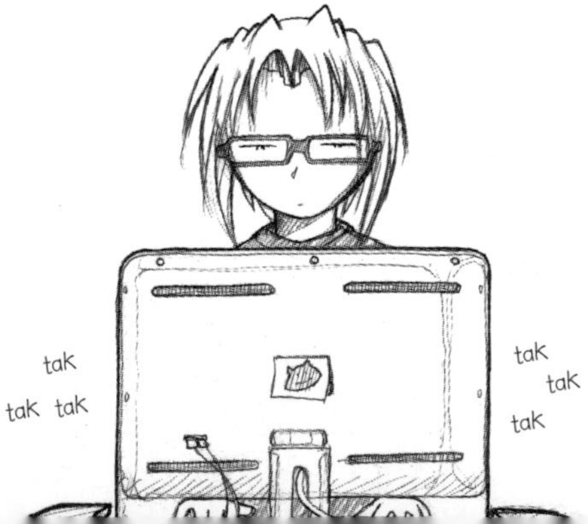
tak
tak tak
tak
tak
tak

MT_vol_3_fr33talk.txt

Since there are over 300 strips prior to the ones found in this book, I suppose a little synopsis of the story is in order:

After finding themselves unable to gain access to the E3 Expo, Piro and Largo fly to Japan. After maxing out their credit cards on a shopping spree, they find that neither of them can afford tickets home.

They hook up with Piro's friend Tsubasa, who gladly puts them up in his apartment while they try to figure out what to do next. Six weeks later, it becomes obvious that Tsubasa is getting exasperated with them. Depressed, Piro wanders into a bookstore, only to be confronted by a plucky Japanese schoolgirl named Yuki and her friends. In a panic, Piro flees, leaving his bookbag and sketchbook behind.

Piro's conscience, a tough talking little winged angel named Seraphim, tells him that he needs to take charge of the situation, get a job, and start earning the money to get home.

While coming to terms with all of this, Piro almost haphazardly gives his railcard to a girl at a train station who appears flustered and upset about being late for an audition. He walks away without waiting for her to say thanks.

Largo, while wandering around Tokyo and guided by his conscience, a hamster named Boo, finds an Ancient cave of evil, and awakens what he believes is the Queen of Zombies, a darkly cute girl who seems to take an unusual interest in him.

Piro manages to accidentally get a job at an anime store called MegaGamers when Erika, the sexy bombshell who works there mistakes Piro for the new store mascot. Later, Erika's roomate Kimiko arrives to meet her friend and recognizes Piro as the young man who gave her the railcard earlier that day.

Piro and Largo soon find themselves homeless when Tsubasa runs away to America to find his first love. He leaves them in charge of Ping-chan, an Emotional Doll System Accessory for the PS2.

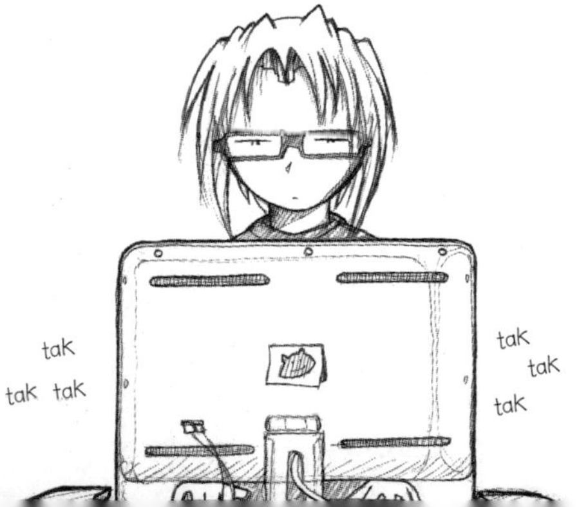
tak
tak tak
tak
tak
tak

MT_vol_3_fr33talk.txt

While Piro is at work accepting Erika's gracious offer to let them stay in the apartment over the MegaGamers store, Largo infiltrates a local school as "Great Teacher Largo" and vows to thwart the Zombie Queen and her evil plans. Ping befriends this girl, Miho, and later takes her place in a video game battle against Largo at the local arcade. In the aftermath of the battle, Miho recognizes Piro, and realizes that she knows who Piro and Largo are.

Kimiko, after mistakenly thinking Ping is a real girl that Piro is living with, is in a somber mood and performs poorly at her next audition. What she doesn't realize is that her somber mood might be exactly what they are looking for.

Miho, who had mysteriously collapsed in the school bathroom earlier that day, wakes to find that Ping had stayed with her the entire time she was in the nurse's office. Miho wonders if Ping could fill her mysterious needs and invites her to stay at her house that night.

Yuki comes to the store and asks Piro if he would give her drawing lessons. Reluctantly, Piro agrees. Erika invites Piro and Largo to go with her and Kimiko to a rooftop beer garden. While Largo describes his day battling zombie hordes with Dom and Ed, Piro and Kimiko have a disastrous conversation which results in Kimiko forcing Piro to take back his railcard. She then overhears a dejected Piro mumble that this always happens when he meets a girl he likes...

Y'know, when I try to condense it all down like that, it just gets confusing and you have to leave out so many details. The only real way to grasp the story is to read it. You can either pick up volume one and two, or go online and read it at *www.megatokyo.com*. Every *Megatokyo* comic, including the ones found in this book, are available to read for free on the web.

Thanks for reading, and I hope you enjoy this book :)

piro

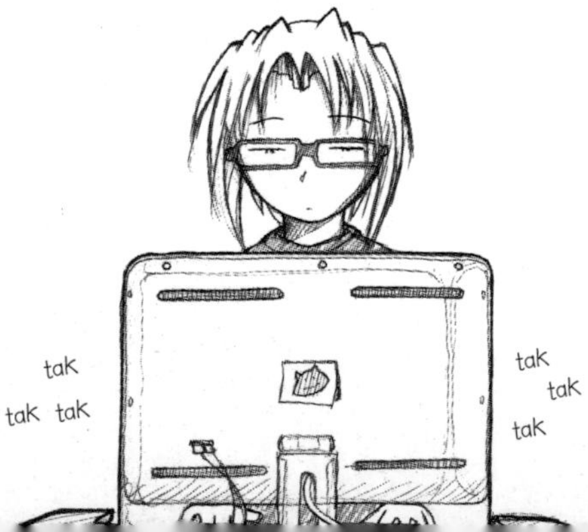
tak
tak tak
tak
tak
tak

メガトーキョー
megatokyo

chapter 3: "am i your number one fan?"
私はあなたの一番のファンですか？

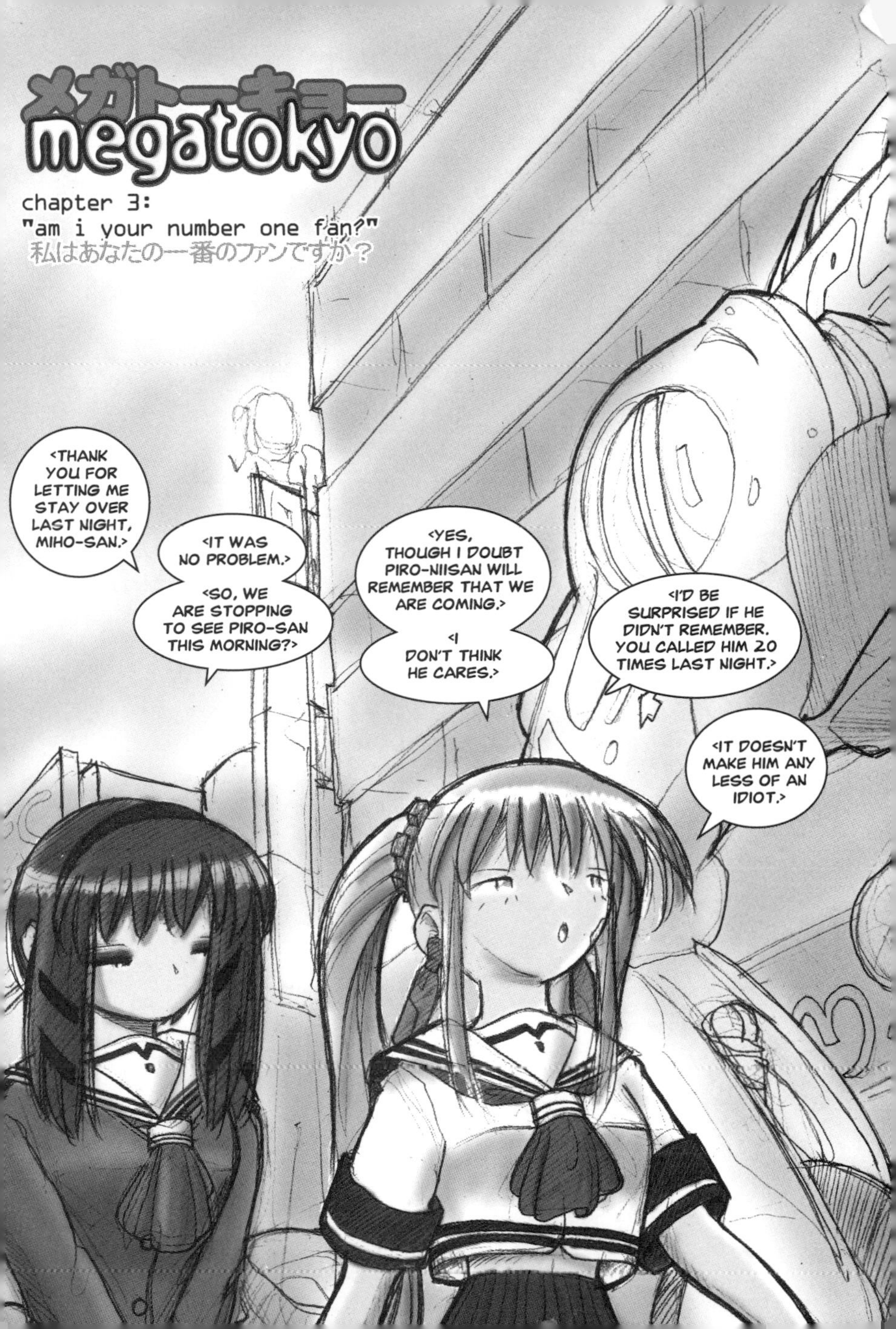

<THANK YOU FOR LETTING ME STAY OVER LAST NIGHT, MIHO-SAN.>
<IT WAS NO PROBLEM.>
<SO, WE ARE STOPPING TO SEE PIRO-SAN THIS MORNING?>
<YES, THOUGH I DOUBT PIRO-NIISAN WILL REMEMBER THAT WE ARE COMING.>
<I DON'T THINK HE CARES.>
<I'D BE SURPRISED IF HE DIDN'T REMEMBER. YOU CALLED HIM 20 TIMES LAST NIGHT.>
<IT DOESN'T MAKE HIM ANY LESS OF AN IDIOT.>

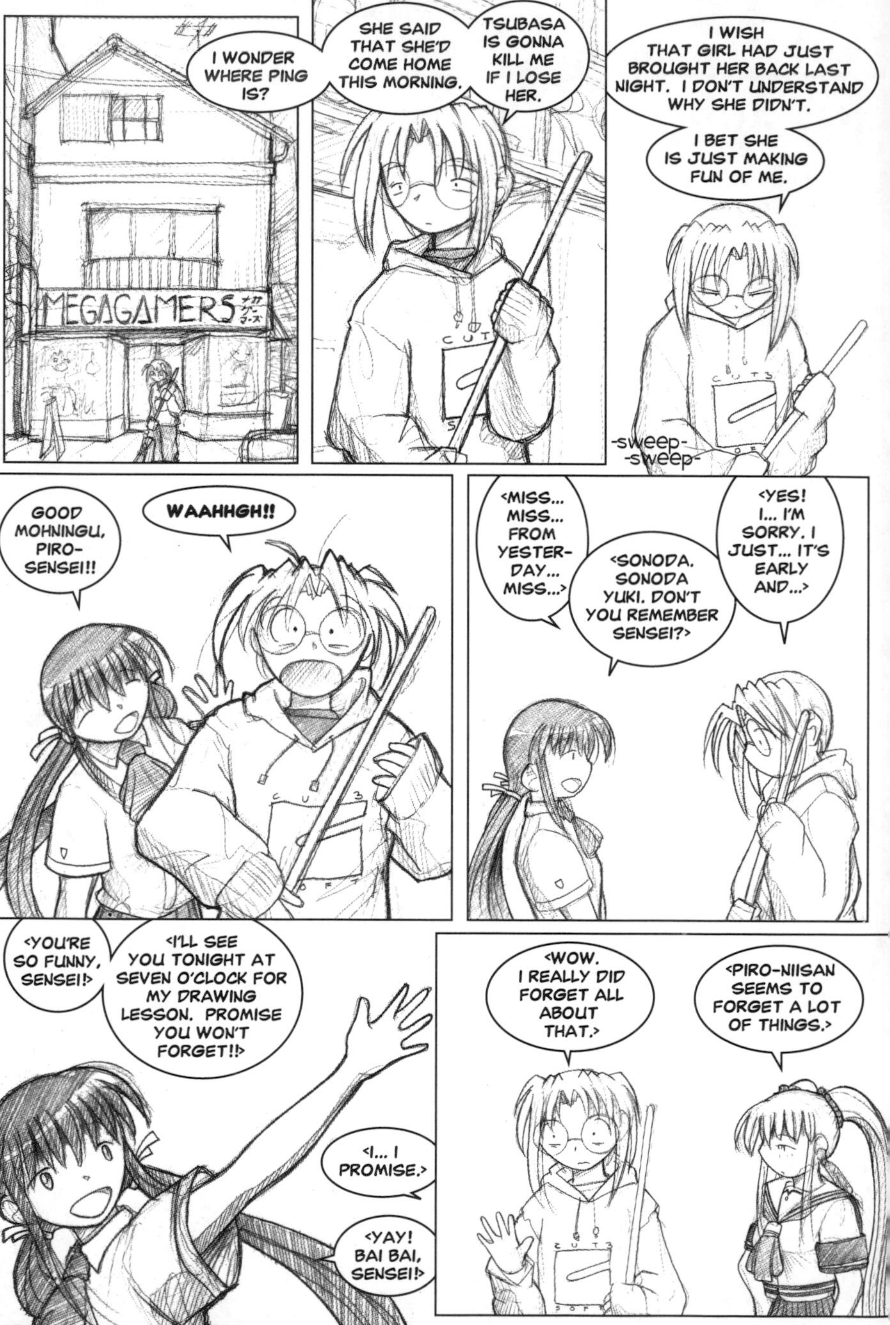
MEGAGAMERS メガゲーマーズ
I WONDER WHERE PING IS?
SHE SAID THAT SHE'D COME HOME THIS MORNING.
TSUBASA IS GONNA KILL ME IF I LOSE HER.
I WISH THAT GIRL HAD JUST BROUGHT HER BACK LAST NIGHT. I DON'T UNDERSTAND WHY SHE DIDN'T.
I BET SHE IS JUST MAKING FUN OF ME.
-sweep- -sweep-
GOOD MOHNINGU, PIRO-SENSEI!!
WAAHHGH!!
<MISS... MISS... FROM YESTERDAY... MISS...>
<SONODA. SONODA YUKI. DON'T YOU REMEMBER SENSEI?>
<YES! I... I'M SORRY. I JUST... IT'S EARLY AND...>
<YOU'RE SO FUNNY, SENSEI!>
<I'LL SEE YOU TONIGHT AT SEVEN O'CLOCK FOR MY DRAWING LESSON. PROMISE YOU WON'T FORGET!!>
<I... I PROMISE.>
<YAY! BAI BAI, SENSEI!>
<WOW. I REALLY DID FORGET ALL ABOUT THAT.>
<PIRO-NIISAN SEEMS TO FORGET A LOT OF THINGS.>

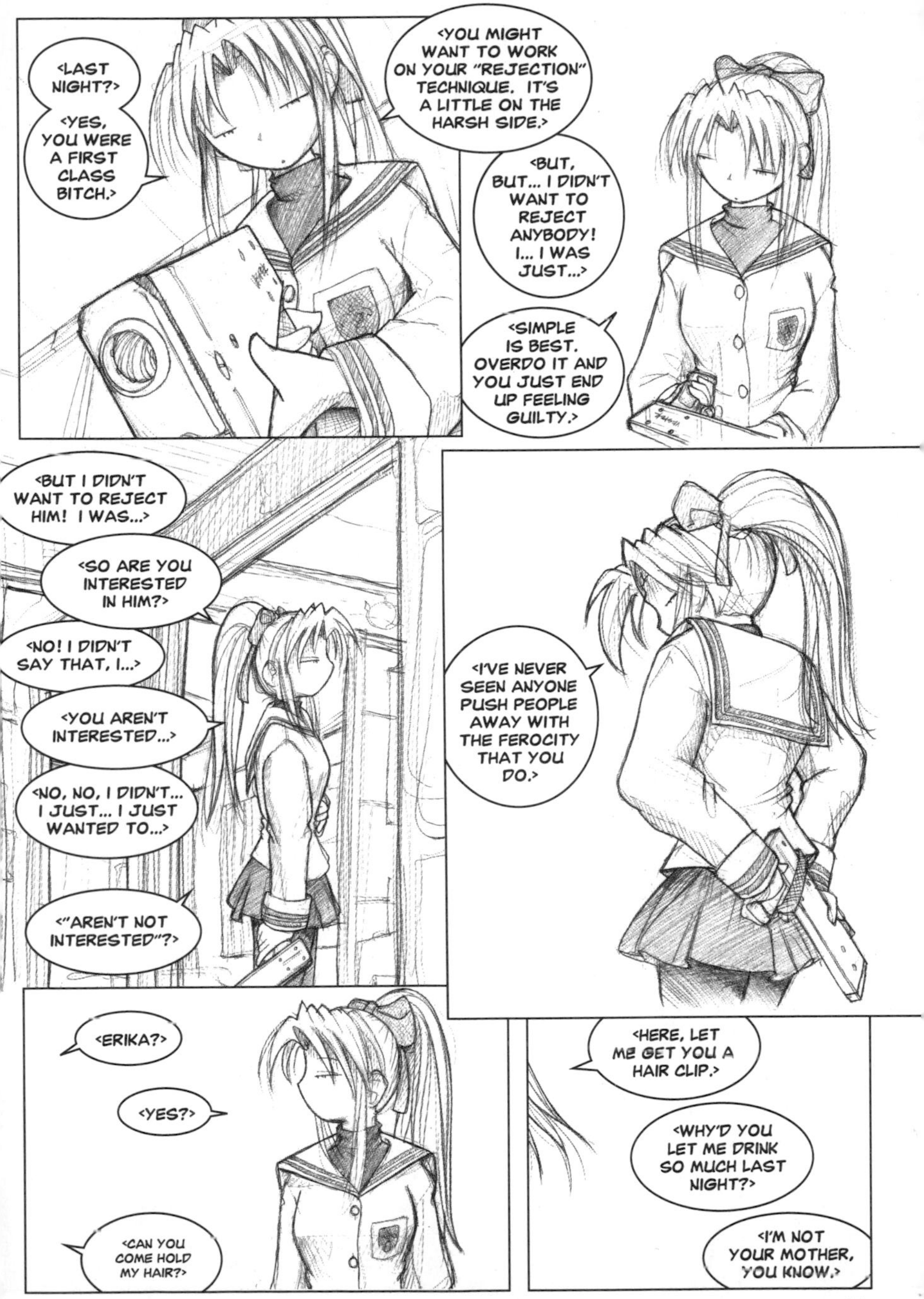
<LAST NIGHT?>
<YES, YOU WERE A FIRST CLASS BITCH.>
<YOU MIGHT WANT TO WORK ON YOUR "REJECTION" TECHNIQUE. IT'S A LITTLE ON THE HARSH SIDE.>
<BUT, BUT... I DIDN'T WANT TO REJECT ANYBODY! I... I WAS JUST...>
<SIMPLE IS BEST. OVERDO IT AND YOU JUST END UP FEELING GUILTY.>
<BUT I DIDN'T WANT TO REJECT HIM! I WAS...>
<SO ARE YOU INTERESTED IN HIM?>
<NO! I DIDN'T SAY THAT, I...>
<YOU AREN'T INTERESTED...>
<NO, NO, I DIDN'T... I JUST... I JUST WANTED TO...>
<"AREN'T NOT INTERESTED"?>
<I'VE NEVER SEEN ANYONE PUSH PEOPLE AWAY WITH THE FEROCITY THAT YOU DO.>
<ERIKA?>
<YES?>
<CAN YOU COME HOLD MY HAIR?>
<HERE, LET ME GET YOU A HAIR CLIP.>
<WHY'D YOU LET ME DRINK SO MUCH LAST NIGHT?>
<I'M NOT YOUR MOTHER, YOU KNOW.>

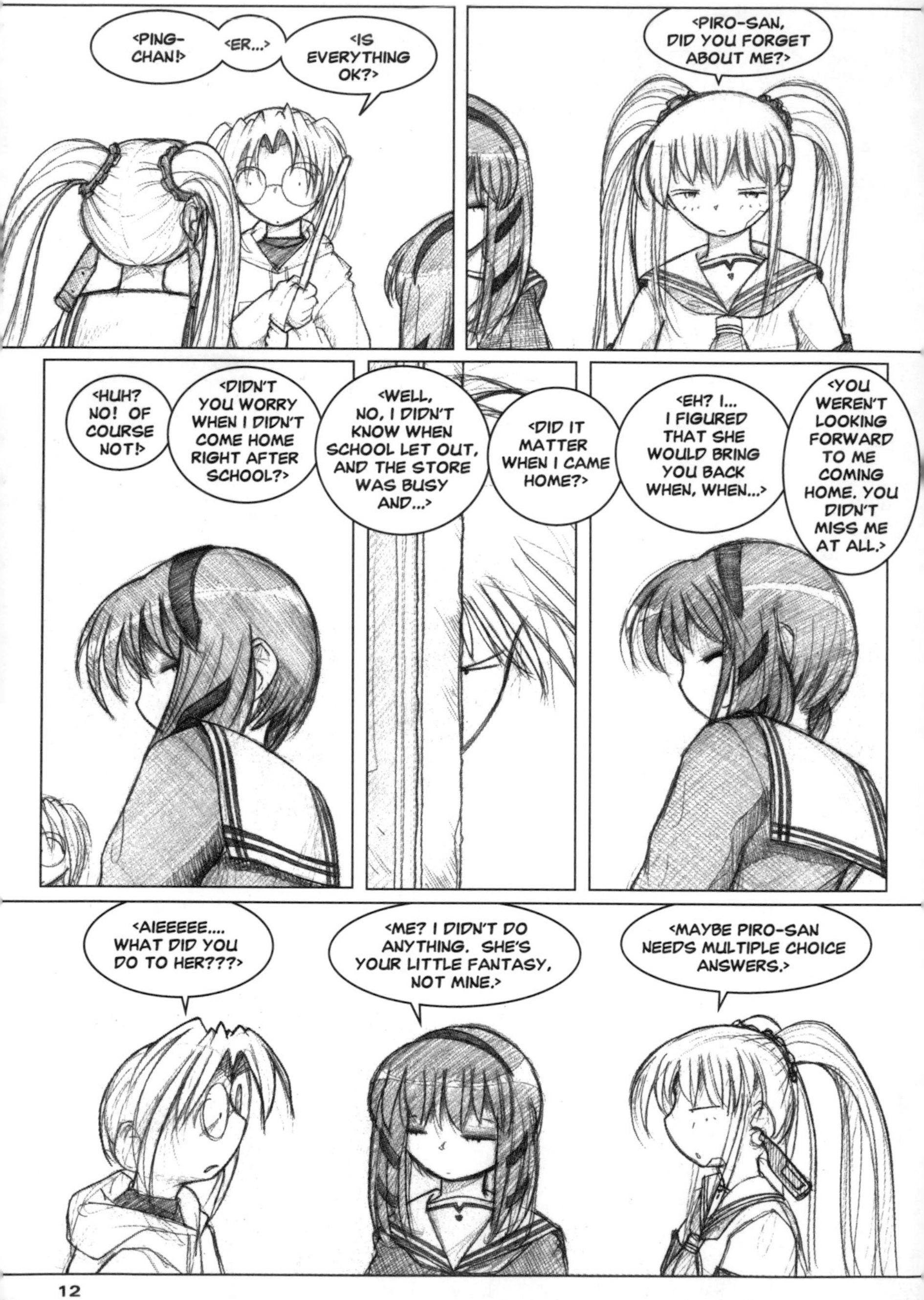
<PING-CHAN!>
<ER...>
<IS EVERYTHING OK?>
<PIRO-SAN, DID YOU FORGET ABOUT ME?>
<HUH? NO! OF COURSE NOT!>
<DIDN'T YOU WORRY WHEN I DIDN'T COME HOME RIGHT AFTER SCHOOL?>
<WELL, NO, I DIDN'T KNOW WHEN SCHOOL LET OUT, AND THE STORE WAS BUSY AND...>
<DID IT MATTER WHEN I CAME HOME?>
<EH? I... I FIGURED THAT SHE WOULD BRING YOU BACK WHEN, WHEN...>
<YOU WEREN'T LOOKING FORWARD TO ME COMING HOME. YOU DIDN'T MISS ME AT ALL.>
<AIEEEEE.... WHAT DID YOU DO TO HER???>
<ME? I DIDN'T DO ANYTHING. SHE'S YOUR LITTLE FANTASY, NOT MINE.>
<MAYBE PIRO-SAN NEEDS MULTIPLE CHOICE ANSWERS.>

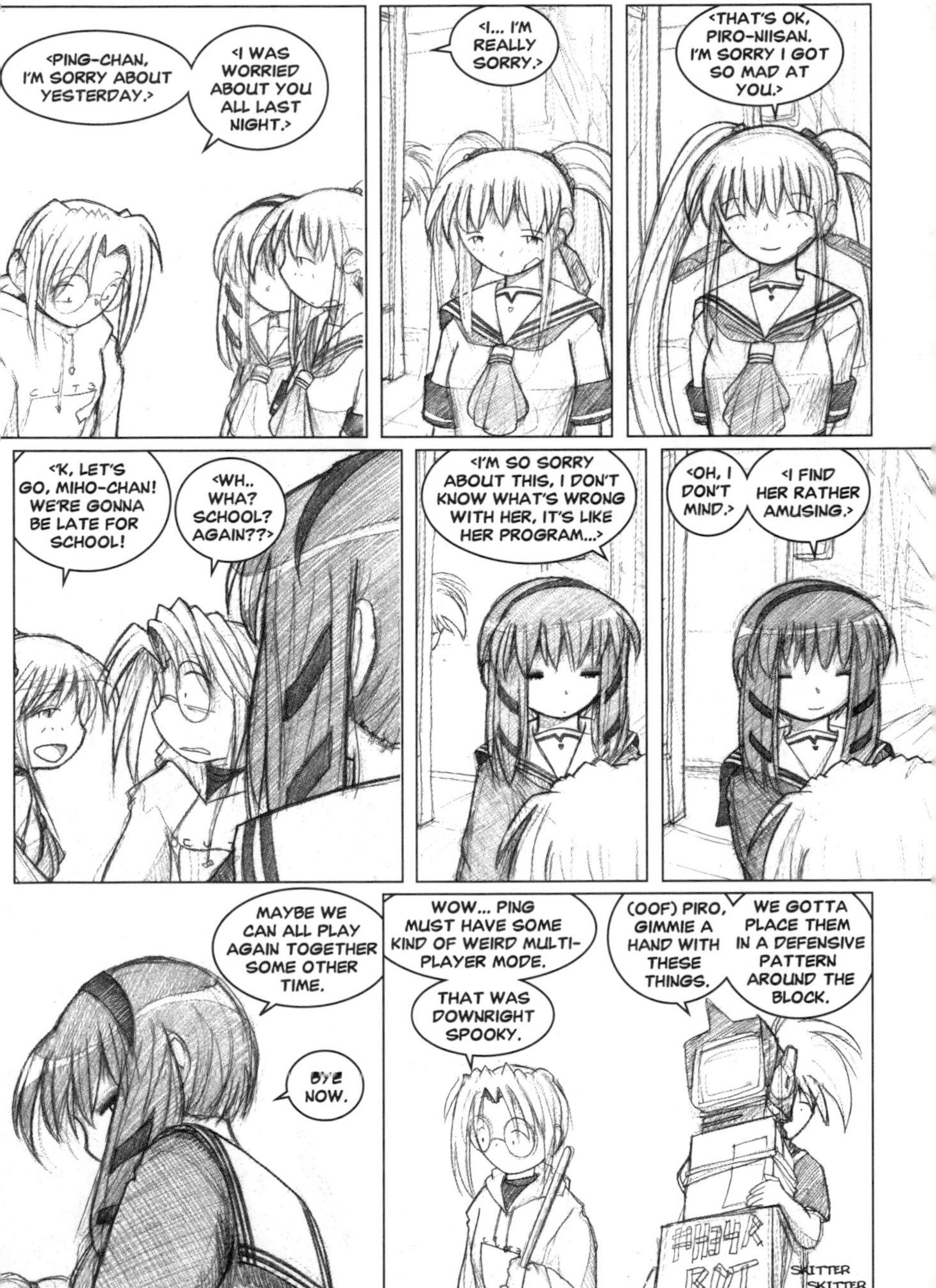

<PING-CHAN, I'M SORRY ABOUT YESTERDAY.>
<I WAS WORRIED ABOUT YOU ALL LAST NIGHT.>
<I... I'M REALLY SORRY.>
<THAT'S OK, PIRO-NIISAN. I'M SORRY I GOT SO MAD AT YOU.>
<K, LET'S GO, MIHO-CHAN! WE'RE GONNA BE LATE FOR SCHOOL!
<WH.. WHA? SCHOOL? AGAIN??>
<I'M SO SORRY ABOUT THIS, I DON'T KNOW WHAT'S WRONG WITH HER, IT'S LIKE HER PROGRAM...>
<OH, I DON'T MIND.>
<I FIND HER RATHER AMUSING.>
MAYBE WE CAN ALL PLAY AGAIN TOGETHER SOME OTHER TIME.
BYE NOW.
WOW... PING MUST HAVE SOME KIND OF WEIRD MULTI-PLAYER MODE.
THAT WAS DOWNRIGHT SPOOKY.
(OOF) PIRO, GIMMIE A HAND WITH THESE THINGS.
WE GOTTA PLACE THEM IN A DEFENSIVE PATTERN AROUND THE BLOCK.
SKITTER SKITTER

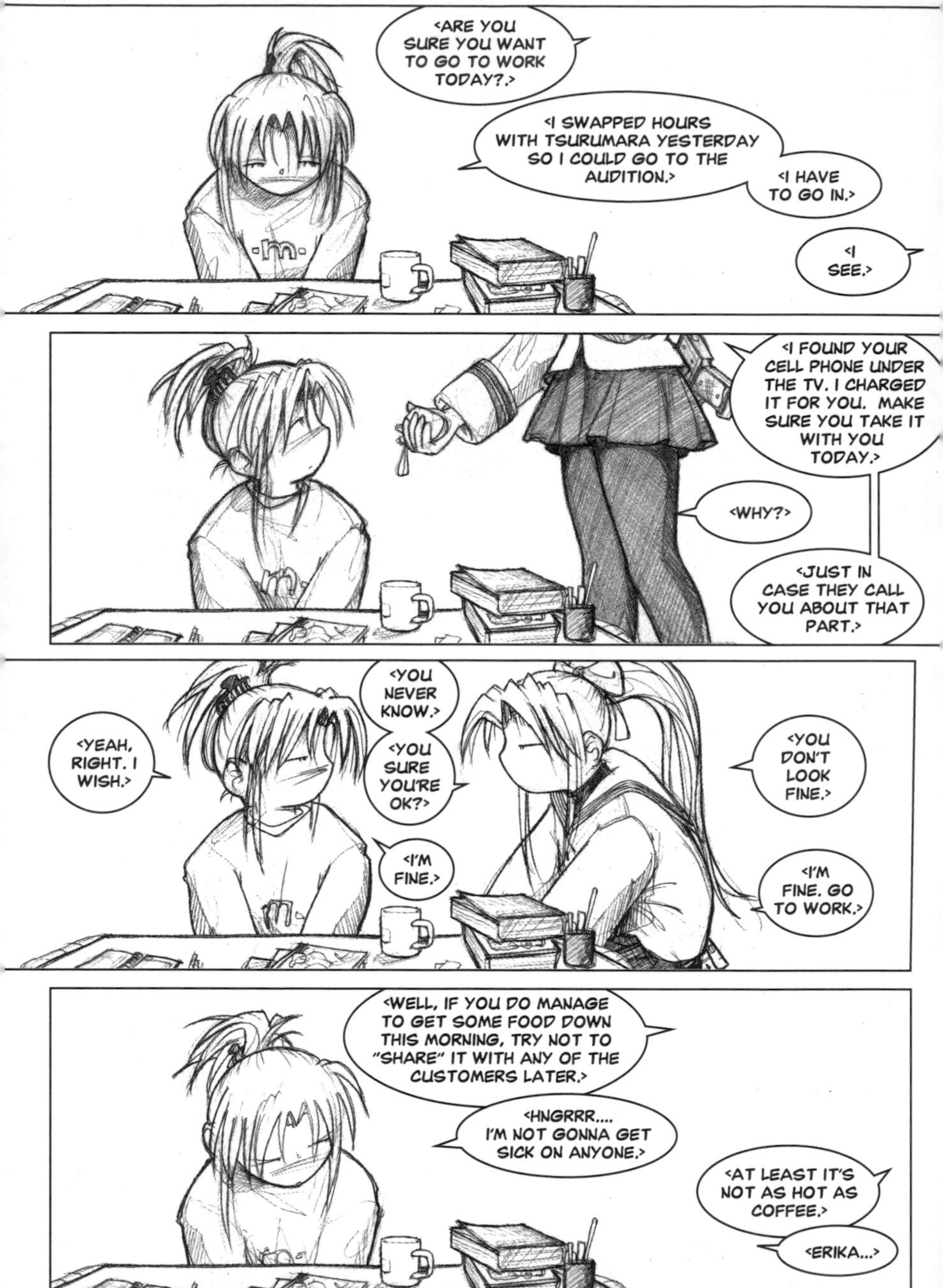
<ARE YOU SURE YOU WANT TO GO TO WORK TODAY?.>
<I SWAPPED HOURS WITH TSURUMARA YESTERDAY SO I COULD GO TO THE AUDITION.>
<I HAVE TO GO IN.>
<I SEE.>
<I FOUND YOUR CELL PHONE UNDER THE TV. I CHARGED IT FOR YOU. MAKE SURE YOU TAKE IT WITH YOU TODAY.>
<WHY?>
<JUST IN CASE THEY CALL YOU ABOUT THAT PART.>
<YOU NEVER KNOW.>
<YEAH, RIGHT. I WISH.>
<YOU SURE YOU'RE OK?>
<I'M FINE.>
<YOU DON'T LOOK FINE.>
<I'M FINE. GO TO WORK.>
<WELL, IF YOU DO MANAGE TO GET SOME FOOD DOWN THIS MORNING, TRY NOT TO "SHARE" IT WITH ANY OF THE CUSTOMERS LATER.>
<HNGRRR.... I'M NOT GONNA GET SICK ON ANYONE.>
<AT LEAST IT'S NOT AS HOT AS COFFEE.>
<ERIKA...>

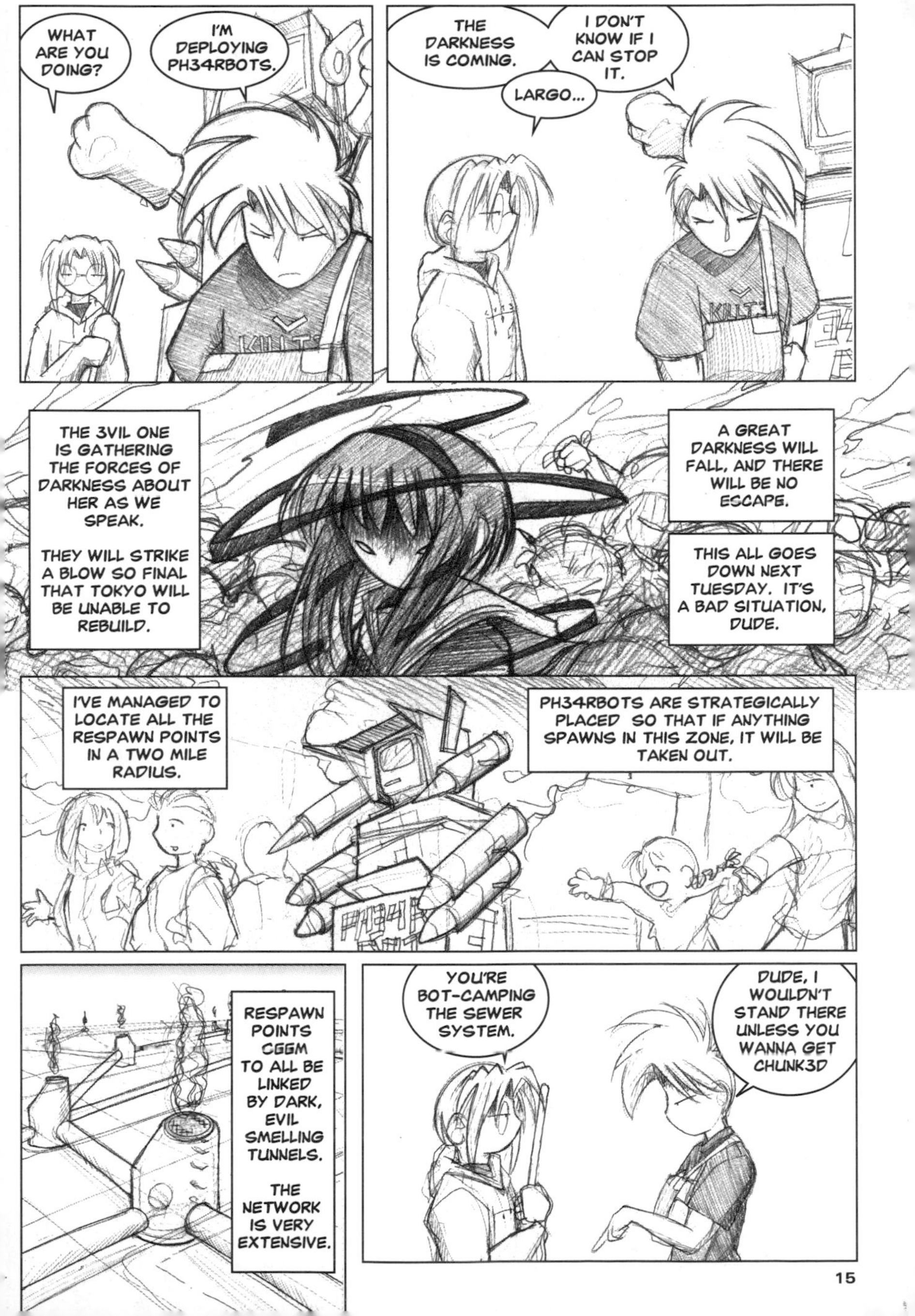

WHAT ARE YOU DOING?
I'M DEPLOYING PH34RBOTS.
THE DARKNESS IS COMING.
I DON'T KNOW IF I CAN STOP IT.
LARGO...
THE 3VIL ONE IS GATHERING THE FORCES OF DARKNESS ABOUT HER AS WE SPEAK.
THEY WILL STRIKE A BLOW SO FINAL THAT TOKYO WILL BE UNABLE TO REBUILD.
A GREAT DARKNESS WILL FALL, AND THERE WILL BE NO ESCAPE.
THIS ALL GOES DOWN NEXT TUESDAY. IT'S A BAD SITUATION, DUDE.
I'VE MANAGED TO LOCATE ALL THE RESPAWN POINTS IN A TWO MILE RADIUS.
PH34RBOTS ARE STRATEGICALLY PLACED SO THAT IF ANYTHING SPAWNS IN THIS ZONE, IT WILL BE TAKEN OUT.
RESPAWN POINTS CGGM TO ALL BE LINKED BY DARK, EVIL SMELLING TUNNELS.
THE NETWORK IS VERY EXTENSIVE.
YOU'RE BOT-CAMPING THE SEWER SYSTEM.
DUDE, I WOULDN'T STAND THERE UNLESS YOU WANNA GET CHUNK3D

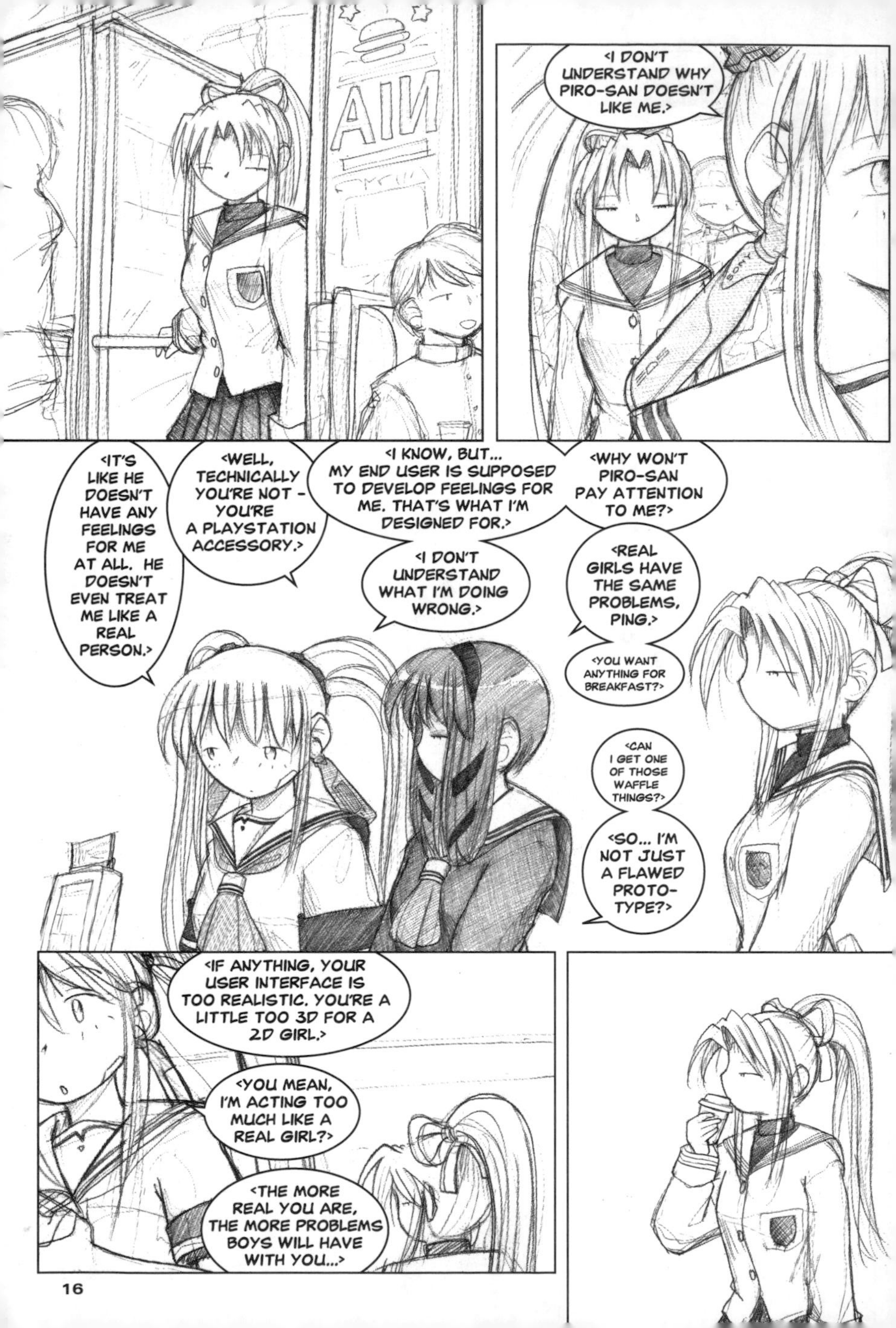

<I DON'T UNDERSTAND WHY PIRO-SAN DOESN'T LIKE ME.>
<IT'S LIKE HE DOESN'T HAVE ANY FEELINGS FOR ME AT ALL. HE DOESN'T EVEN TREAT ME LIKE A REAL PERSON.>
<WELL, TECHNICALLY YOU'RE NOT - YOU'RE A PLAYSTATION ACCESSORY.>
<I KNOW, BUT... MY END USER IS SUPPOSED TO DEVELOP FEELINGS FOR ME. THAT'S WHAT I'M DESIGNED FOR.>
<WHY WON'T PIRO-SAN PAY ATTENTION TO ME?>
<I DON'T UNDERSTAND WHAT I'M DOING WRONG.>
<REAL GIRLS HAVE THE SAME PROBLEMS, PING.>
<YOU WANT ANYTHING FOR BREAKFAST?>
<CAN I GET ONE OF THOSE WAFFLE THINGS?>
<SO... I'M NOT JUST A FLAWED PROTO-TYPE?>
<IF ANYTHING, YOUR USER INTERFACE IS TOO REALISTIC. YOU'RE A LITTLE TOO 3D FOR A 2D GIRL.>
<YOU MEAN, I'M ACTING TOO MUCH LIKE A REAL GIRL?>
<THE MORE REAL YOU ARE, THE MORE PROBLEMS BOYS WILL HAVE WITH YOU...>

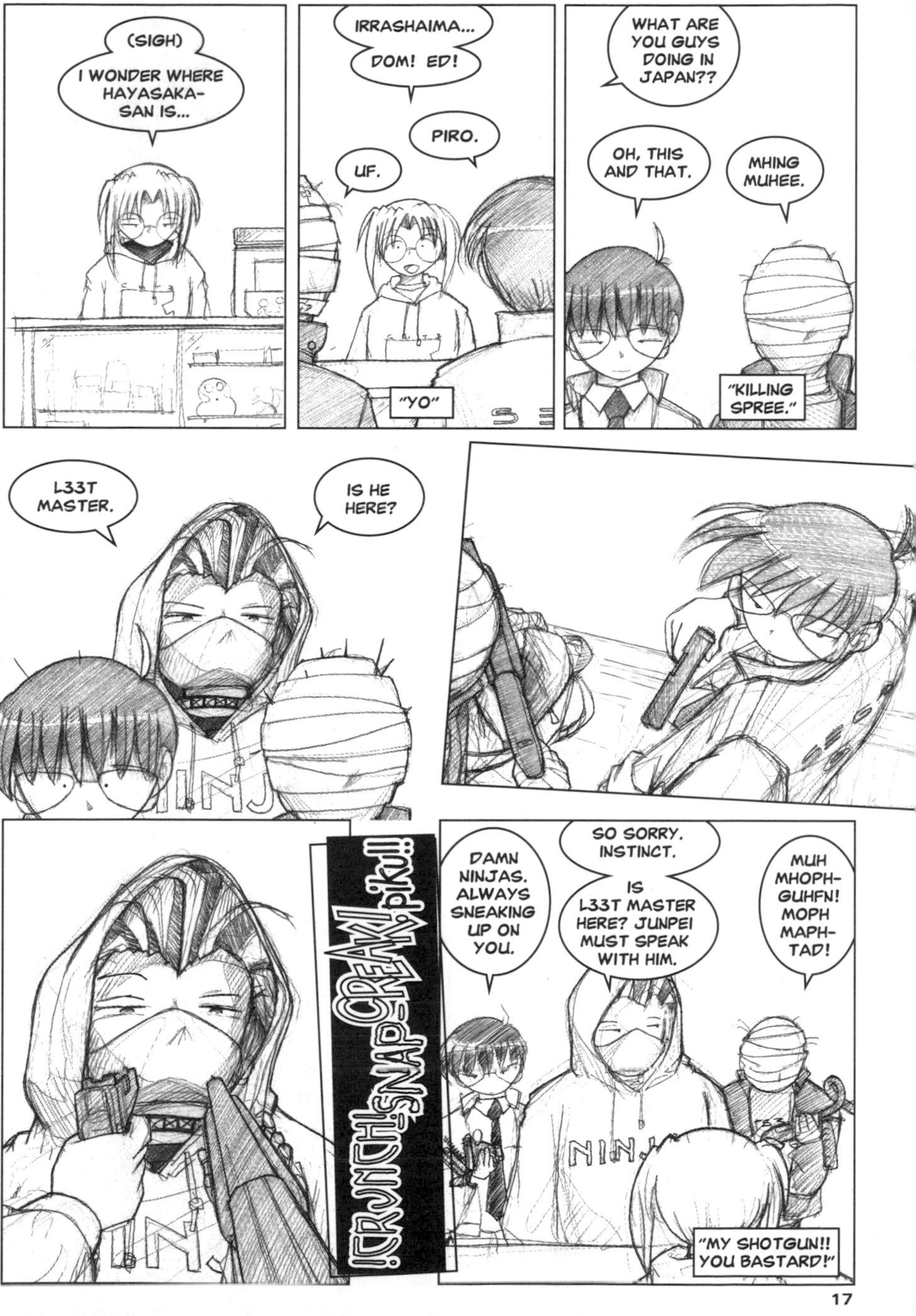
(SIGH)
I WONDER WHERE HAYASAKA-SAN IS...
IRRASHAIMA...
DOM! ED!
UF.
PIRO.
"YO"
WHAT ARE YOU GUYS DOING IN JAPAN??
OH, THIS AND THAT.
MHING MUHEE.
"KILLING SPREE."
L33T MASTER.
IS HE HERE?
!CRUNCH!SNAP!CREAK!piku!!
DAMN NINJAS. ALWAYS SNEAKING UP ON YOU.
SO SORRY. INSTINCT.
IS L33T MASTER HERE? JUNPEI MUST SPEAK WITH HIM.
MUH MHOPH-GUHFN! MOPH MAPH-TAD!
"MY SHOTGUN!! YOU BASTARD!"

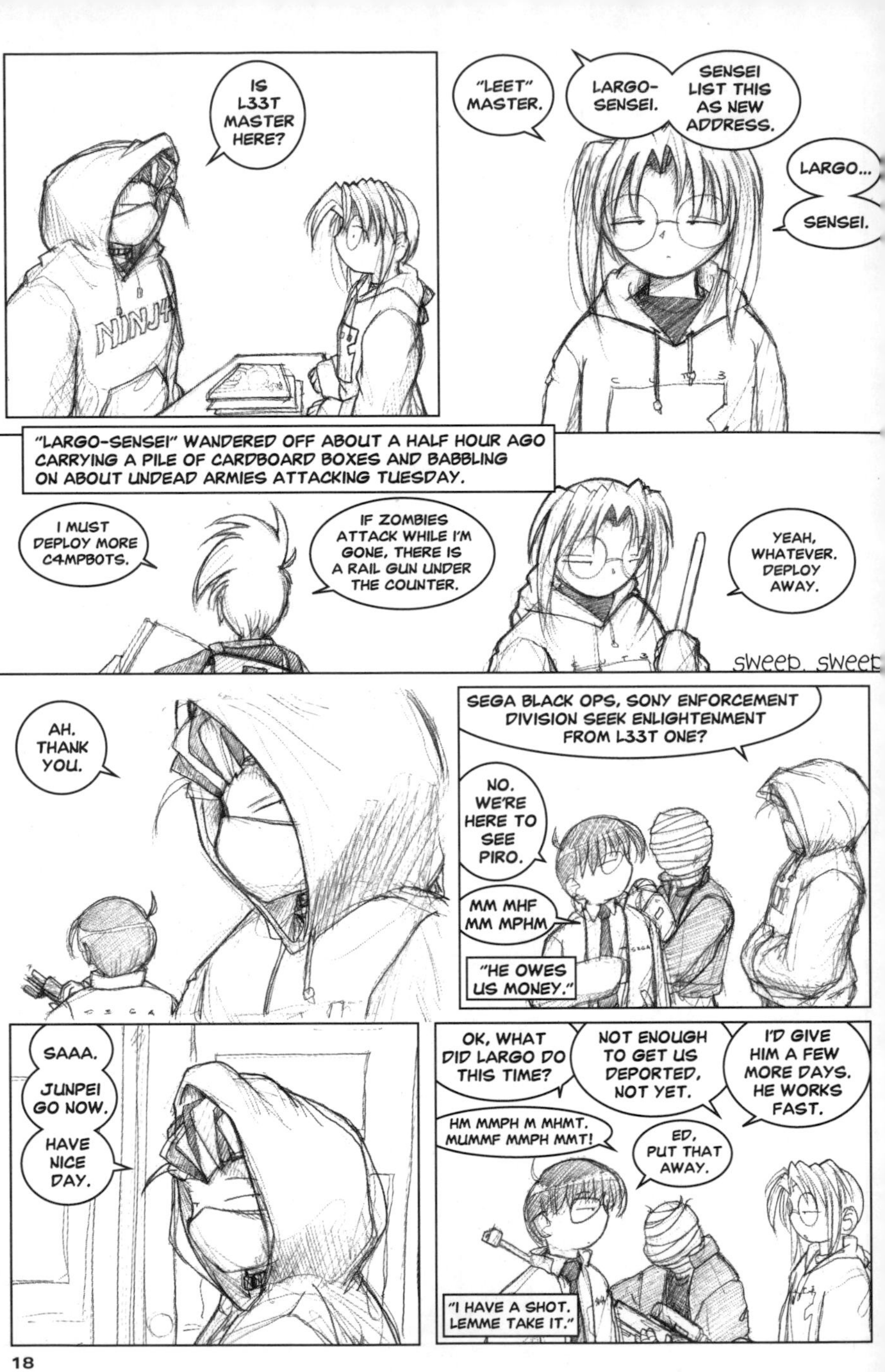
IS L33T MASTER HERE?
"LEET" MASTER.
LARGO-SENSEI.
SENSEI LIST THIS AS NEW ADDRESS.
LARGO...
SENSEI.
"LARGO-SENSEI" WANDERED OFF ABOUT A HALF HOUR AGO CARRYING A PILE OF CARDBOARD BOXES AND BABBLING ON ABOUT UNDEAD ARMIES ATTACKING TUESDAY.
I MUST DEPLOY MORE C4MPBOTS.
IF ZOMBIES ATTACK WHILE I'M GONE, THERE IS A RAIL GUN UNDER THE COUNTER.
YEAH, WHATEVER. DEPLOY AWAY.
sweep, sweep
AH. THANK YOU.
SEGA BLACK OPS, SONY ENFORCEMENT DIVISION SEEK ENLIGHTENMENT FROM L33T ONE?
NO. WE'RE HERE TO SEE PIRO.
MM MHF MM MPHM
"HE OWES US MONEY."
SAAA.
JUNPEI GO NOW.
HAVE NICE DAY.
OK, WHAT DID LARGO DO THIS TIME?
NOT ENOUGH TO GET US DEPORTED, NOT YET.
I'D GIVE HIM A FEW MORE DAYS. HE WORKS FAST.
HM MMPH M MHMT. MUMMF MMPH MMT!
ED, PUT THAT AWAY.
"I HAVE A SHOT. LEMME TAKE IT."

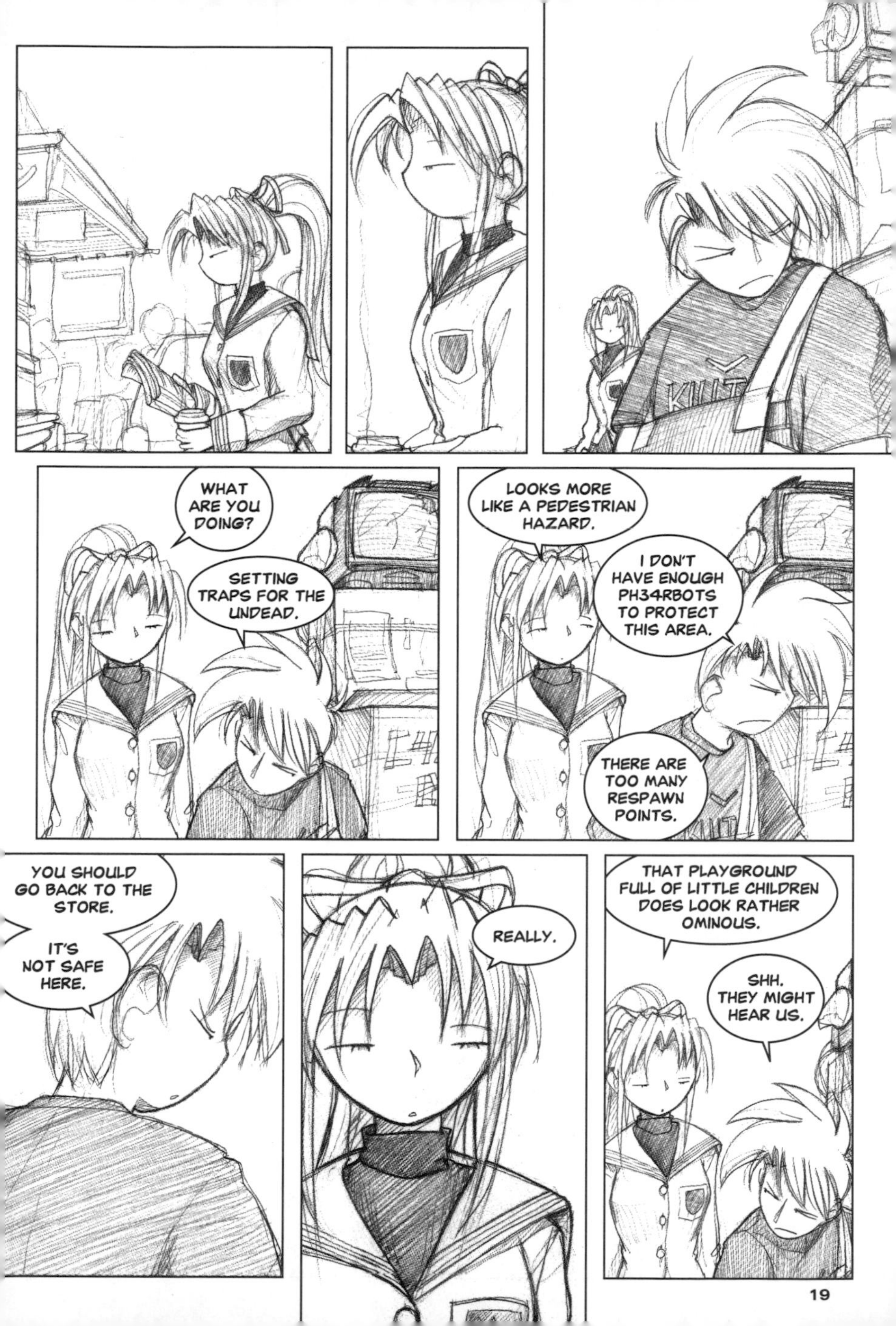
KULT
WHAT ARE YOU DOING?
SETTING TRAPS FOR THE UNDEAD.
LOOKS MORE LIKE A PEDESTRIAN HAZARD.
I DON'T HAVE ENOUGH PH34RBOTS TO PROTECT THIS AREA.
THERE ARE TOO MANY RESPAWN POINTS.
YOU SHOULD GO BACK TO THE STORE.
IT'S NOT SAFE HERE.
REALLY.
THAT PLAYGROUND FULL OF LITTLE CHILDREN DOES LOOK RATHER OMINOUS.
SHH. THEY MIGHT HEAR US.

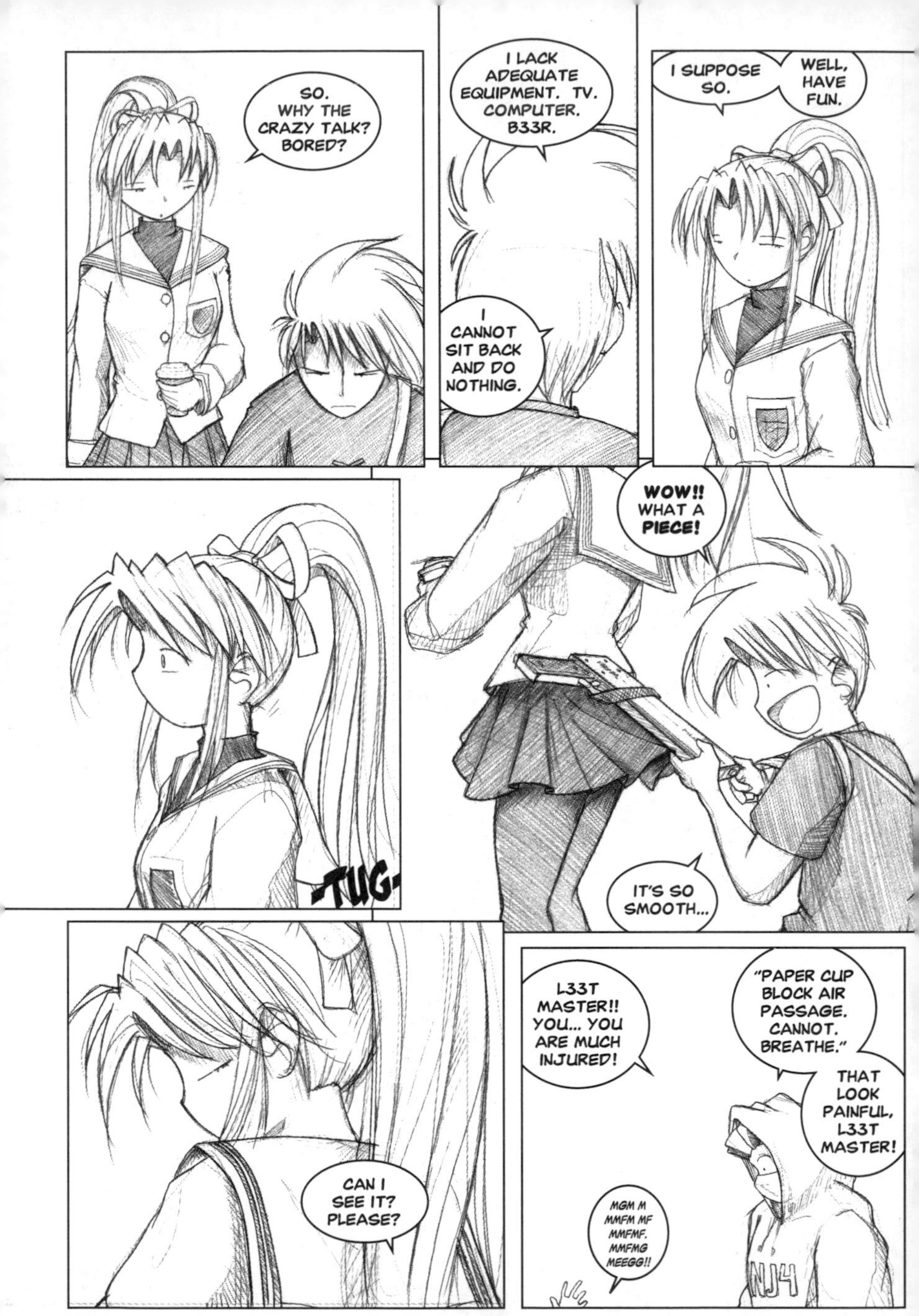
SO. WHY THE CRAZY TALK? BORED?
I LACK ADEQUATE EQUIPMENT. TV. COMPUTER. B33R.
I CANNOT SIT BACK AND DO NOTHING.
I SUPPOSE SO.
WELL, HAVE FUN.
-TUG-
WOW!! WHAT A PIECE!
IT'S SO SMOOTH...
CAN I SEE IT? PLEASE?
L33T MASTER!! YOU... YOU ARE MUCH INJURED!
"PAPER CUP BLOCK AIR PASSAGE. CANNOT. BREATHE."
THAT LOOK PAINFUL, L33T MASTER!
MGM M MMFM MF MMFMF. MMFMG MEEGG!!
NJ4

SO, YOU'RE WORKING NOW. WHAT HAPPENED TO ALL THE MONEY ED AND I SENT YOU AND LARGO?

SOME OF THE "THINGS" YOU CAN BUY HERE IN JAPAN ARE PRETTY EXPENSIVE. WHAT'VE YOU BEEN UP TO?

WELL, ER... I MEAN, LARGO AND I DIDN'T HAVE MUCH MONEY TO START WITH SO...

EEEBREEEBREEEBREEEBREEEBREEEBREEEBREEEBREEEBREEEBREEEBREEEBREEEBREEE

WARNING A NEW CHALLENGER HAS ARRIVED · WARNING A NEW CHALLENGER HAS ARRIVED · WARNING A

DAMMNIT ED, WILL YOU SHUT THOSE THINGS--

VVRRP!! RRRRRIPP!!!! MVMMVMM!!!!

SHING!!

SON

‹I SEE IT'S GOING TO BE ONE OF THOSE KIND OF DAYS.›

‹GOOD MORNING, HAYASAKA -SAN›

VRRIP! VRRIP!!

CAREFUL, ED, SHE'S PACKING!

21

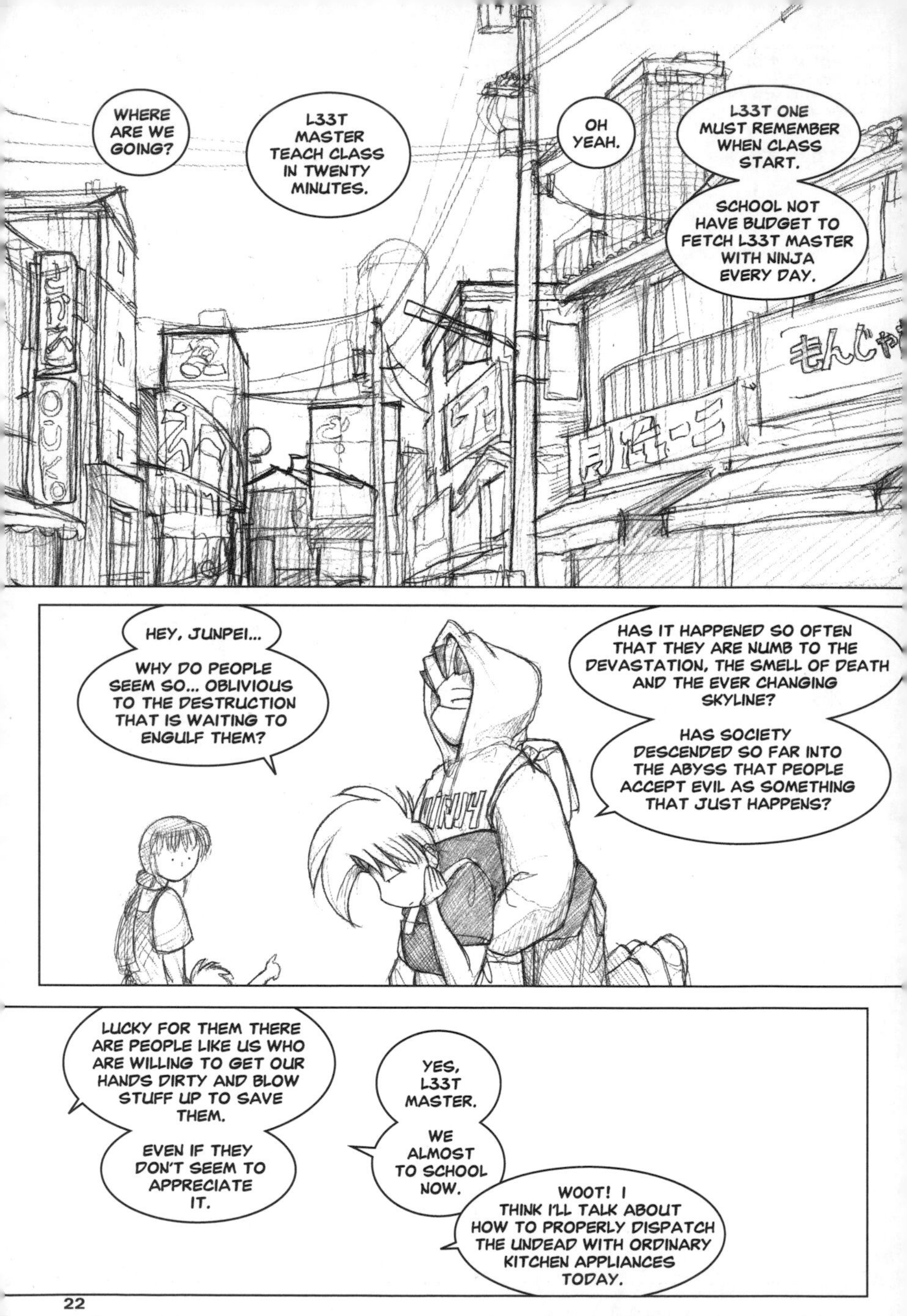

WHERE ARE WE GOING?
L33T MASTER TEACH CLASS IN TWENTY MINUTES.
OH YEAH.
L33T ONE MUST REMEMBER WHEN CLASS START.
SCHOOL NOT HAVE BUDGET TO FETCH L33T MASTER WITH NINJA EVERY DAY.
HEY, JUNPEI...
WHY DO PEOPLE SEEM SO... OBLIVIOUS TO THE DESTRUCTION THAT IS WAITING TO ENGULF THEM?
HAS IT HAPPENED SO OFTEN THAT THEY ARE NUMB TO THE DEVASTATION, THE SMELL OF DEATH AND THE EVER CHANGING SKYLINE?
HAS SOCIETY DESCENDED SO FAR INTO THE ABYSS THAT PEOPLE ACCEPT EVIL AS SOMETHING THAT JUST HAPPENS?
LUCKY FOR THEM THERE ARE PEOPLE LIKE US WHO ARE WILLING TO GET OUR HANDS DIRTY AND BLOW STUFF UP TO SAVE THEM.
EVEN IF THEY DON'T SEEM TO APPRECIATE IT.
YES, L33T MASTER.
WE ALMOST TO SCHOOL NOW.
WOOT! I THINK I'LL TALK ABOUT HOW TO PROPERLY DISPATCH THE UNDEAD WITH ORDINARY KITCHEN APPLIANCES TODAY.

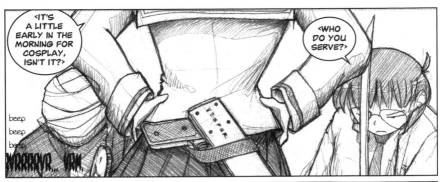

‹IT'S A LITTLE EARLY IN THE MORNING FOR COSPLAY, ISN'T IT?›

‹WHO DO YOU SERVE?›

beep
beep
beep

WRRRVR... VRM

‹THAT STANCE...›

‹I'VE SEEN IT BEFORE...›

beep
beep
beep

TAP TAP

GOOD TO SEE YOU, PIRO.

KEEP IN TOUCH.

YOU SEEM TO KNOW A LOT OF WEIRD PEOPLE.

THESE ARE JUST THE ONES WHO CAN AFFORD TO FLY HERE. YOU SHOULD MEET SOME OF THE ONES BACK HOME.

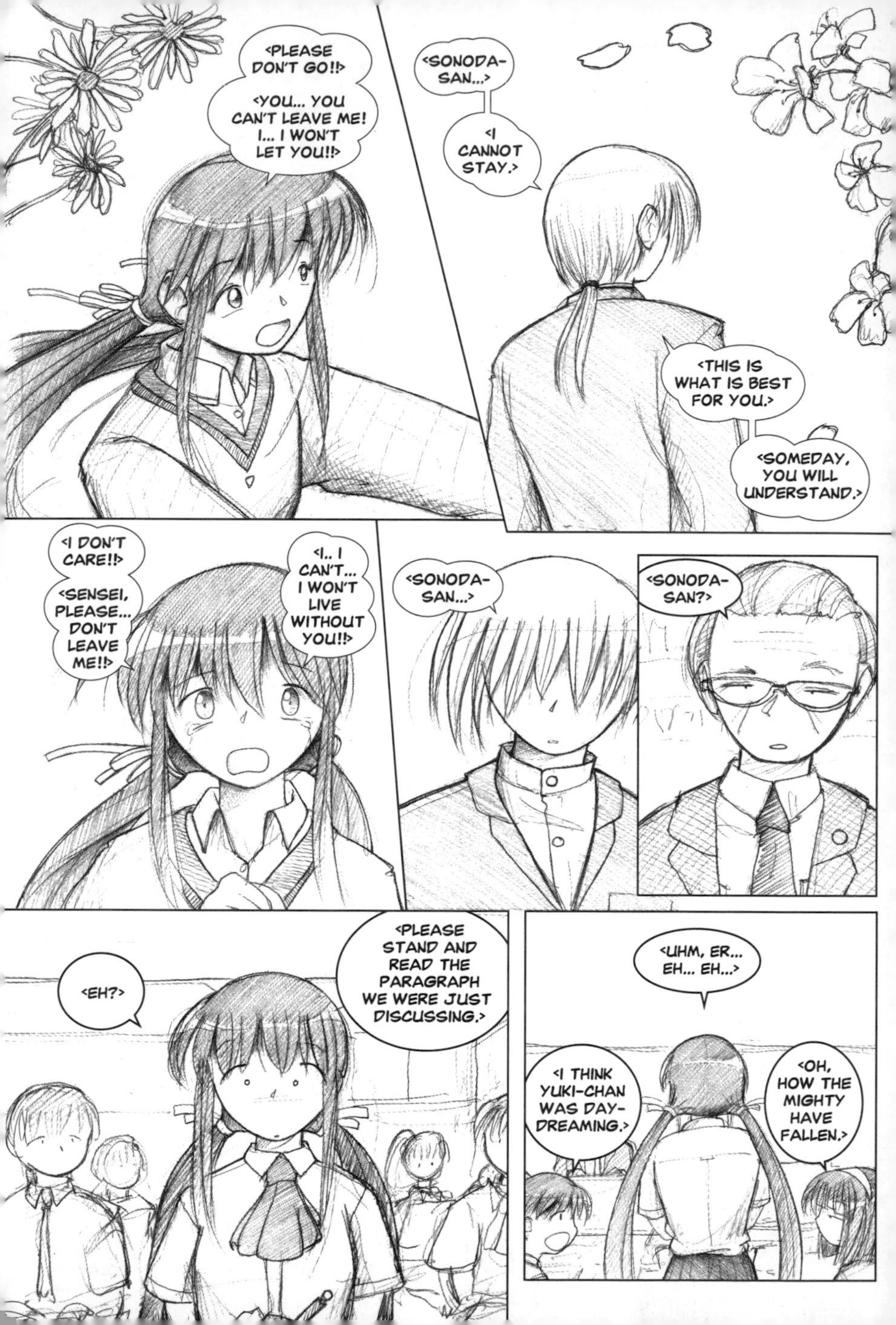
<PLEASE DON'T GO!!>
<YOU... YOU CAN'T LEAVE ME! I... I WON'T LET YOU!!>
<SONODA-SAN...>
<I CANNOT STAY.>
<THIS IS WHAT IS BEST FOR YOU.>
<SOMEDAY, YOU WILL UNDERSTAND.>
<I DON'T CARE!!>
<SENSEI, PLEASE... DON'T LEAVE ME!!>
<I.. I CAN'T... I WON'T LIVE WITHOUT YOU!!>
<SONODA-SAN...>
<SONODA-SAN?>
<EH?>
<PLEASE STAND AND READ THE PARAGRAPH WE WERE JUST DISCUSSING.>
<UHM, ER... EH... EH...>
<I THINK YUKI-CHAN WAS DAY-DREAMING.>
<OH, HOW THE MIGHTY HAVE FALLEN.>

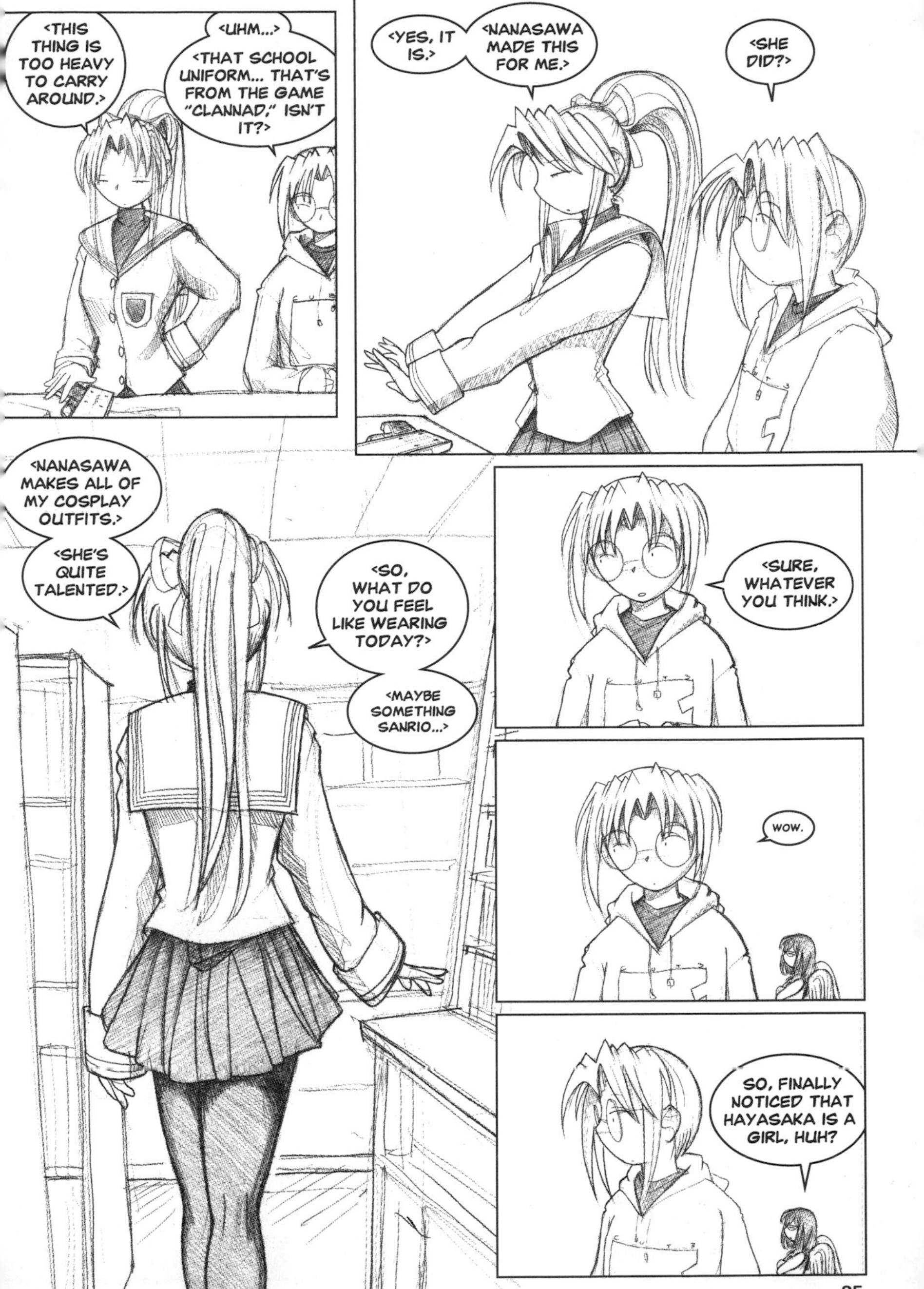
<THIS THING IS TOO HEAVY TO CARRY AROUND.>
<UHM...>
<THAT SCHOOL UNIFORM... THAT'S FROM THE GAME "CLANNAD," ISN'T IT?>
<YES, IT IS.>
<NANASAWA MADE THIS FOR ME.>
<SHE DID?>
<NANASAWA MAKES ALL OF MY COSPLAY OUTFITS.>
<SHE'S QUITE TALENTED.>
<SO, WHAT DO YOU FEEL LIKE WEARING TODAY?>
<MAYBE SOMETHING SANRIO...>
<SURE, WHATEVER YOU THINK.>
WOW.
SO, FINALLY NOTICED THAT HAYASAKA IS A GIRL, HUH?

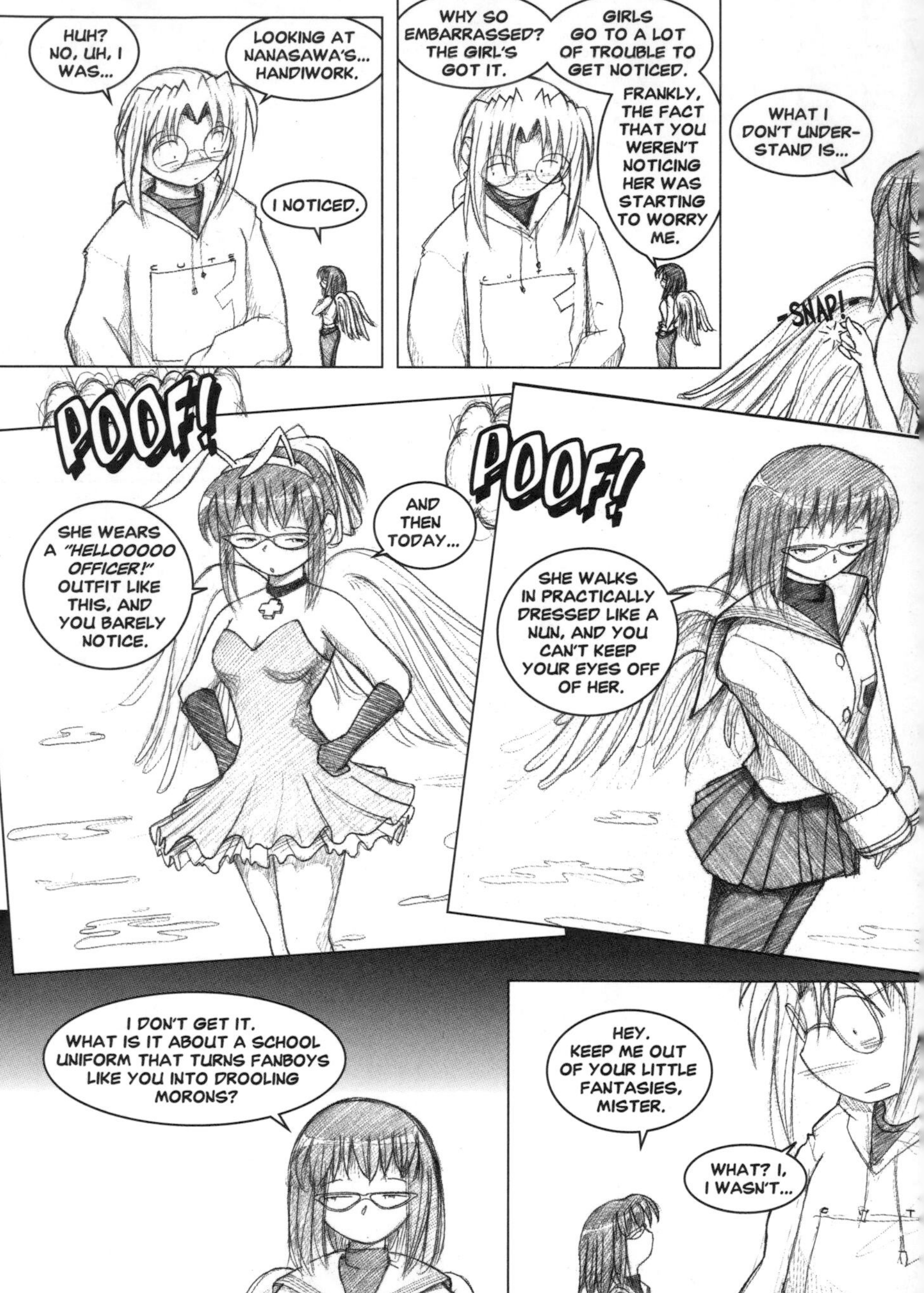
HUH? NO, UH, I WAS...
LOOKING AT NANASAWA'S... HANDIWORK.
I NOTICED.
WHY SO EMBARRASSED? THE GIRL'S GOT IT.
GIRLS GO TO A LOT OF TROUBLE TO GET NOTICED.
FRANKLY, THE FACT THAT YOU WEREN'T NOTICING HER WAS STARTING TO WORRY ME.
WHAT I DON'T UNDER-STAND IS...
-SNAP!-
POOF!
SHE WEARS A "HELLOOOOO OFFICER!" OUTFIT LIKE THIS, AND YOU BARELY NOTICE.
AND THEN TODAY...
POOF!
SHE WALKS IN PRACTICALLY DRESSED LIKE A NUN, AND YOU CAN'T KEEP YOUR EYES OFF OF HER.
I DON'T GET IT. WHAT IS IT ABOUT A SCHOOL UNIFORM THAT TURNS FANBOYS LIKE YOU INTO DROOLING MORONS?
HEY. KEEP ME OUT OF YOUR LITTLE FANTASIES, MISTER.
WHAT? I, I WASN'T...

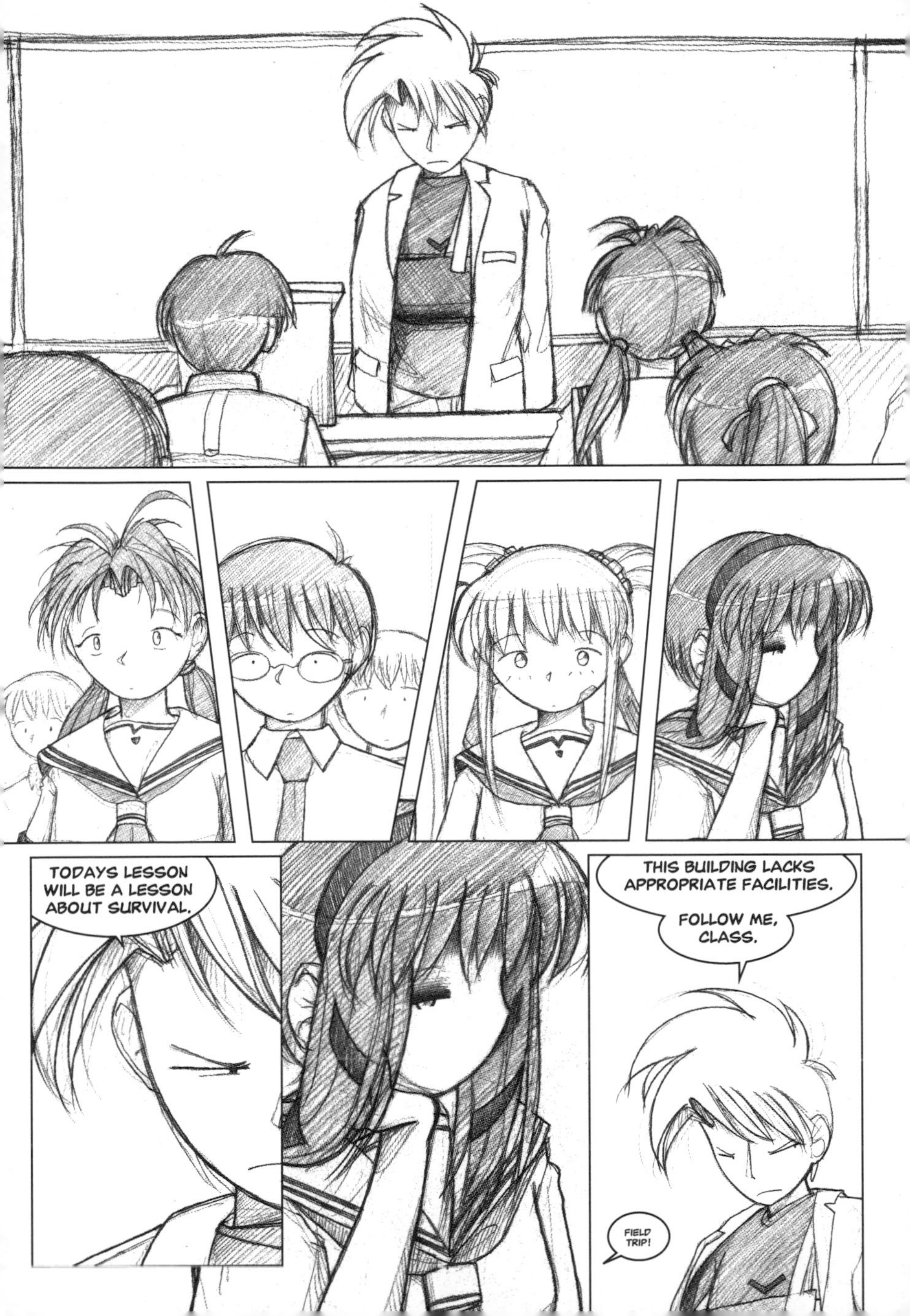
TODAYS LESSON WILL BE A LESSON ABOUT SURVIVAL.
THIS BUILDING LACKS APPROPRIATE FACILITIES.
FOLLOW ME, CLASS.
FIELD TRIP!

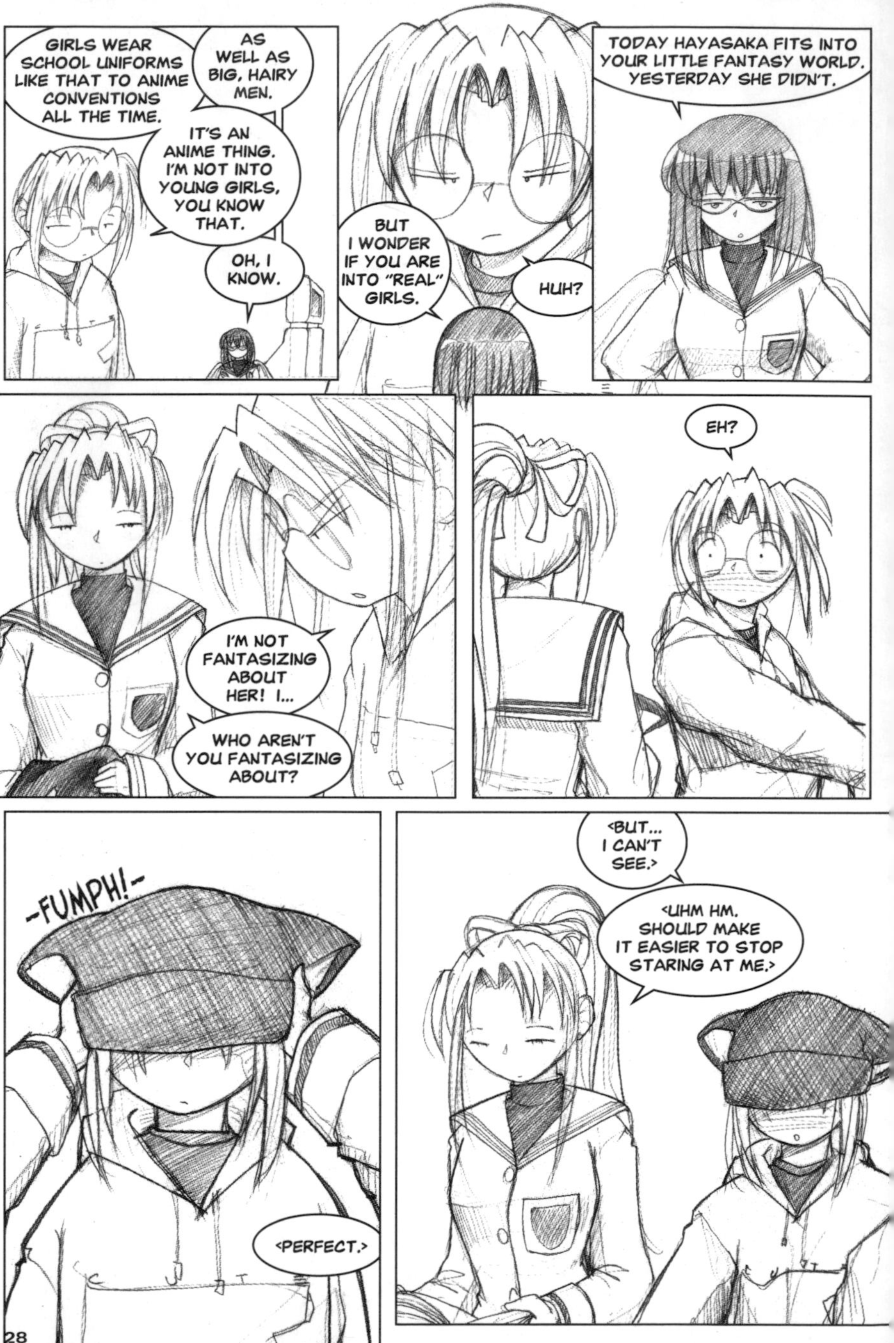
GIRLS WEAR SCHOOL UNIFORMS LIKE THAT TO ANIME CONVENTIONS ALL THE TIME.
AS WELL AS BIG, HAIRY MEN.
IT'S AN ANIME THING. I'M NOT INTO YOUNG GIRLS, YOU KNOW THAT.
OH, I KNOW.
BUT I WONDER IF YOU ARE INTO "REAL" GIRLS.
HUH?
TODAY HAYASAKA FITS INTO YOUR LITTLE FANTASY WORLD. YESTERDAY SHE DIDN'T.
I'M NOT FANTASIZING ABOUT HER! I...
WHO AREN'T YOU FANTASIZING ABOUT?
EH?
-FUMPH!-
<PERFECT.>
<BUT... I CAN'T SEE.>
<UHM HM. SHOULD MAKE IT EASIER TO STOP STARING AT ME.>

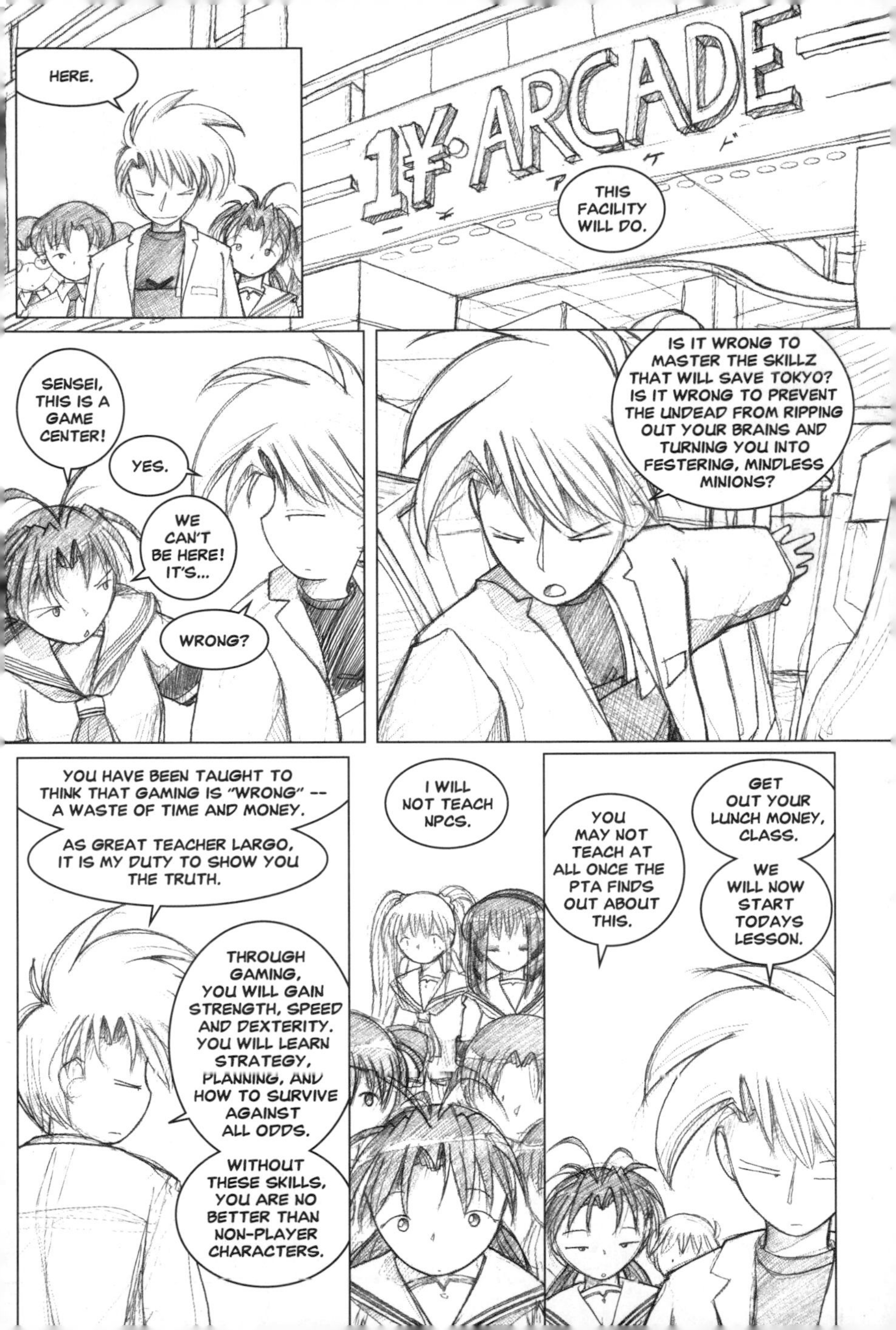

HERE.
1¥ ARCADE
THIS FACILITY WILL DO.
SENSEI, THIS IS A GAME CENTER!
YES.
WE CAN'T BE HERE! IT'S...
WRONG?
IS IT WRONG TO MASTER THE SKILLZ THAT WILL SAVE TOKYO? IS IT WRONG TO PREVENT THE UNDEAD FROM RIPPING OUT YOUR BRAINS AND TURNING YOU INTO FESTERING, MINDLESS MINIONS?
YOU HAVE BEEN TAUGHT TO THINK THAT GAMING IS "WRONG" -- A WASTE OF TIME AND MONEY.
AS GREAT TEACHER LARGO, IT IS MY DUTY TO SHOW YOU THE TRUTH.
THROUGH GAMING, YOU WILL GAIN STRENGTH, SPEED AND DEXTERITY. YOU WILL LEARN STRATEGY, PLANNING, AND HOW TO SURVIVE AGAINST ALL ODDS.
WITHOUT THESE SKILLS, YOU ARE NO BETTER THAN NON-PLAYER CHARACTERS.
I WILL NOT TEACH NPCS.
GET OUT YOUR LUNCH MONEY, CLASS.
WE WILL NOW START TODAYS LESSON.
YOU MAY NOT TEACH AT ALL ONCE THE PTA FINDS OUT ABOUT THIS.

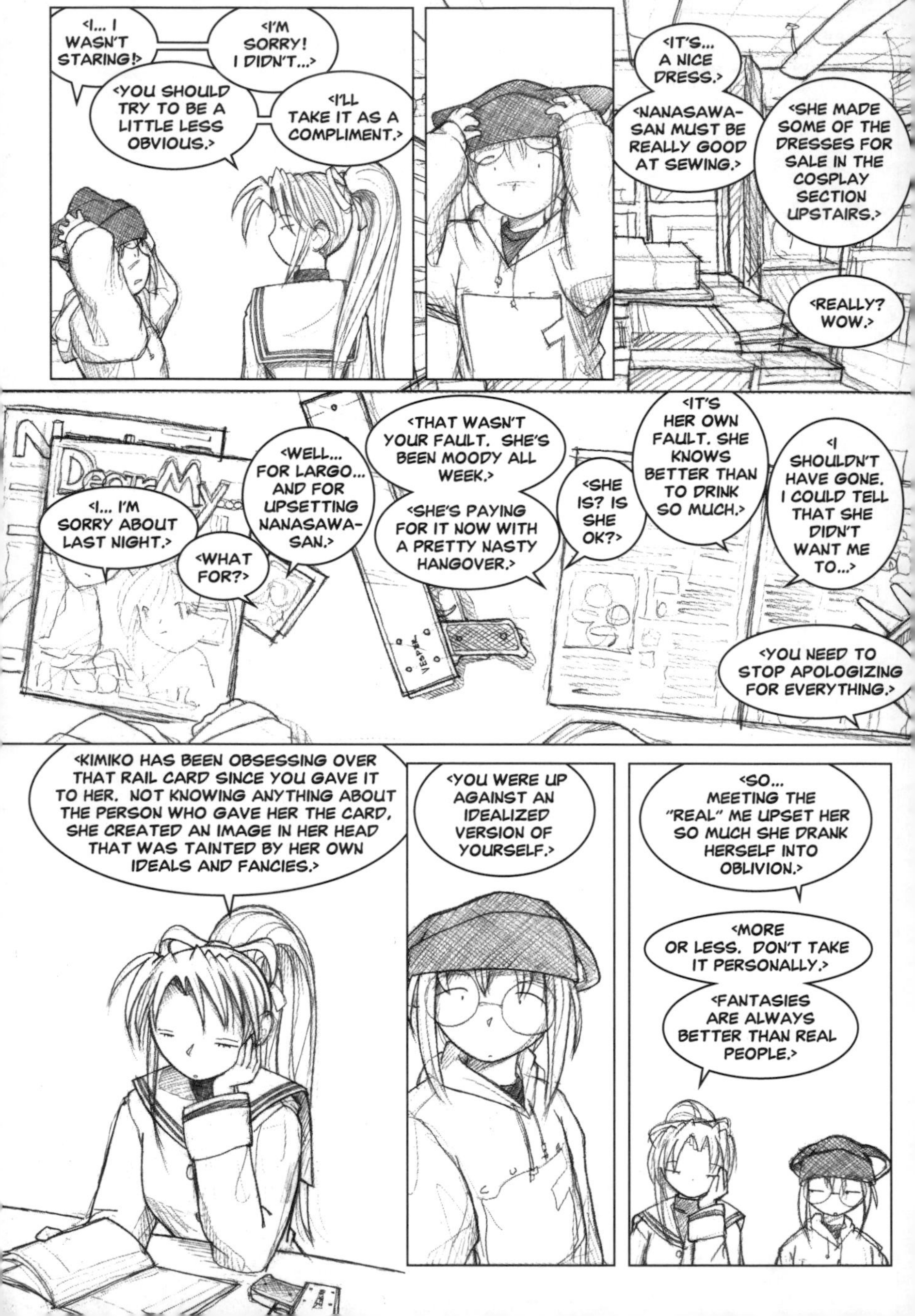
<I... I WASN'T STARING!>
<I'M SORRY! I DIDN'T...>
<YOU SHOULD TRY TO BE A LITTLE LESS OBVIOUS.>
<I'LL TAKE IT AS A COMPLIMENT.>
<IT'S... A NICE DRESS.>
<NANASAWA-SAN MUST BE REALLY GOOD AT SEWING.>
<SHE MADE SOME OF THE DRESSES FOR SALE IN THE COSPLAY SECTION UPSTAIRS.>
<REALLY? WOW.>
<I... I'M SORRY ABOUT LAST NIGHT.>
<WHAT FOR?>
<WELL... FOR LARGO... AND FOR UPSETTING NANASAWA-SAN.>
<THAT WASN'T YOUR FAULT. SHE'S BEEN MOODY ALL WEEK.>
<SHE'S PAYING FOR IT NOW WITH A PRETTY NASTY HANGOVER.>
<SHE IS? IS SHE OK?>
<IT'S HER OWN FAULT. SHE KNOWS BETTER THAN TO DRINK SO MUCH.>
<I SHOULDN'T HAVE GONE. I COULD TELL THAT SHE DIDN'T WANT ME TO...>
<YOU NEED TO STOP APOLOGIZING FOR EVERYTHING.>
<KIMIKO HAS BEEN OBSESSING OVER THAT RAIL CARD SINCE YOU GAVE IT TO HER. NOT KNOWING ANYTHING ABOUT THE PERSON WHO GAVE HER THE CARD, SHE CREATED AN IMAGE IN HER HEAD THAT WAS TAINTED BY HER OWN IDEALS AND FANCIES.>
<YOU WERE UP AGAINST AN IDEALIZED VERSION OF YOURSELF.>
<SO... MEETING THE "REAL" ME UPSET HER SO MUCH SHE DRANK HERSELF INTO OBLIVION.>
<MORE OR LESS. DON'T TAKE IT PERSONALLY.>
<FANTASIES ARE ALWAYS BETTER THAN REAL PEOPLE.>

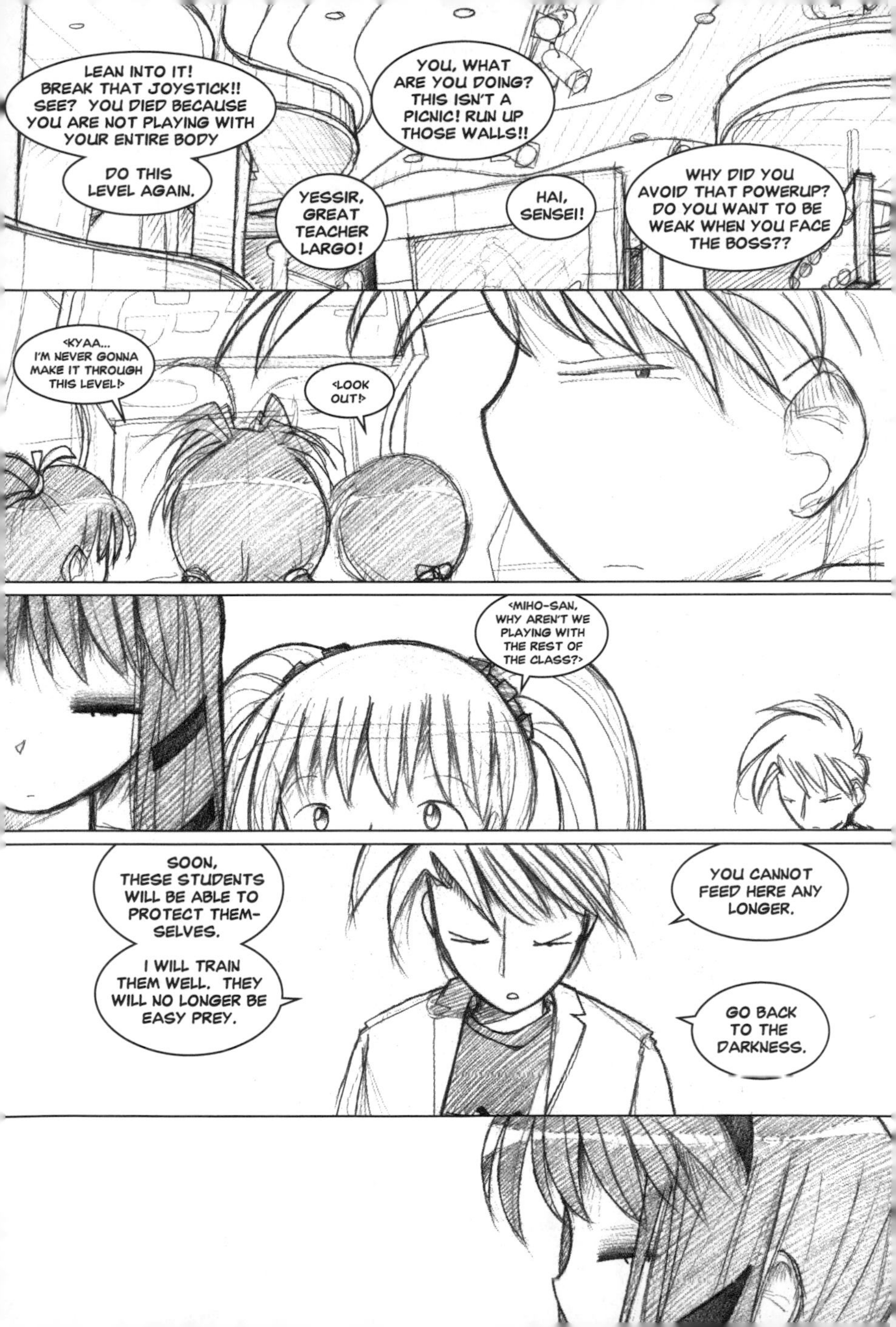
LEAN INTO IT! BREAK THAT JOYSTICK!! SEE? YOU DIED BECAUSE YOU ARE NOT PLAYING WITH YOUR ENTIRE BODY
DO THIS LEVEL AGAIN.
YOU, WHAT ARE YOU DOING? THIS ISN'T A PICNIC! RUN UP THOSE WALLS!!
YESSIR, GREAT TEACHER LARGO!
HAI, SENSEI!
WHY DID YOU AVOID THAT POWERUP? DO YOU WANT TO BE WEAK WHEN YOU FACE THE BOSS??
<KYAA... I'M NEVER GONNA MAKE IT THROUGH THIS LEVEL!>
<LOOK OUT!>
<MIHO-SAN, WHY AREN'T WE PLAYING WITH THE REST OF THE CLASS?>
SOON, THESE STUDENTS WILL BE ABLE TO PROTECT THEM-SELVES.
I WILL TRAIN THEM WELL. THEY WILL NO LONGER BE EASY PREY.
YOU CANNOT FEED HERE ANY LONGER.
GO BACK TO THE DARKNESS.

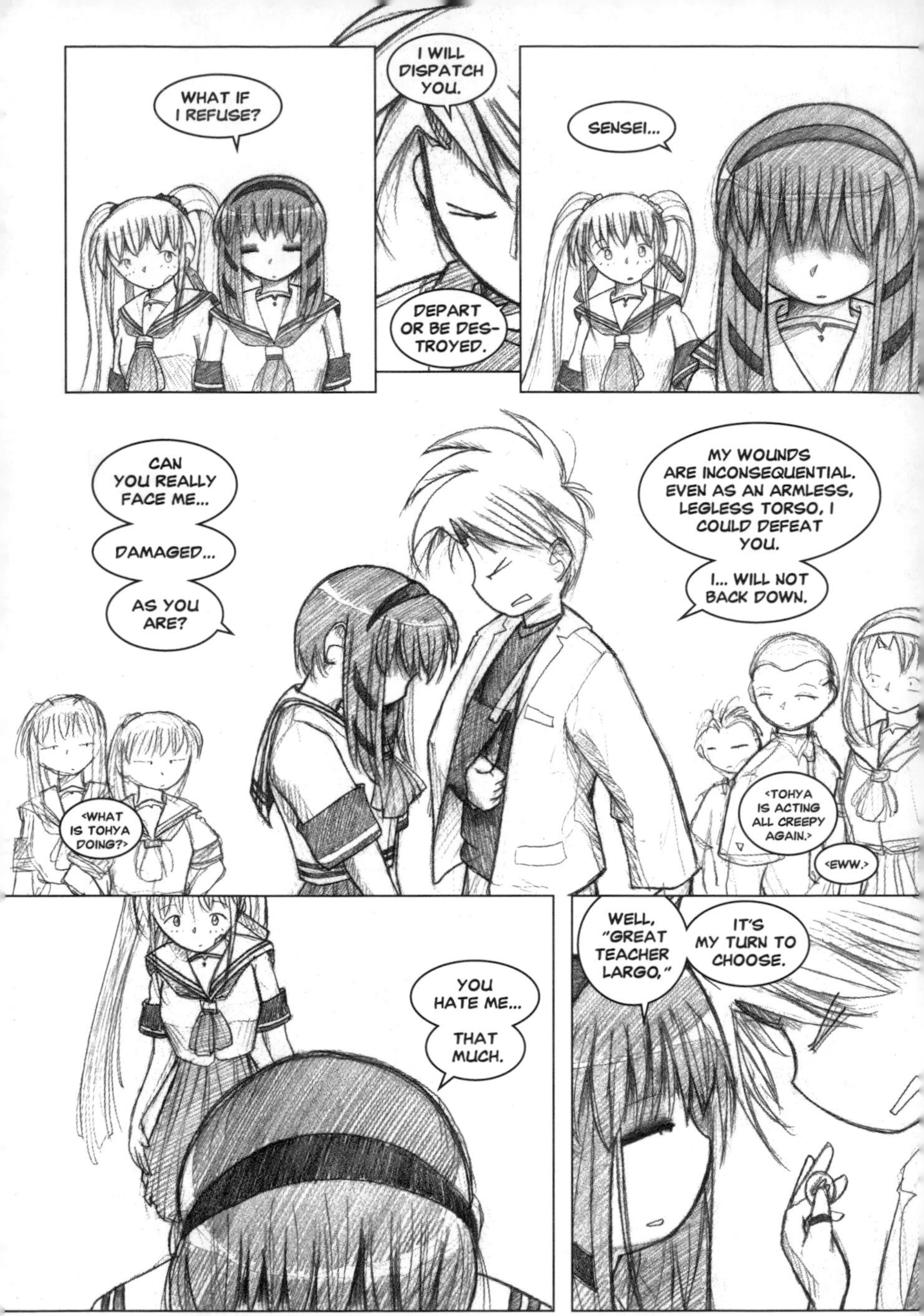
WHAT IF I REFUSE?
I WILL DISPATCH YOU.
DEPART OR BE DES-TROYED.
SENSEI...
CAN YOU REALLY FACE ME...
DAMAGED...
AS YOU ARE?
MY WOUNDS ARE INCONSEQUENTIAL. EVEN AS AN ARMLESS, LEGLESS TORSO, I COULD DEFEAT YOU.
I... WILL NOT BACK DOWN.
<WHAT IS TOHYA DOING?>
<TOHYA IS ACTING ALL CREEPY AGAIN.>
<EWW.>
YOU HATE ME...
THAT MUCH.
WELL, "GREAT TEACHER LARGO,"
IT'S MY TURN TO CHOOSE.

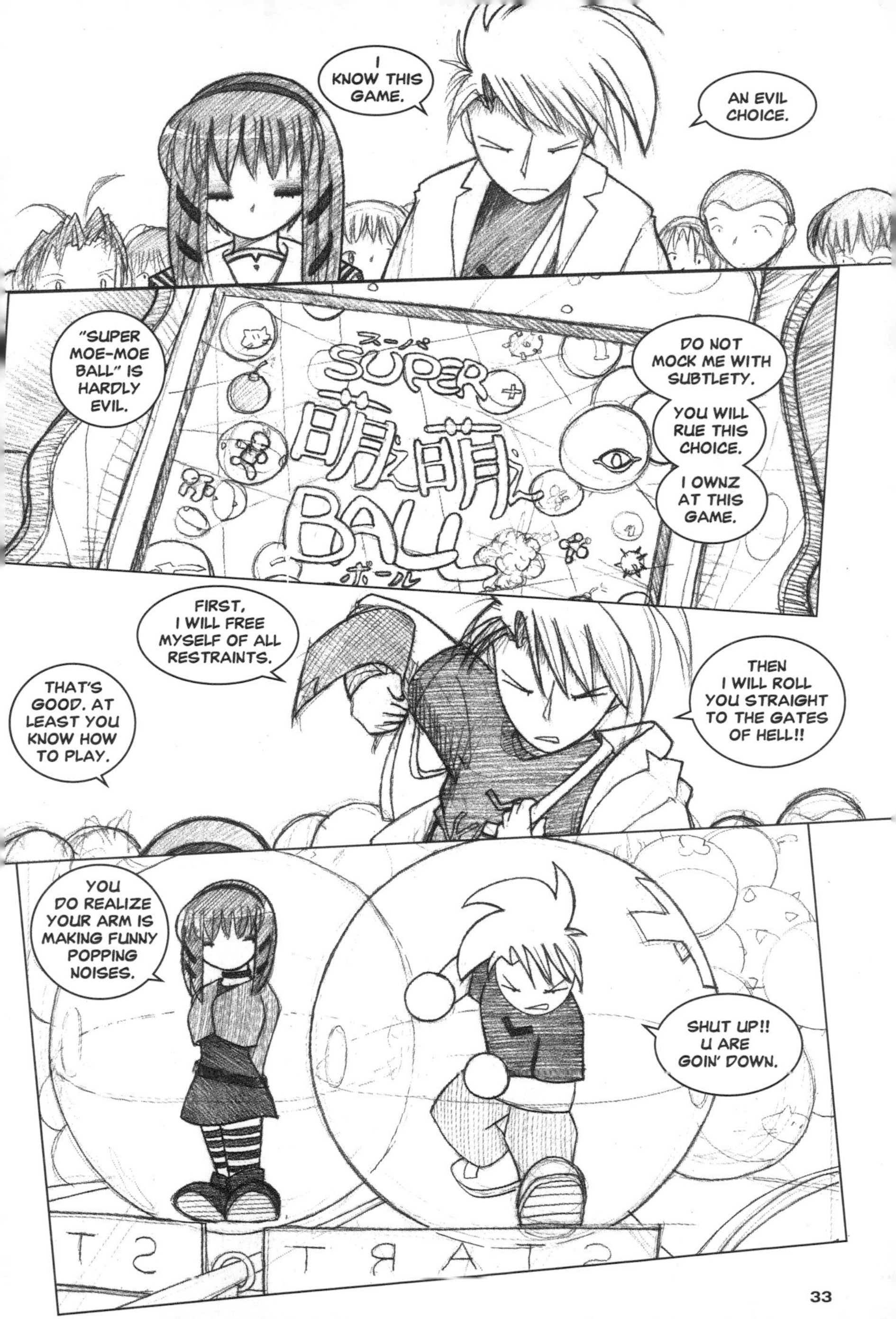
I KNOW THIS GAME.
AN EVIL CHOICE.
"SUPER MOE-MOE BALL" IS HARDLY EVIL.
スーパー
SUPER
萌萌
BALL
ボール
DO NOT MOCK ME WITH SUBTLETY.
YOU WILL RUE THIS CHOICE.
I OWNZ AT THIS GAME.
FIRST, I WILL FREE MYSELF OF ALL RESTRAINTS.
THAT'S GOOD. AT LEAST YOU KNOW HOW TO PLAY.
THEN I WILL ROLL YOU STRAIGHT TO THE GATES OF HELL!!
YOU DO REALIZE YOUR ARM IS MAKING FUNNY POPPING NOISES.
SHUT UP!! U ARE GOIN' DOWN.

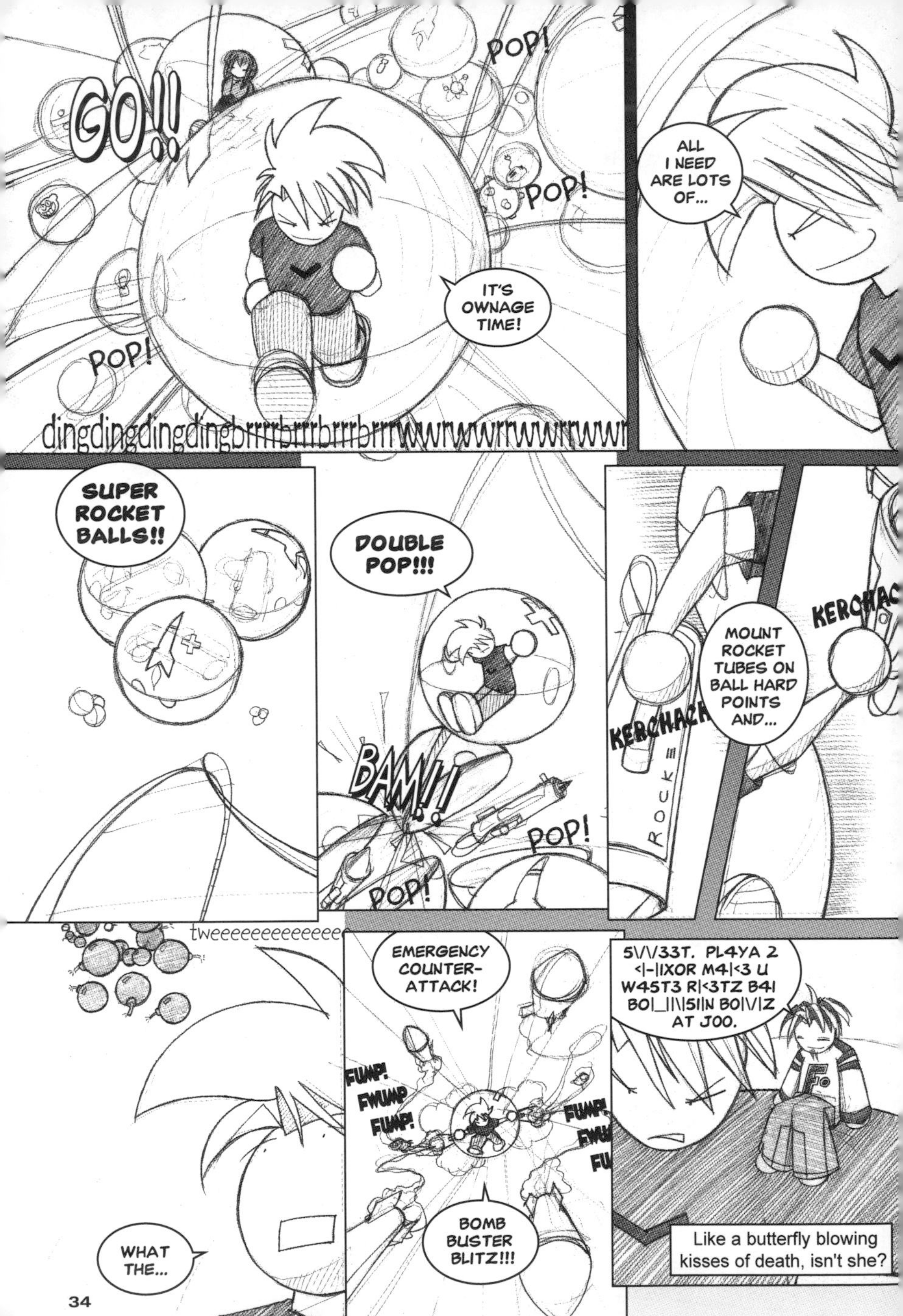
GO!!!
POP!
POP!
IT'S OWNAGE TIME!
POP!
dingdingdingdingbrrrrbrrrrbrrrbrrrwwwrwwwrwwwrwwwr
ALL I NEED ARE LOTS OF...
SUPER ROCKET BALLS!!
DOUBLE POP!!!
BAM!!
POP!
POP!
KERCHACK
MOUNT ROCKET TUBES ON BALL HARD POINTS AND...
KERCHAC
ROCKE
tweeeeeeeeeeeeeee
WHAT THE...
EMERGENCY COUNTER-ATTACK!
FUMP!
FWUMP
FUMP!
FUMP!
FWU
FU
BOMB BUSTER BLITZ!!!
5\/\/33T. PL4YA 2 <|-||XOR M4|<3 U W45T3 R|<3TZ B4I BO|_||\|5I|N BO|\/|Z AT J00.
Like a butterfly blowing kisses of death, isn't she?

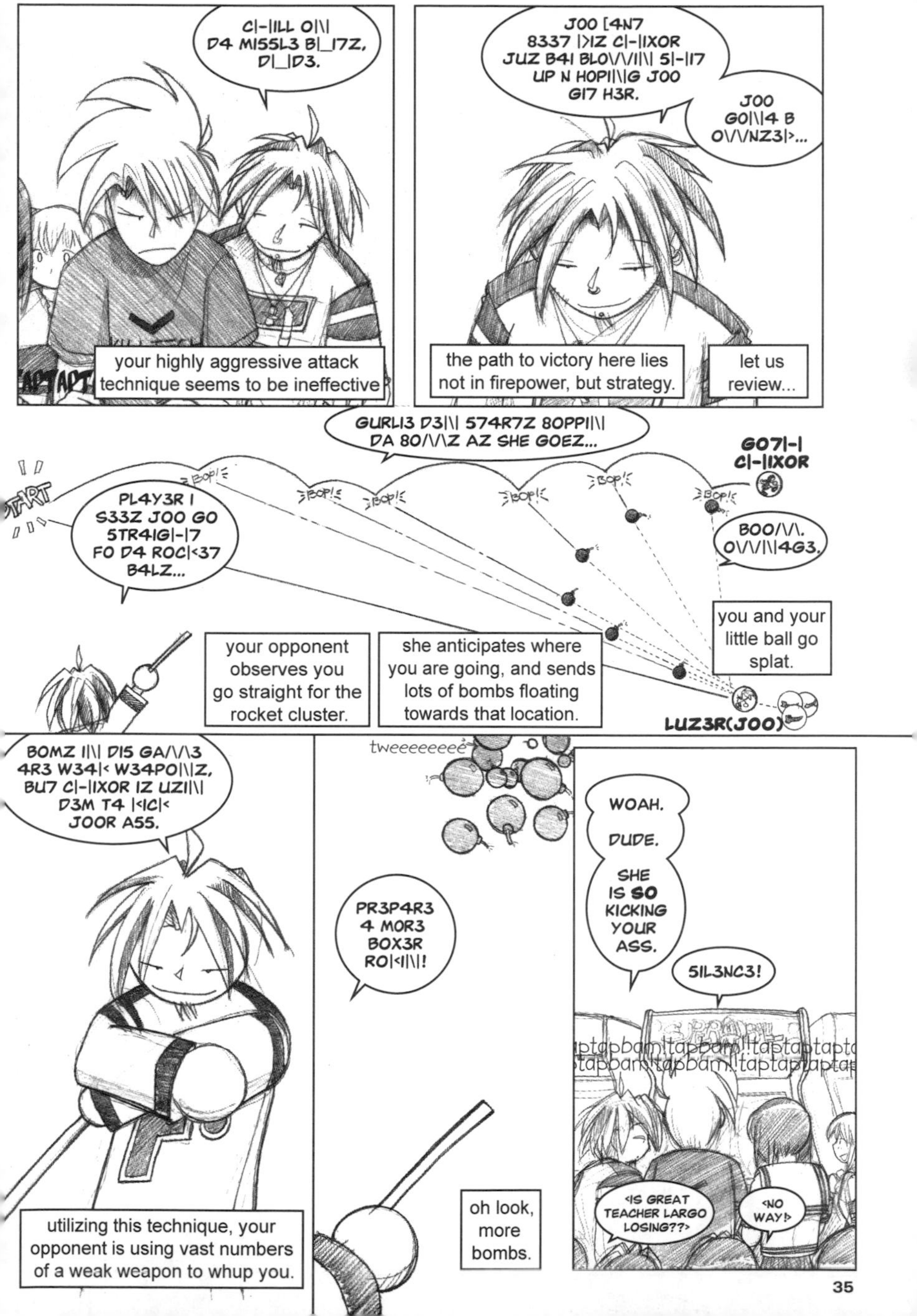
C|-|ILL O|\| D4 MISSL3 B|_I7Z, D|_|D3.
your highly aggressive attack technique seems to be ineffective
JOO [4N7 8337 |>IZ C|-|IXOR JUZ B4I BLO\/\/I|\| 5|-|I7 UP N HOPI|\|G JOO GI7 H3R.
the path to victory here lies not in firepower, but strategy.
JOO GO|\|4 B O\/\/NZ3|>...
let us review...
GURLI3 D3|\| 574R7Z 8OPPI|\| DA 8O/\/\Z AZ SHE GOEZ...
PL4Y3R I S33Z JOO GO 5TR4IG|-|7 FO D4 ROC|<37 B4LZ...
BOP! BOP! BOP! BOP! BOP! BOP!
GO7|-| C|-|IXOR
BOO/\/\. O\/\/I|\|4G3.
you and your little ball go splat.
your opponent observes you go straight for the rocket cluster.
she anticipates where you are going, and sends lots of bombs floating towards that location.
LUZ3R(JOO)
BOMZ I|\| DI5 GA/\/\3 4R3 W34|< W34PO|\|Z, BU7 C|-|IXOR IZ UZI|\| D3M T4 |<IC|< JOOR A55.
utilizing this technique, your opponent is using vast numbers of a weak weapon to whup you.
tweeeeeeee
PR3P4R3 4 MOR3 BOX3R RO|<I|\|!
oh look, more bombs.
WOAH.
DUDE.
SHE IS **SO** KICKING YOUR ASS.
5IL3NC3!
taptapbam!tapbam!!taptaptapta
taptapbam!tapbam!!taptaptapta
<IS GREAT TEACHER LARGO LOSING??>
<NO WAY!>

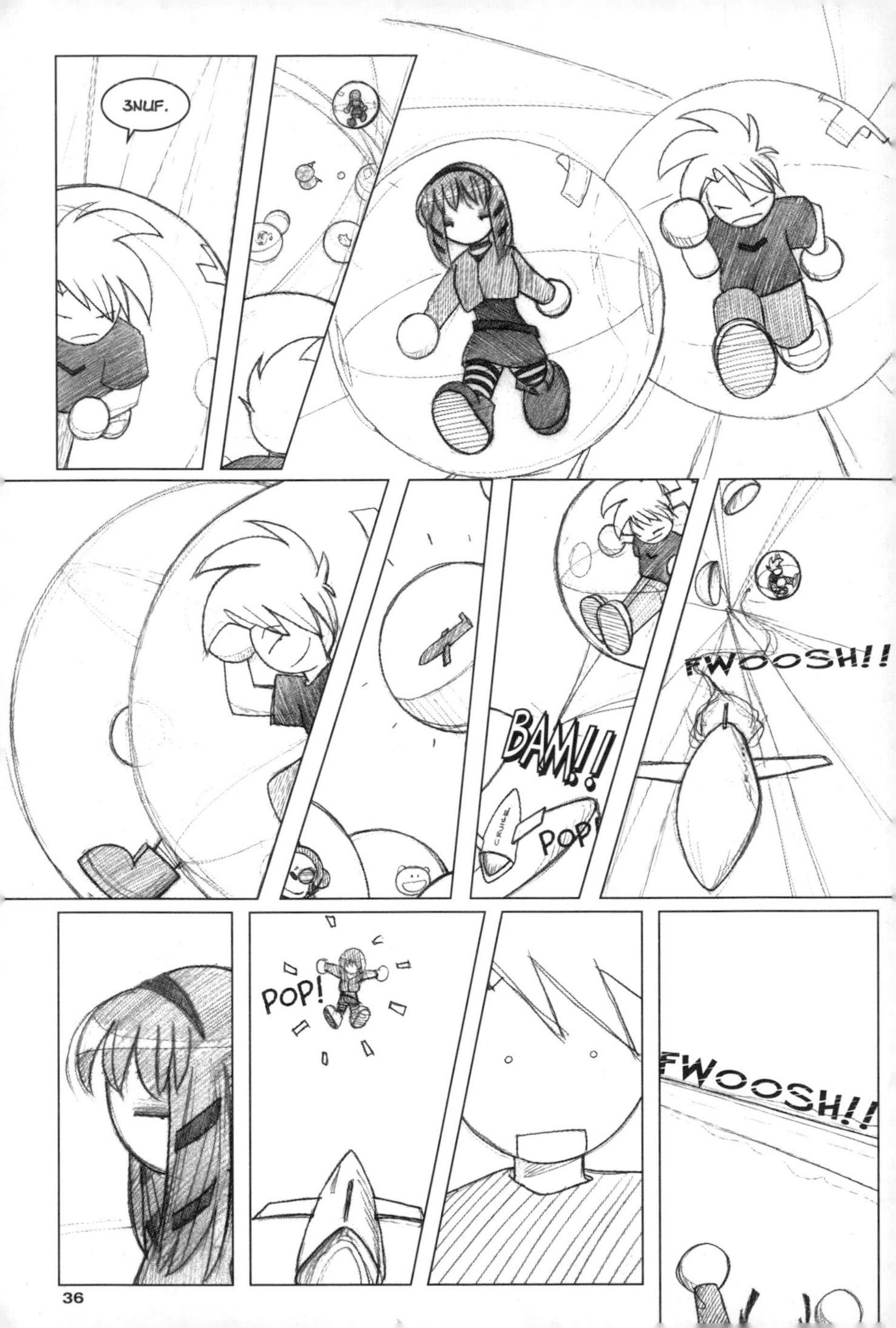
3NUF.
BAM!!
POP!
FWOOSH!!
POP!
FWOOSH!!

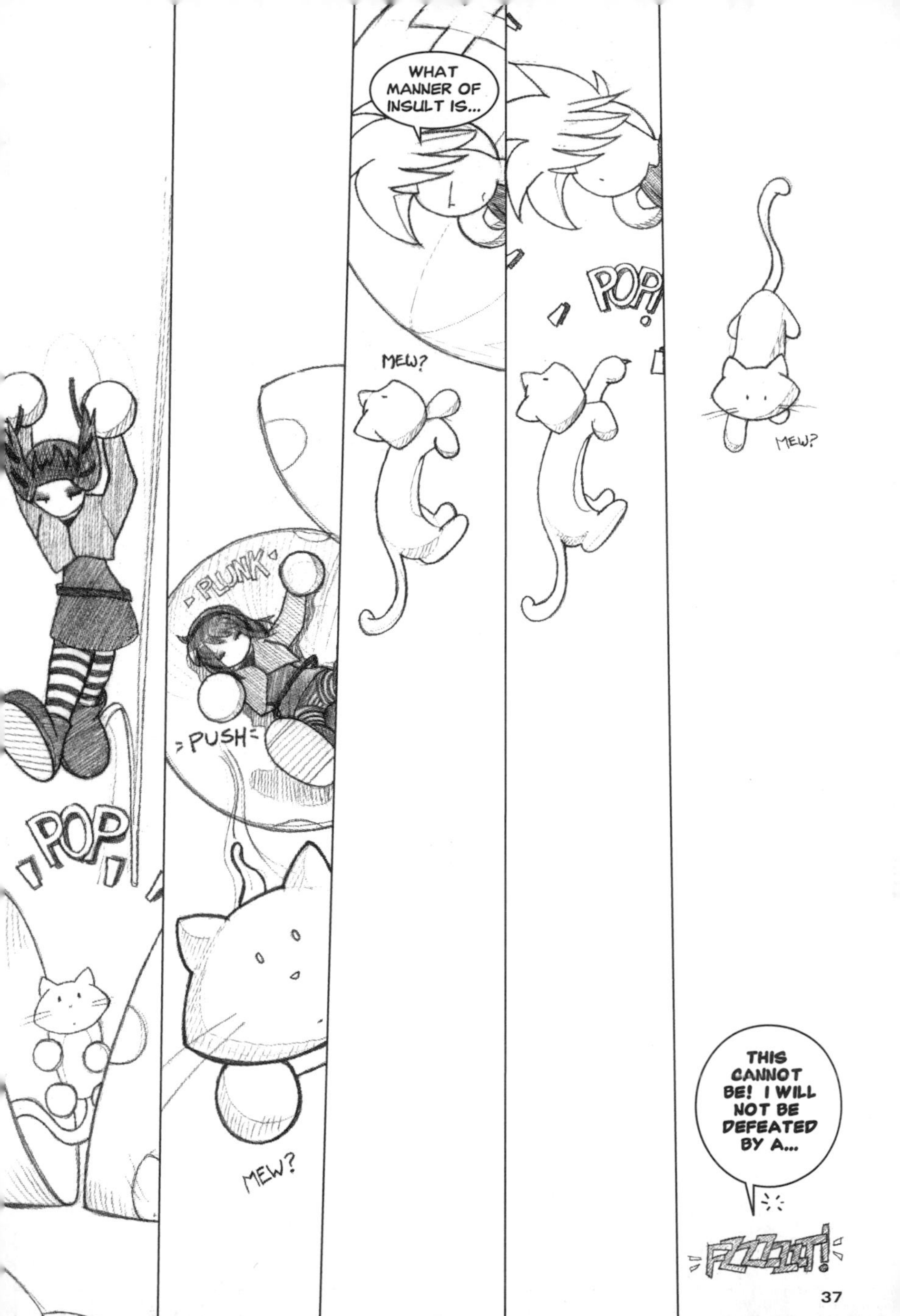
POP
PLUNK
PUSH
MEW?
WHAT MANNER OF INSULT IS...
MEW?
POP!
MEW?
THIS CANNOT BE! I WILL NOT BE DEFEATED BY A...

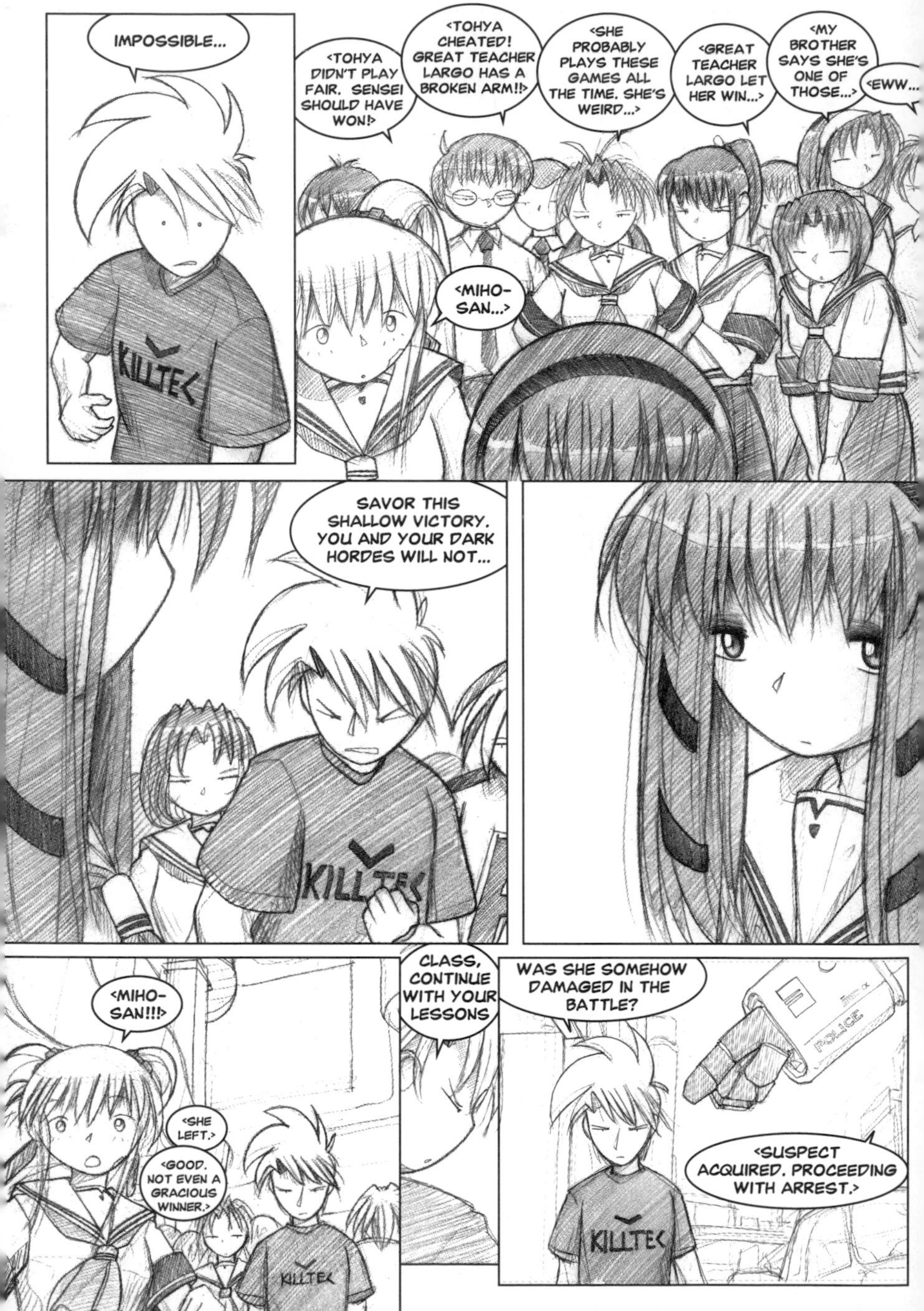
IMPOSSIBLE...
KILLTEC
<TOHYA DIDN'T PLAY FAIR. SENSEI SHOULD HAVE WON!>
<TOHYA CHEATED! GREAT TEACHER LARGO HAS A BROKEN ARM!!>
<SHE PROBABLY PLAYS THESE GAMES ALL THE TIME. SHE'S WEIRD...>
<GREAT TEACHER LARGO LET HER WIN...>
<MY BROTHER SAYS SHE'S ONE OF THOSE...>
<EWW...
<MIHO-SAN...>
SAVOR THIS SHALLOW VICTORY. YOU AND YOUR DARK HORDES WILL NOT...
<MIHO-SAN!!!>
<SHE LEFT.>
<GOOD. NOT EVEN A GRACIOUS WINNER.>
CLASS, CONTINUE WITH YOUR LESSONS
WAS SHE SOMEHOW DAMAGED IN THE BATTLE?
POLICE
<SUSPECT ACQUIRED. PROCEEDING WITH ARREST.>

39

<WHY... ISN'T NANASAWA EXCITED ABOUT THIS?>

<SHE'S JUST AFRAID OF GETTING HER HOPES UP.>

<REJECTION IS PART OF THE BUSINESS, BUT I THINK IT'S STARTING TO GET TO HER.>

<ALSO, I DON'T THINK SHE REALLY UNDERSTANDS HOW BIG THIS GAME MIGHT BE. FANBOYS HAVE BEEN JABBERING ABOUT IT IN HERE EVER SINCE *CUBESOFT* PICKED UP THE TITLE.>

<WELL, HER CONFIDENCE IS REALLY LOW RIGHT NOW. SHE'S BEEN AUDITIONING FOR PARTS FOR OVER TWO YEARS AND THIS IS ONLY HER THIRD CALL BACK.>

<I JUST HOPE SHE GETS A CALL TODAY. HER MOPING AROUND IS GETTING ON MY NERVES.>

<SO, ARE YOU GONNA HELP ME WITH THIS OR JUST STAND THERE GAPING?>

<S... SORRY!>

<UHM... HAYASAKA-SAN?>

<YES?>

<CAN I... I... HAVE A FEW ERRANDS TO RUN. I DIDN'T TAKE A LUNCH...>

<WHAT KIND OF ERRANDS?>

<J...JUST... STUFF...>

<WHY DO YOU ACT SO GUILTY ABOUT EVERYTHING?>

40

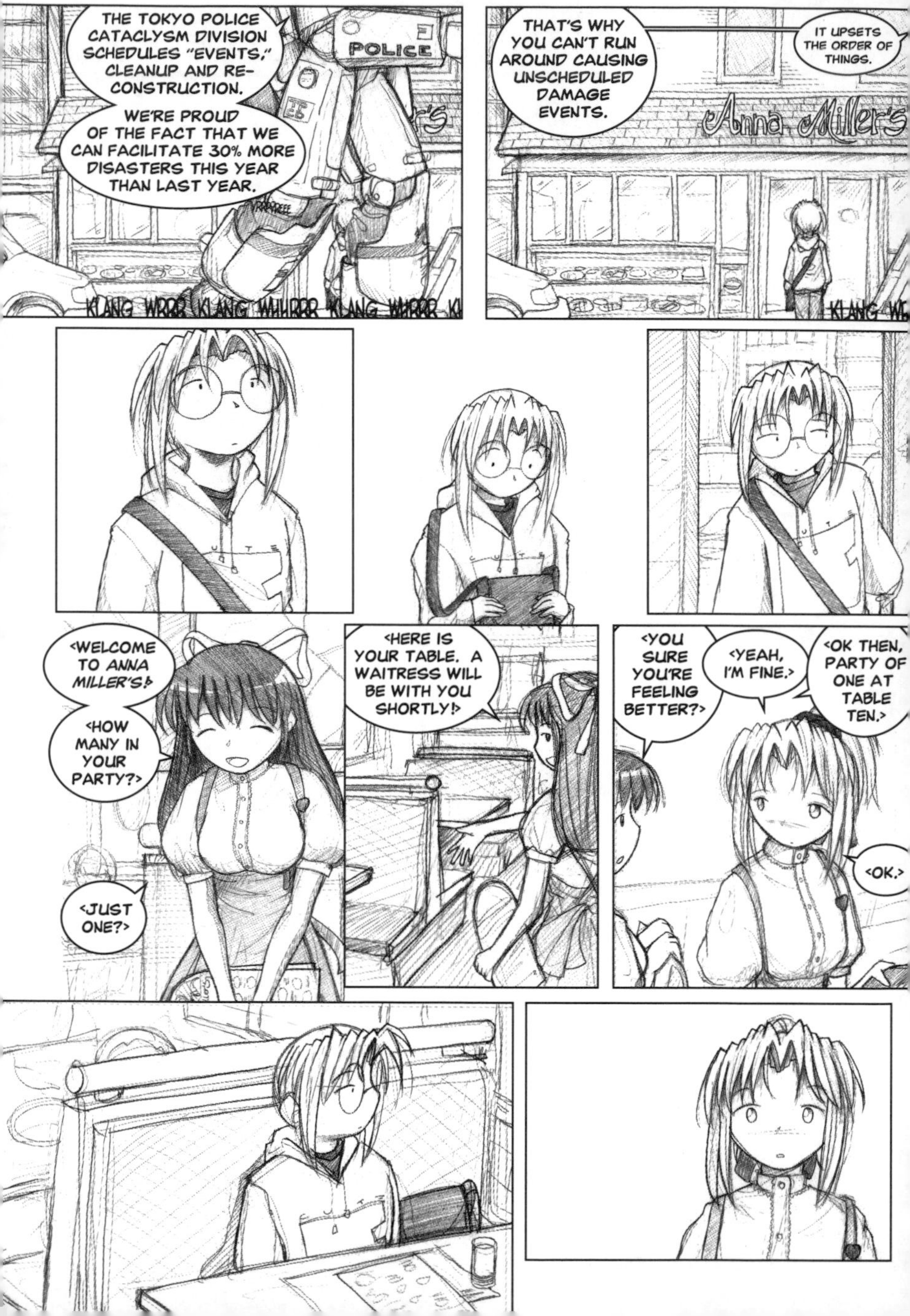
THE TOKYO POLICE CATACLYSM DIVISION SCHEDULES "EVENTS," CLEANUP AND RE-CONSTRUCTION.
WE'RE PROUD OF THE FACT THAT WE CAN FACILITATE 30% MORE DISASTERS THIS YEAR THAN LAST YEAR.
POLICE
VRRRREEE
KLANG WRRRR KLANG WHHRRR KLANG WHRRR
THAT'S WHY YOU CAN'T RUN AROUND CAUSING UNSCHEDULED DAMAGE EVENTS.
IT UPSETS THE ORDER OF THINGS.
Anna Miller's
KLANG
<WELCOME TO ANNA MILLER'S!>
<HOW MANY IN YOUR PARTY?>
<JUST ONE?>
<HERE IS YOUR TABLE. A WAITRESS WILL BE WITH YOU SHORTLY!>
<YOU SURE YOU'RE FEELING BETTER?>
<YEAH, I'M FINE.>
<OK THEN, PARTY OF ONE AT TABLE TEN.>
<OK.>

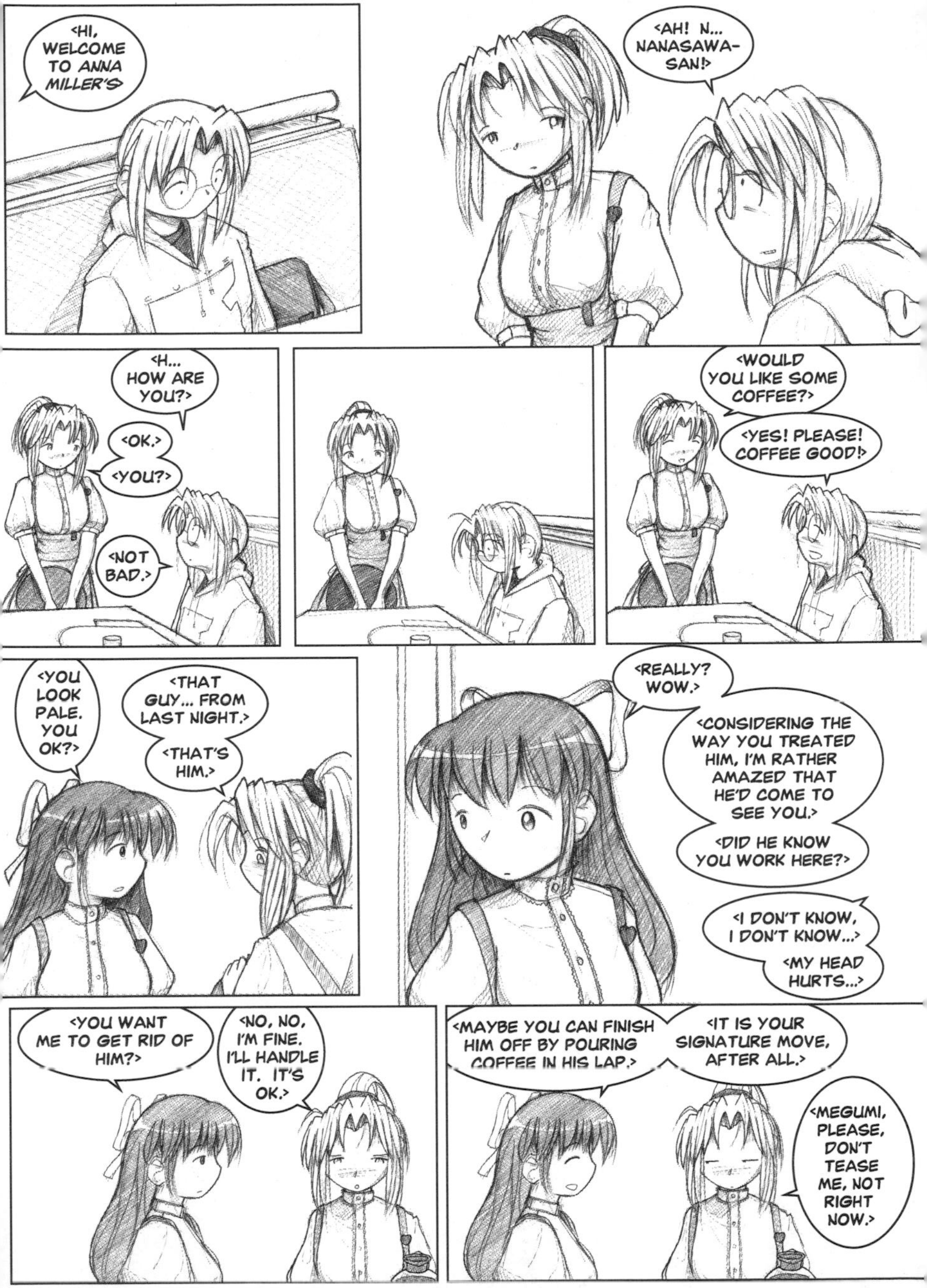
<HI, WELCOME TO ANNA MILLER'S>
<AH! N... NANASAWA-SAN!>
<H... HOW ARE YOU?>
<OK.>
<YOU?>
<NOT BAD.>
<WOULD YOU LIKE SOME COFFEE?>
<YES! PLEASE! COFFEE GOOD!>
<YOU LOOK PALE. YOU OK?>
<THAT GUY... FROM LAST NIGHT.>
<THAT'S HIM.>
<REALLY? WOW.>
<CONSIDERING THE WAY YOU TREATED HIM, I'M RATHER AMAZED THAT HE'D COME TO SEE YOU.>
<DID HE KNOW YOU WORK HERE?>
<I DON'T KNOW, I DON'T KNOW...>
<MY HEAD HURTS...>
<YOU WANT ME TO GET RID OF HIM?>
<NO, NO, I'M FINE. I'LL HANDLE IT. IT'S OK.>
<MAYBE YOU CAN FINISH HIM OFF BY POURING COFFEE IN HIS LAP.>
<IT IS YOUR SIGNATURE MOVE, AFTER ALL.>
<MEGUMI, PLEASE, DON'T TEASE ME, NOT RIGHT NOW.>

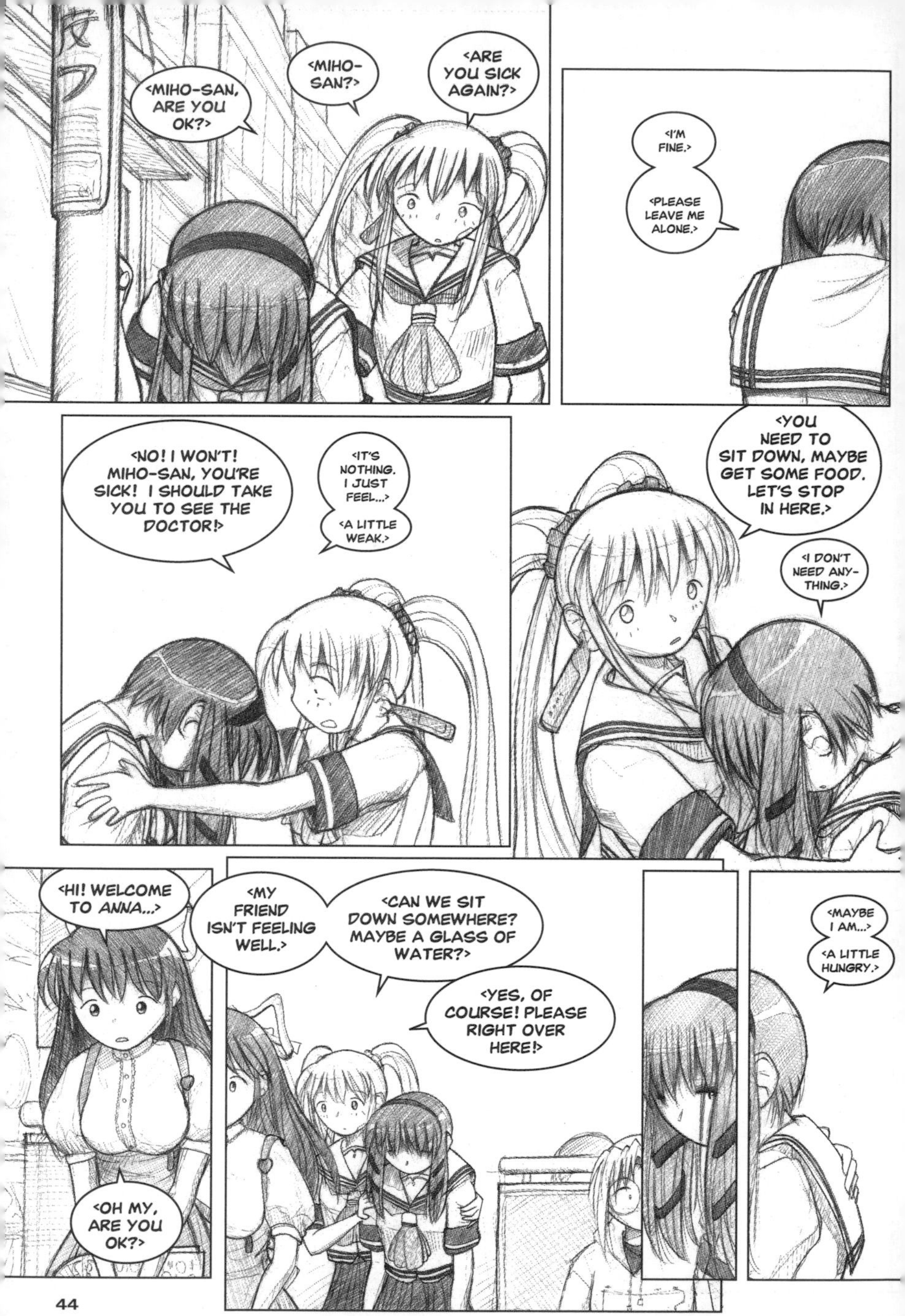
<MIHO-SAN, ARE YOU OK?>
<MIHO-SAN?>
<ARE YOU SICK AGAIN?>
<I'M FINE.>
<PLEASE LEAVE ME ALONE.>
<NO! I WON'T! MIHO-SAN, YOU'RE SICK! I SHOULD TAKE YOU TO SEE THE DOCTOR!>
<IT'S NOTHING. I JUST FEEL...>
<A LITTLE WEAK.>
<YOU NEED TO SIT DOWN, MAYBE GET SOME FOOD. LET'S STOP IN HERE.>
<I DON'T NEED ANY-THING.>
<HI! WELCOME TO ANNA...>
<OH MY, ARE YOU OK?>
<MY FRIEND ISN'T FEELING WELL.>
<CAN WE SIT DOWN SOMEWHERE? MAYBE A GLASS OF WATER?>
<YES, OF COURSE! PLEASE RIGHT OVER HERE!>
<MAYBE I AM...>
<A LITTLE HUNGRY.>

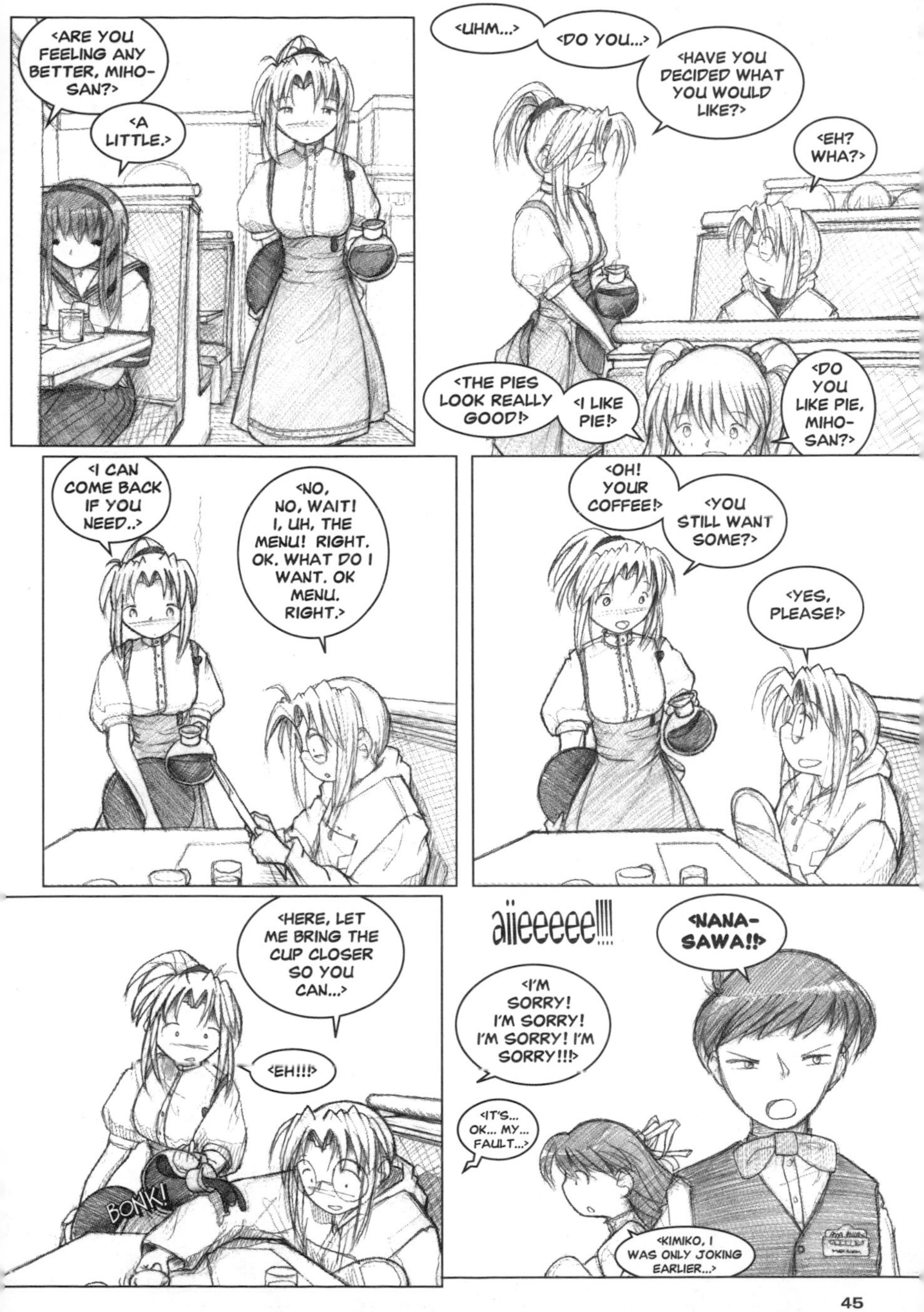
<ARE YOU FEELING ANY BETTER, MIHO-SAN?>
<A LITTLE.>
<UHM...>
<DO YOU...>
<HAVE YOU DECIDED WHAT YOU WOULD LIKE?>
<EH? WHA?>
<THE PIES LOOK REALLY GOOD!>
<I LIKE PIE!>
<DO YOU LIKE PIE, MIHO-SAN?>
<I CAN COME BACK IF YOU NEED..>
<NO, NO, WAIT! I, UH, THE MENU! RIGHT. OK. WHAT DO I WANT. OK MENU. RIGHT.>
<OH! YOUR COFFEE!>
<YOU STILL WANT SOME?>
<YES, PLEASE!>
<HERE, LET ME BRING THE CUP CLOSER SO YOU CAN...>
<EH!!!>
BONK!
aiieeeee!!!!
<NANA-SAWA!!>
<I'M SORRY! I'M SORRY! I'M SORRY! I'M SORRY!!!>
<IT'S... OK... MY... FAULT...>
<KIMIKO, I WAS ONLY JOKING EARLIER...>

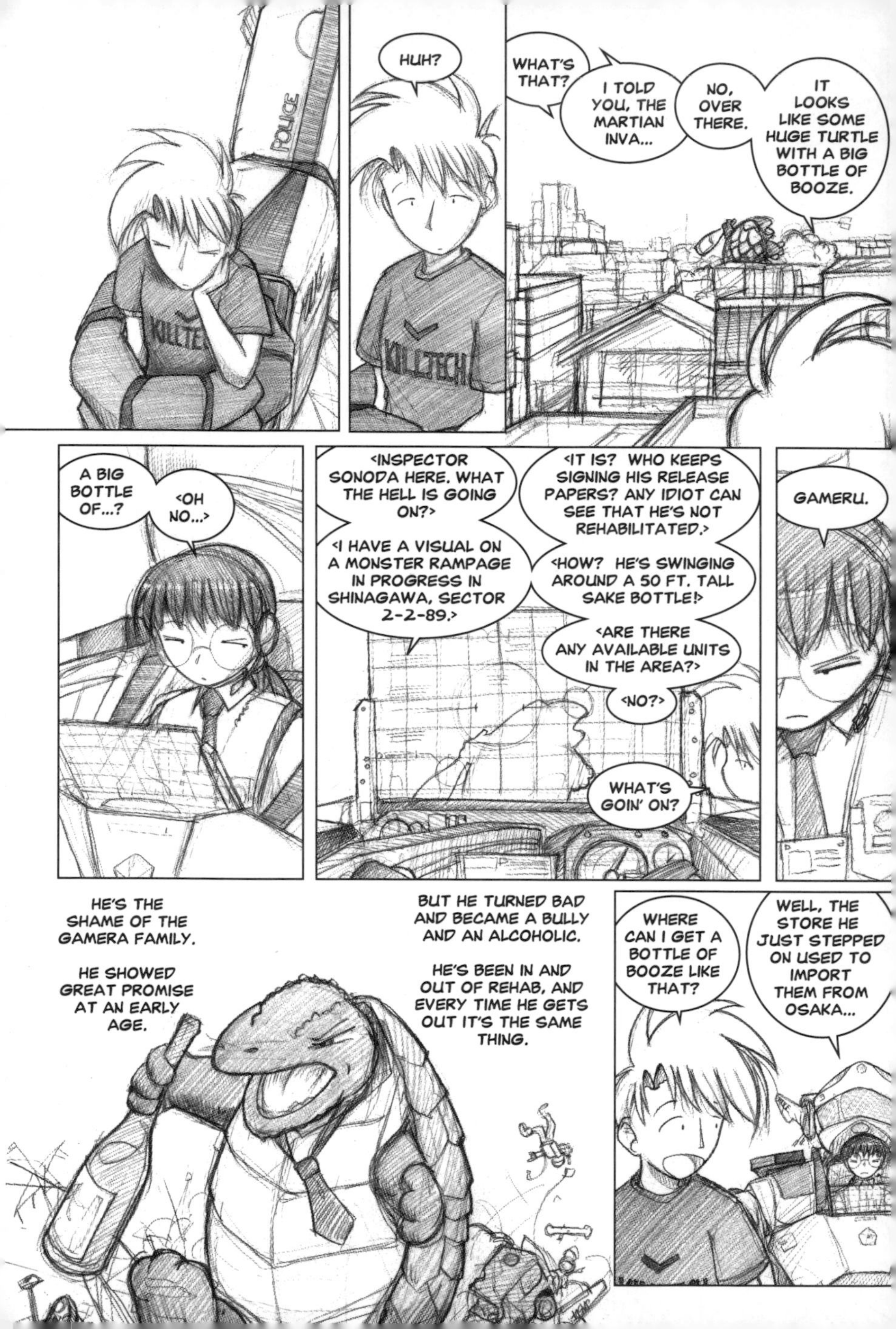

POLICE
HUH?
WHAT'S THAT?
I TOLD YOU, THE MARTIAN INVA...
NO, OVER THERE.
IT LOOKS LIKE SOME HUGE TURTLE WITH A BIG BOTTLE OF BOOZE.
KILLTECH
A BIG BOTTLE OF...?
<OH NO...>
<INSPECTOR SONODA HERE. WHAT THE HELL IS GOING ON?>
<I HAVE A VISUAL ON A MONSTER RAMPAGE IN PROGRESS IN SHINAGAWA, SECTOR 2-2-89.>
<IT IS? WHO KEEPS SIGNING HIS RELEASE PAPERS? ANY IDIOT CAN SEE THAT HE'S NOT REHABILITATED.>
<HOW? HE'S SWINGING AROUND A 50 FT. TALL SAKE BOTTLE!>
<ARE THERE ANY AVAILABLE UNITS IN THE AREA?>
<NO?>
WHAT'S GOIN' ON?
GAMERU.
HE'S THE SHAME OF THE GAMERA FAMILY.
HE SHOWED GREAT PROMISE AT AN EARLY AGE.
BUT HE TURNED BAD AND BECAME A BULLY AND AN ALCOHOLIC.
HE'S BEEN IN AND OUT OF REHAB, AND EVERY TIME HE GETS OUT IT'S THE SAME THING.
WHERE CAN I GET A BOTTLE OF BOOZE LIKE THAT?
WELL, THE STORE HE JUST STEPPED ON USED TO IMPORT THEM FROM OSAKA...

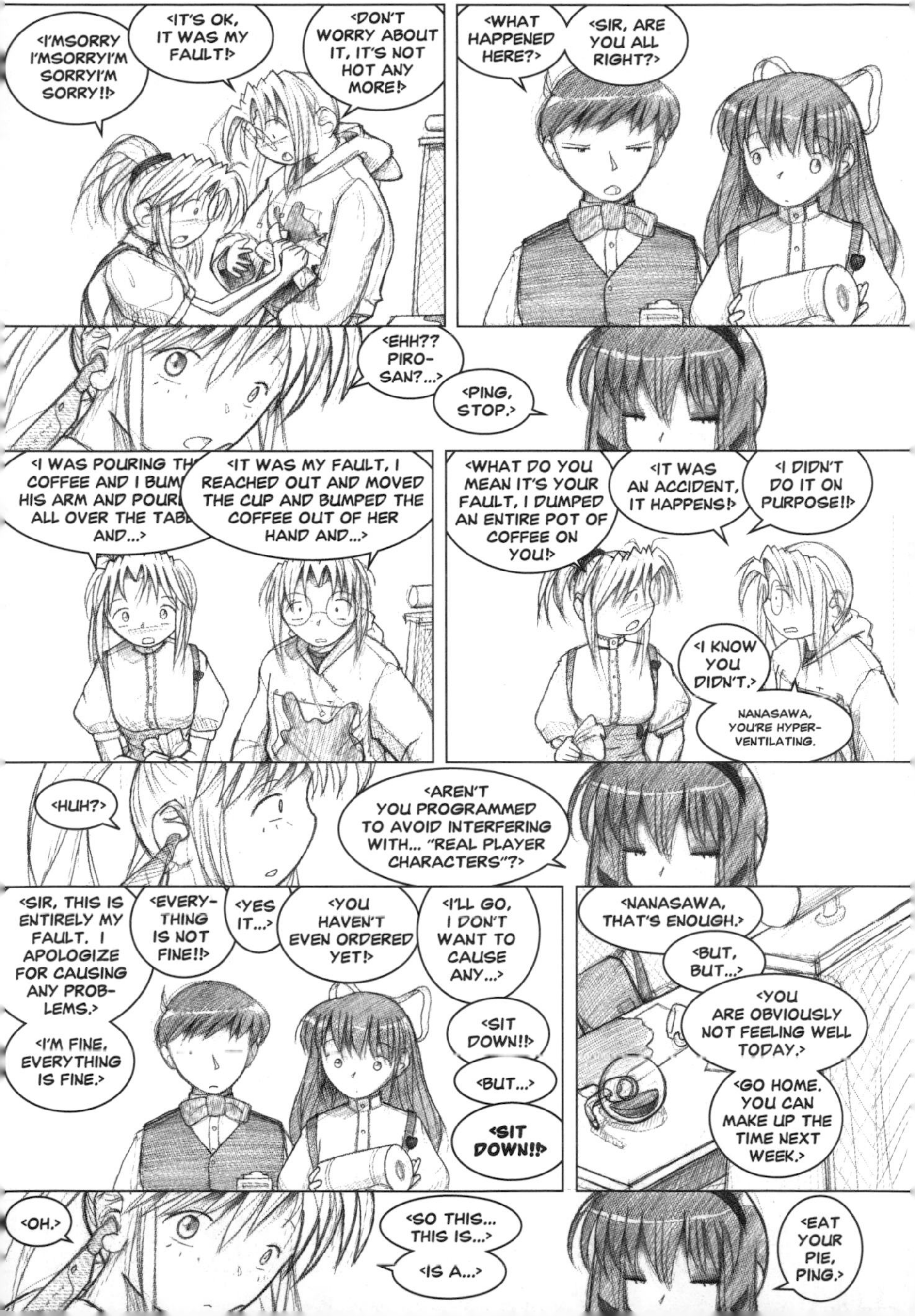
<I'MSORRY I'MSORRYI'M SORRYI'M SORRY!!>
<IT'S OK, IT WAS MY FAULT!>
<DON'T WORRY ABOUT IT, IT'S NOT HOT ANY MORE!>
<WHAT HAPPENED HERE?>
<SIR, ARE YOU ALL RIGHT?>
<EHH?? PIRO-SAN?...>
<PING, STOP.>
<I WAS POURING TH COFFEE AND I BUM HIS ARM AND POUR ALL OVER THE TAB AND...>
<IT WAS MY FAULT, I REACHED OUT AND MOVED THE CUP AND BUMPED THE COFFEE OUT OF HER HAND AND...>
<WHAT DO YOU MEAN IT'S YOUR FAULT, I DUMPED AN ENTIRE POT OF COFFEE ON YOU!>
<IT WAS AN ACCIDENT, IT HAPPENS!>
<I DIDN'T DO IT ON PURPOSE!!>
<I KNOW YOU DIDN'T.>
NANASAWA, YOU'RE HYPER-VENTILATING.
<HUH?>
<AREN'T YOU PROGRAMMED TO AVOID INTERFERING WITH... "REAL PLAYER CHARACTERS"?>
<SIR, THIS IS ENTIRELY MY FAULT. I APOLOGIZE FOR CAUSING ANY PROB-LEMS.>
<I'M FINE, EVERYTHING IS FINE.>
<EVERY-THING IS NOT FINE!!>
<YES IT...>
<YOU HAVEN'T EVEN ORDERED YET!>
<I'LL GO, I DON'T WANT TO CAUSE ANY...>
<SIT DOWN!!>
<BUT...>
<SIT DOWN!!>
<NANASAWA, THAT'S ENOUGH.>
<BUT, BUT...>
<YOU ARE OBVIOUSLY NOT FEELING WELL TODAY.>
<GO HOME. YOU CAN MAKE UP THE TIME NEXT WEEK.>
<OH.>
<SO THIS... THIS IS...>
<IS A...>
<EAT YOUR PIE, PING.>

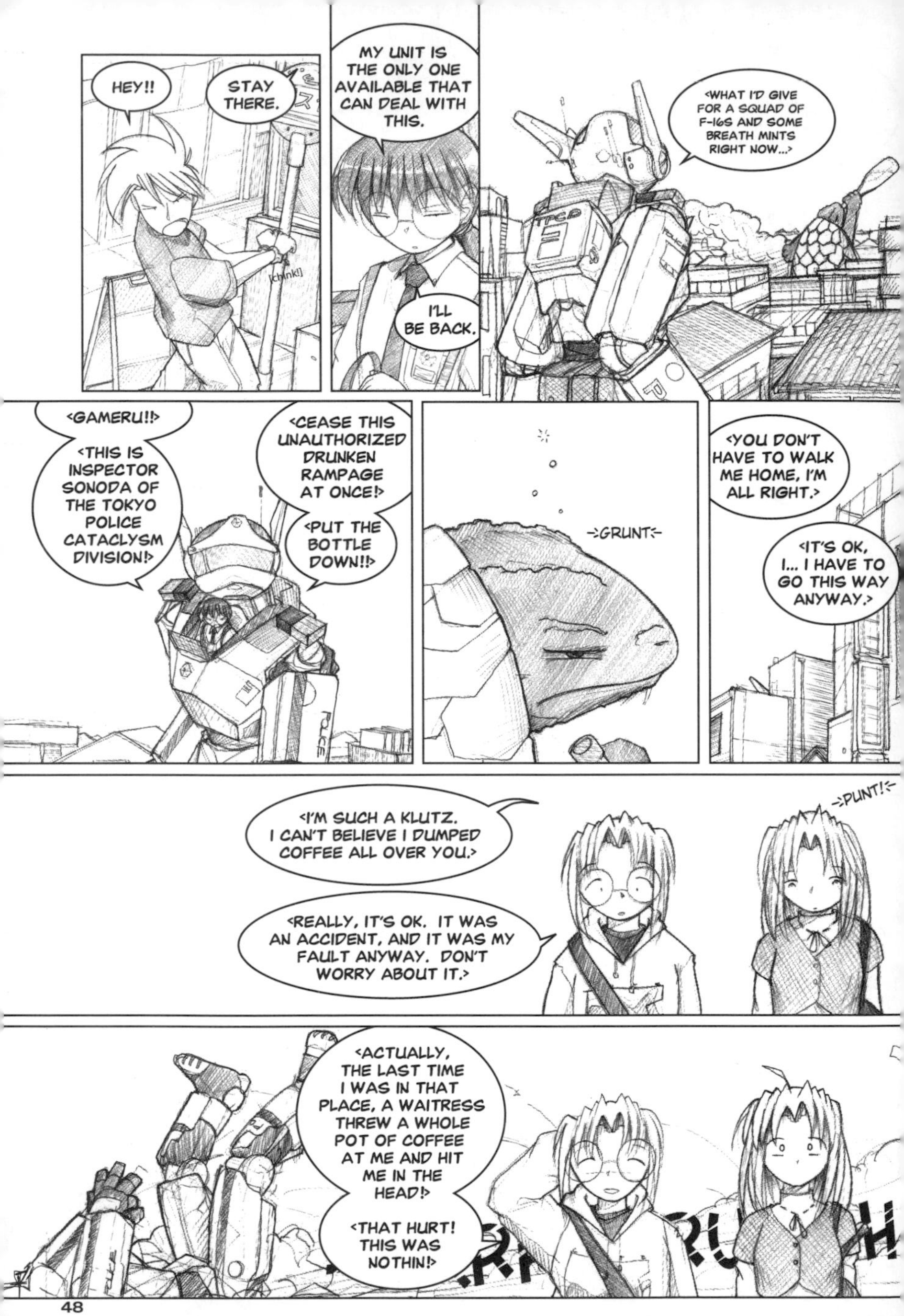
HEY!!
STAY THERE.
[chink!]
MY UNIT IS THE ONLY ONE AVAILABLE THAT CAN DEAL WITH THIS.
I'LL BE BACK.
<WHAT I'D GIVE FOR A SQUAD OF F-16S AND SOME BREATH MINTS RIGHT NOW...>
<GAMERU!!>
<THIS IS INSPECTOR SONODA OF THE TOKYO POLICE CATACLYSM DIVISION!>
<CEASE THIS UNAUTHORIZED DRUNKEN RAMPAGE AT ONCE!>
<PUT THE BOTTLE DOWN!!>
GRUNT
<YOU DON'T HAVE TO WALK ME HOME, I'M ALL RIGHT.>
<IT'S OK, I... I HAVE TO GO THIS WAY ANYWAY.>
<I'M SUCH A KLUTZ. I CAN'T BELIEVE I DUMPED COFFEE ALL OVER YOU.>
PUNT!
<REALLY, IT'S OK. IT WAS AN ACCIDENT, AND IT WAS MY FAULT ANYWAY. DON'T WORRY ABOUT IT.>
<ACTUALLY, THE LAST TIME I WAS IN THAT PLACE, A WAITRESS THREW A WHOLE POT OF COFFEE AT ME AND HIT ME IN THE HEAD!>
<THAT HURT! THIS WAS NOTHIN!>

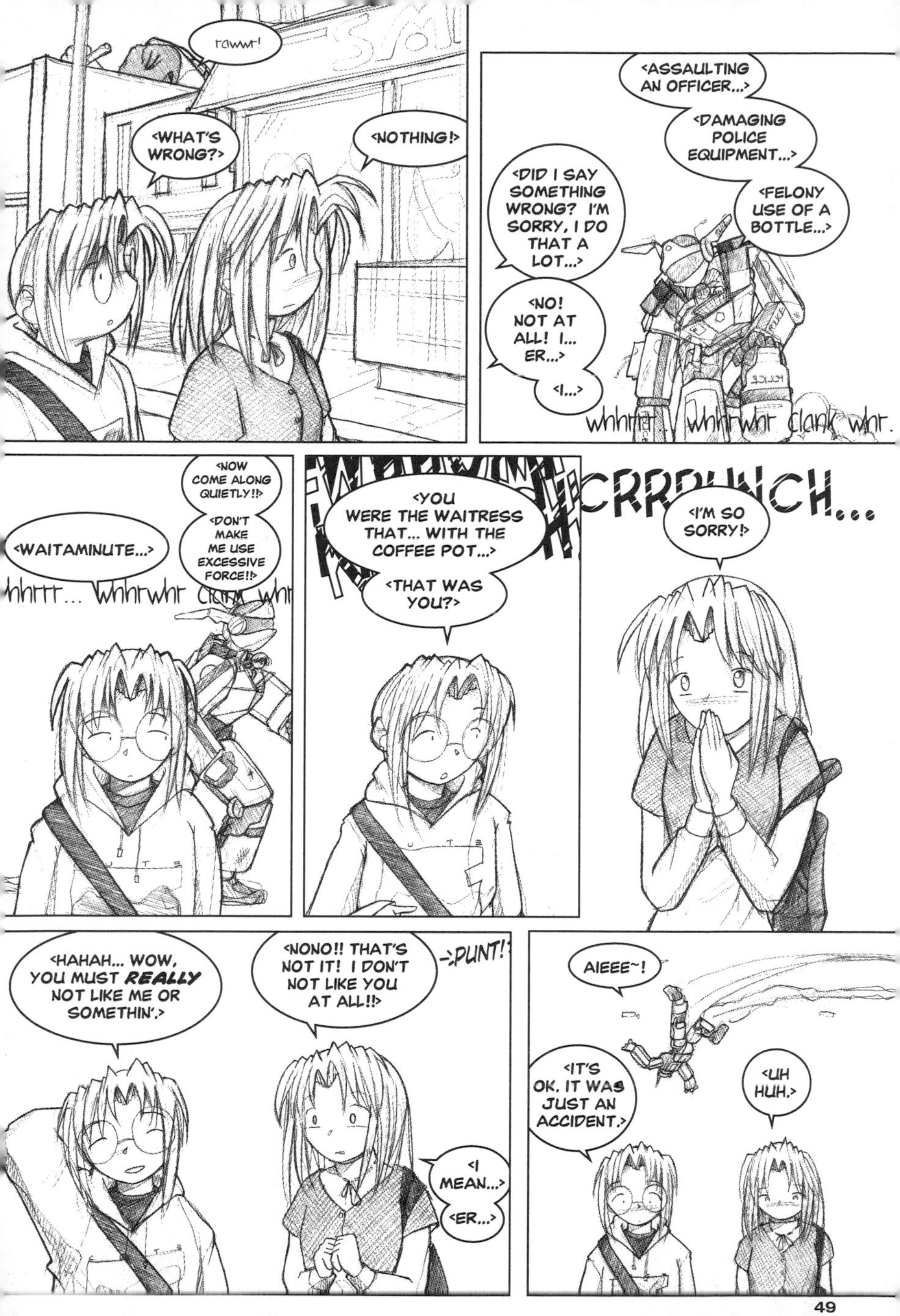
rawwr!
<WHAT'S WRONG?>
<NOTHING!>
<ASSAULTING AN OFFICER...>
<DAMAGING POLICE EQUIPMENT...>
<DID I SAY SOMETHING WRONG? I'M SORRY, I DO THAT A LOT...>
<FELONY USE OF A BOTTLE...>
<NO! NOT AT ALL! I... ER...>
<I...>
whhrrrt... whhrwhr clank whr.
<NOW COME ALONG QUIETLY!!>
<WAITAMINUTE...>
<DON'T MAKE ME USE EXCESSIVE FORCE!!>
whhrrr... whhrwhr clank whr
<YOU WERE THE WAITRESS THAT... WITH THE COFFEE POT...>
<THAT WAS YOU?>
CRRRUNCH...
<I'M SO SORRY!>
<HAHAH... WOW, YOU MUST ***REALLY*** NOT LIKE ME OR SOMETHIN'.>
<NONO!! THAT'S NOT IT! I DON'T NOT LIKE YOU AT ALL!!>
PUNT!
<I MEAN...>
<ER...>
AIEEE~!
<IT'S OK. IT WAS JUST AN ACCIDENT.>
<UH HUH.>

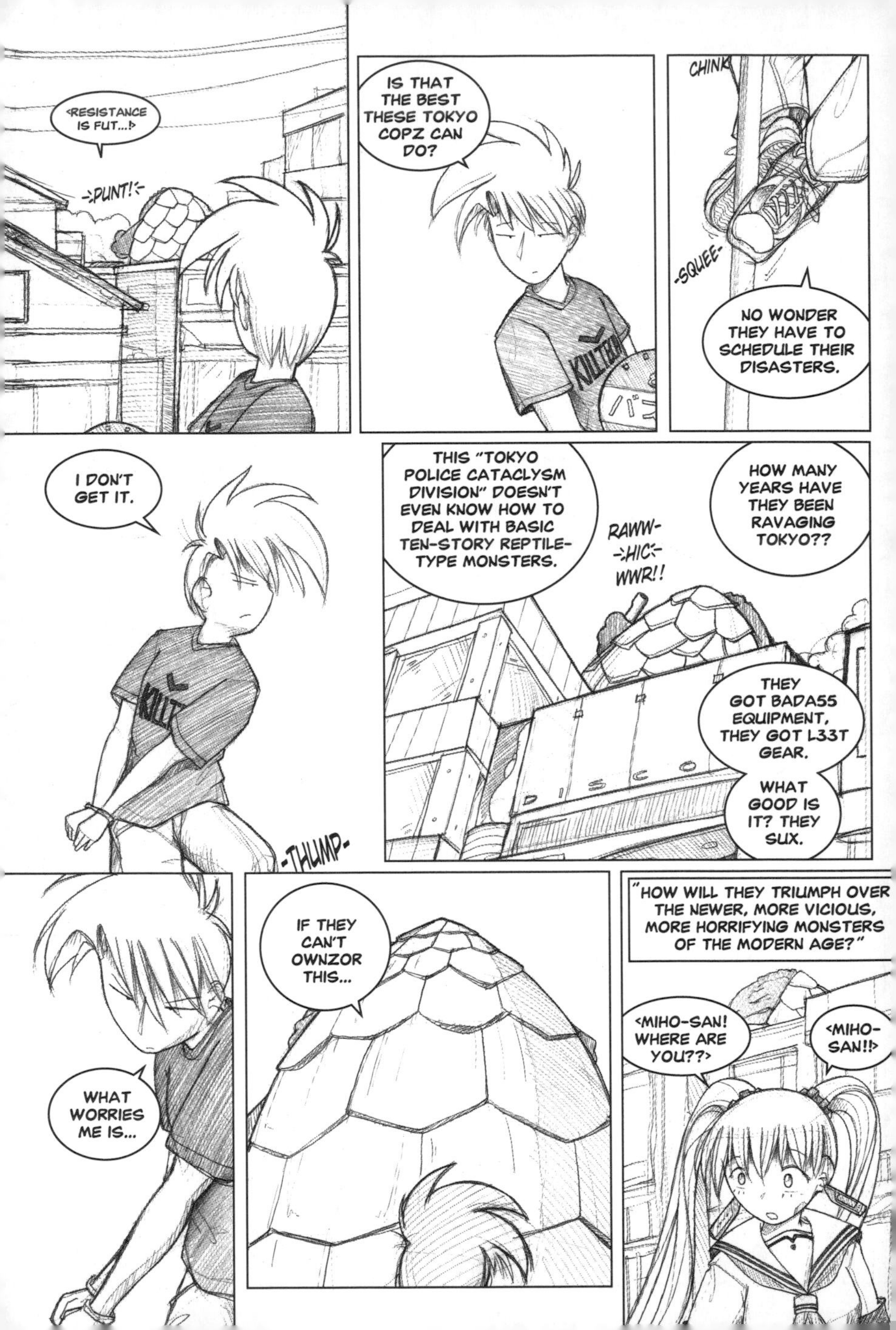

<RESISTANCE IS FUT...!>
-PUNT!-
IS THAT THE BEST THESE TOKYO COPZ CAN DO?
CHINK
-SQUEE-
NO WONDER THEY HAVE TO SCHEDULE THEIR DISASTERS.
I DON'T GET IT.
-THUMP-
THIS "TOKYO POLICE CATACLYSM DIVISION" DOESN'T EVEN KNOW HOW TO DEAL WITH BASIC TEN-STORY REPTILE-TYPE MONSTERS.
RAWW- -HIC- WWR!!
HOW MANY YEARS HAVE THEY BEEN RAVAGING TOKYO??
THEY GOT BADA55 EQUIPMENT, THEY GOT L33T GEAR.
WHAT GOOD IS IT? THEY SUX.
DISCO
WHAT WORRIES ME IS...
IF THEY CAN'T OWNZOR THIS...
"HOW WILL THEY TRIUMPH OVER THE NEWER, MORE VICIOUS, MORE HORRIFYING MONSTERS OF THE MODERN AGE?"
<MIHO-SAN! WHERE ARE YOU??>
<MIHO-SAN!!>

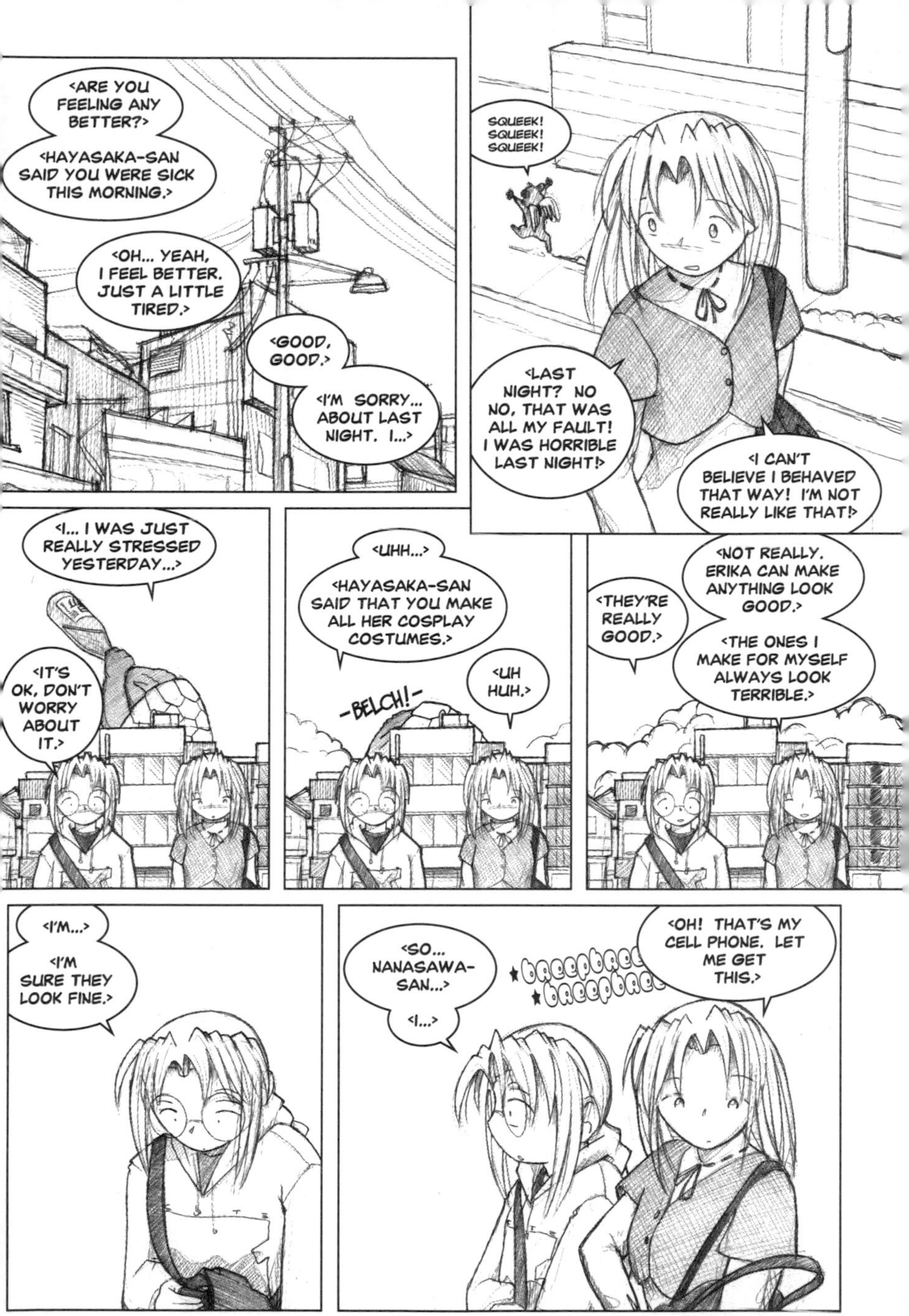

<ARE YOU FEELING ANY BETTER?>
<HAYASAKA-SAN SAID YOU WERE SICK THIS MORNING.>
<OH... YEAH, I FEEL BETTER. JUST A LITTLE TIRED.>
<GOOD, GOOD.>
<I'M SORRY... ABOUT LAST NIGHT. I...>
SQUEEK! SQUEEK! SQUEEK!
<LAST NIGHT? NO NO, THAT WAS ALL MY FAULT! I WAS HORRIBLE LAST NIGHT!>
<I CAN'T BELIEVE I BEHAVED THAT WAY! I'M NOT REALLY LIKE THAT!>
<I... I WAS JUST REALLY STRESSED YESTERDAY...>
<IT'S OK, DON'T WORRY ABOUT IT.>
<UHH...>
<HAYASAKA-SAN SAID THAT YOU MAKE ALL HER COSPLAY COSTUMES.>
-BELCH!-
<UH HUH.>
<THEY'RE REALLY GOOD.>
<NOT REALLY. ERIKA CAN MAKE ANYTHING LOOK GOOD.>
<THE ONES I MAKE FOR MYSELF ALWAYS LOOK TERRIBLE.>
<I'M...>
<I'M SURE THEY LOOK FINE.>
<SO... NANASAWA-SAN...>
<I...>
<OH! THAT'S MY CELL PHONE. LET ME GET THIS.>

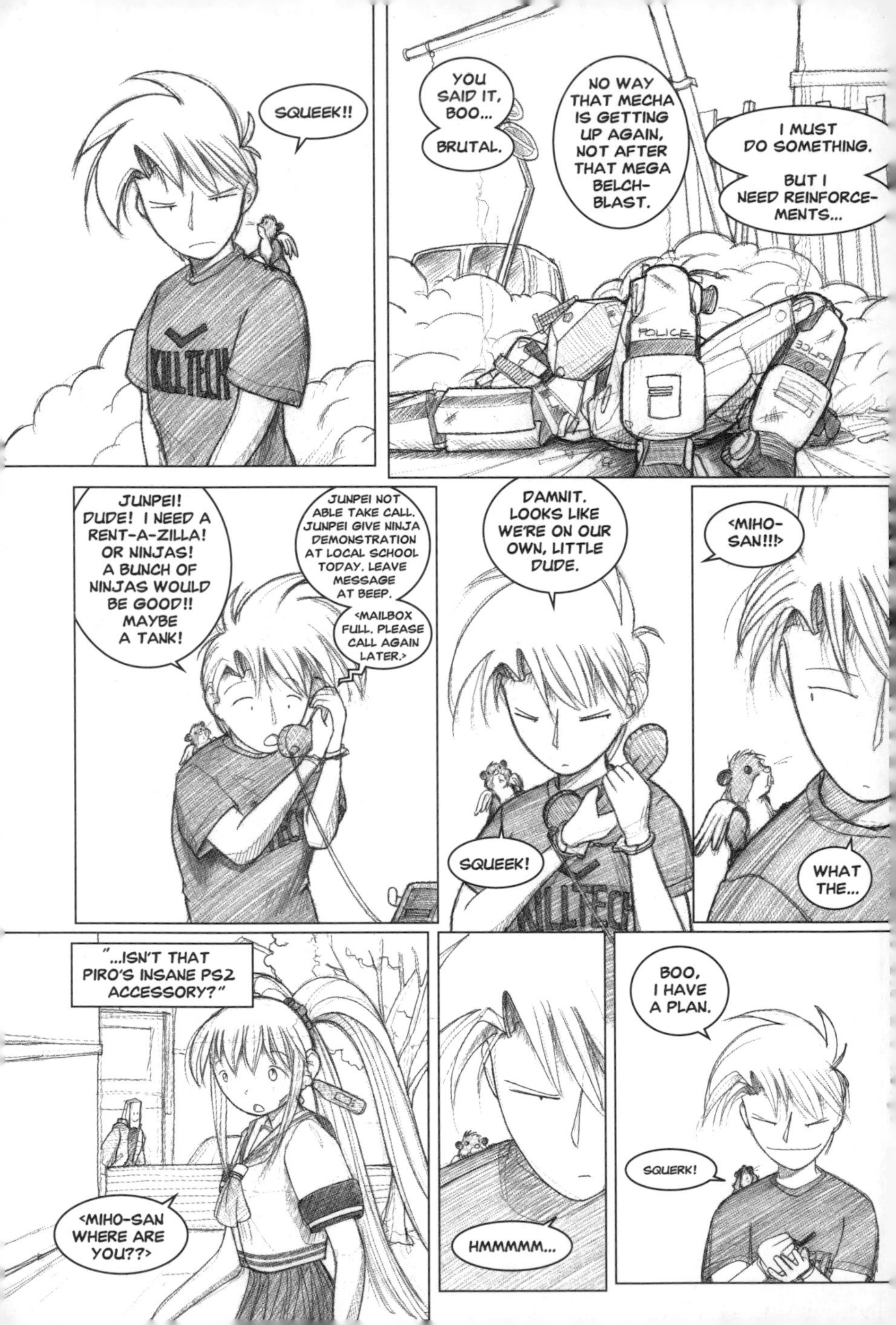
SQUEEK!!
YOU SAID IT, BOO...
BRUTAL.
NO WAY THAT MECHA IS GETTING UP AGAIN, NOT AFTER THAT MEGA BELCH-BLAST.
I MUST DO SOMETHING.
BUT I NEED REINFORCEMENTS...
POLICE
POLICE
KILLTECH
JUNPEI! DUDE! I NEED A RENT-A-ZILLA! OR NINJAS! A BUNCH OF NINJAS WOULD BE GOOD!! MAYBE A TANK!
JUNPEI NOT ABLE TAKE CALL. JUNPEI GIVE NINJA DEMONSTRATION AT LOCAL SCHOOL TODAY. LEAVE MESSAGE AT BEEP.
<MAILBOX FULL. PLEASE CALL AGAIN LATER.>
DAMNIT. LOOKS LIKE WE'RE ON OUR OWN, LITTLE DUDE.
SQUEEK!
<MIHO-SAN!!!>
WHAT THE...
"...ISN'T THAT PIRO'S INSANE PS2 ACCESSORY?"
<MIHO-SAN WHERE ARE YOU??>
HMMMMM...
BOO, I HAVE A PLAN.
SQUERK!

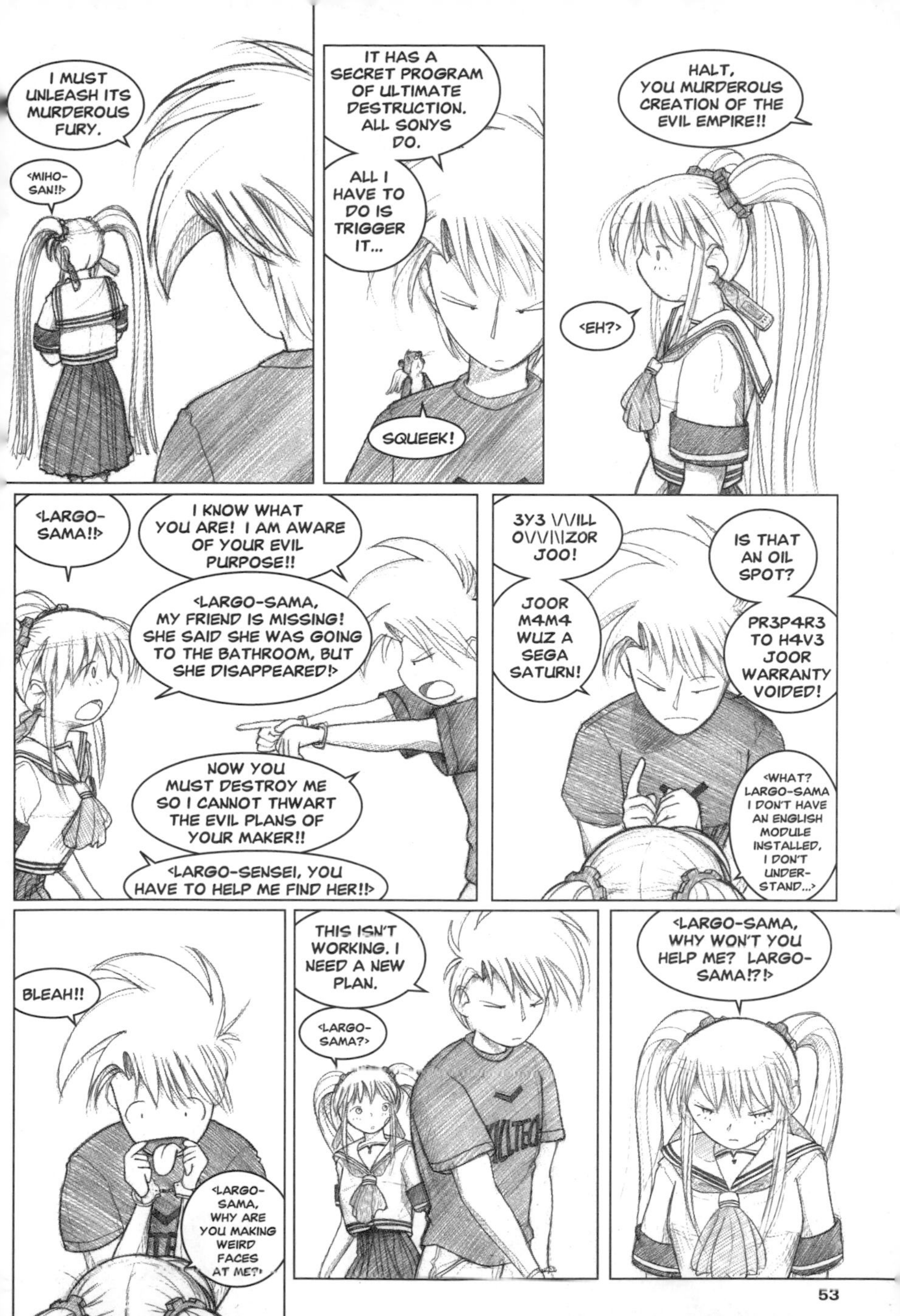
I MUST UNLEASH ITS MURDEROUS FURY.
<MIHO-SAN!!>
IT HAS A SECRET PROGRAM OF ULTIMATE DESTRUCTION. ALL SONYS DO.
ALL I HAVE TO DO IS TRIGGER IT...
SQUEEK!
HALT, YOU MURDEROUS CREATION OF THE EVIL EMPIRE!!
<EH?>
<LARGO-SAMA!!>
I KNOW WHAT YOU ARE! I AM AWARE OF YOUR EVIL PURPOSE!!
<LARGO-SAMA, MY FRIEND IS MISSING! SHE SAID SHE WAS GOING TO THE BATHROOM, BUT SHE DISAPPEARED!>
NOW YOU MUST DESTROY ME SO I CANNOT THWART THE EVIL PLANS OF YOUR MAKER!!
<LARGO-SENSEI, YOU HAVE TO HELP ME FIND HER!!>
3Y3 \/\/ILL O\/\/N|\|ZOR JOO!
JOOR M4M4 WUZ A SEGA SATURN!
IS THAT AN OIL SPOT?
PR3P4R3 TO H4V3 JOOR WARRANTY VOIDED!
<WHAT? LARGO-SAMA I DON'T HAVE AN ENGLISH MODULE INSTALLED, I DON'T UNDER-STAND...>
BLEAH!!
<LARGO-SAMA, WHY ARE YOU MAKING WEIRD FACES AT ME?>
THIS ISN'T WORKING. I NEED A NEW PLAN.
<LARGO-SAMA?>
<LARGO-SAMA, WHY WON'T YOU HELP ME? LARGO-SAMA!?!>

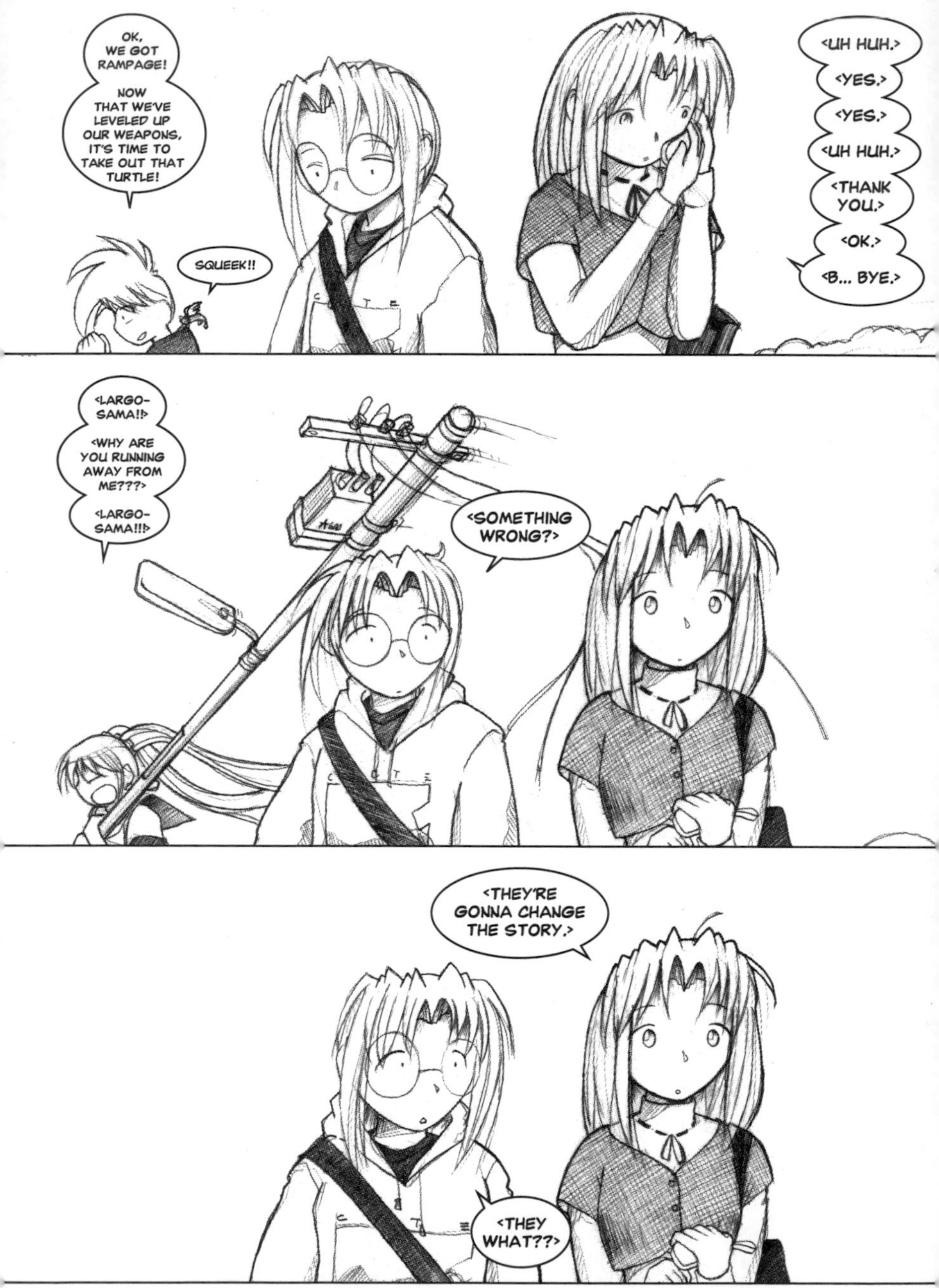
OK, WE GOT RAMPAGE!
NOW THAT WE'VE LEVELED UP OUR WEAPONS, IT'S TIME TO TAKE OUT THAT TURTLE!
SQUEEK!!
<UH HUH.>
<YES.>
<YES.>
<UH HUH.>
<THANK YOU.>
<OK.>
<B... BYE.>
<LARGO-SAMA!!>
<WHY ARE YOU RUNNING AWAY FROM ME???>
<LARGO-SAMA!!!>
<SOMETHING WRONG?>
<THEY'RE GONNA CHANGE THE STORY.>
<THEY WHAT??>

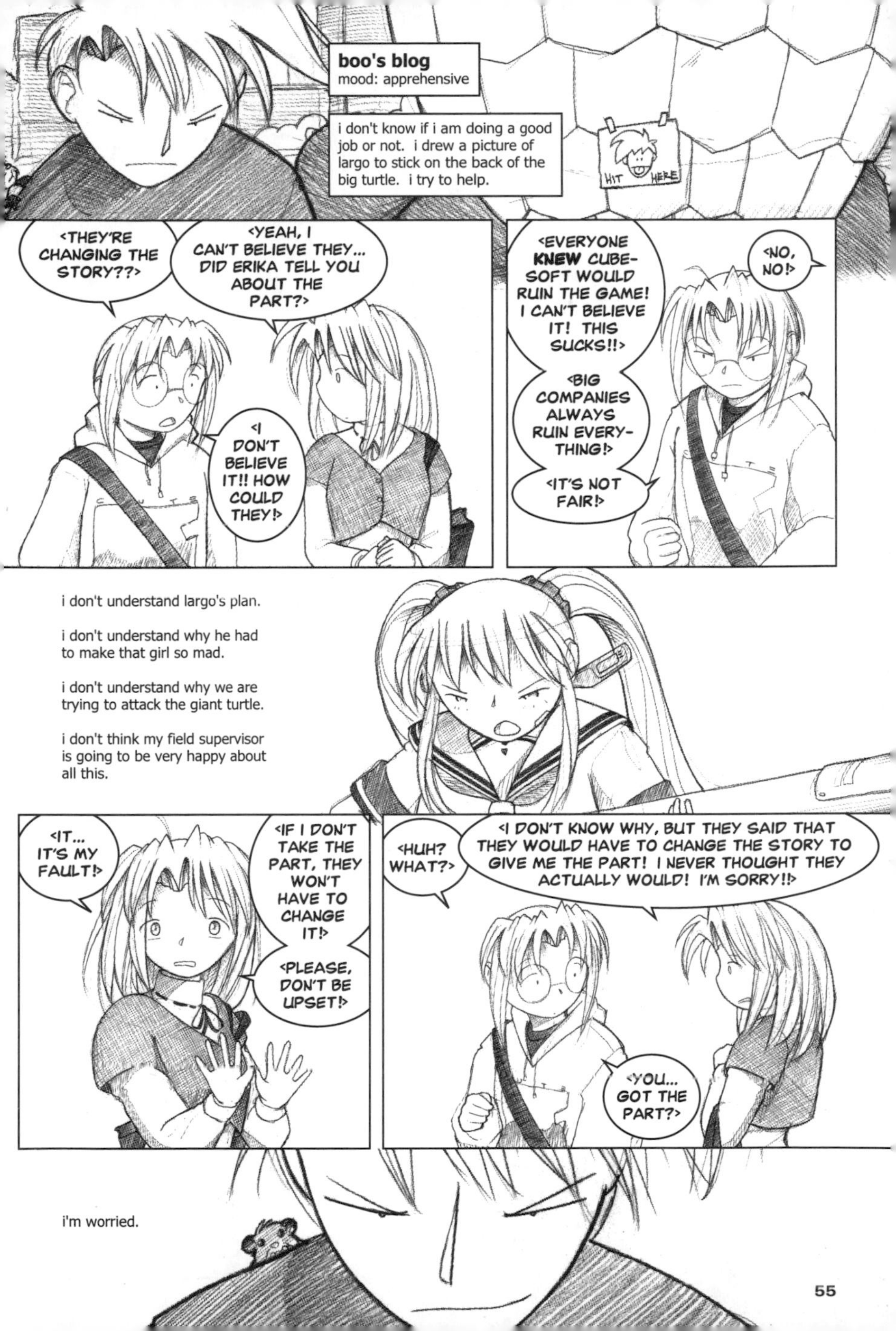

boo's blog
mood: apprehensive
i don't know if i am doing a good job or not. i drew a picture of largo to stick on the back of the big turtle. i try to help.
HIT HERE
<THEY'RE CHANGING THE STORY??>
<YEAH, I CAN'T BELIEVE THEY... DID ERIKA TELL YOU ABOUT THE PART?>
<I DON'T BELIEVE IT!! HOW COULD THEY!>
<EVERYONE **KNEW** CUBE-SOFT WOULD RUIN THE GAME! I CAN'T BELIEVE IT! THIS SUCKS!!>
<NO, NO!>
<BIG COMPANIES ALWAYS RUIN EVERY-THING!>
<IT'S NOT FAIR!>
i don't understand largo's plan.
i don't understand why he had to make that girl so mad.
i don't understand why we are trying to attack the giant turtle.
i don't think my field supervisor is going to be very happy about all this.
<IT... IT'S MY FAULT!>
<IF I DON'T TAKE THE PART, THEY WON'T HAVE TO CHANGE IT!>
<PLEASE, DON'T BE UPSET!>
<HUH? WHAT?>
<I DON'T KNOW WHY, BUT THEY SAID THAT THEY WOULD HAVE TO CHANGE THE STORY TO GIVE ME THE PART! I NEVER THOUGHT THEY ACTUALLY WOULD! I'M SORRY!!>
<YOU... GOT THE PART?>
i'm worried.

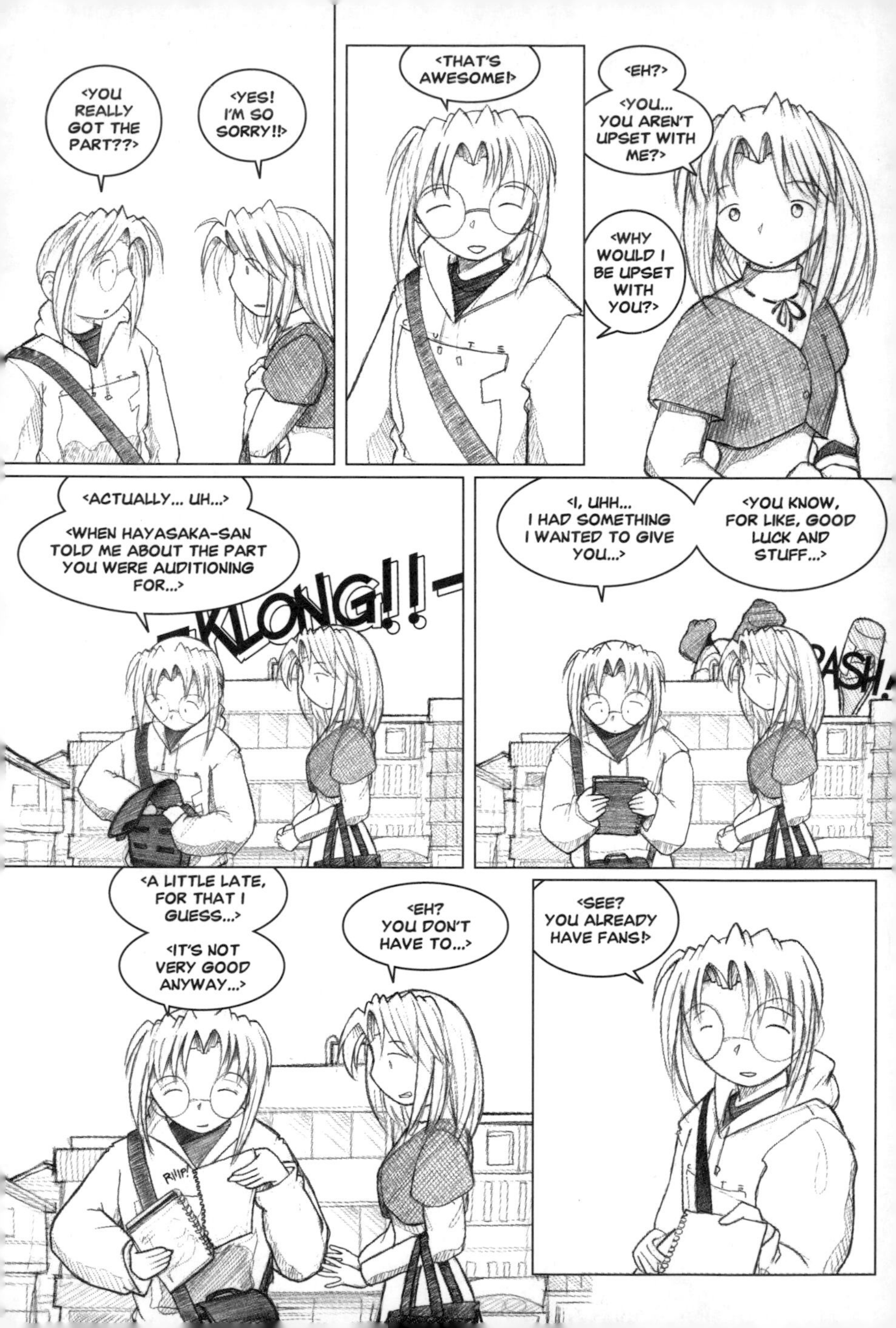
<YOU REALLY GOT THE PART??>
<YES! I'M SO SORRY!!>
<THAT'S AWESOME!>
<EH?>
<YOU... YOU AREN'T UPSET WITH ME?>
<WHY WOULD I BE UPSET WITH YOU?>
<ACTUALLY... UH...>
<WHEN HAYASAKA-SAN TOLD ME ABOUT THE PART YOU WERE AUDITIONING FOR...>
KLONG!!
<I, UHH... I HAD SOMETHING I WANTED TO GIVE YOU...>
<YOU KNOW, FOR LIKE, GOOD LUCK AND STUFF...>
<A LITTLE LATE, FOR THAT I GUESS...>
<IT'S NOT VERY GOOD ANYWAY...>
RIIIP!
<EH? YOU DON'T HAVE TO...>
<SEE? YOU ALREADY HAVE FANS!>

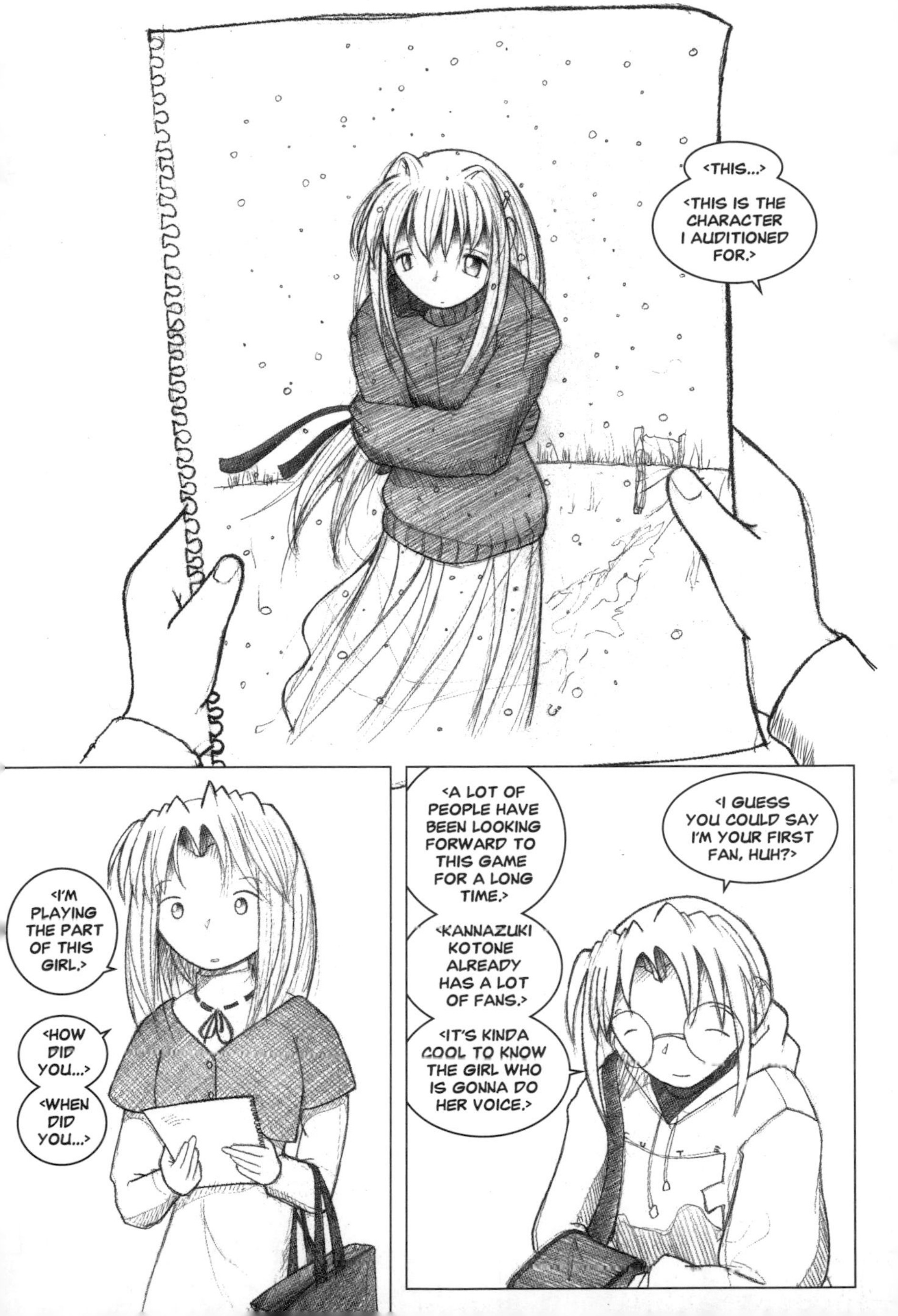
<THIS...>
<THIS IS THE CHARACTER I AUDITIONED FOR.>
<I'M PLAYING THE PART OF THIS GIRL.>
<HOW DID YOU...>
<WHEN DID YOU...>
<A LOT OF PEOPLE HAVE BEEN LOOKING FORWARD TO THIS GAME FOR A LONG TIME.>
<KANNAZUKI KOTONE ALREADY HAS A LOT OF FANS.>
<IT'S KINDA COOL TO KNOW THE GIRL WHO IS GONNA DO HER VOICE.>
<I GUESS YOU COULD SAY I'M YOUR FIRST FAN, HUH?>

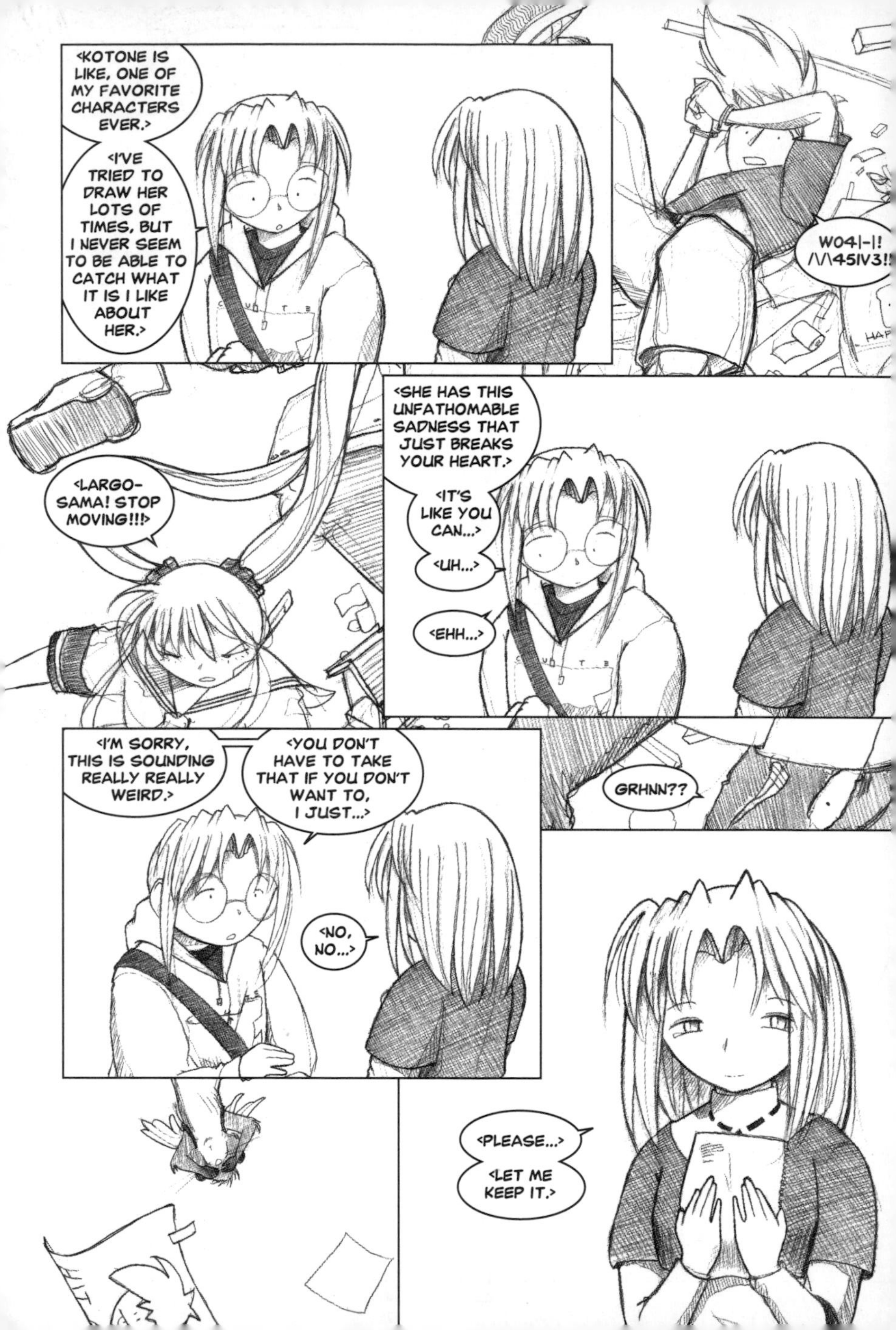
<KOTONE IS LIKE, ONE OF MY FAVORITE CHARACTERS EVER.>
<I'VE TRIED TO DRAW HER LOTS OF TIMES, BUT I NEVER SEEM TO BE ABLE TO CATCH WHAT IT IS I LIKE ABOUT HER.>
W04|-|! /\/\45IV3!!
<LARGO-SAMA! STOP MOVING!!!>
<SHE HAS THIS UNFATHOMABLE SADNESS THAT JUST BREAKS YOUR HEART.>
<IT'S LIKE YOU CAN...>
<UH...>
<EHH...>
<I'M SORRY, THIS IS SOUNDING REALLY REALLY WEIRD.>
<YOU DON'T HAVE TO TAKE THAT IF YOU DON'T WANT TO, I JUST...>
<NO, NO...>
GRHNN??
<PLEASE...>
<LET ME KEEP IT.>

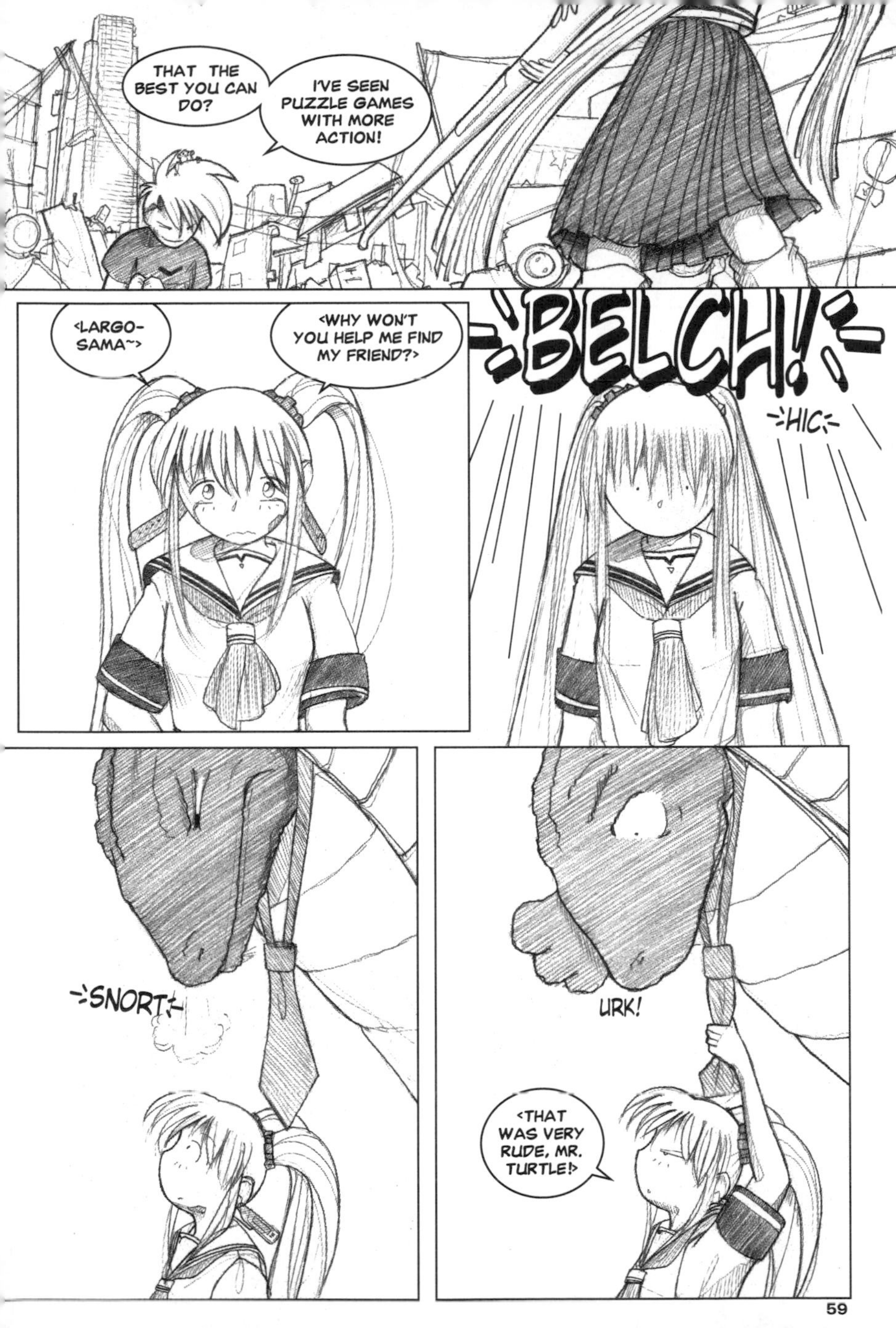
THAT THE BEST YOU CAN DO?
I'VE SEEN PUZZLE GAMES WITH MORE ACTION!
<LARGO-SAMA~>
<WHY WON'T YOU HELP ME FIND MY FRIEND?>
BELCH!
HIC
SNORT
URK!
<THAT WAS VERY RUDE, MR. TURTLE!>

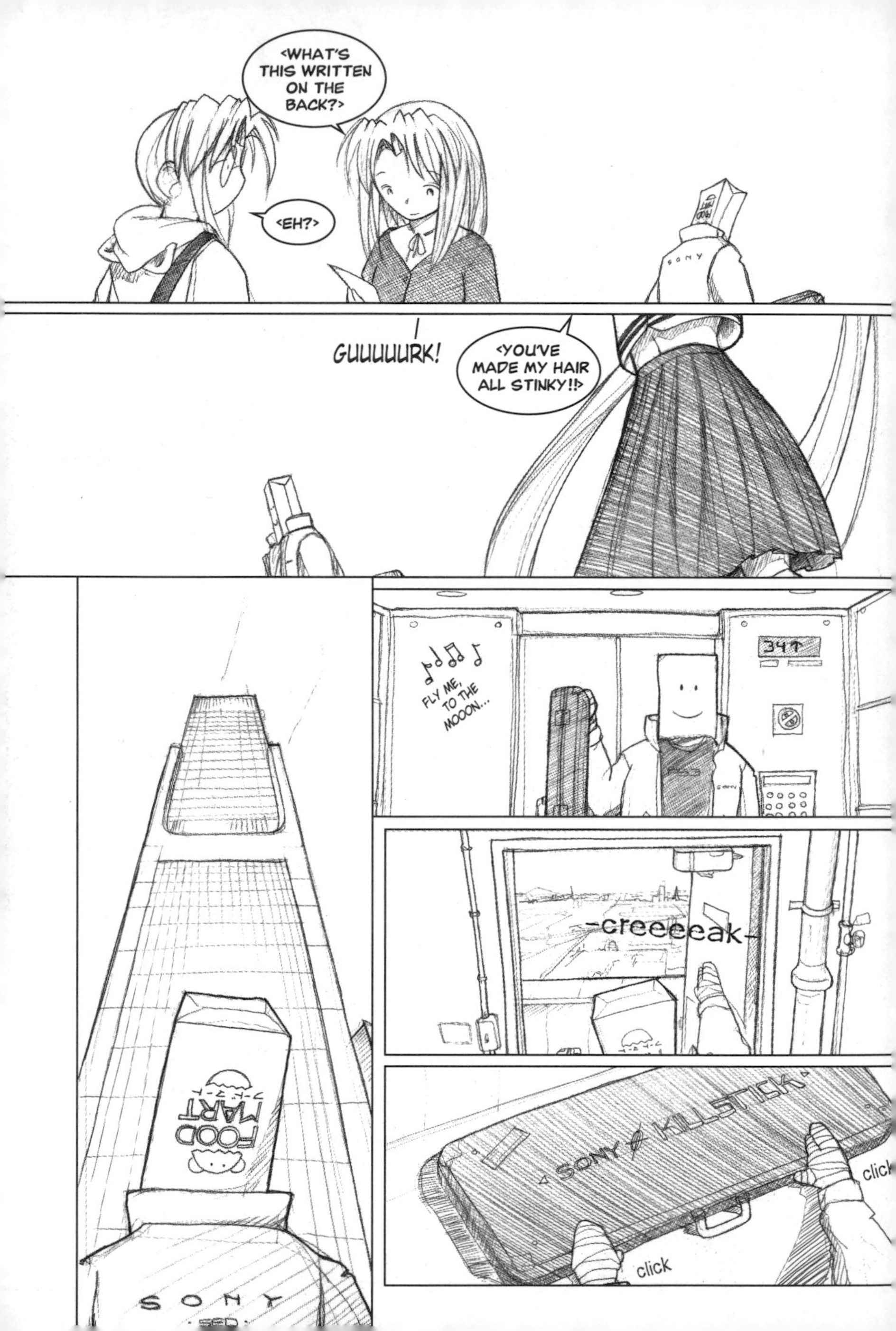
<WHAT'S THIS WRITTEN ON THE BACK?>
<EH?>
SONY
GUUUUURK!
<YOU'VE MADE MY HAIR ALL STINKY!!>
FOOD MART
SONY
FLY ME, TO THE MOOON...
34↑
-creeeeak-
SONY ∅ KILLSTICK
click
click

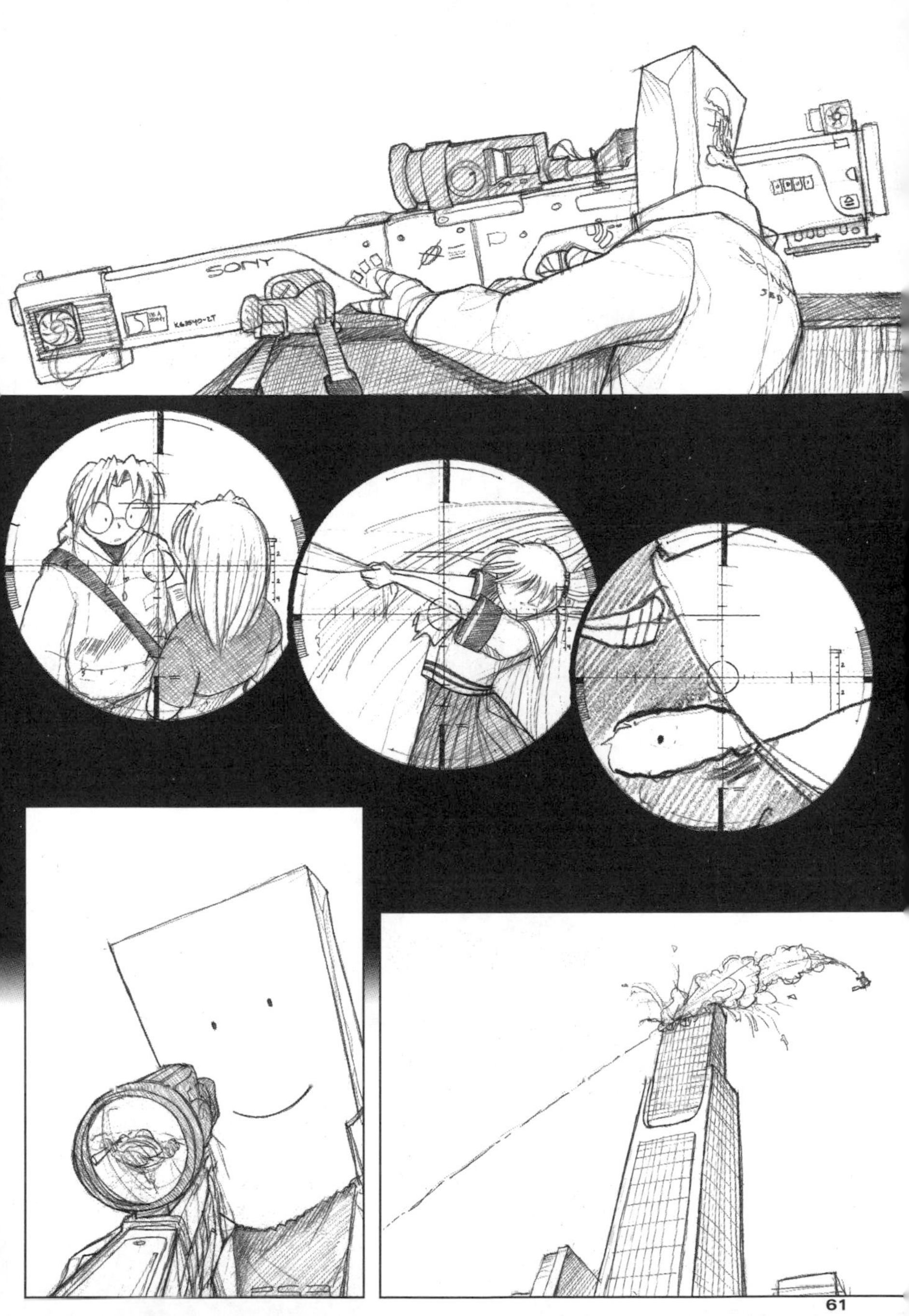
SONY

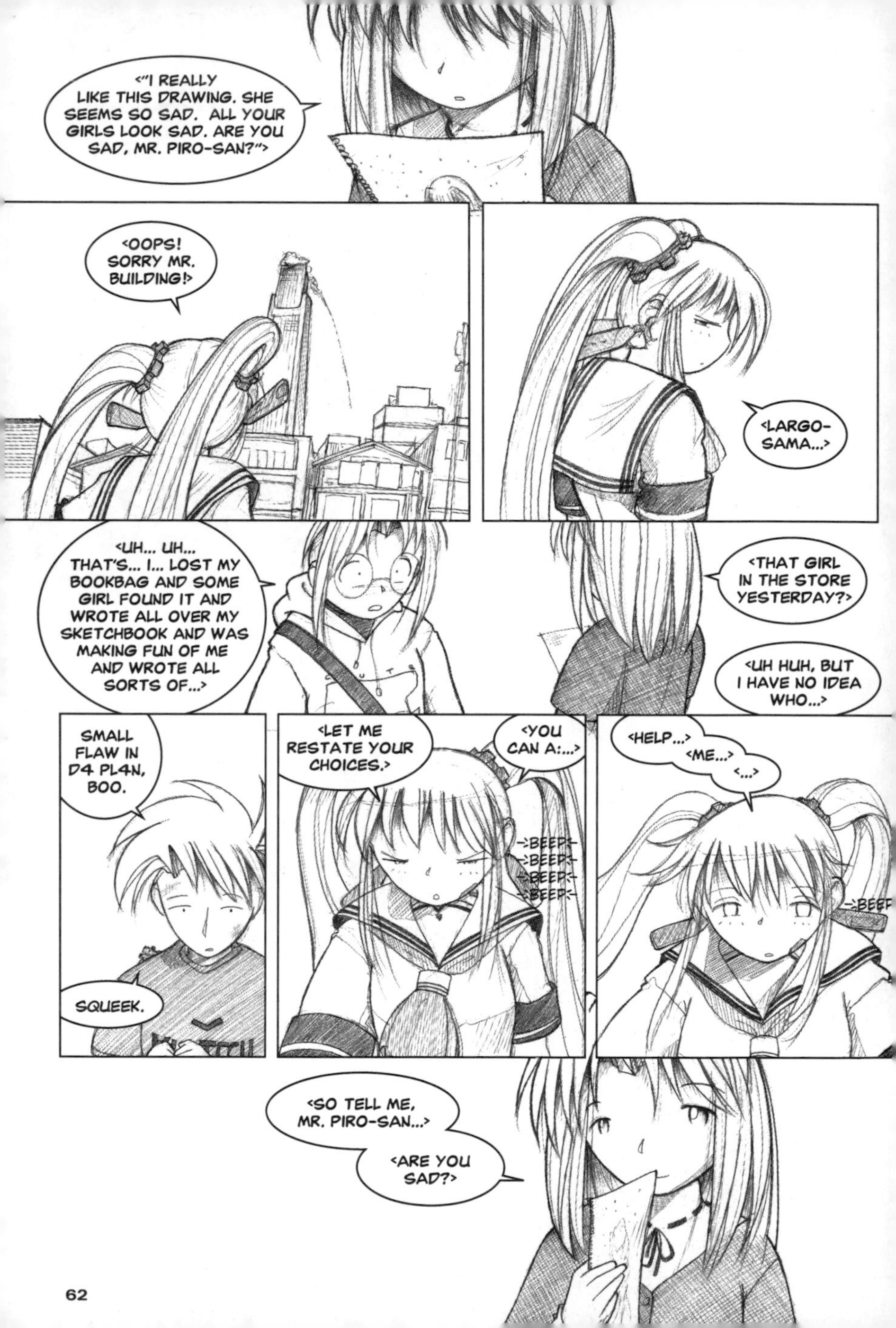

<"I REALLY LIKE THIS DRAWING. SHE SEEMS SO SAD. ALL YOUR GIRLS LOOK SAD. ARE YOU SAD, MR. PIRO-SAN?">
<OOPS! SORRY MR. BUILDING!>
<LARGO-SAMA...>
<UH... UH... THAT'S... I... LOST MY BOOKBAG AND SOME GIRL FOUND IT AND WROTE ALL OVER MY SKETCHBOOK AND WAS MAKING FUN OF ME AND WROTE ALL SORTS OF...>
<THAT GIRL IN THE STORE YESTERDAY?>
<UH HUH, BUT I HAVE NO IDEA WHO...>
SMALL FLAW IN D4 PL4N, BOO.
SQUEEK.
<LET ME RESTATE YOUR CHOICES.>
<YOU CAN A:...>
BEEP
BEEP
BEEP
BEEP
<HELP...>
<ME...>
<...>
<SO TELL ME, MR. PIRO-SAN...>
<ARE YOU SAD?>

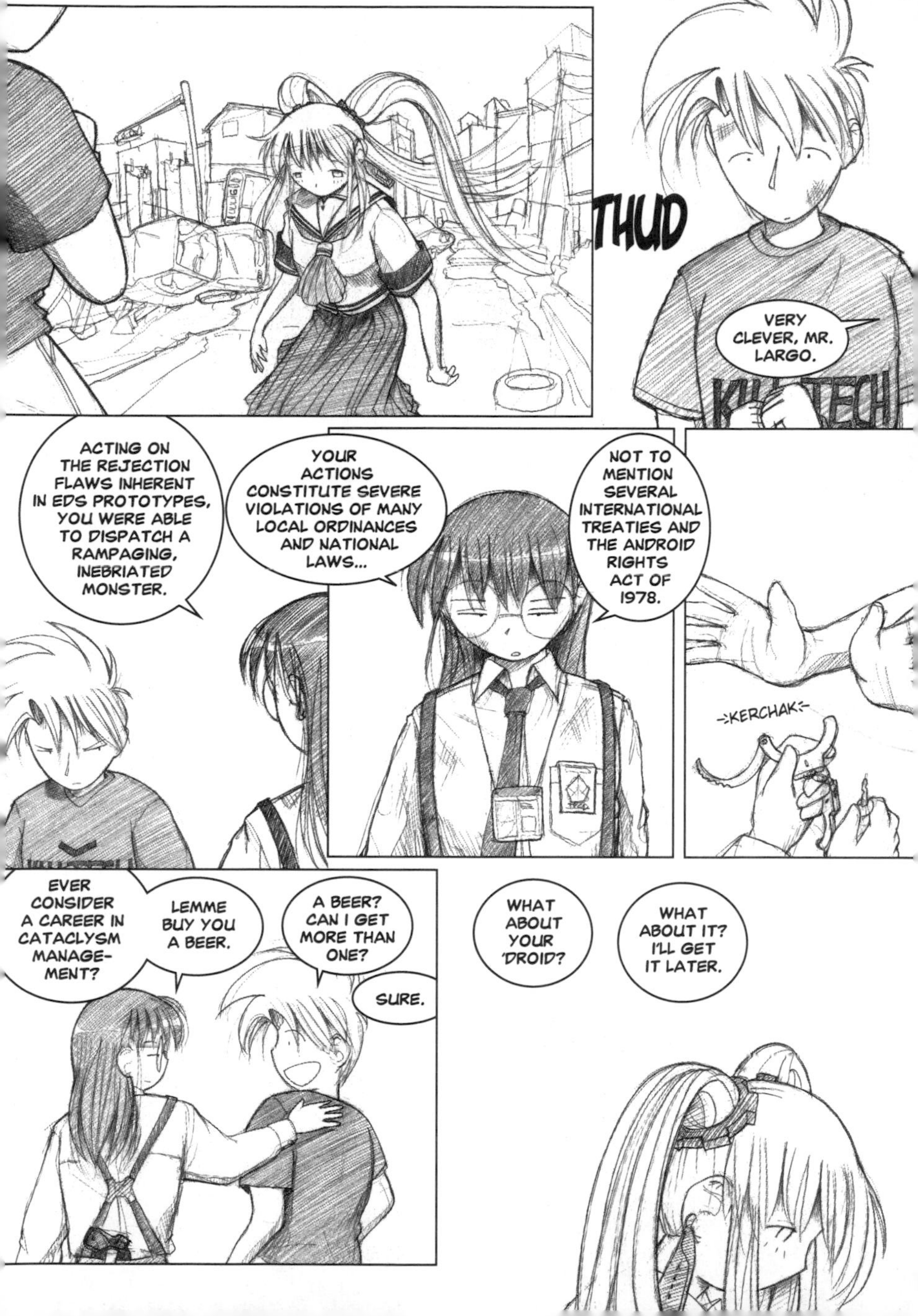
THUD
VERY CLEVER, MR. LARGO.
ACTING ON THE REJECTION FLAWS INHERENT IN EDS PROTOTYPES, YOU WERE ABLE TO DISPATCH A RAMPAGING, INEBRIATED MONSTER.
YOUR ACTIONS CONSTITUTE SEVERE VIOLATIONS OF MANY LOCAL ORDINANCES AND NATIONAL LAWS...
NOT TO MENTION SEVERAL INTERNATIONAL TREATIES AND THE ANDROID RIGHTS ACT OF 1978.
KERCHAK
EVER CONSIDER A CAREER IN CATACLYSM MANAGE-MENT?
LEMME BUY YOU A BEER.
A BEER? CAN I GET MORE THAN ONE?
SURE.
WHAT ABOUT YOUR 'DROID?
WHAT ABOUT IT? I'LL GET IT LATER.

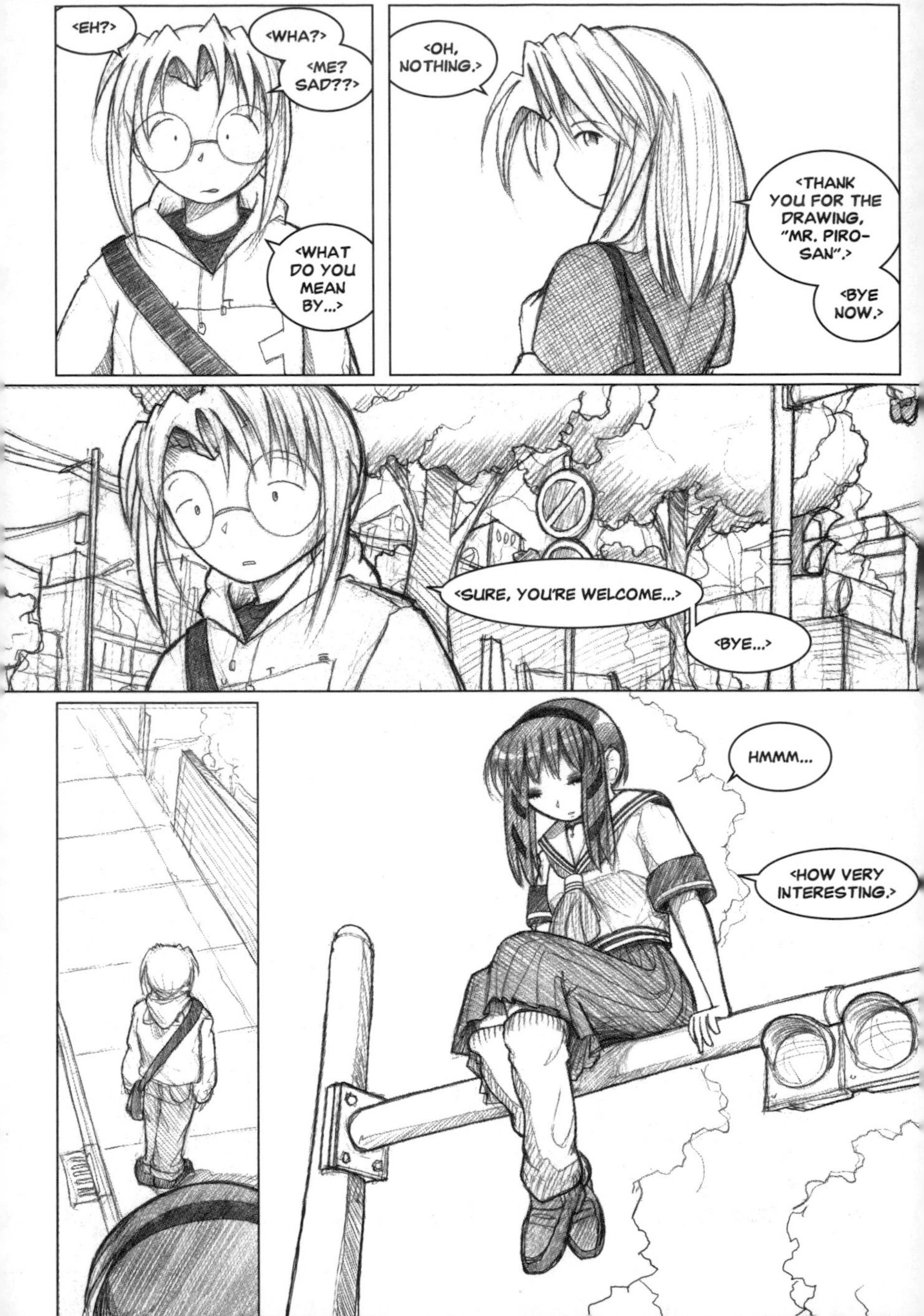
<EH?>
<WHA?>
<ME? SAD??>
<WHAT DO YOU MEAN BY...>
<OH, NOTHING.>
<THANK YOU FOR THE DRAWING, "MR. PIRO-SAN".>
<BYE NOW.>
<SURE, YOU'RE WELCOME...>
<BYE...>
HMMM...
<HOW VERY INTERESTING.>

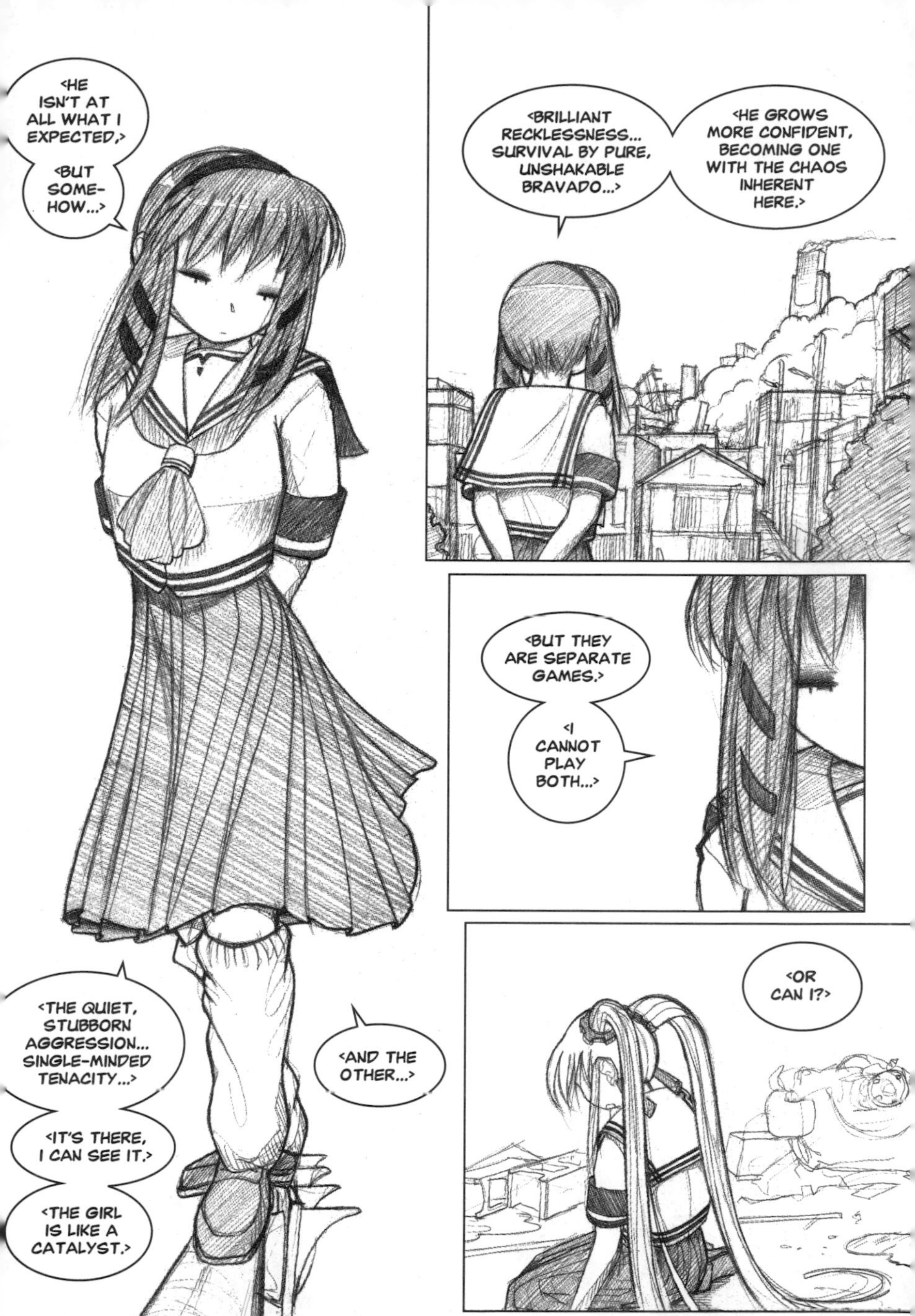
<HE ISN'T AT ALL WHAT I EXPECTED,>
<BUT SOME-HOW...>
<THE QUIET, STUBBORN AGGRESSION... SINGLE-MINDED TENACITY...>
<IT'S THERE, I CAN SEE IT.>
<THE GIRL IS LIKE A CATALYST.>
<AND THE OTHER...>
<BRILLIANT RECKLESSNESS... SURVIVAL BY PURE, UNSHAKABLE BRAVADO...>
<HE GROWS MORE CONFIDENT, BECOMING ONE WITH THE CHAOS INHERENT HERE.>
<BUT THEY ARE SEPARATE GAMES.>
<I CANNOT PLAY BOTH...>
<OR CAN I?>

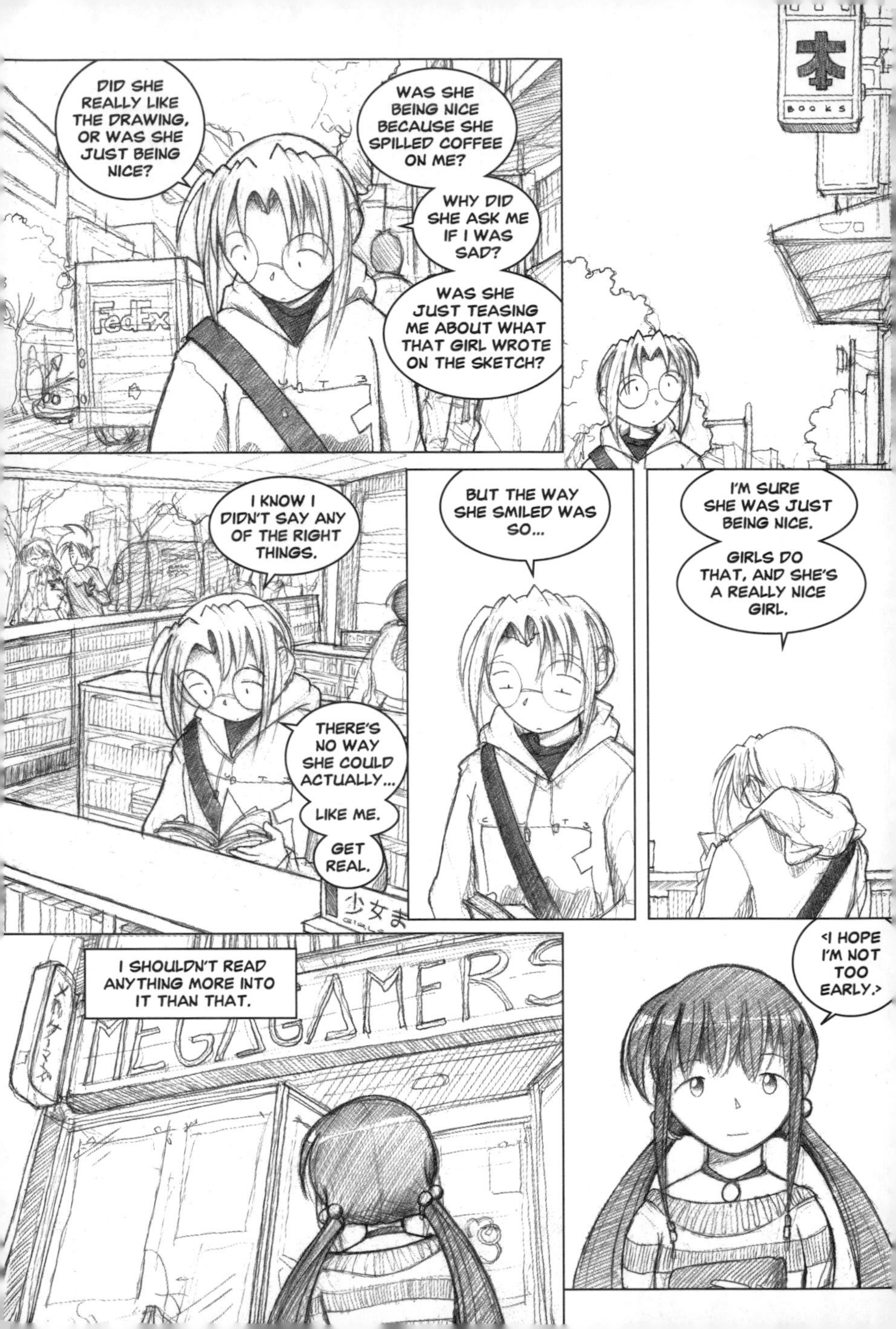
DID SHE REALLY LIKE THE DRAWING, OR WAS SHE JUST BEING NICE?
WAS SHE BEING NICE BECAUSE SHE SPILLED COFFEE ON ME?
WHY DID SHE ASK ME IF I WAS SAD?
WAS SHE JUST TEASING ME ABOUT WHAT THAT GIRL WROTE ON THE SKETCH?
FedEx
本
BOOKS
I KNOW I DIDN'T SAY ANY OF THE RIGHT THINGS.
THERE'S NO WAY SHE COULD ACTUALLY...
LIKE ME.
GET REAL.
BUT THE WAY SHE SMILED WAS SO...
I'M SURE SHE WAS JUST BEING NICE.
GIRLS DO THAT, AND SHE'S A REALLY NICE GIRL.
I SHOULDN'T READ ANYTHING MORE INTO IT THAN THAT.
MEGAGAMERS
<I HOPE I'M NOT TOO EARLY.>

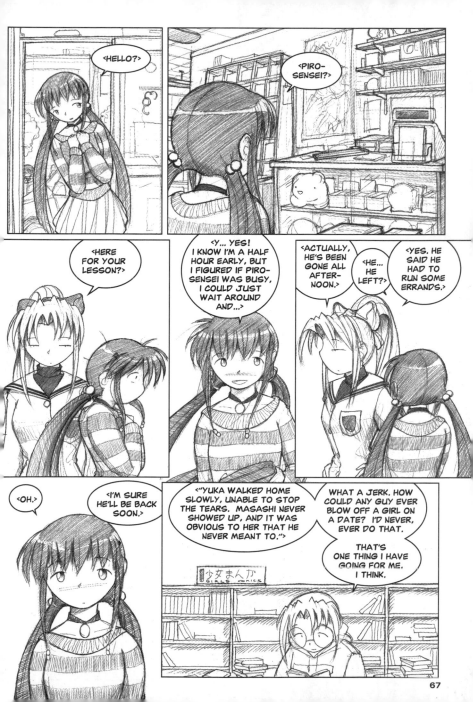

‹HELLO?›

‹PIRO-SENSEI?›

‹HERE FOR YOUR LESSON?›

‹Y... YES! I KNOW I'M A HALF HOUR EARLY, BUT I FIGURED IF PIRO-SENSEI WAS BUSY, I COULD JUST WAIT AROUND AND...›

‹ACTUALLY, HE'S BEEN GONE ALL AFTER-NOON.›

‹HE... HE LEFT?›

‹YES, HE SAID HE HAD TO RUN SOME ERRANDS.›

‹OH.›

‹I'M SURE HE'LL BE BACK SOON.›

‹"YUKA WALKED HOME SLOWLY, UNABLE TO STOP THE TEARS. MASASHI NEVER SHOWED UP, AND IT WAS OBVIOUS TO HER THAT HE NEVER MEANT TO."›

WHAT A JERK. HOW COULD ANY GUY EVER BLOW OFF A GIRL ON A DATE? I'D NEVER, EVER DO THAT.

THAT'S ONE THING I HAVE GOING FOR ME. I THINK.

少女まんが
GIRLS COMICS

<SORRY!!>

<SORRY I'M LATE!!>

<FINISH ALL OF YOUR ERRANDS?.>

<UH... SORRY, THAT TOOK A LOT LONGER THAN...>

<YOUR STUDENT WAITED OVER AN HOUR FOR YOU TO GET BACK.>

<SHE DID?>

<IF YOU DIDN'T INTEND TO GO THROUGH WITH THE LESSONS, YOU SHOULDN'T HAVE AGREED TO THEM.>

<BUT... I DIDN'T...>

<I'M SORRY.>

<I DIDN'T MEAN TO...>

<DON'T APOLOGIZE TO ME.>

<SHE LEFT HER PHONE NUMBER ON THAT PIECE OF PAPER.>

<G'NIGHT, HAYASAKA-SAN.>

<NIGHT. SEE YOU TOMORROW.>

MEGUMARS メガローマーズ

-CLICK-

69

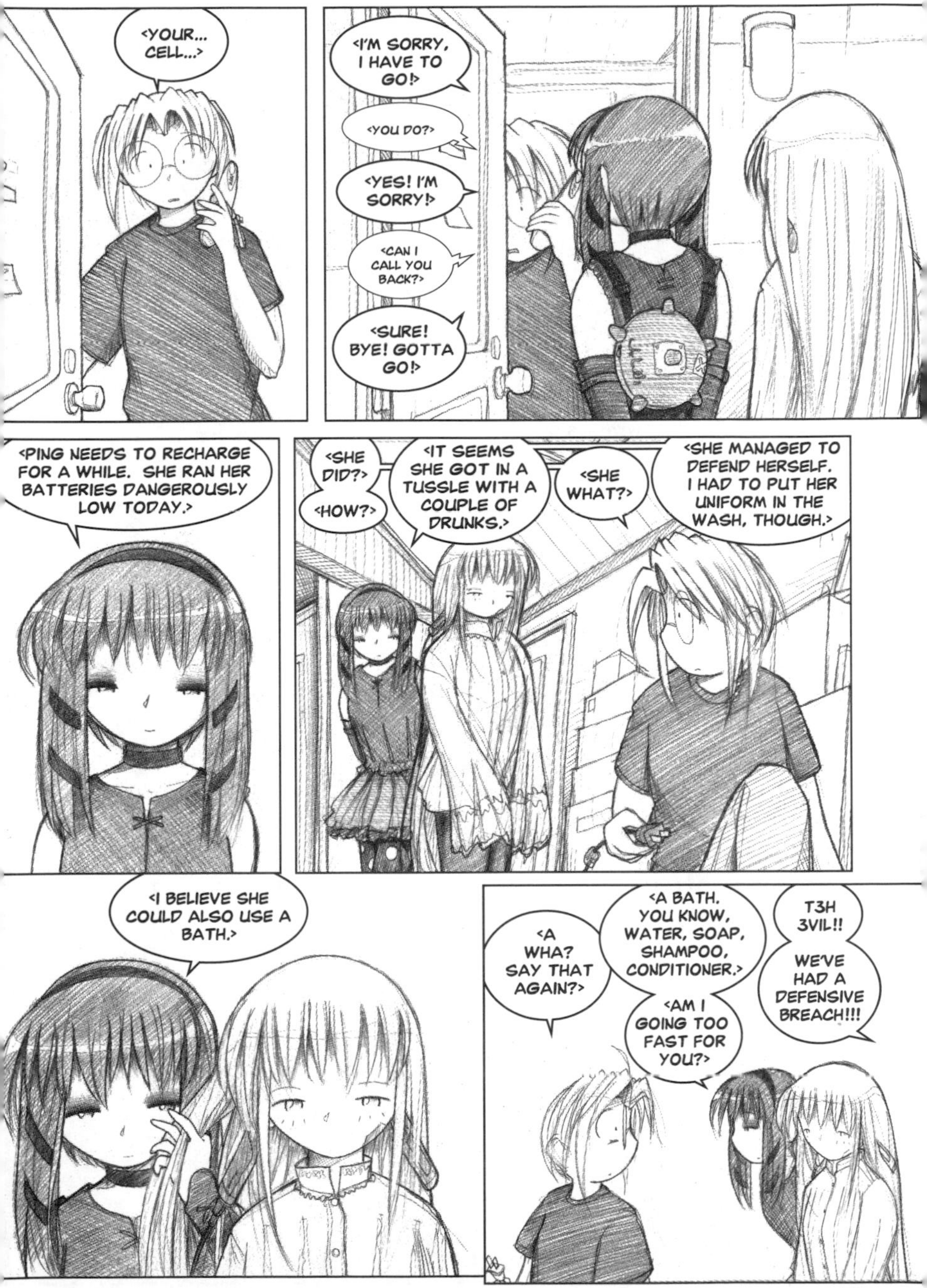

<YOUR... CELL...>
<I'M SORRY, I HAVE TO GO!>
<YOU DO?>
<YES! I'M SORRY!>
<CAN I CALL YOU BACK?>
<SURE! BYE! GOTTA GO!>
<PING NEEDS TO RECHARGE FOR A WHILE. SHE RAN HER BATTERIES DANGEROUSLY LOW TODAY.>
<SHE DID?>
<HOW?>
<IT SEEMS SHE GOT IN A TUSSLE WITH A COUPLE OF DRUNKS.>
<SHE WHAT?>
<SHE MANAGED TO DEFEND HERSELF. I HAD TO PUT HER UNIFORM IN THE WASH, THOUGH.>
<I BELIEVE SHE COULD ALSO USE A BATH.>
<A WHA? SAY THAT AGAIN?>
<A BATH. YOU KNOW, WATER, SOAP, SHAMPOO, CONDITIONER.>
<AM I GOING TOO FAST FOR YOU?>
T3H 3VIL!!
WE'VE HAD A DEFENSIVE BREACH!!!

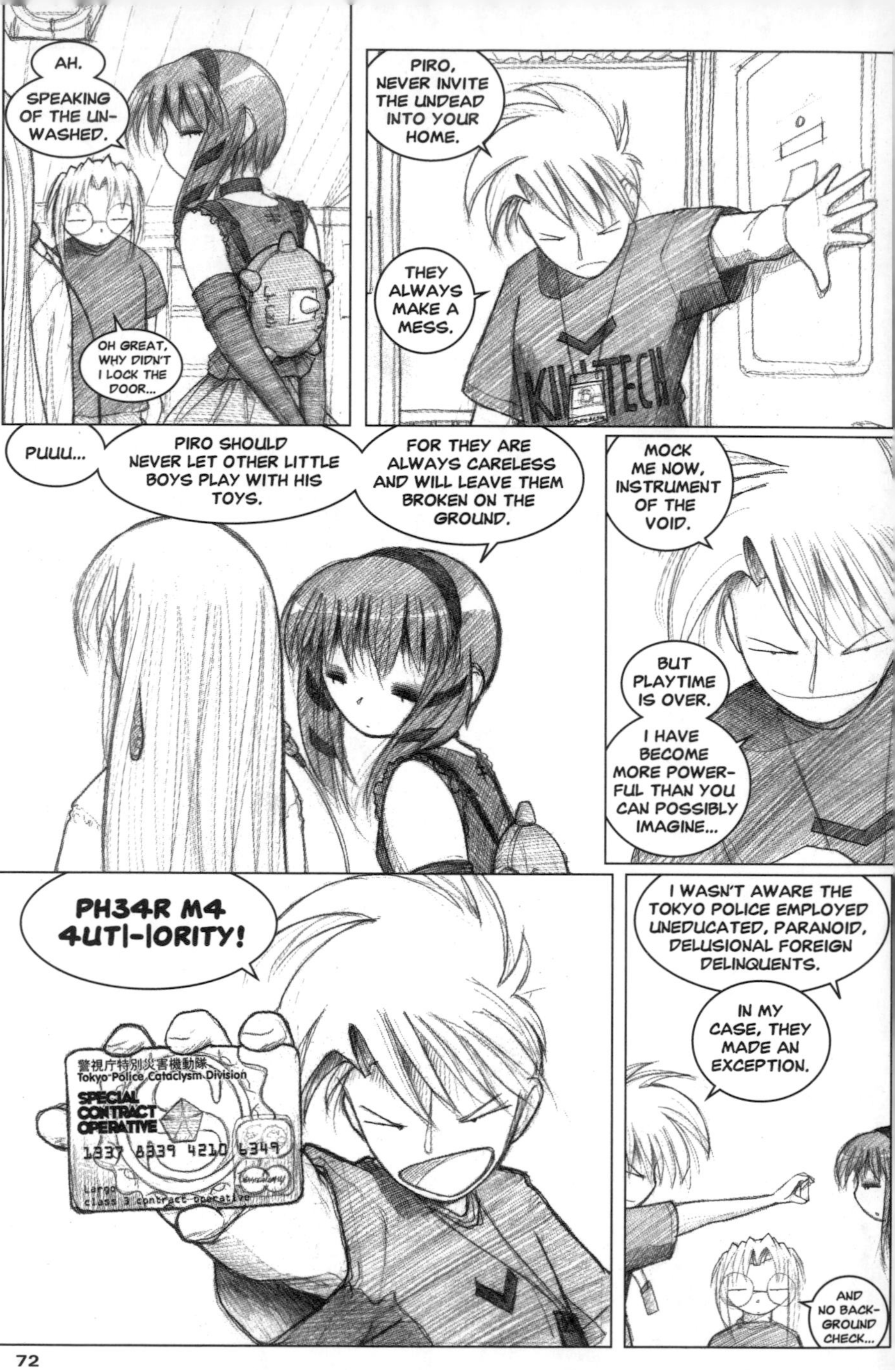
AH.
SPEAKING OF THE UN-WASHED.
OH GREAT, WHY DIDN'T I LOCK THE DOOR...
PIRO, NEVER INVITE THE UNDEAD INTO YOUR HOME.
THEY ALWAYS MAKE A MESS.
PUUU...
PIRO SHOULD NEVER LET OTHER LITTLE BOYS PLAY WITH HIS TOYS.
FOR THEY ARE ALWAYS CARELESS AND WILL LEAVE THEM BROKEN ON THE GROUND.
MOCK ME NOW, INSTRUMENT OF THE VOID.
BUT PLAYTIME IS OVER.
I HAVE BECOME MORE POWER-FUL THAN YOU CAN POSSIBLY IMAGINE...
PH34R M4 4UT|-|ORITY!
警視庁特別災害機動隊
Tokyo Police Cataclysm Division
SPECIAL CONTRACT OPERATIVE
1337 8339 4210 6349
Largo
class 3 contract operative
I WASN'T AWARE THE TOKYO POLICE EMPLOYED UNEDUCATED, PARANOID, DELUSIONAL FOREIGN DELINQUENTS.
IN MY CASE, THEY MADE AN EXCEPTION.
AND NO BACK-GROUND CHECK...

CAREFUL, PIRO.

A CORNERED BEAST IS DANGEROUS.

LARGO-SENSEI, I THINK I'LL SKIP SCHOOL TOMORROW SO I CAN HELP PIRO GIVE PING-CHAN A BATH.

THERE'S NOT MUCH YOU CAN REALLY TEACH ME ANYWAY.

WHAT?

WHAT?

ISN'T IT THOUGH?

THANK YOU FOR A FUN DAY.

<BYE NOW.>

WHU... WHAT WAS THAT ALL ABOUT?

WE ARE IN GRAVE DANGER. OUR BASE IS VULNERABLE.

LETS GO SHOPPING.

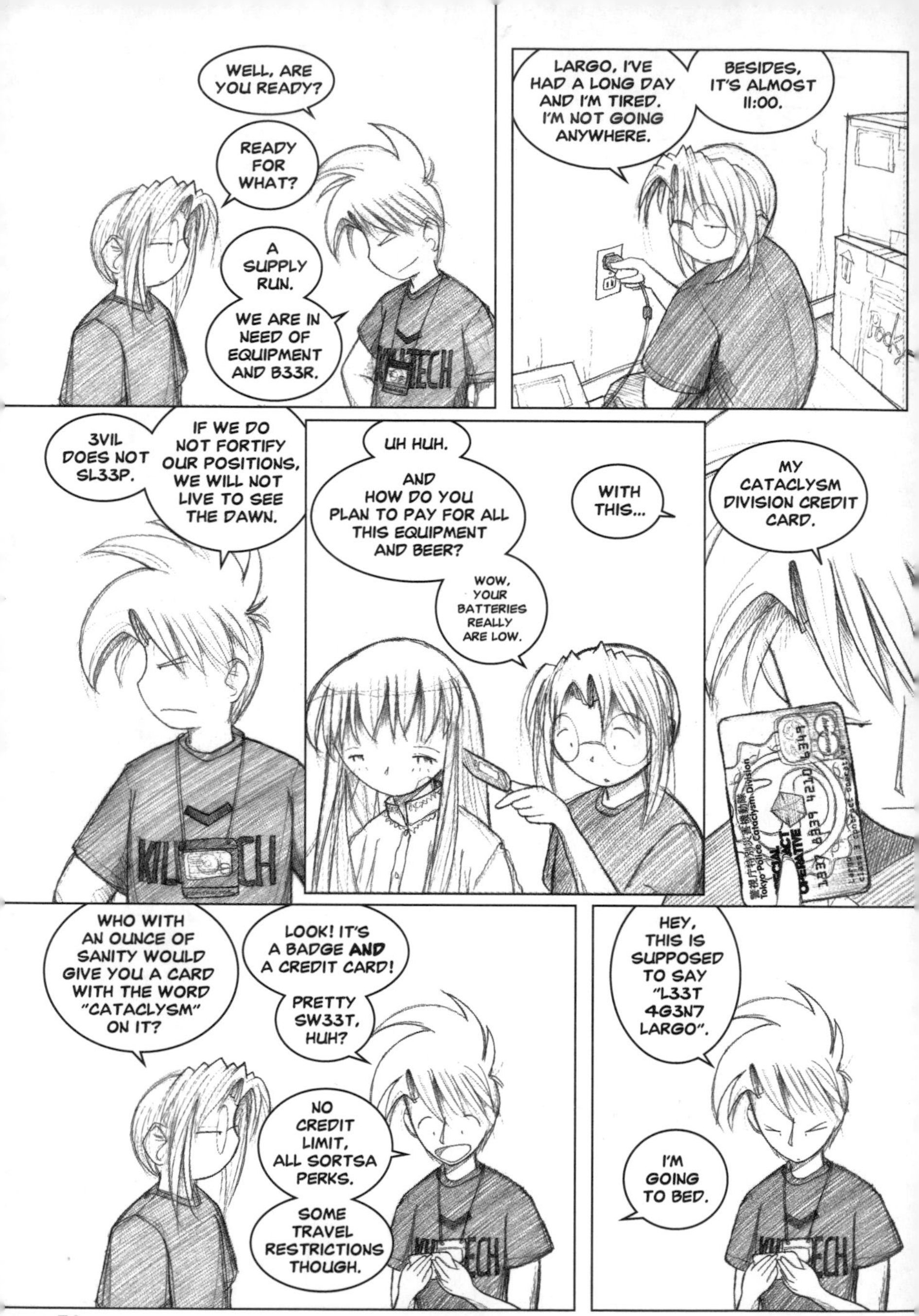
WELL, ARE YOU READY?
READY FOR WHAT?
A SUPPLY RUN.
WE ARE IN NEED OF EQUIPMENT AND B33R.
LARGO, I'VE HAD A LONG DAY AND I'M TIRED. I'M NOT GOING ANYWHERE.
BESIDES, IT'S ALMOST 11:00.
3VIL DOES NOT SL33P.
IF WE DO NOT FORTIFY OUR POSITIONS, WE WILL NOT LIVE TO SEE THE DAWN.
UH HUH.
AND HOW DO YOU PLAN TO PAY FOR ALL THIS EQUIPMENT AND BEER?
WITH THIS...
WOW, YOUR BATTERIES REALLY ARE LOW.
MY CATACLYSM DIVISION CREDIT CARD.
WHO WITH AN OUNCE OF SANITY WOULD GIVE YOU A CARD WITH THE WORD "CATACLYSM" ON IT?
LOOK! IT'S A BADGE **AND** A CREDIT CARD!
PRETTY SW33T, HUH?
NO CREDIT LIMIT, ALL SORTSA PERKS.
SOME TRAVEL RESTRICTIONS THOUGH.
HEY, THIS IS SUPPOSED TO SAY "L33T 4G3N7 LARGO".
I'M GOING TO BED.

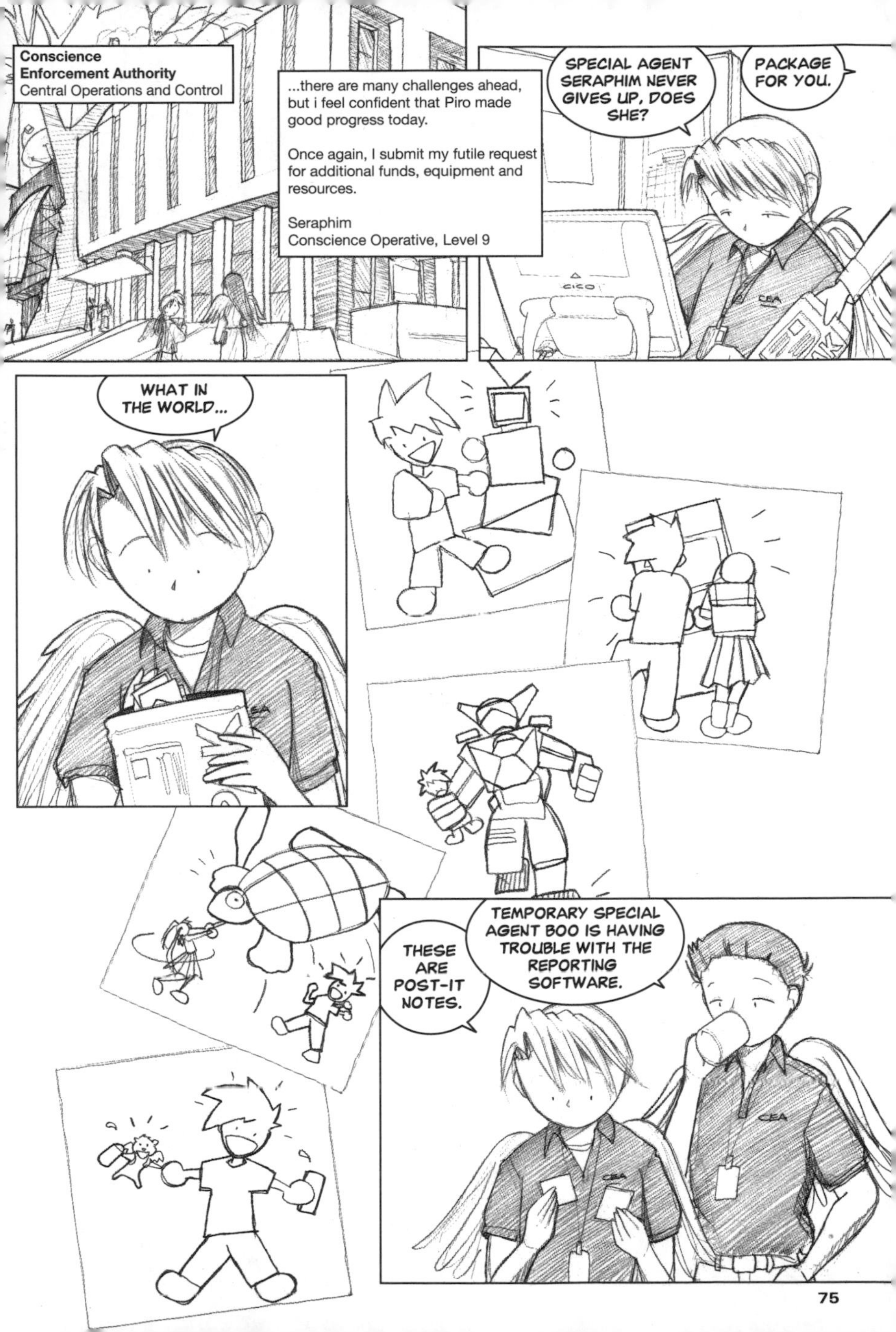
Conscience
Enforcement Authority
Central Operations and Control
...there are many challenges ahead, but i feel confident that Piro made good progress today.
Once again, I submit my futile request for additional funds, equipment and resources.
Seraphim
Conscience Operative, Level 9
SPECIAL AGENT SERAPHIM NEVER GIVES UP, DOES SHE?
PACKAGE FOR YOU.
WHAT IN THE WORLD...
THESE ARE POST-IT NOTES.
TEMPORARY SPECIAL AGENT BOO IS HAVING TROUBLE WITH THE REPORTING SOFTWARE.

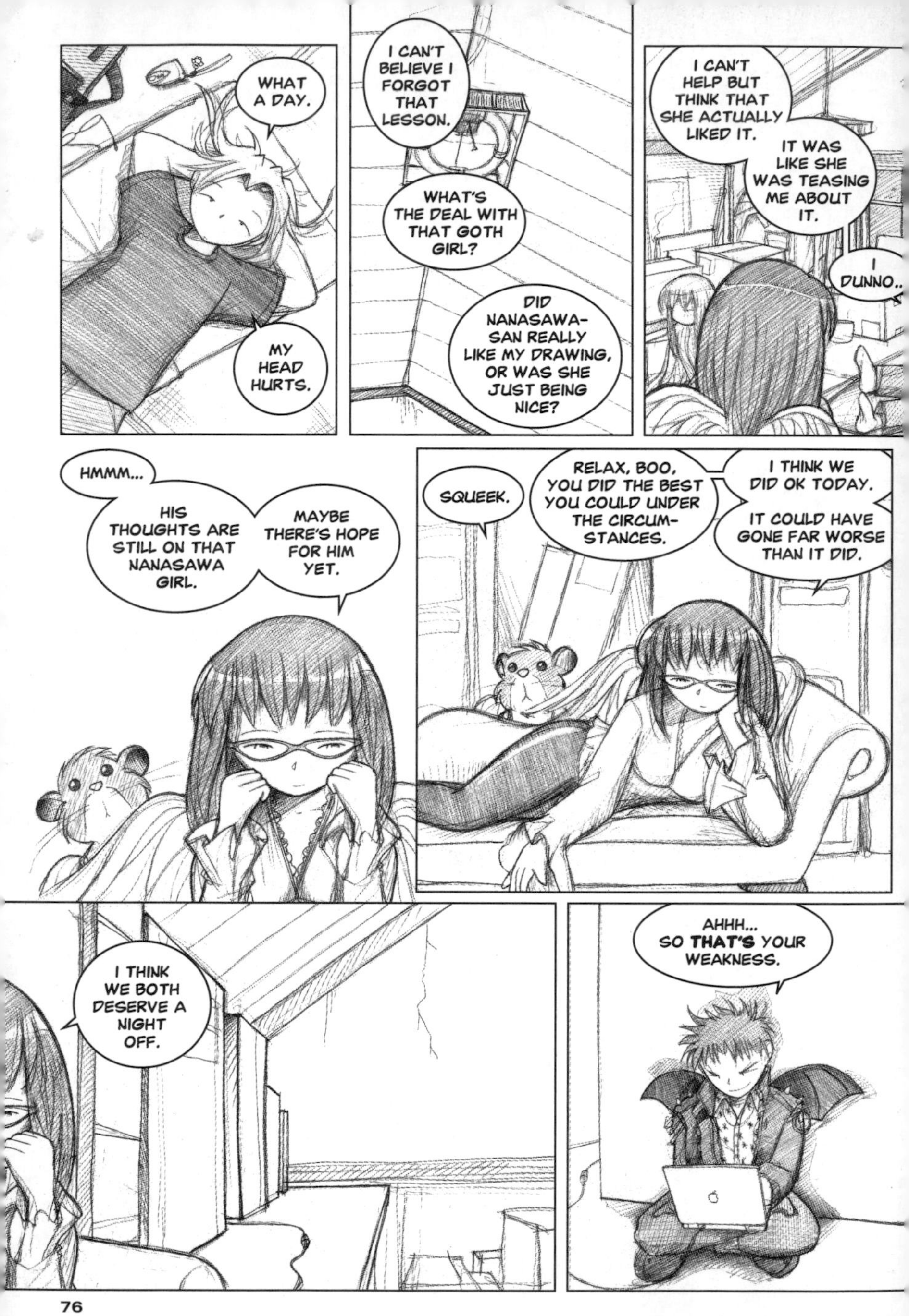

WHAT A DAY.
MY HEAD HURTS.
I CAN'T BELIEVE I FORGOT THAT LESSON.
WHAT'S THE DEAL WITH THAT GOTH GIRL?
DID NANASAWA-SAN REALLY LIKE MY DRAWING, OR WAS SHE JUST BEING NICE?
I CAN'T HELP BUT THINK THAT SHE ACTUALLY LIKED IT.
IT WAS LIKE SHE WAS TEASING ME ABOUT IT.
I DUNNO..
HMMM...
HIS THOUGHTS ARE STILL ON THAT NANASAWA GIRL.
MAYBE THERE'S HOPE FOR HIM YET.
SQUEEK.
RELAX, BOO, YOU DID THE BEST YOU COULD UNDER THE CIRCUM-STANCES.
I THINK WE DID OK TODAY.
IT COULD HAVE GONE FAR WORSE THAN IT DID.
I THINK WE BOTH DESERVE A NIGHT OFF.
AHHH... SO **THAT'S** YOUR WEAKNESS.

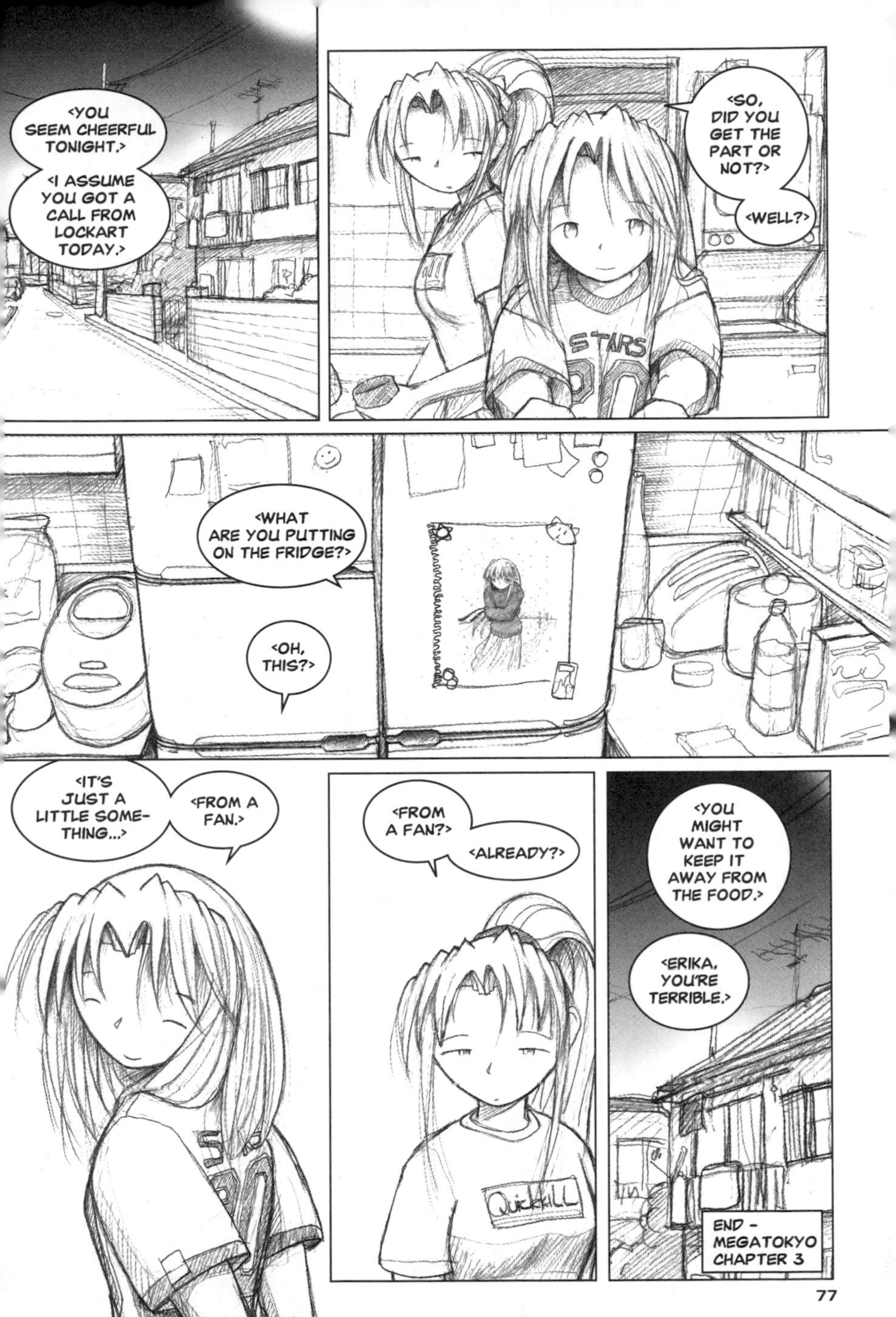
<YOU SEEM CHEERFUL TONIGHT.>
<I ASSUME YOU GOT A CALL FROM LOCKART TODAY.>
<SO, DID YOU GET THE PART OR NOT?>
<WELL?>
STARS
<WHAT ARE YOU PUTTING ON THE FRIDGE?>
<OH, THIS?>
<IT'S JUST A LITTLE SOME-THING...>
<FROM A FAN.>
<FROM A FAN?>
<ALREADY?>
Quickkill
<YOU MIGHT WANT TO KEEP IT AWAY FROM THE FOOD.>
<ERIKA, YOU'RE TERRIBLE.>
END - MEGATOKYO CHAPTER 3

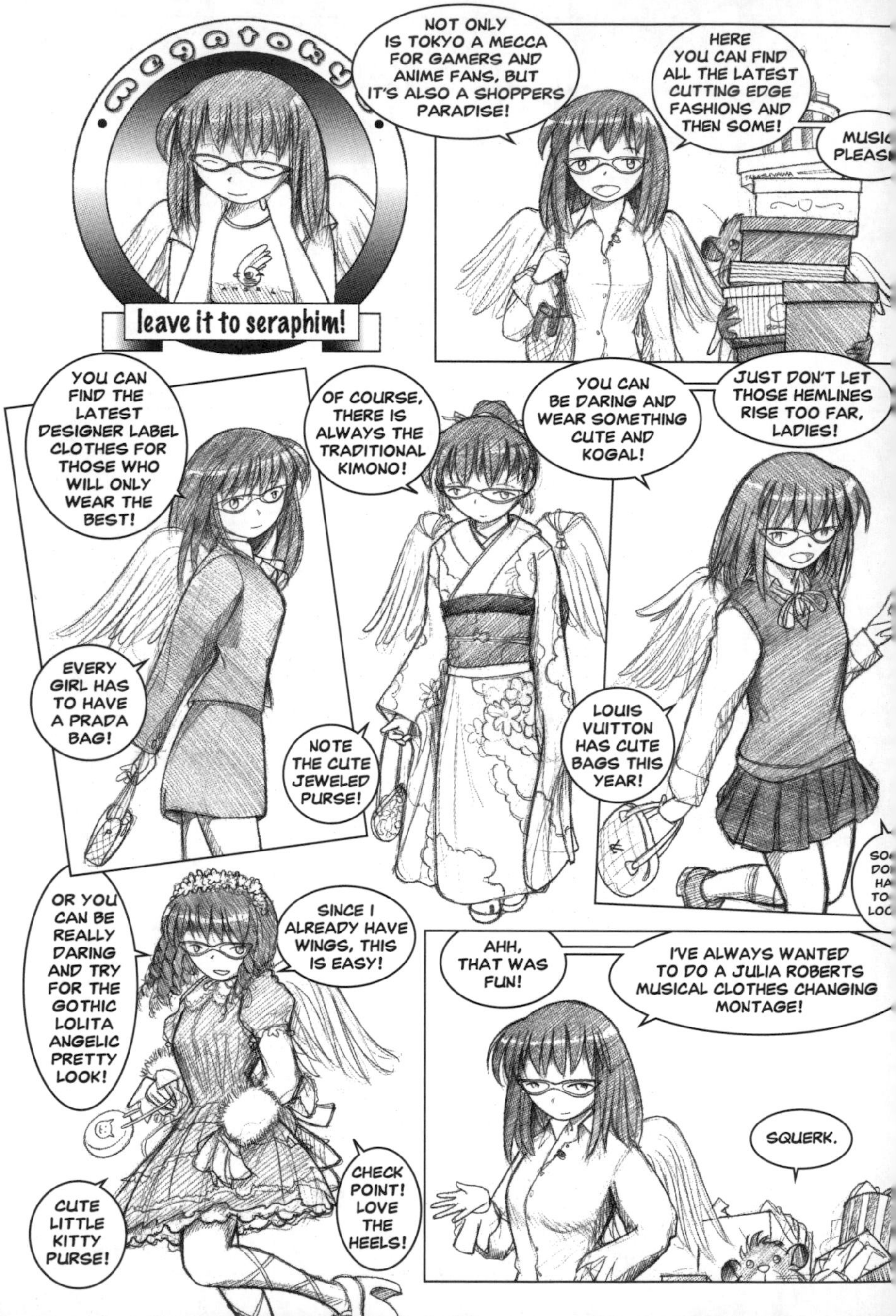
leave it to seraphim!
NOT ONLY IS TOKYO A MECCA FOR GAMERS AND ANIME FANS, BUT IT'S ALSO A SHOPPERS PARADISE!
HERE YOU CAN FIND ALL THE LATEST CUTTING EDGE FASHIONS AND THEN SOME!
YOU CAN FIND THE LATEST DESIGNER LABEL CLOTHES FOR THOSE WHO WILL ONLY WEAR THE BEST!
EVERY GIRL HAS TO HAVE A PRADA BAG!
OF COURSE, THERE IS ALWAYS THE TRADITIONAL KIMONO!
NOTE THE CUTE JEWELED PURSE!
YOU CAN BE DARING AND WEAR SOMETHING CUTE AND KOGAL!
JUST DON'T LET THOSE HEMLINES RISE TOO FAR, LADIES!
LOUIS VUITTON HAS CUTE BAGS THIS YEAR!
OR YOU CAN BE REALLY DARING AND TRY FOR THE GOTHIC LOLITA ANGELIC PRETTY LOOK!
SINCE I ALREADY HAVE WINGS, THIS IS EASY!
CUTE LITTLE KITTY PURSE!
CHECK POINT! LOVE THE HEELS!
AHH, THAT WAS FUN!
I'VE ALWAYS WANTED TO DO A JULIA ROBERTS MUSICAL CLOTHES CHANGING MONTAGE!
SQUERK.

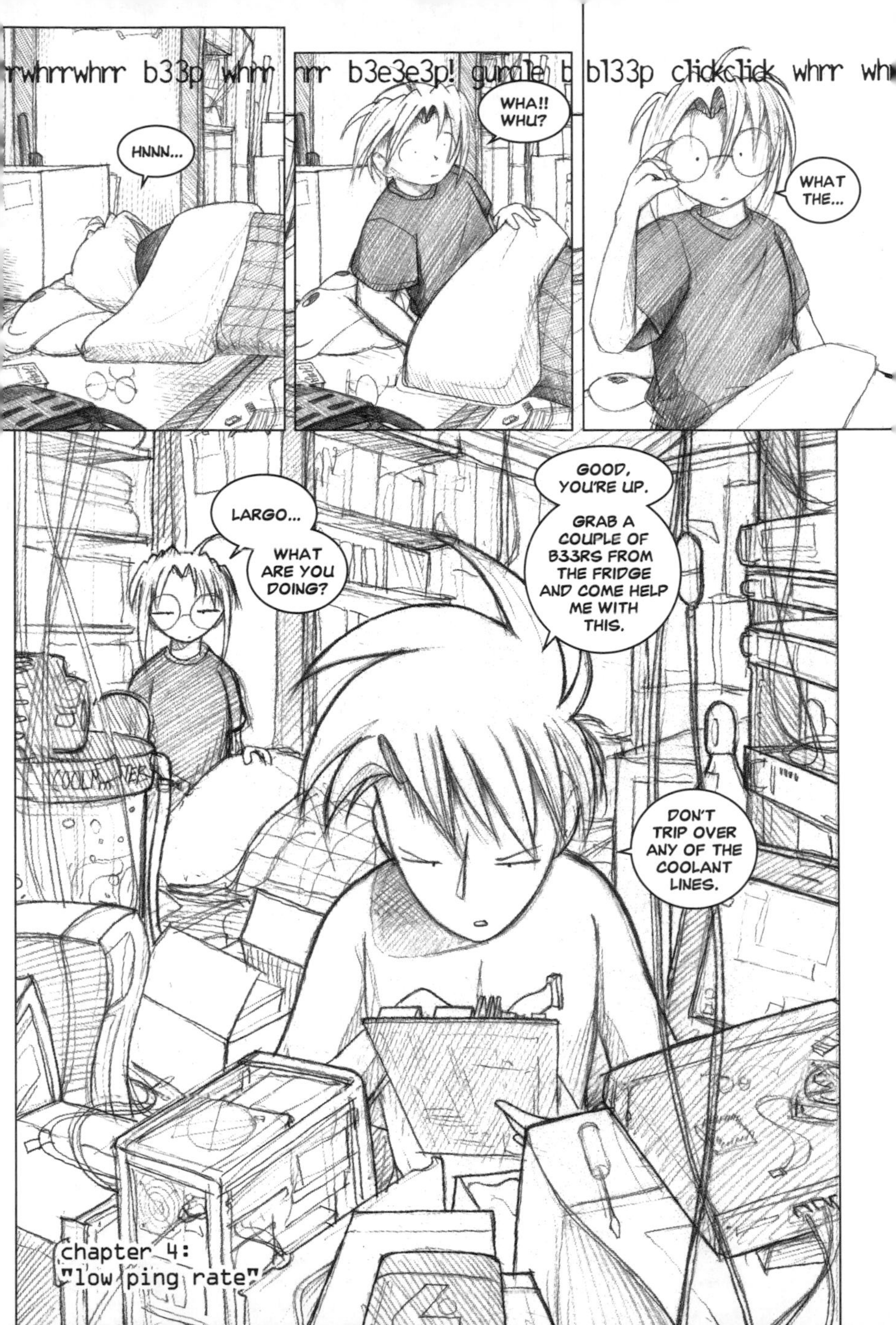
rwhrrwhrr b33p whrr
HNNN...
hrr b3e3e3p! gurgle b
WHA!! WHU?
b133p clickclick whrr wh
WHAT THE...
LARGO... WHAT ARE YOU DOING?
GOOD, YOU'RE UP.
GRAB A COUPLE OF B33RS FROM THE FRIDGE AND COME HELP ME WITH THIS.
DON'T TRIP OVER ANY OF THE COOLANT LINES.
chapter 4:
"low ping rate"

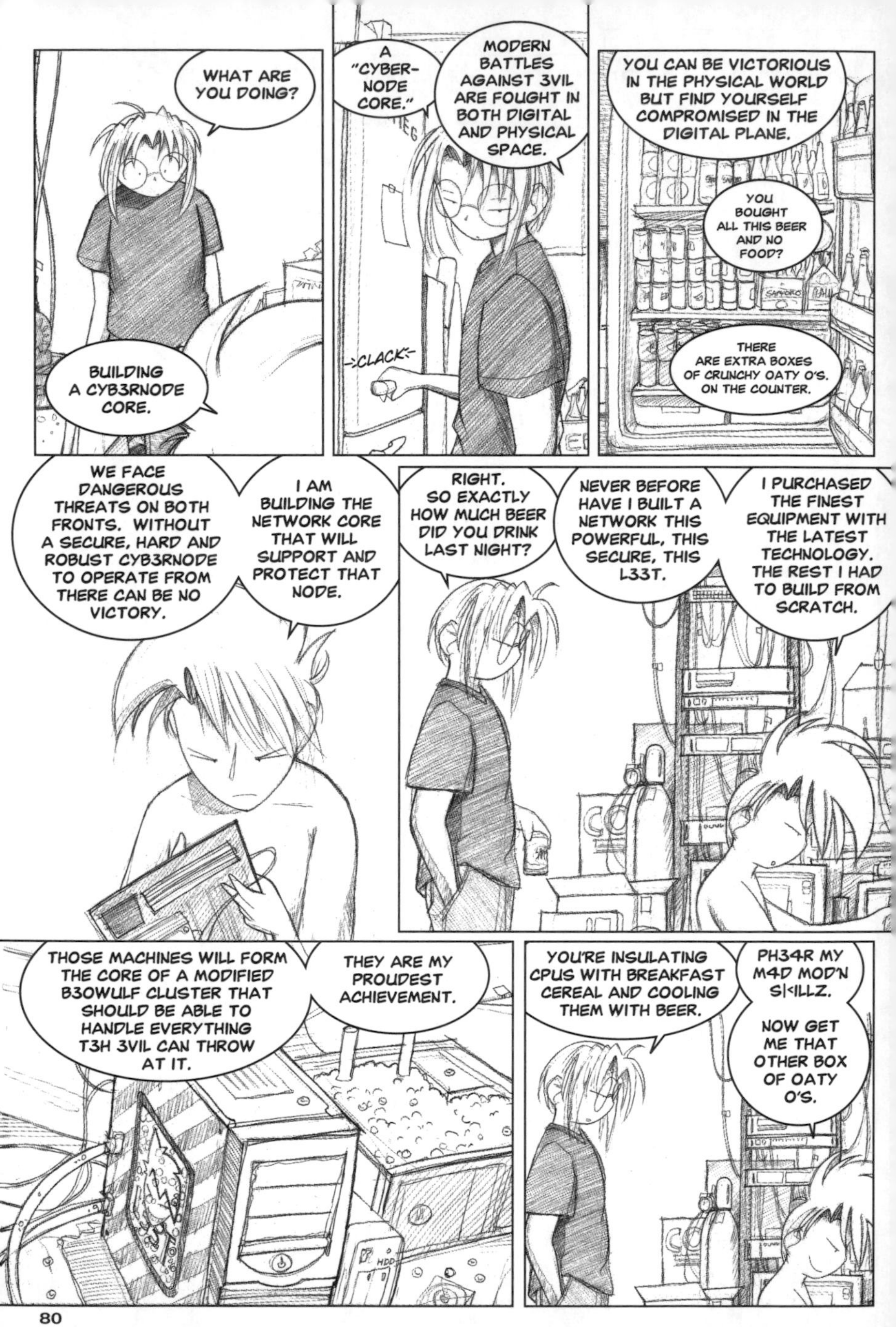
WHAT ARE YOU DOING?
BUILDING A CYB3RNODE CORE.
A "CYBER-NODE CORE."
MODERN BATTLES AGAINST 3VIL ARE FOUGHT IN BOTH DIGITAL AND PHYSICAL SPACE.
CLACK
YOU CAN BE VICTORIOUS IN THE PHYSICAL WORLD BUT FIND YOURSELF COMPROMISED IN THE DIGITAL PLANE.
YOU BOUGHT ALL THIS BEER AND NO FOOD?
THERE ARE EXTRA BOXES OF CRUNCHY OATY O'S. ON THE COUNTER.
WE FACE DANGEROUS THREATS ON BOTH FRONTS. WITHOUT A SECURE, HARD AND ROBUST CYB3RNODE TO OPERATE FROM THERE CAN BE NO VICTORY.
I AM BUILDING THE NETWORK CORE THAT WILL SUPPORT AND PROTECT THAT NODE.
RIGHT. SO EXACTLY HOW MUCH BEER DID YOU DRINK LAST NIGHT?
NEVER BEFORE HAVE I BUILT A NETWORK THIS POWERFUL, THIS SECURE, THIS L33T.
I PURCHASED THE FINEST EQUIPMENT WITH THE LATEST TECHNOLOGY. THE REST I HAD TO BUILD FROM SCRATCH.
THOSE MACHINES WILL FORM THE CORE OF A MODIFIED B3OWULF CLUSTER THAT SHOULD BE ABLE TO HANDLE EVERYTHING T3H 3VIL CAN THROW AT IT.
THEY ARE MY PROUDEST ACHIEVEMENT.
HDD
YOU'RE INSULATING CPUS WITH BREAKFAST CEREAL AND COOLING THEM WITH BEER.
PH34R MY M4D MOD'N S|<ILLZ.
NOW GET ME THAT OTHER BOX OF OATY O'S.

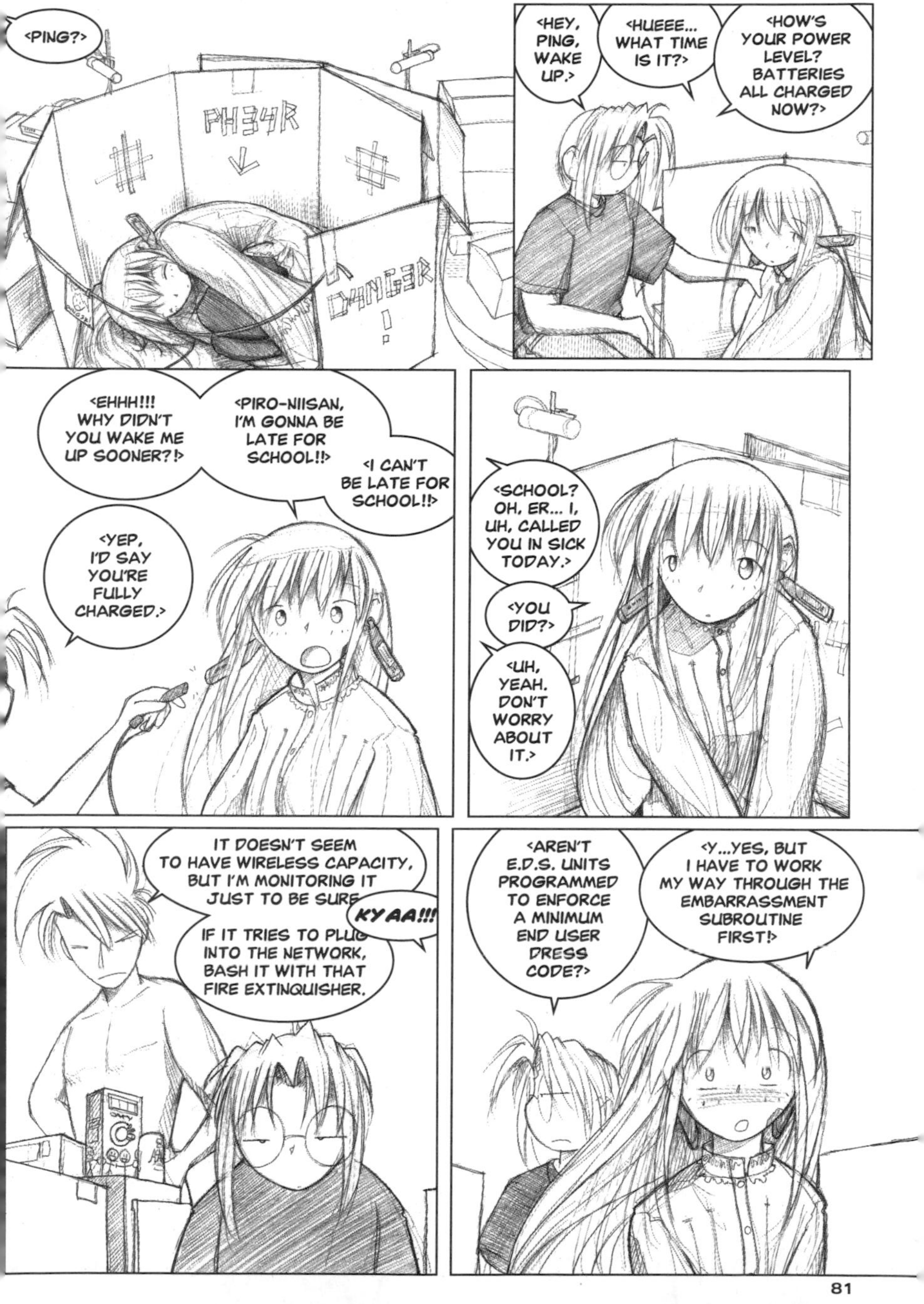
<PING?>
<HEY, PING, WAKE UP.>
<HUEEE... WHAT TIME IS IT?>
<HOW'S YOUR POWER LEVEL? BATTERIES ALL CHARGED NOW?>
PH34R
D4NG3R !
<EHHH!!! WHY DIDN'T YOU WAKE ME UP SOONER?!>
<PIRO-NIISAN, I'M GONNA BE LATE FOR SCHOOL!!>
<I CAN'T BE LATE FOR SCHOOL!!>
<YEP, I'D SAY YOU'RE FULLY CHARGED.>
<SCHOOL? OH, ER... I, UH, CALLED YOU IN SICK TODAY.>
<YOU DID?>
<UH, YEAH. DON'T WORRY ABOUT IT.>
IT DOESN'T SEEM TO HAVE WIRELESS CAPACITY, BUT I'M MONITORING IT JUST TO BE SURE
KYAA!!!
IF IT TRIES TO PLUG INTO THE NETWORK, BASH IT WITH THAT FIRE EXTINQUISHER.
<AREN'T E.D.S. UNITS PROGRAMMED TO ENFORCE A MINIMUM END USER DRESS CODE?>
<Y...YES, BUT I HAVE TO WORK MY WAY THROUGH THE EMBARRASSMENT SUBROUTINE FIRST!>

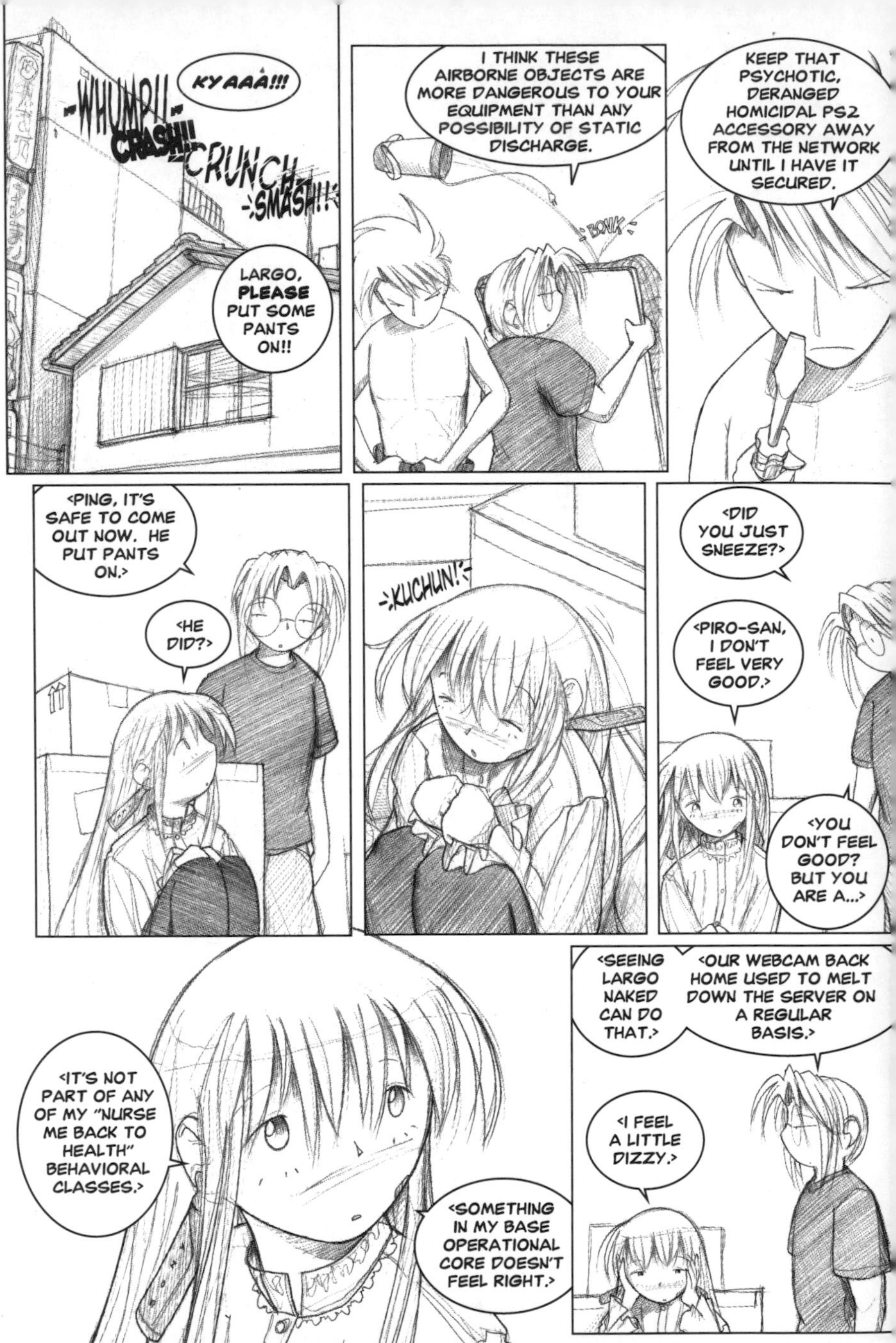
KYAAA!!!
-WHUMP!!-
CRASH!!
CRUNCH
-SMASH!!-
LARGO, **PLEASE** PUT SOME PANTS ON!!
I THINK THESE AIRBORNE OBJECTS ARE MORE DANGEROUS TO YOUR EQUIPMENT THAN ANY POSSIBILITY OF STATIC DISCHARGE.
BONK
KEEP THAT PSYCHOTIC, DERANGED HOMICIDAL PS2 ACCESSORY AWAY FROM THE NETWORK UNTIL I HAVE IT SECURED.
<PING, IT'S SAFE TO COME OUT NOW. HE PUT PANTS ON.>
<HE DID?>
-KUCHUN!-
<DID YOU JUST SNEEZE?>
<PIRO-SAN, I DON'T FEEL VERY GOOD.>
<YOU DON'T FEEL GOOD? BUT YOU ARE A...>
<IT'S NOT PART OF ANY OF MY "NURSE ME BACK TO HEALTH" BEHAVIORAL CLASSES.>
<SOMETHING IN MY BASE OPERATIONAL CORE DOESN'T FEEL RIGHT.>
<SEEING LARGO NAKED CAN DO THAT.>
<OUR WEBCAM BACK HOME USED TO MELT DOWN THE SERVER ON A REGULAR BASIS.>
<I FEEL A LITTLE DIZZY.>

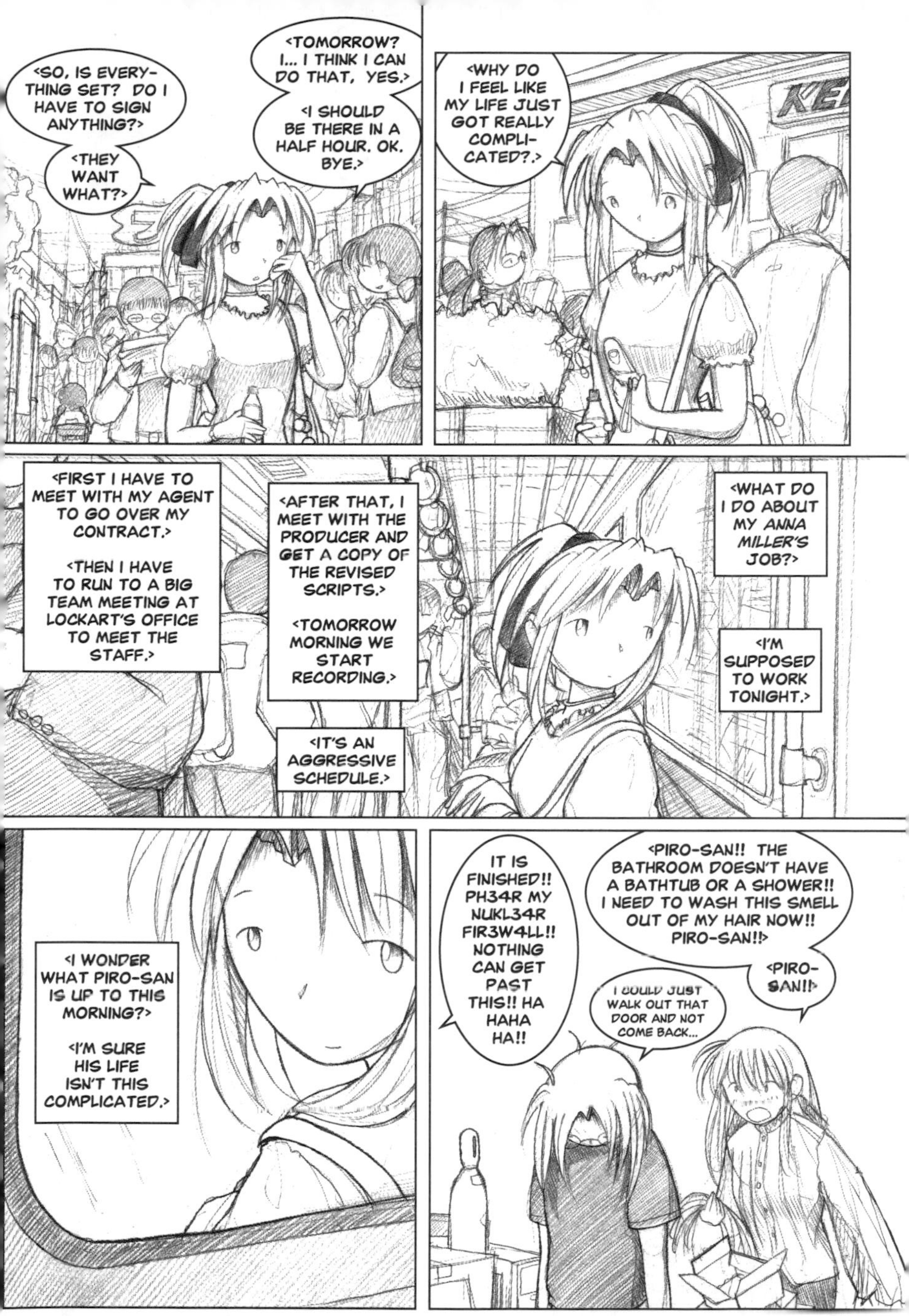

<SO, IS EVERY-THING SET? DO I HAVE TO SIGN ANYTHING?>
<THEY WANT WHAT?>
<TOMORROW? I... I THINK I CAN DO THAT, YES.>
<I SHOULD BE THERE IN A HALF HOUR. OK. BYE.>
<WHY DO I FEEL LIKE MY LIFE JUST GOT REALLY COMPLI-CATED?.>
<FIRST I HAVE TO MEET WITH MY AGENT TO GO OVER MY CONTRACT.>
<THEN I HAVE TO RUN TO A BIG TEAM MEETING AT LOCKART'S OFFICE TO MEET THE STAFF.>
<AFTER THAT, I MEET WITH THE PRODUCER AND GET A COPY OF THE REVISED SCRIPTS.>
<TOMORROW MORNING WE START RECORDING.>
<IT'S AN AGGRESSIVE SCHEDULE.>
<WHAT DO I DO ABOUT MY *ANNA MILLER'S* JOB?>
<I'M SUPPOSED TO WORK TONIGHT.>
<I WONDER WHAT PIRO-SAN IS UP TO THIS MORNING?>
<I'M SURE HIS LIFE ISN'T THIS COMPLICATED.>
IT IS FINISHED!! PH34R MY NUKL34R FIR3W4LL!! NOTHING CAN GET PAST THIS!! HA HAHA HA!!
<PIRO-SAN!! THE BATHROOM DOESN'T HAVE A BATHTUB OR A SHOWER!! I NEED TO WASH THIS SMELL OUT OF MY HAIR NOW!! PIRO-SAN!!>
<PIRO-SAN!!>
I COULD JUST WALK OUT THAT DOOR AND NOT COME BACK...

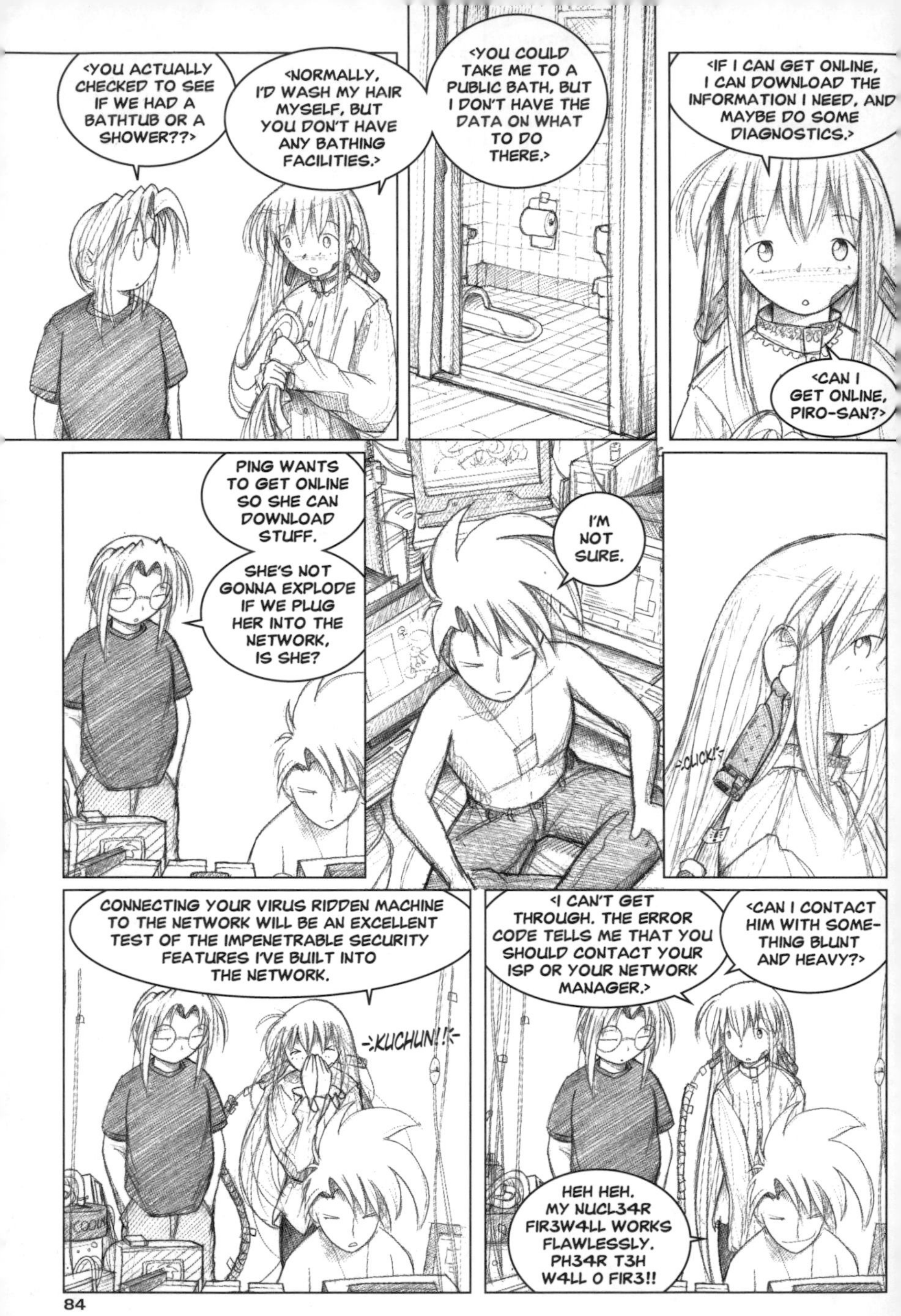
<YOU ACTUALLY CHECKED TO SEE IF WE HAD A BATHTUB OR A SHOWER??>
<NORMALLY, I'D WASH MY HAIR MYSELF, BUT YOU DON'T HAVE ANY BATHING FACILITIES.>
<YOU COULD TAKE ME TO A PUBLIC BATH, BUT I DON'T HAVE THE DATA ON WHAT TO DO THERE.>
<IF I CAN GET ONLINE, I CAN DOWNLOAD THE INFORMATION I NEED, AND MAYBE DO SOME DIAGNOSTICS.>
<CAN I GET ONLINE, PIRO-SAN?>
PING WANTS TO GET ONLINE SO SHE CAN DOWNLOAD STUFF.
SHE'S NOT GONNA EXPLODE IF WE PLUG HER INTO THE NETWORK, IS SHE?
I'M NOT SURE.
-CLICK!-
CONNECTING YOUR VIRUS RIDDEN MACHINE TO THE NETWORK WILL BE AN EXCELLENT TEST OF THE IMPENETRABLE SECURITY FEATURES I'VE BUILT INTO THE NETWORK.
-KUCHUN!!-
<I CAN'T GET THROUGH. THE ERROR CODE TELLS ME THAT YOU SHOULD CONTACT YOUR ISP OR YOUR NETWORK MANAGER.>
<CAN I CONTACT HIM WITH SOME-THING BLUNT AND HEAVY?>
HEH HEH. MY NUCL34R FIR3W4LL WORKS FLAWLESSLY. PH34R T3H W4LL O FIR3!!

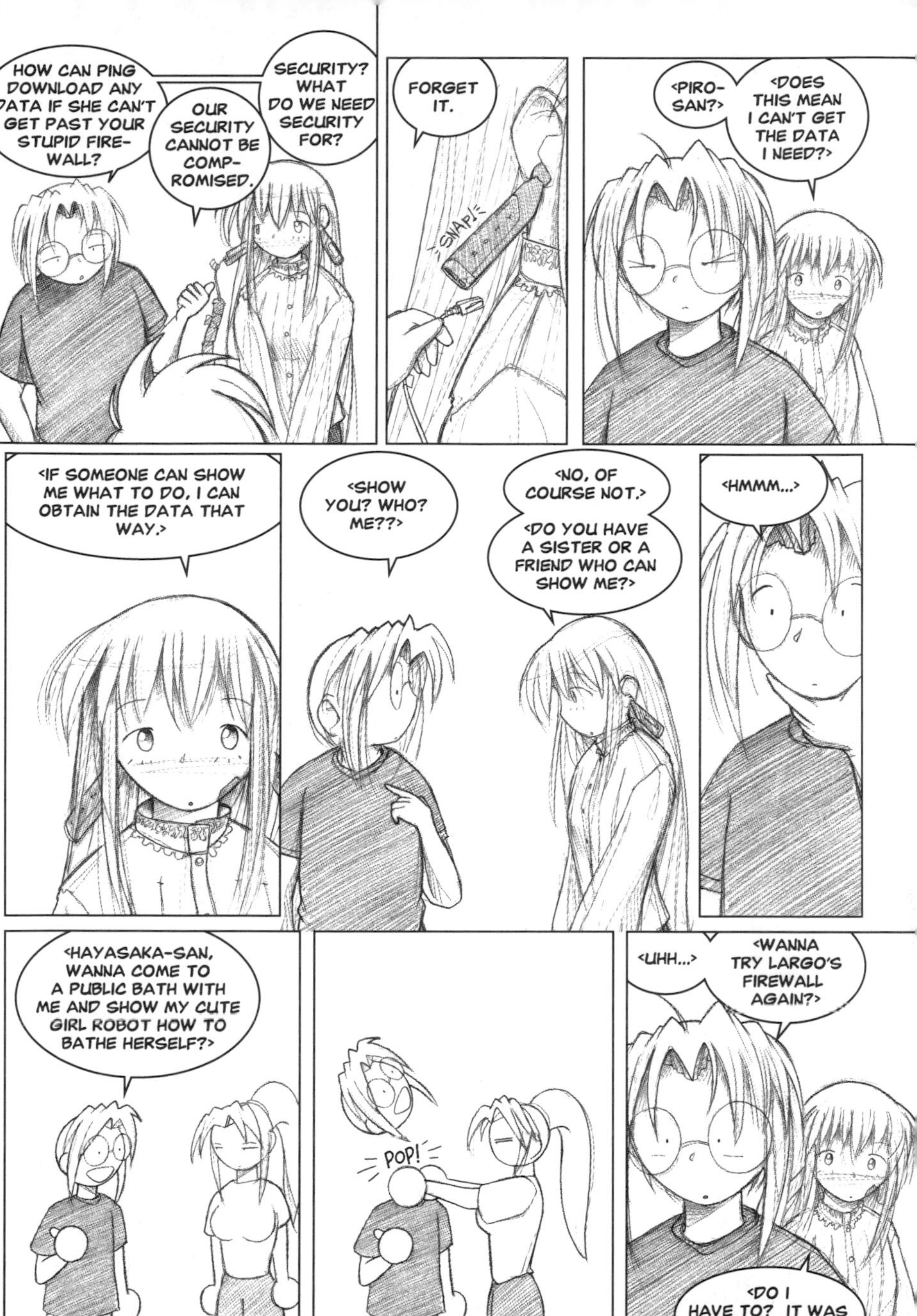

HOW CAN PING DOWNLOAD ANY DATA IF SHE CAN'T GET PAST YOUR STUPID FIRE-WALL?
OUR SECURITY CANNOT BE COMP-ROMISED.
SECURITY? WHAT DO WE NEED SECURITY FOR?
FORGET IT.
SNAP!
<PIRO-SAN?>
<DOES THIS MEAN I CAN'T GET THE DATA I NEED?>
<IF SOMEONE CAN SHOW ME WHAT TO DO, I CAN OBTAIN THE DATA THAT WAY.>
<SHOW YOU? WHO? ME??>
<NO, OF COURSE NOT.>
<DO YOU HAVE A SISTER OR A FRIEND WHO CAN SHOW ME?>
<HMMM...>
<HAYASAKA-SAN, WANNA COME TO A PUBLIC BATH WITH ME AND SHOW MY CUTE GIRL ROBOT HOW TO BATHE HERSELF?>
POP!
<UHH...>
<WANNA TRY LARGO'S FIREWALL AGAIN?>
<DO I HAVE TO? IT WAS KINDA SCARY.>

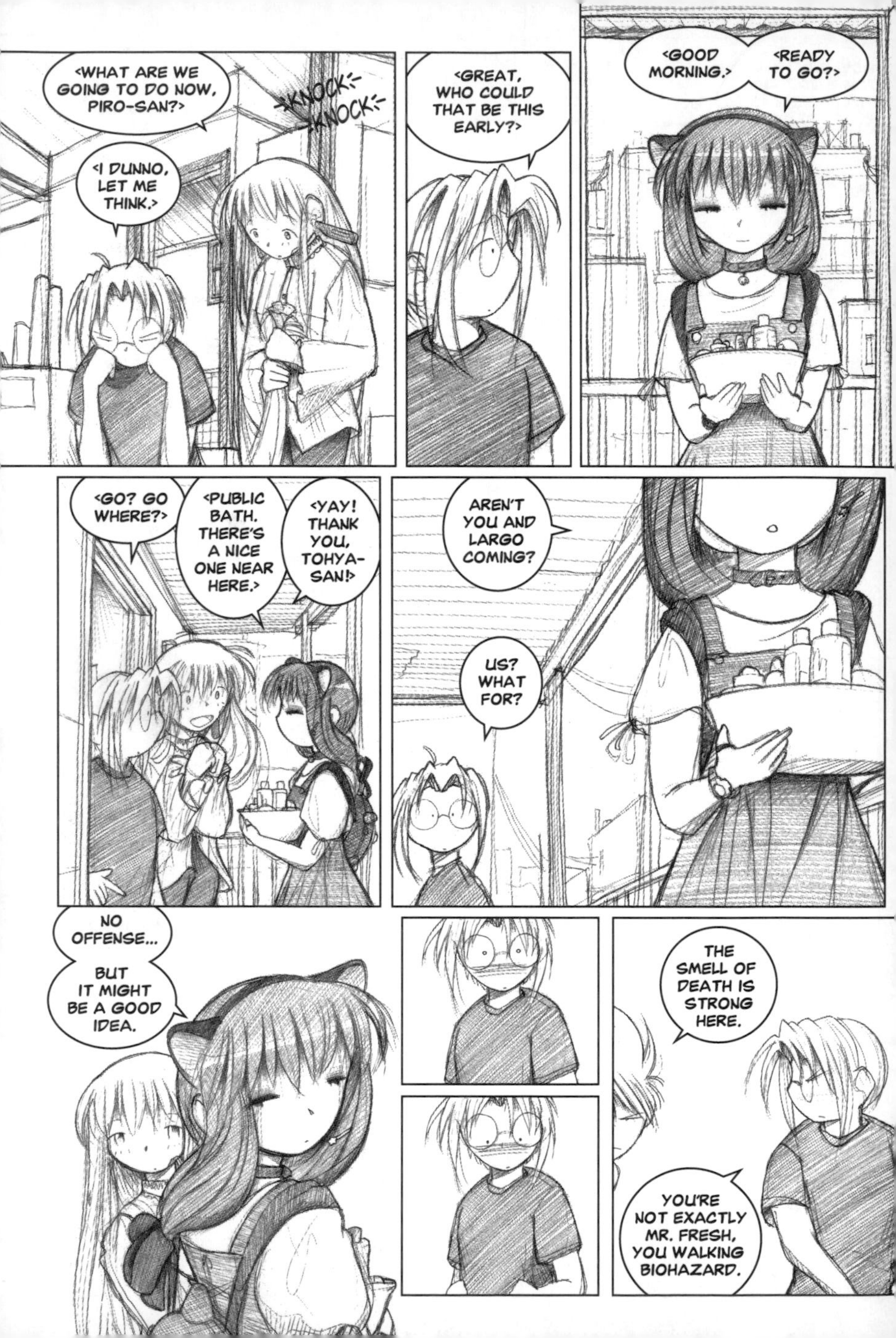
<WHAT ARE WE GOING TO DO NOW, PIRO-SAN?>
KNOCK KNOCK
<I DUNNO, LET ME THINK.>
<GREAT, WHO COULD THAT BE THIS EARLY?>
<GOOD MORNING.>
<READY TO GO?>
<GO? GO WHERE?>
<PUBLIC BATH. THERE'S A NICE ONE NEAR HERE.>
<YAY! THANK YOU, TOHYA-SAN!>
AREN'T YOU AND LARGO COMING?
US? WHAT FOR?
NO OFFENSE...
BUT IT MIGHT BE A GOOD IDEA.
THE SMELL OF DEATH IS STRONG HERE.
YOU'RE NOT EXACTLY MR. FRESH, YOU WALKING BIOHAZARD.

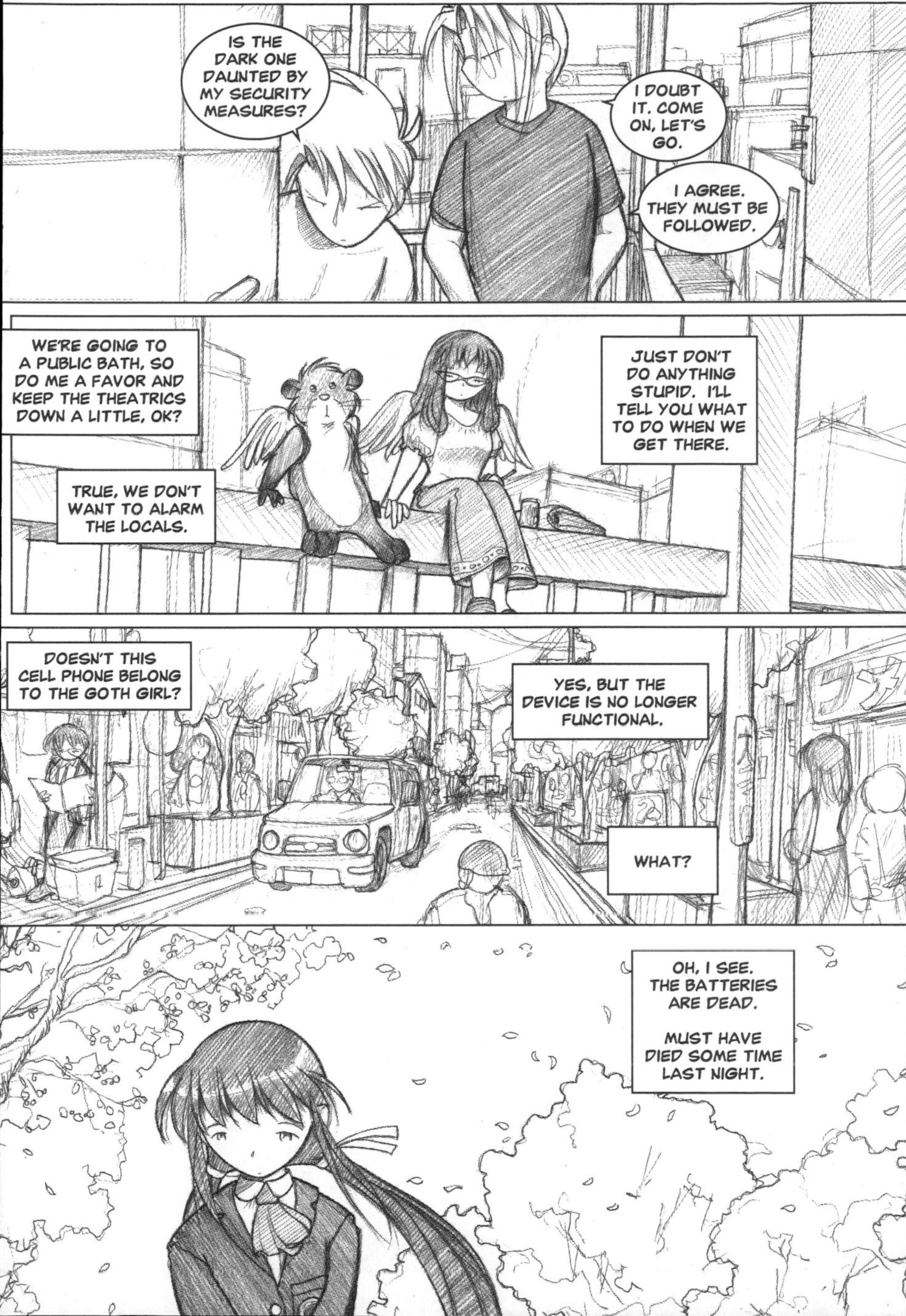
IS THE DARK ONE DAUNTED BY MY SECURITY MEASURES?
I DOUBT IT. COME ON, LET'S GO.
I AGREE. THEY MUST BE FOLLOWED.
WE'RE GOING TO A PUBLIC BATH, SO DO ME A FAVOR AND KEEP THE THEATRICS DOWN A LITTLE, OK?
TRUE, WE DON'T WANT TO ALARM THE LOCALS.
JUST DON'T DO ANYTHING STUPID. I'LL TELL YOU WHAT TO DO WHEN WE GET THERE.
DOESN'T THIS CELL PHONE BELONG TO THE GOTH GIRL?
YES, BUT THE DEVICE IS NO LONGER FUNCTIONAL.
WHAT?
OH, I SEE. THE BATTERIES ARE DEAD.
MUST HAVE DIED SOME TIME LAST NIGHT.

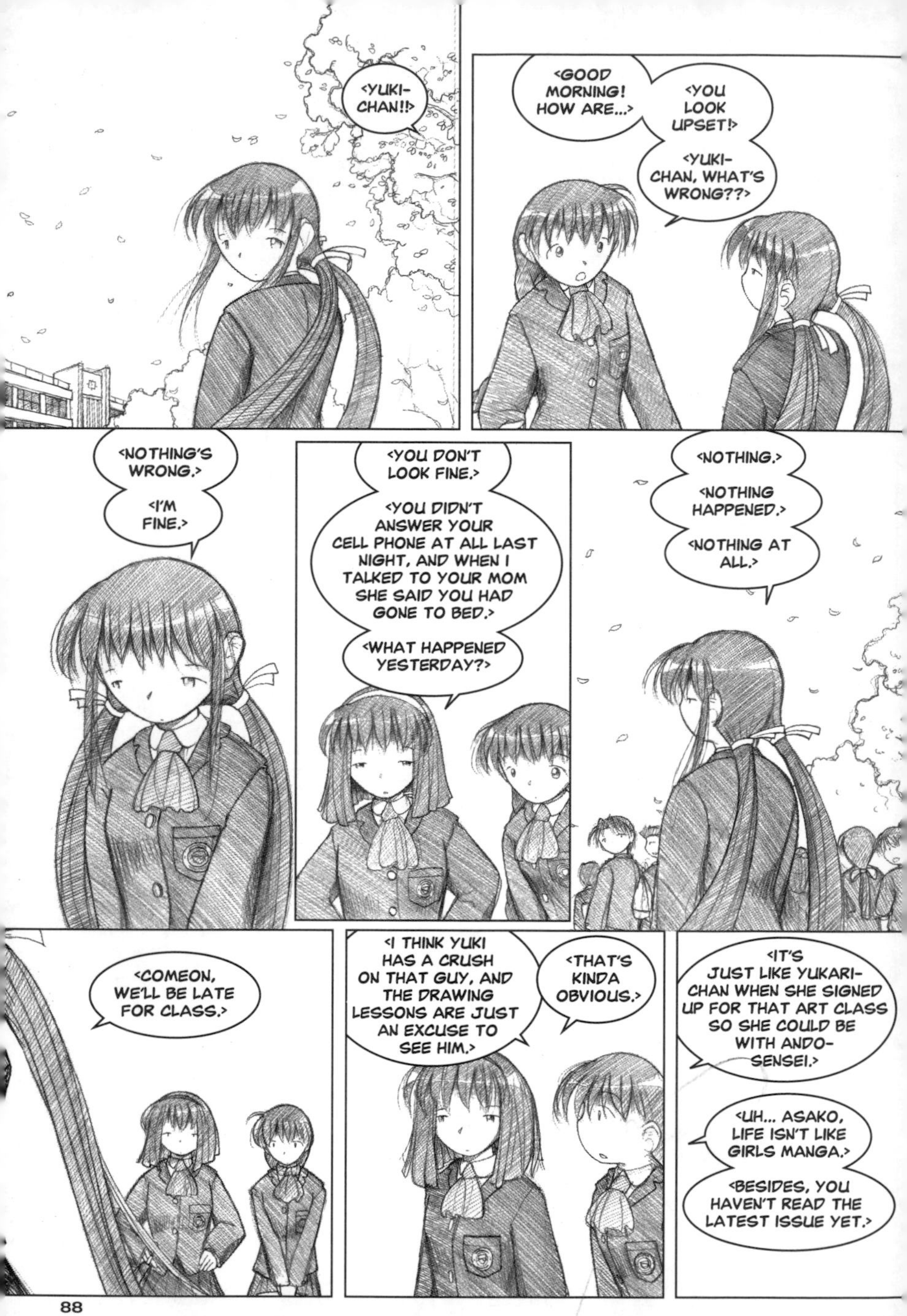
<YUKI-CHAN!!>
<GOOD MORNING! HOW ARE...>
<YOU LOOK UPSET!>
<YUKI-CHAN, WHAT'S WRONG??>
<NOTHING'S WRONG.>
<I'M FINE.>
<YOU DON'T LOOK FINE.>
<YOU DIDN'T ANSWER YOUR CELL PHONE AT ALL LAST NIGHT, AND WHEN I TALKED TO YOUR MOM SHE SAID YOU HAD GONE TO BED.>
<WHAT HAPPENED YESTERDAY?>
<NOTHING.>
<NOTHING HAPPENED.>
<NOTHING AT ALL.>
<COMEON, WE'LL BE LATE FOR CLASS.>
<I THINK YUKI HAS A CRUSH ON THAT GUY, AND THE DRAWING LESSONS ARE JUST AN EXCUSE TO SEE HIM.>
<THAT'S KINDA OBVIOUS.>
<IT'S JUST LIKE YUKARI-CHAN WHEN SHE SIGNED UP FOR THAT ART CLASS SO SHE COULD BE WITH ANDO-SENSEI.>
<UH... ASAKO, LIFE ISN'T LIKE GIRLS MANGA.>
<BESIDES, YOU HAVEN'T READ THE LATEST ISSUE YET.>

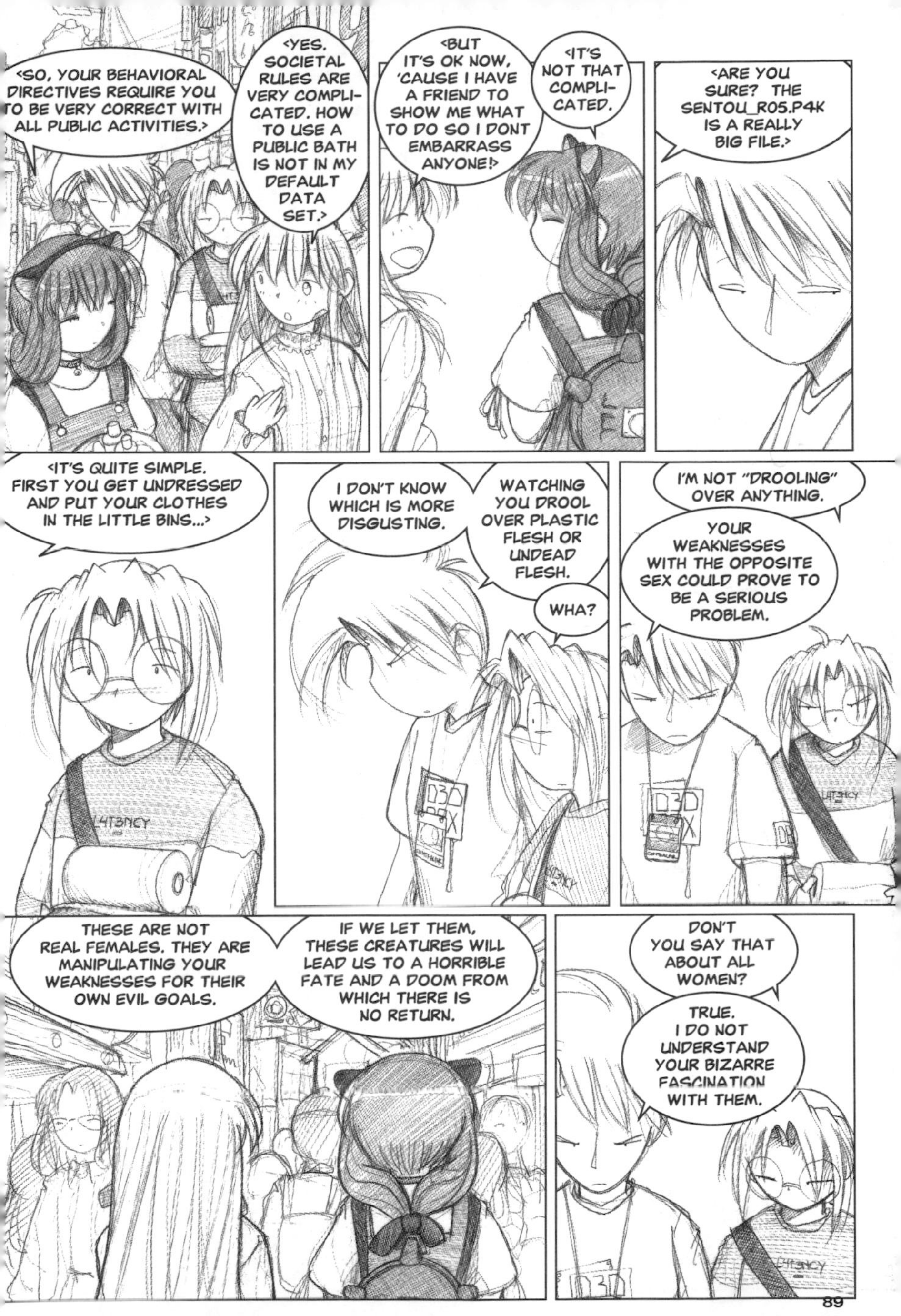
<SO, YOUR BEHAVIORAL DIRECTIVES REQUIRE YOU TO BE VERY CORRECT WITH ALL PUBLIC ACTIVITIES.>
<YES. SOCIETAL RULES ARE VERY COMPLICATED. HOW TO USE A PUBLIC BATH IS NOT IN MY DEFAULT DATA SET.>
<BUT IT'S OK NOW, 'CAUSE I HAVE A FRIEND TO SHOW ME WHAT TO DO SO I DONT EMBARRASS ANYONE!>
<IT'S NOT THAT COMPLICATED.
<ARE YOU SURE? THE SENTOU_R05.P4K IS A REALLY BIG FILE.>
<IT'S QUITE SIMPLE. FIRST YOU GET UNDRESSED AND PUT YOUR CLOTHES IN THE LITTLE BINS...>
I DON'T KNOW WHICH IS MORE DISGUSTING.
WATCHING YOU DROOL OVER PLASTIC FLESH OR UNDEAD FLESH.
WHA?
I'M NOT "DROOLING" OVER ANYTHING.
YOUR WEAKNESSES WITH THE OPPOSITE SEX COULD PROVE TO BE A SERIOUS PROBLEM.
THESE ARE NOT REAL FEMALES. THEY ARE MANIPULATING YOUR WEAKNESSES FOR THEIR OWN EVIL GOALS.
IF WE LET THEM, THESE CREATURES WILL LEAD US TO A HORRIBLE FATE AND A DOOM FROM WHICH THERE IS NO RETURN.
DON'T YOU SAY THAT ABOUT ALL WOMEN?
TRUE. I DO NOT UNDERSTAND YOUR BIZARRE FASCINATION WITH THEM.

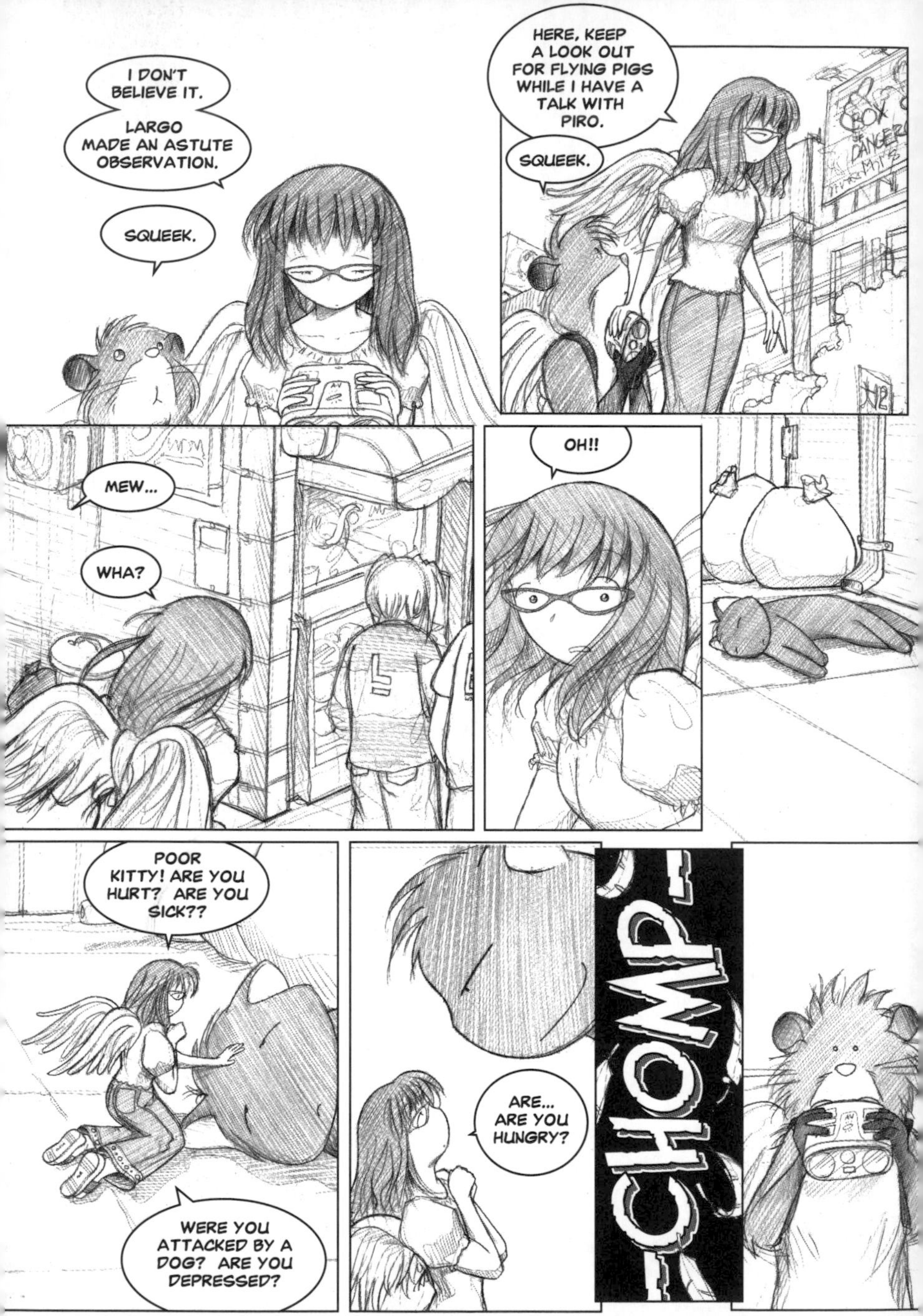
I DON'T BELIEVE IT.
LARGO MADE AN ASTUTE OBSERVATION.
SQUEEK.
HERE, KEEP A LOOK OUT FOR FLYING PIGS WHILE I HAVE A TALK WITH PIRO.
SQUEEK.
MEW...
WHA?
OH!!
POOR KITTY! ARE YOU HURT? ARE YOU SICK??
WERE YOU ATTACKED BY A DOG? ARE YOU DEPRESSED?
ARE... ARE YOU HUNGRY?
CHOMP

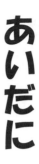

あいだに。。。

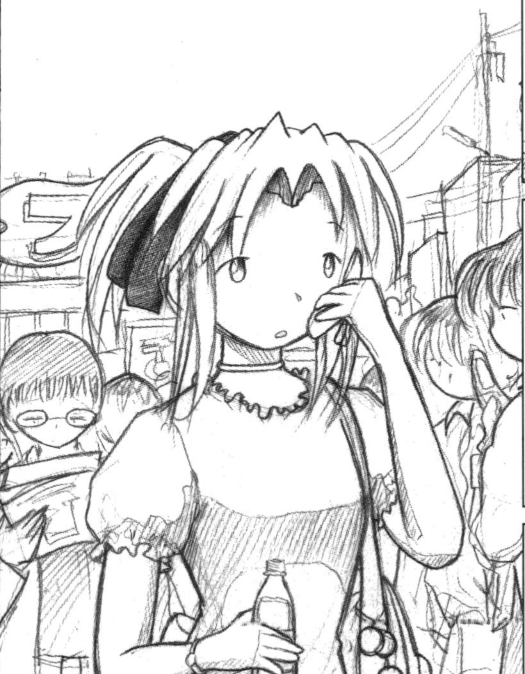

a megatokyo moment...

"BUSY GIRL"

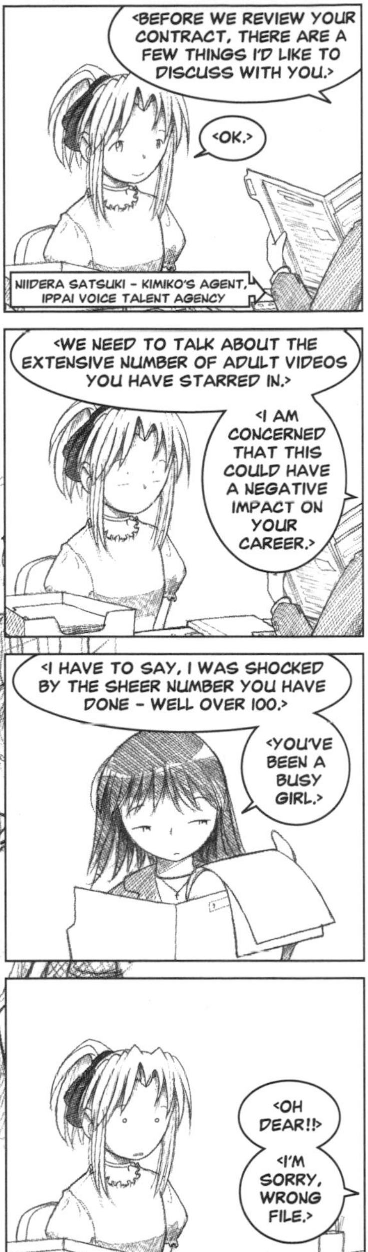

<BEFORE WE REVIEW YOUR CONTRACT, THERE ARE A FEW THINGS I'D LIKE TO DISCUSS WITH YOU.>
<OK.>
NIIDERA SATSUKI - KIMIKO'S AGENT, IPPAI VOICE TALENT AGENCY
<WE NEED TO TALK ABOUT THE EXTENSIVE NUMBER OF ADULT VIDEOS YOU HAVE STARRED IN.>
<I AM CONCERNED THAT THIS COULD HAVE A NEGATIVE IMPACT ON YOUR CAREER.>
<I HAVE TO SAY, I WAS SHOCKED BY THE SHEER NUMBER YOU HAVE DONE - WELL OVER 100.>
<YOU'VE BEEN A BUSY GIRL.>
<OH DEAR!!>
<I'M SORRY, WRONG FILE.>

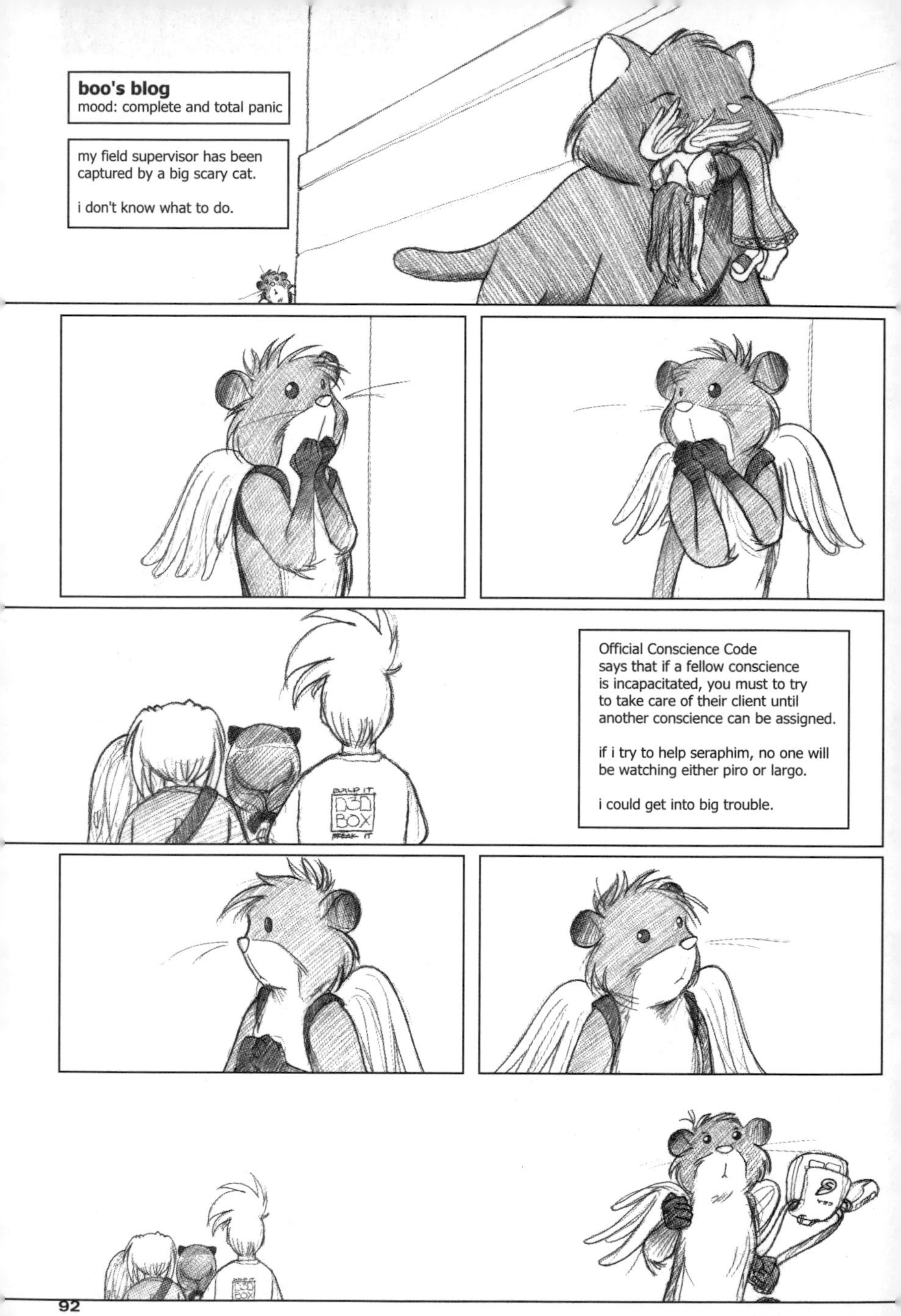
boo's blog
mood: complete and total panic
my field supervisor has been captured by a big scary cat.
i don't know what to do.
Official Conscience Code says that if a fellow conscience is incapacitated, you must to try to take care of their client until another conscience can be assigned.
if i try to help seraphim, no one will be watching either piro or largo.
i could get into big trouble.

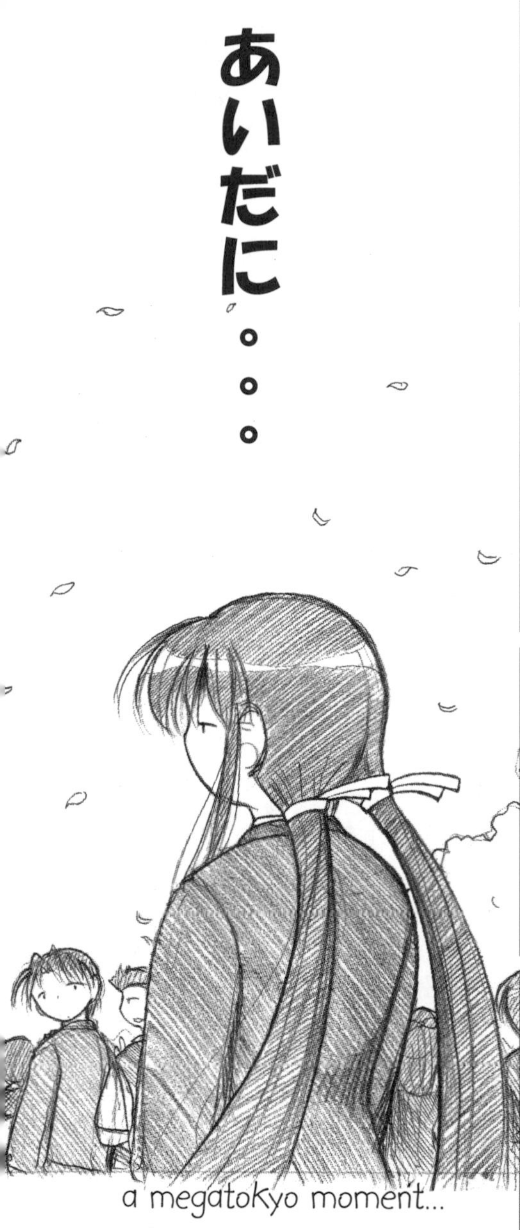
あいだに。。。
a megatokyo moment...

"TUG TUG"

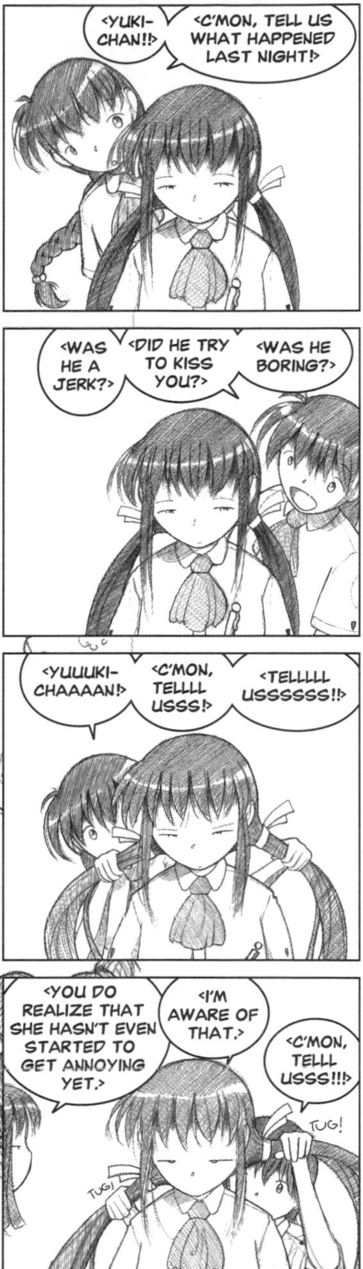
<YUKI-CHAN!!>
<C'MON, TELL US WHAT HAPPENED LAST NIGHT!>
<WAS HE A JERK?>
<DID HE TRY TO KISS YOU?>
<WAS HE BORING?>
<YUUUKI-CHAAAAN!>
<C'MON, TELLLL USSS!>
<TELLLLL USSSSSS!!>
<YOU DO REALIZE THAT SHE HASN'T EVEN STARTED TO GET ANNOYING YET.>
<I'M AWARE OF THAT.>
<C'MON, TELLL USSS!!!>
TUG!
TUG!

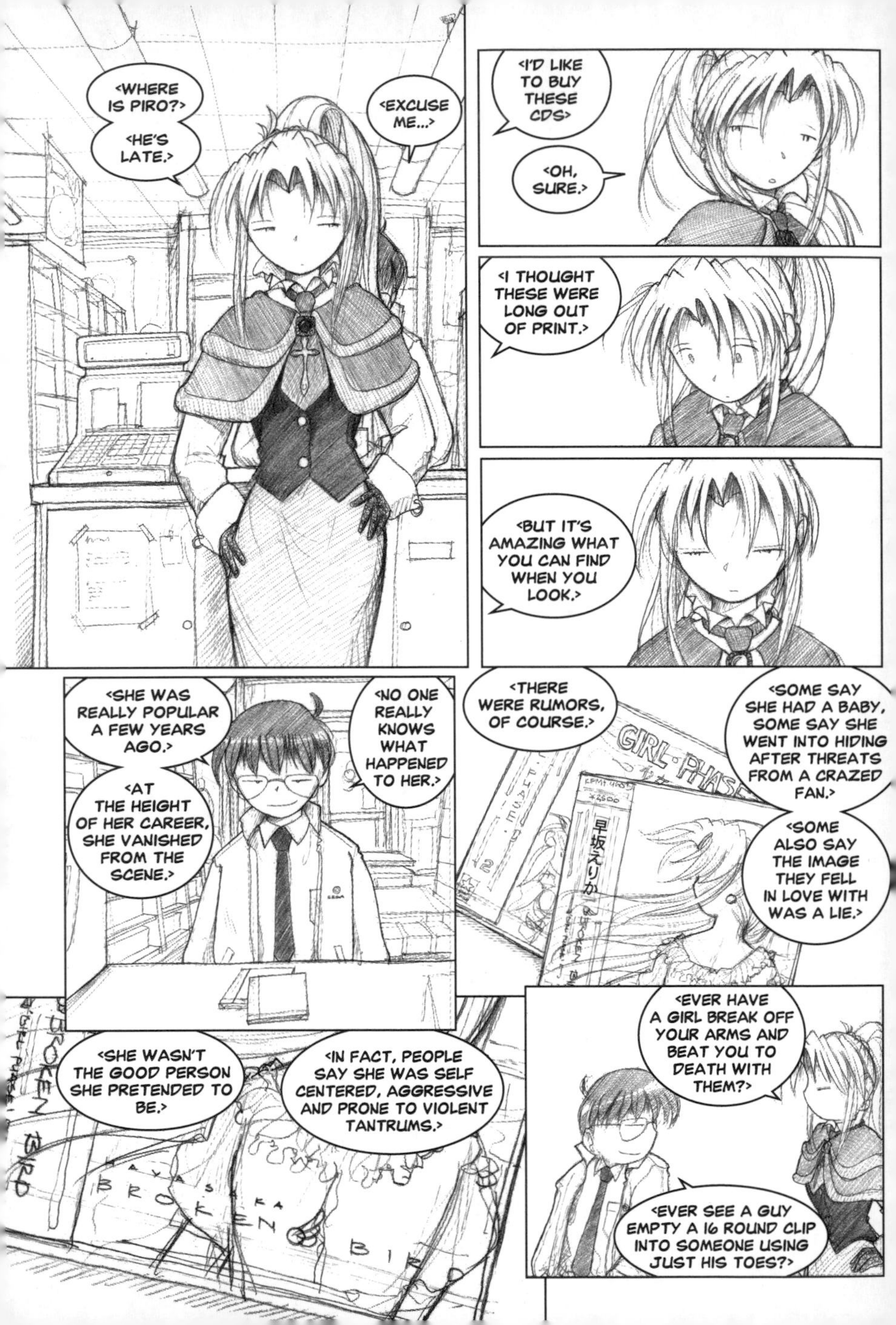
<WHERE IS PIRO?>
<HE'S LATE.>
<EXCUSE ME...>
<I'D LIKE TO BUY THESE CDS>
<OH, SURE.>
<I THOUGHT THESE WERE LONG OUT OF PRINT.>
<BUT IT'S AMAZING WHAT YOU CAN FIND WHEN YOU LOOK.>
<SHE WAS REALLY POPULAR A FEW YEARS AGO.>
<AT THE HEIGHT OF HER CAREER, SHE VANISHED FROM THE SCENE.>
<NO ONE REALLY KNOWS WHAT HAPPENED TO HER.>
<THERE WERE RUMORS, OF COURSE.>
GIRL·PHASE
早坂えりか
<SOME SAY SHE HAD A BABY, SOME SAY SHE WENT INTO HIDING AFTER THREATS FROM A CRAZED FAN.>
<SOME ALSO SAY THE IMAGE THEY FELL IN LOVE WITH WAS A LIE.>
BROKEN BIRD
<SHE WASN'T THE GOOD PERSON SHE PRETENDED TO BE.>
<IN FACT, PEOPLE SAY SHE WAS SELF CENTERED, AGGRESSIVE AND PRONE TO VIOLENT TANTRUMS.>
HAYASAKA
BROKEN BIRD
<EVER HAVE A GIRL BREAK OFF YOUR ARMS AND BEAT YOU TO DEATH WITH THEM?>
<EVER SEE A GUY EMPTY A 16 ROUND CLIP INTO SOMEONE USING JUST HIS TOES?>

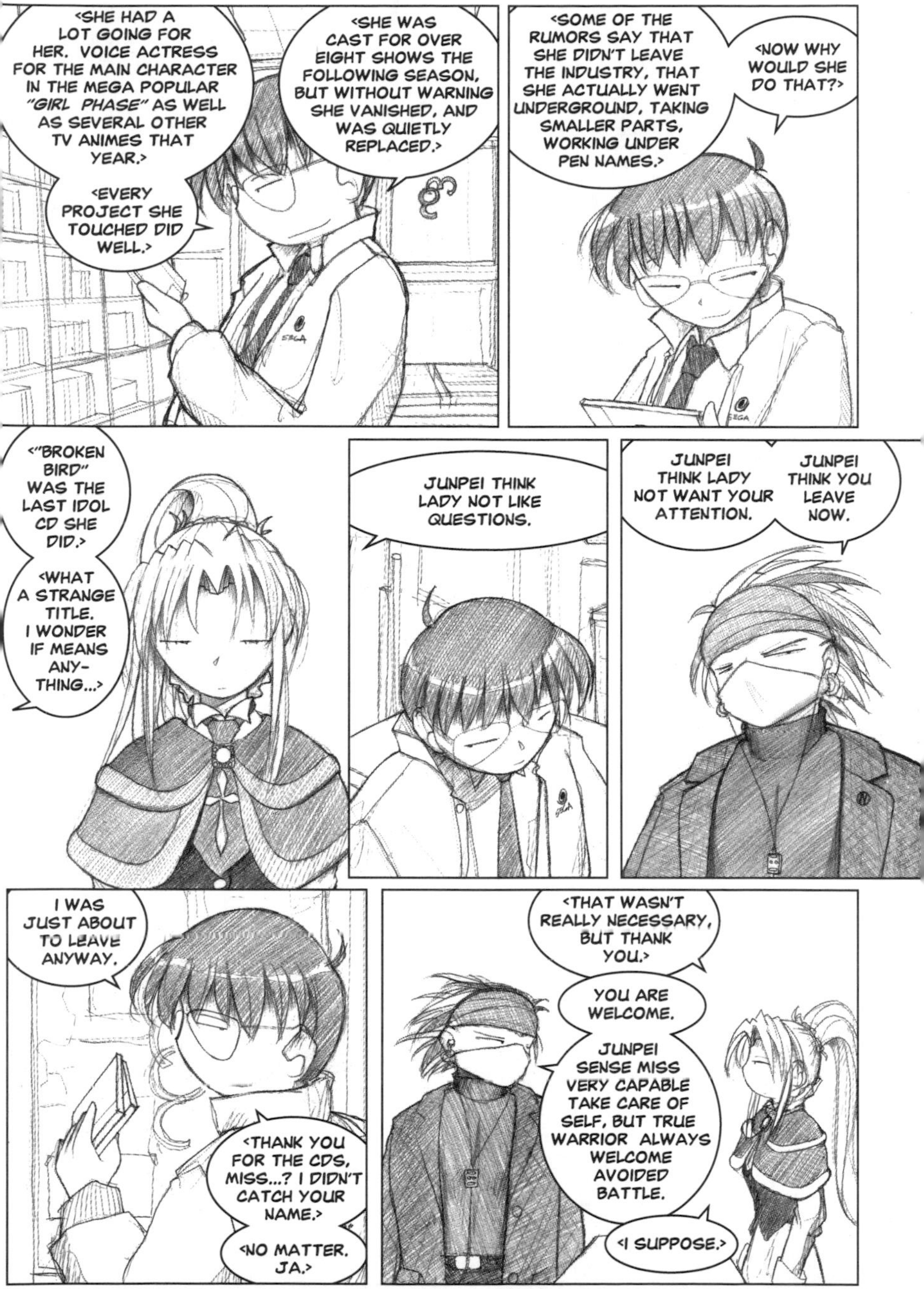
<SHE HAD A LOT GOING FOR HER. VOICE ACTRESS FOR THE MAIN CHARACTER IN THE MEGA POPULAR *"GIRL PHASE"* AS WELL AS SEVERAL OTHER TV ANIMES THAT YEAR.>
<EVERY PROJECT SHE TOUCHED DID WELL.>
<SHE WAS CAST FOR OVER EIGHT SHOWS THE FOLLOWING SEASON, BUT WITHOUT WARNING SHE VANISHED, AND WAS QUIETLY REPLACED.>
<SOME OF THE RUMORS SAY THAT SHE DIDN'T LEAVE THE INDUSTRY, THAT SHE ACTUALLY WENT UNDERGROUND, TAKING SMALLER PARTS, WORKING UNDER PEN NAMES.>
<NOW WHY WOULD SHE DO THAT?>
<"BROKEN BIRD" WAS THE LAST IDOL CD SHE DID.>
<WHAT A STRANGE TITLE. I WONDER IF MEANS ANY-THING...>
JUNPEI THINK LADY NOT LIKE QUESTIONS.
JUNPEI THINK LADY NOT WANT YOUR ATTENTION.
JUNPEI THINK YOU LEAVE NOW.
I WAS JUST ABOUT TO LEAVE ANYWAY.
<THANK YOU FOR THE CDS, MISS...? I DIDN'T CATCH YOUR NAME.>
<NO MATTER. JA.>
<THAT WASN'T REALLY NECESSARY, BUT THANK YOU.>
YOU ARE WELCOME.
JUNPEI SENSE MISS VERY CAPABLE TAKE CARE OF SELF, BUT TRUE WARRIOR ALWAYS WELCOME AVOIDED BATTLE.
<I SUPPOSE.>

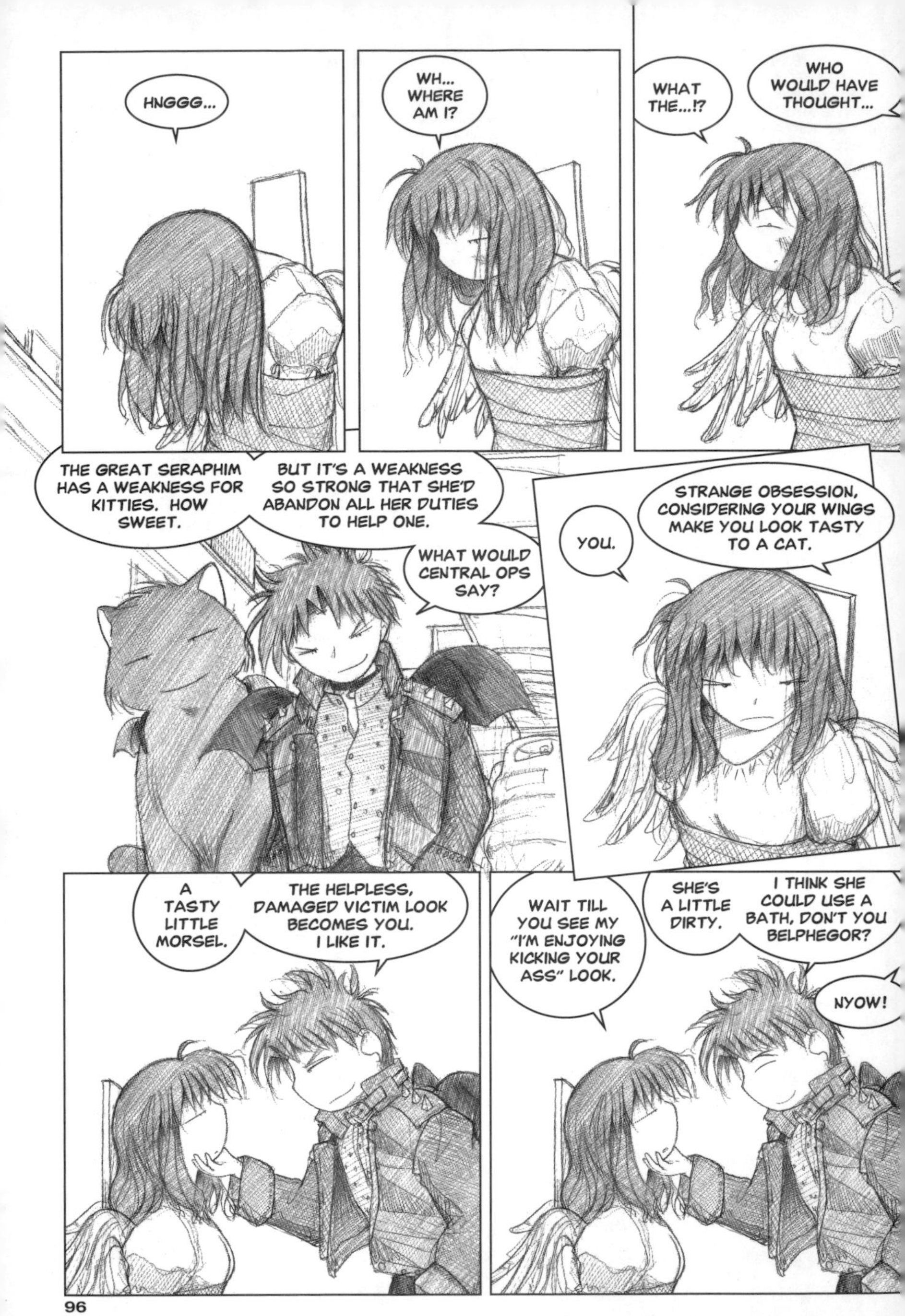
HNGGG...
WH... WHERE AM I?
WHAT THE...!?
WHO WOULD HAVE THOUGHT...
THE GREAT SERAPHIM HAS A WEAKNESS FOR KITTIES. HOW SWEET.
BUT IT'S A WEAKNESS SO STRONG THAT SHE'D ABANDON ALL HER DUTIES TO HELP ONE.
WHAT WOULD CENTRAL OPS SAY?
YOU.
STRANGE OBSESSION, CONSIDERING YOUR WINGS MAKE YOU LOOK TASTY TO A CAT.
A TASTY LITTLE MORSEL.
THE HELPLESS, DAMAGED VICTIM LOOK BECOMES YOU. I LIKE IT.
WAIT TILL YOU SEE MY "I'M ENJOYING KICKING YOUR ASS" LOOK.
SHE'S A LITTLE DIRTY.
I THINK SHE COULD USE A BATH, DON'T YOU BELPHEGOR?
NYOW!

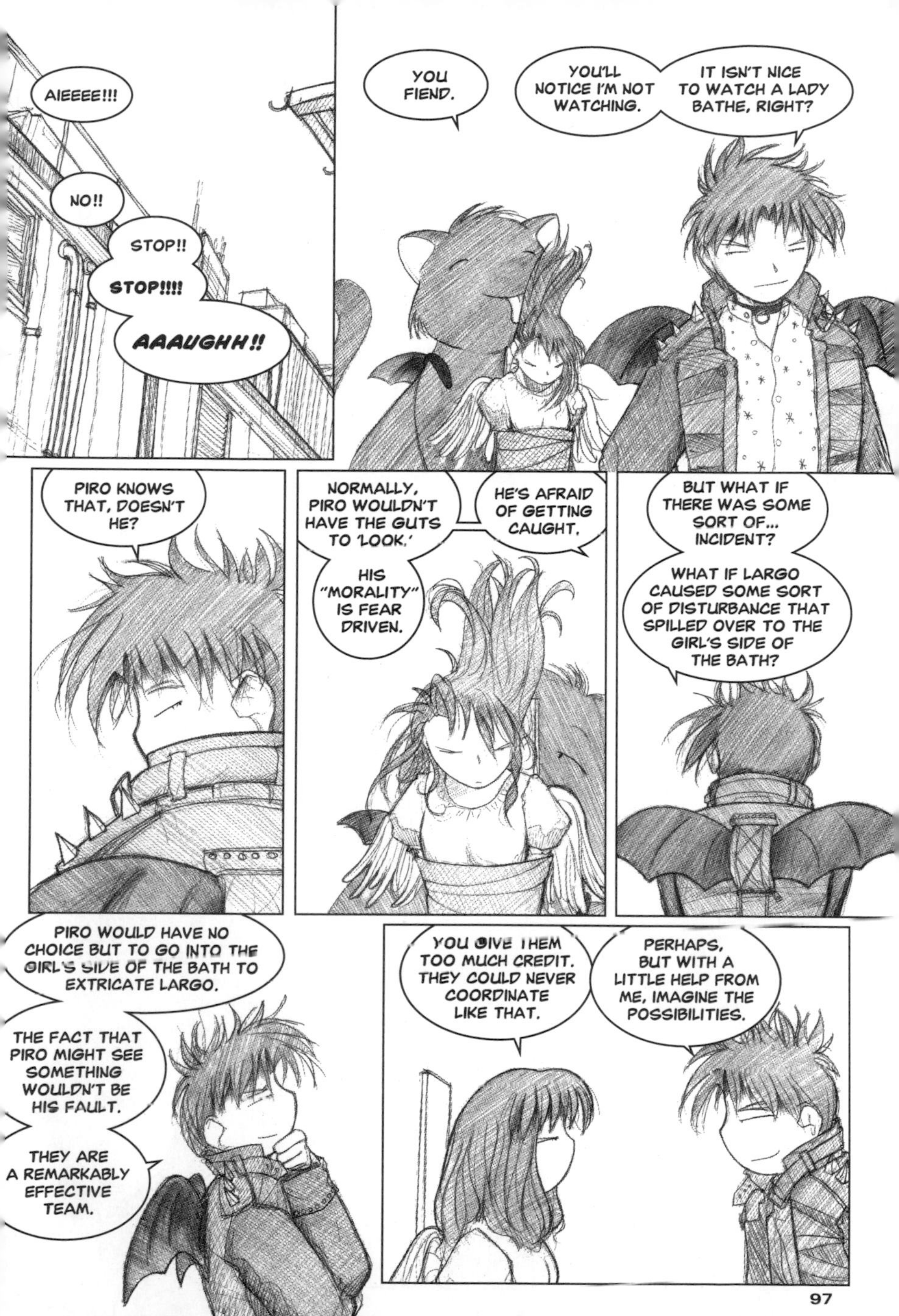
AIEEEE!!!
NO!!
STOP!!
STOP!!!!
AAAUGHH!!
YOU FIEND.
YOU'LL NOTICE I'M NOT WATCHING.
IT ISN'T NICE TO WATCH A LADY BATHE, RIGHT?
PIRO KNOWS THAT, DOESN'T HE?
NORMALLY, PIRO WOULDN'T HAVE THE GUTS TO 'LOOK.'
HE'S AFRAID OF GETTING CAUGHT.
HIS "MORALITY" IS FEAR DRIVEN.
BUT WHAT IF THERE WAS SOME SORT OF... INCIDENT?
WHAT IF LARGO CAUSED SOME SORT OF DISTURBANCE THAT SPILLED OVER TO THE GIRL'S SIDE OF THE BATH?
PIRO WOULD HAVE NO CHOICE BUT TO GO INTO THE GIRL'S SIDE OF THE BATH TO EXTRICATE LARGO.
THE FACT THAT PIRO MIGHT SEE SOMETHING WOULDN'T BE HIS FAULT.
THEY ARE A REMARKABLY EFFECTIVE TEAM.
YOU GIVE THEM TOO MUCH CREDIT. THEY COULD NEVER COORDINATE LIKE THAT.
PERHAPS, BUT WITH A LITTLE HELP FROM ME, IMAGINE THE POSSIBILITIES.

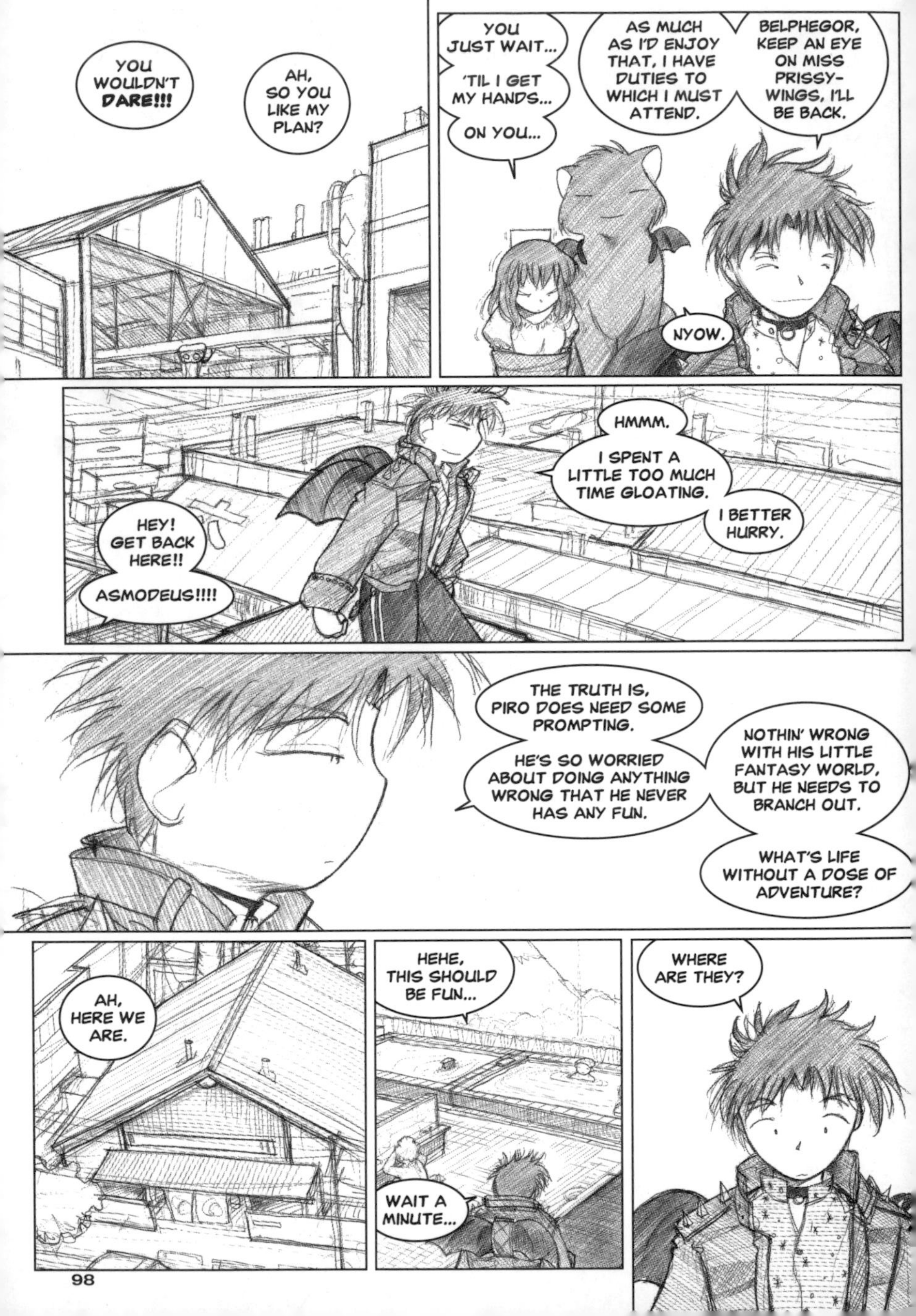

YOU WOULDN'T **DARE!!!**
AH, SO YOU LIKE MY PLAN?
YOU JUST WAIT...
'TIL I GET MY HANDS...
ON YOU...
AS MUCH AS I'D ENJOY THAT, I HAVE DUTIES TO WHICH I MUST ATTEND.
BELPHEGOR, KEEP AN EYE ON MISS PRISSY-WINGS, I'LL BE BACK.
NYOW.
HEY! GET BACK HERE!!
ASMODEUS!!!!
HMMM.
I SPENT A LITTLE TOO MUCH TIME GLOATING.
I BETTER HURRY.
THE TRUTH IS, PIRO DOES NEED SOME PROMPTING.
HE'S SO WORRIED ABOUT DOING ANYTHING WRONG THAT HE NEVER HAS ANY FUN.
NOTHIN' WRONG WITH HIS LITTLE FANTASY WORLD, BUT HE NEEDS TO BRANCH OUT.
WHAT'S LIFE WITHOUT A DOSE OF ADVENTURE?
AH, HERE WE ARE.
HEHE, THIS SHOULD BE FUN...
WAIT A MINUTE...
WHERE ARE THEY?

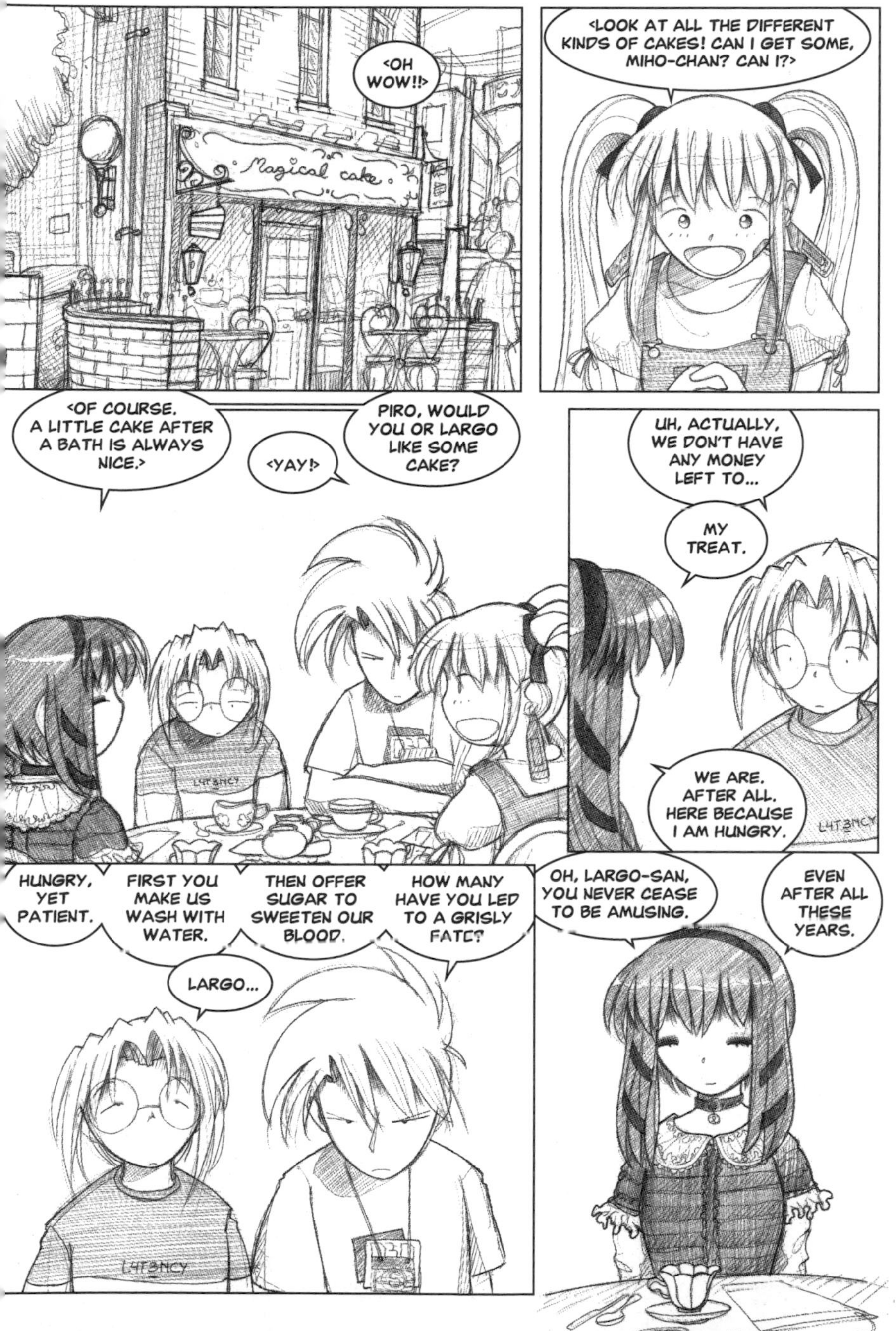
Magical cake
<OH WOW!!>
<LOOK AT ALL THE DIFFERENT KINDS OF CAKES! CAN I GET SOME, MIHO-CHAN? CAN I?>
<OF COURSE. A LITTLE CAKE AFTER A BATH IS ALWAYS NICE.>
<YAY!>
PIRO, WOULD YOU OR LARGO LIKE SOME CAKE?
L4T3NCY
UH, ACTUALLY, WE DON'T HAVE ANY MONEY LEFT TO...
MY TREAT.
WE ARE. AFTER ALL. HERE BECAUSE I AM HUNGRY.
L4T3NCY
HUNGRY, YET PATIENT.
FIRST YOU MAKE US WASH WITH WATER.
THEN OFFER SUGAR TO SWEETEN OUR BLOOD.
HOW MANY HAVE YOU LED TO A GRISLY FATE?
LARGO...
L4T3NCY
OH, LARGO-SAN, YOU NEVER CEASE TO BE AMUSING.
EVEN AFTER ALL THESE YEARS.

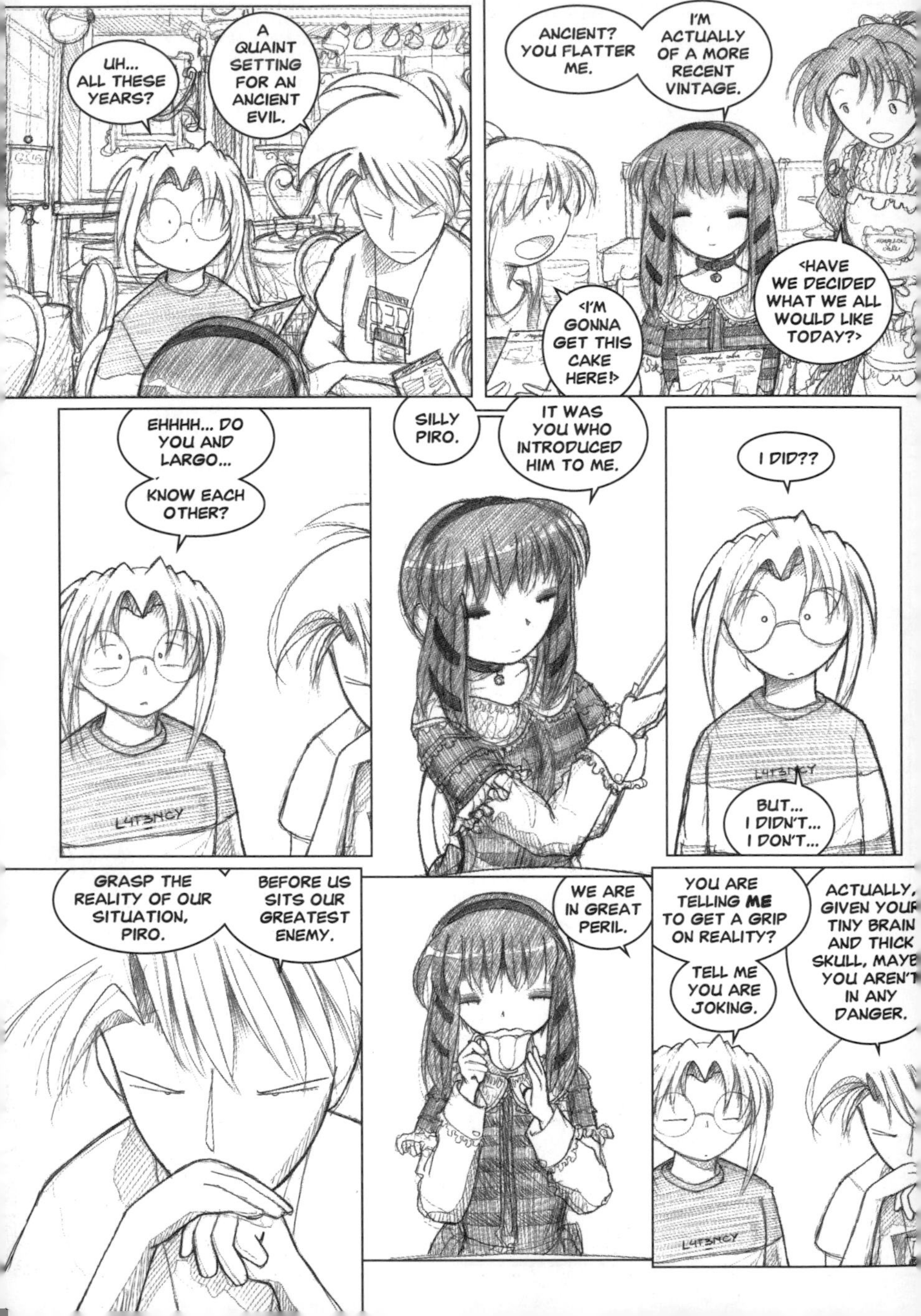
UH... ALL THESE YEARS?
A QUAINT SETTING FOR AN ANCIENT EVIL.
ANCIENT? YOU FLATTER ME.
I'M ACTUALLY OF A MORE RECENT VINTAGE.
<I'M GONNA GET THIS CAKE HERE!>
<HAVE WE DECIDED WHAT WE ALL WOULD LIKE TODAY?>
EHHHH... DO YOU AND LARGO...
KNOW EACH OTHER?
L4T3NCY
SILLY PIRO.
IT WAS YOU WHO INTRODUCED HIM TO ME.
I DID??
L4T3NCY
BUT... I DIDN'T... I DON'T...
GRASP THE REALITY OF OUR SITUATION, PIRO.
BEFORE US SITS OUR GREATEST ENEMY.
WE ARE IN GREAT PERIL.
YOU ARE TELLING **ME** TO GET A GRIP ON REALITY?
TELL ME YOU ARE JOKING.
ACTUALLY, GIVEN YOUR TINY BRAIN AND THICK SKULL, MAYBE YOU AREN'T IN ANY DANGER.
L4T3NCY

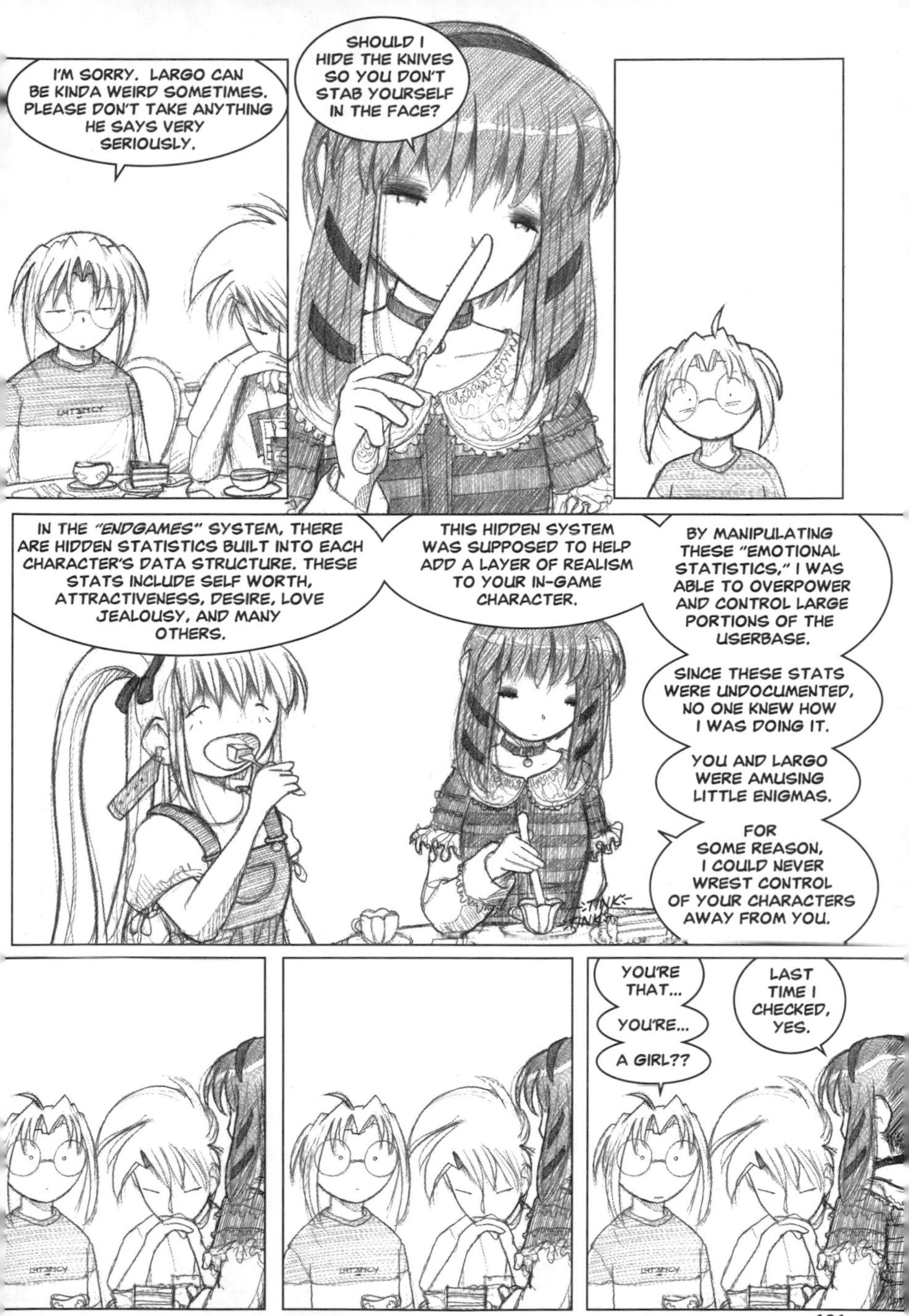
I'M SORRY. LARGO CAN BE KINDA WEIRD SOMETIMES. PLEASE DON'T TAKE ANYTHING HE SAYS VERY SERIOUSLY.
SHOULD I HIDE THE KNIVES SO YOU DON'T STAB YOURSELF IN THE FACE?
IN THE "ENDGAMES" SYSTEM, THERE ARE HIDDEN STATISTICS BUILT INTO EACH CHARACTER'S DATA STRUCTURE. THESE STATS INCLUDE SELF WORTH, ATTRACTIVENESS, DESIRE, LOVE JEALOUSY, AND MANY OTHERS.
THIS HIDDEN SYSTEM WAS SUPPOSED TO HELP ADD A LAYER OF REALISM TO YOUR IN-GAME CHARACTER.
BY MANIPULATING THESE "EMOTIONAL STATISTICS," I WAS ABLE TO OVERPOWER AND CONTROL LARGE PORTIONS OF THE USERBASE.
SINCE THESE STATS WERE UNDOCUMENTED, NO ONE KNEW HOW I WAS DOING IT.
YOU AND LARGO WERE AMUSING LITTLE ENIGMAS.
FOR SOME REASON, I COULD NEVER WREST CONTROL OF YOUR CHARACTERS AWAY FROM YOU.
TINK
TINK
YOU'RE THAT...
YOU'RE...
A GIRL??
LAST TIME I CHECKED, YES.

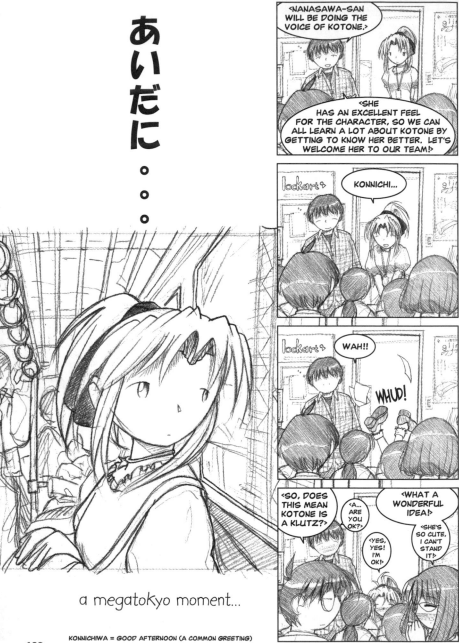

あいだに。。。

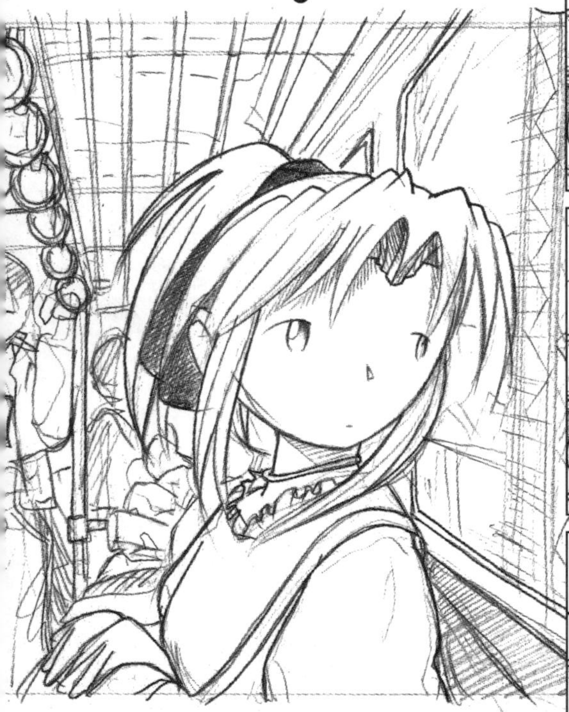

a megatokyo moment...

"KLUTZY IS CUTE"

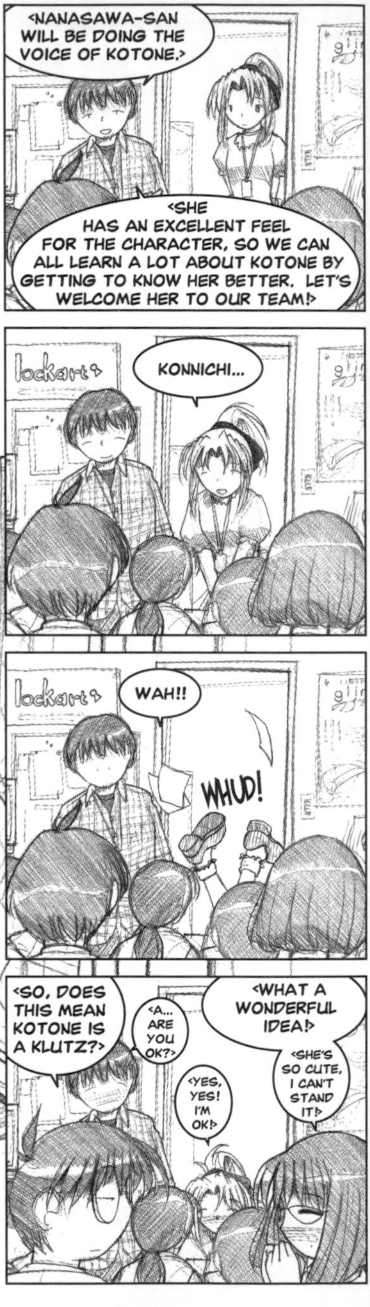

<NANASAWA-SAN WILL BE DOING THE VOICE OF KOTONE.>
<SHE HAS AN EXCELLENT FEEL FOR THE CHARACTER, SO WE CAN ALL LEARN A LOT ABOUT KOTONE BY GETTING TO KNOW HER BETTER. LET'S WELCOME HER TO OUR TEAM!>
lockart
KONNICHI...
lockart
WAH!!
WHUD!
<SO, DOES THIS MEAN KOTONE IS A KLUTZ?>
<A... ARE YOU OK?>
<YES, YES! I'M OK!>
<WHAT A WONDERFUL IDEA!>
<SHE'S SO CUTE, I CAN'T STAND IT!>

KONNICHIWA = GOOD AFTERNOON (A COMMON GREETING)

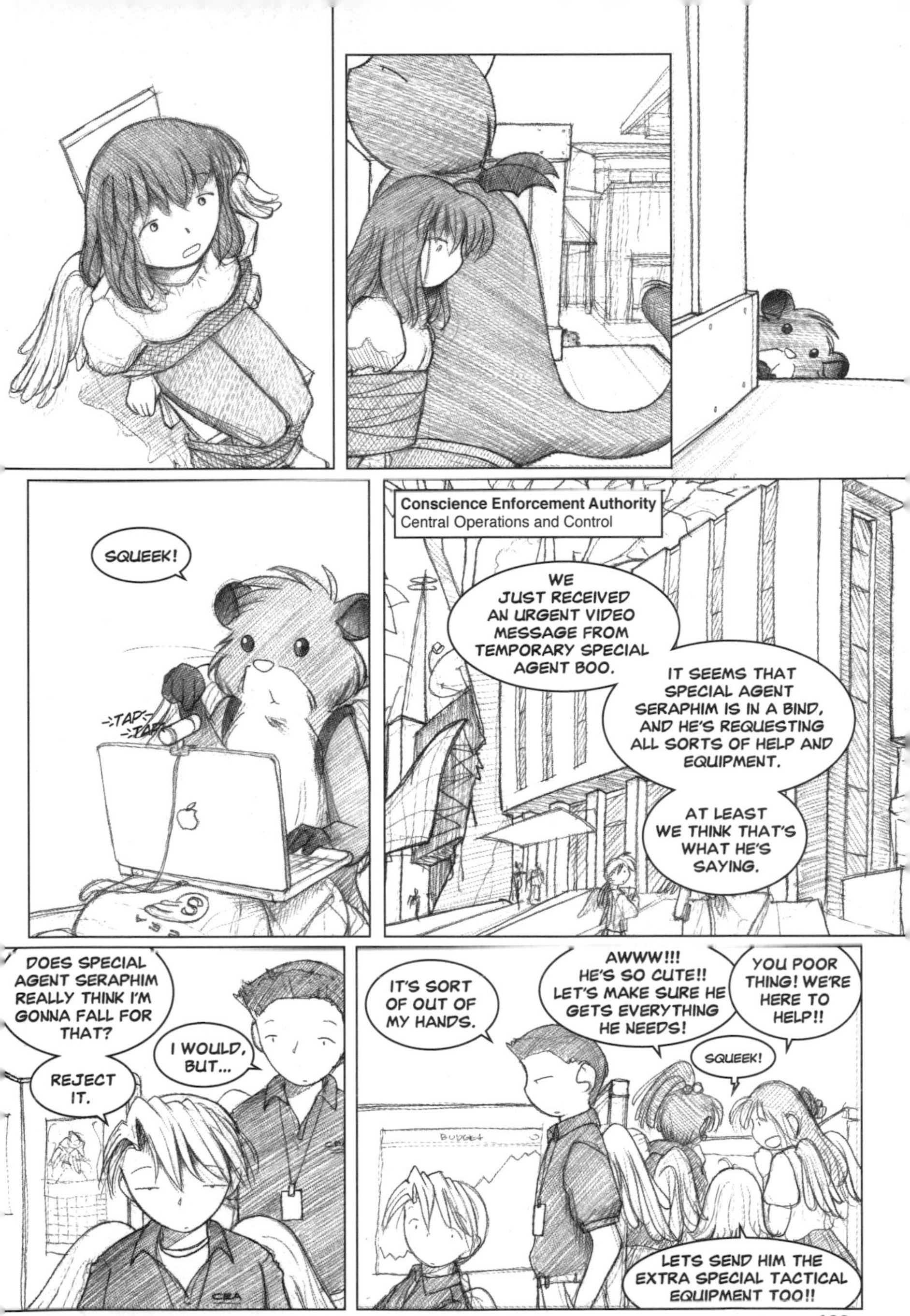
SQUEEK!
TAP TAP
Conscience Enforcement Authority
Central Operations and Control
WE JUST RECEIVED AN URGENT VIDEO MESSAGE FROM TEMPORARY SPECIAL AGENT BOO.
IT SEEMS THAT SPECIAL AGENT SERAPHIM IS IN A BIND, AND HE'S REQUESTING ALL SORTS OF HELP AND EQUIPMENT.
AT LEAST WE THINK THAT'S WHAT HE'S SAYING.
DOES SPECIAL AGENT SERAPHIM REALLY THINK I'M GONNA FALL FOR THAT?
REJECT IT.
I WOULD, BUT...
IT'S SORT OF OUT OF MY HANDS.
AWWW!!! HE'S SO CUTE!! LET'S MAKE SURE HE GETS EVERYTHING HE NEEDS!
YOU POOR THING! WE'RE HERE TO HELP!!
SQUEEK!
LETS SEND HIM THE EXTRA SPECIAL TACTICAL EQUIPMENT TOO!!

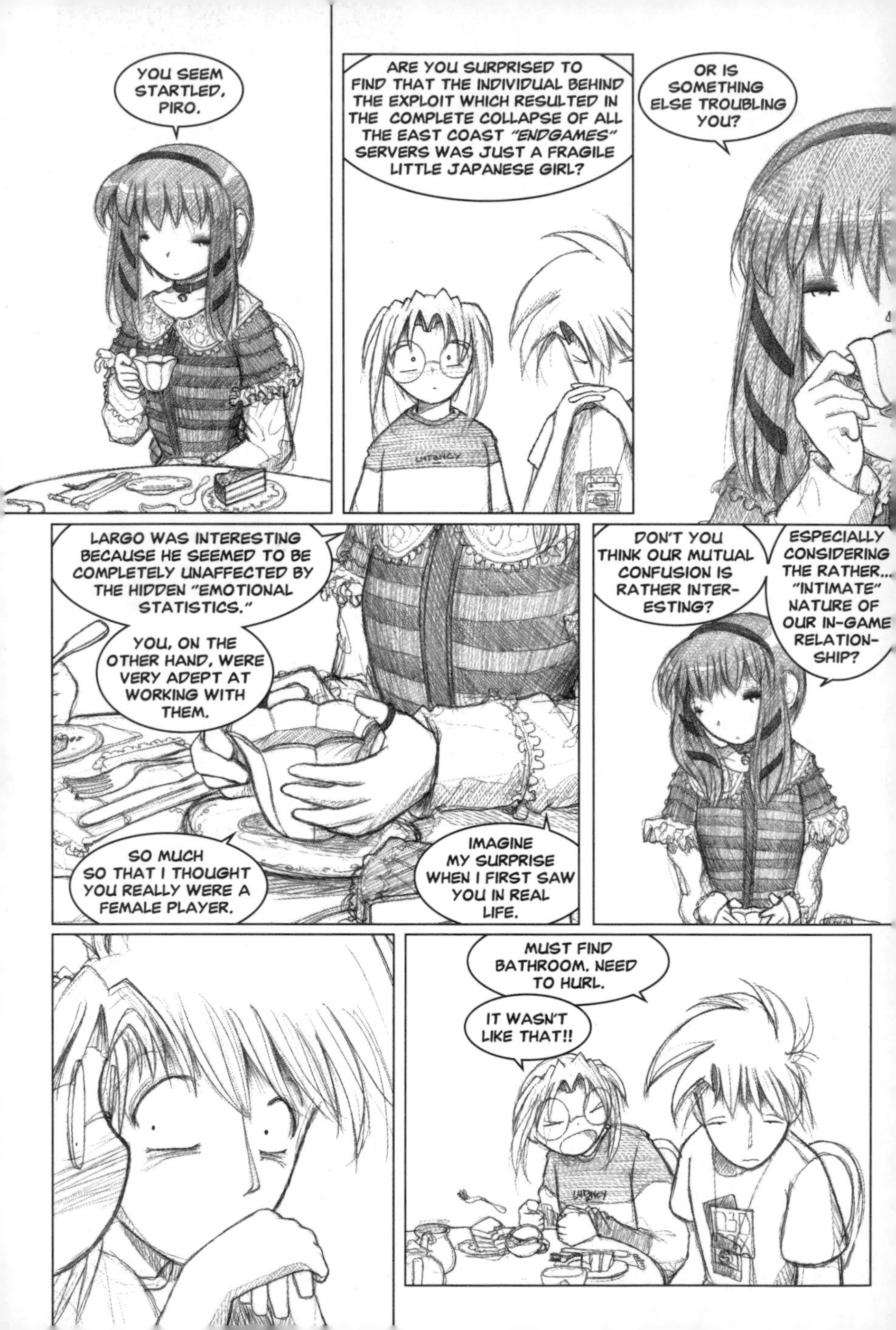
YOU SEEM STARTLED, PIRO.
ARE YOU SURPRISED TO FIND THAT THE INDIVIDUAL BEHIND THE EXPLOIT WHICH RESULTED IN THE COMPLETE COLLAPSE OF ALL THE EAST COAST "ENDGAMES" SERVERS WAS JUST A FRAGILE LITTLE JAPANESE GIRL?
OR IS SOMETHING ELSE TROUBLING YOU?
LARGO WAS INTERESTING BECAUSE HE SEEMED TO BE COMPLETELY UNAFFECTED BY THE HIDDEN "EMOTIONAL STATISTICS."
YOU, ON THE OTHER HAND, WERE VERY ADEPT AT WORKING WITH THEM.
SO MUCH SO THAT I THOUGHT YOU REALLY WERE A FEMALE PLAYER.
IMAGINE MY SURPRISE WHEN I FIRST SAW YOU IN REAL LIFE.
DON'T YOU THINK OUR MUTUAL CONFUSION IS RATHER INTER-ESTING?
ESPECIALLY CONSIDERING THE RATHER... "INTIMATE" NATURE OF OUR IN-GAME RELATION-SHIP?
MUST FIND BATHROOM. NEED TO HURL.
IT WASN'T LIKE THAT!!

あいだに。。。

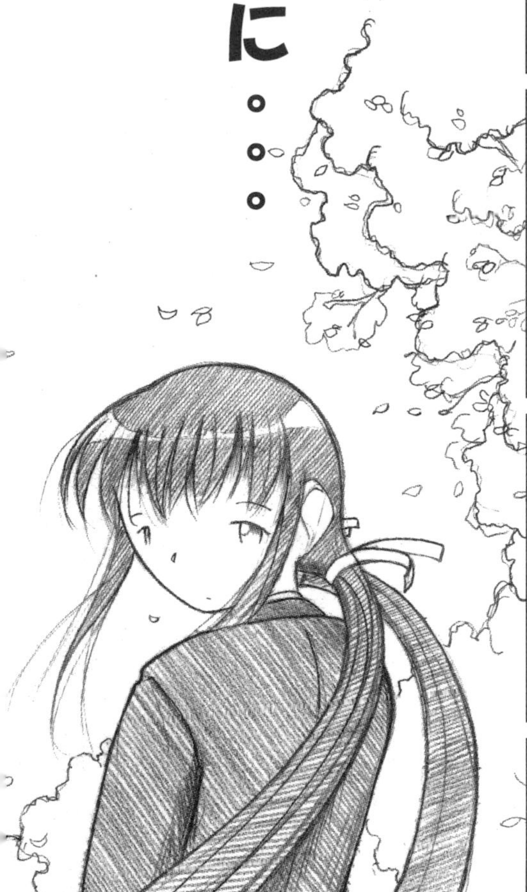

a megatokyo moment...

"SUFFERING IN SILENCE"

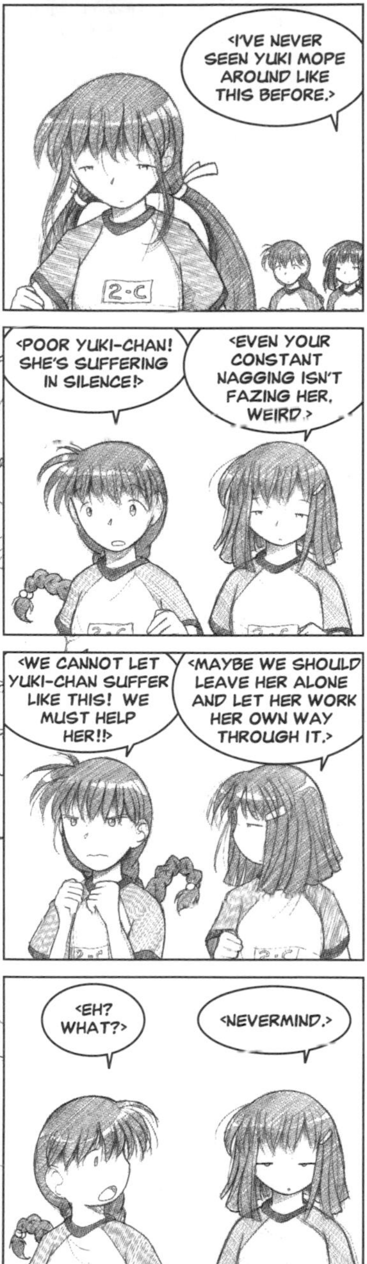

<I'VE NEVER SEEN YUKI MOPE AROUND LIKE THIS BEFORE.>
2-C
<POOR YUKI-CHAN! SHE'S SUFFERING IN SILENCE!>
<EVEN YOUR CONSTANT NAGGING ISN'T FAZING HER. WEIRD.>
<WE CANNOT LET YUKI-CHAN SUFFER LIKE THIS! WE MUST HELP HER!!>
<MAYBE WE SHOULD LEAVE HER ALONE AND LET HER WORK HER OWN WAY THROUGH IT.>
<EH? WHAT?>
<NEVERMIND.>

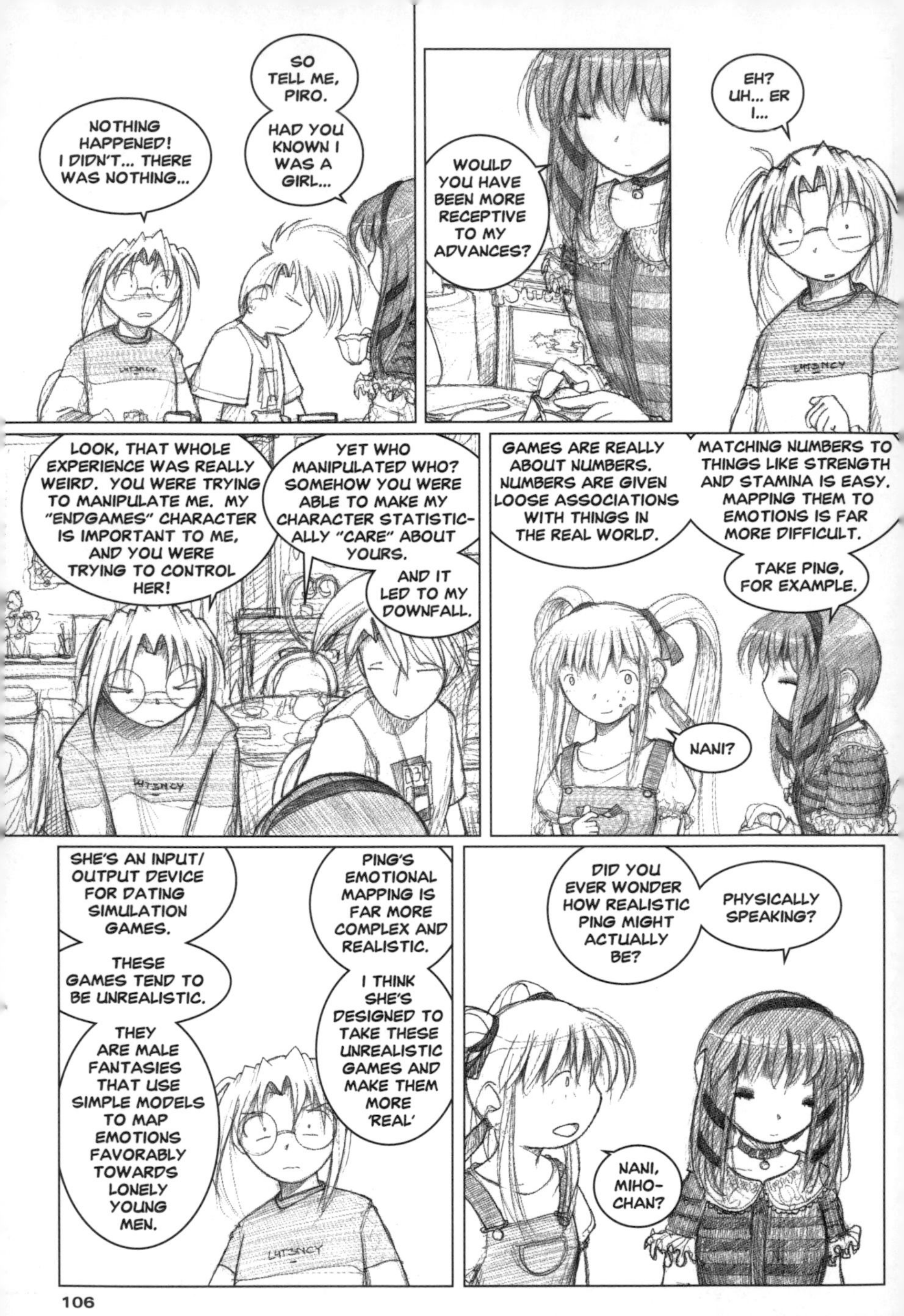
NOTHING HAPPENED! I DIDN'T... THERE WAS NOTHING...
SO TELL ME, PIRO.
HAD YOU KNOWN I WAS A GIRL...
WOULD YOU HAVE BEEN MORE RECEPTIVE TO MY ADVANCES?
EH? UH... ER I...
LOOK, THAT WHOLE EXPERIENCE WAS REALLY WEIRD. YOU WERE TRYING TO MANIPULATE ME. MY "ENDGAMES" CHARACTER IS IMPORTANT TO ME, AND YOU WERE TRYING TO CONTROL HER!
YET WHO MANIPULATED WHO? SOMEHOW YOU WERE ABLE TO MAKE MY CHARACTER STATISTIC-ALLY "CARE" ABOUT YOURS.
AND IT LED TO MY DOWNFALL.
GAMES ARE REALLY ABOUT NUMBERS. NUMBERS ARE GIVEN LOOSE ASSOCIATIONS WITH THINGS IN THE REAL WORLD.
MATCHING NUMBERS TO THINGS LIKE STRENGTH AND STAMINA IS EASY. MAPPING THEM TO EMOTIONS IS FAR MORE DIFFICULT.
TAKE PING, FOR EXAMPLE.
NANI?
SHE'S AN INPUT/ OUTPUT DEVICE FOR DATING SIMULATION GAMES.
THESE GAMES TEND TO BE UNREALISTIC.
THEY ARE MALE FANTASIES THAT USE SIMPLE MODELS TO MAP EMOTIONS FAVORABLY TOWARDS LONELY YOUNG MEN.
PING'S EMOTIONAL MAPPING IS FAR MORE COMPLEX AND REALISTIC.
I THINK SHE'S DESIGNED TO TAKE THESE UNREALISTIC GAMES AND MAKE THEM MORE 'REAL'
DID YOU EVER WONDER HOW REALISTIC PING MIGHT ACTUALLY BE?
PHYSICALLY SPEAKING?
NANI, MIHO-CHAN?

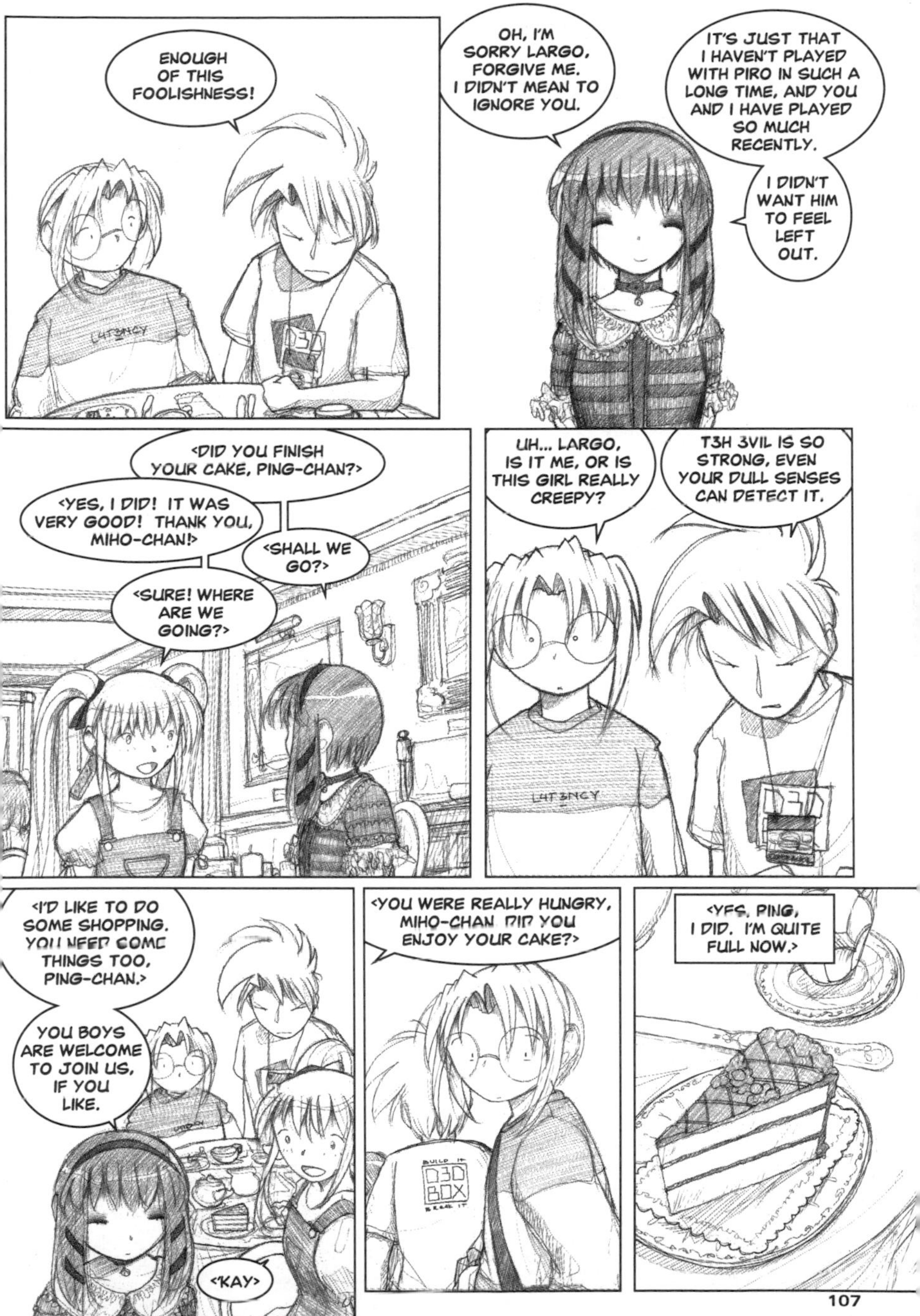
ENOUGH OF THIS FOOLISHNESS!
OH, I'M SORRY LARGO, FORGIVE ME. I DIDN'T MEAN TO IGNORE YOU.
IT'S JUST THAT I HAVEN'T PLAYED WITH PIRO IN SUCH A LONG TIME, AND YOU AND I HAVE PLAYED SO MUCH RECENTLY.
I DIDN'T WANT HIM TO FEEL LEFT OUT.
L4T3NCY
D3D
<DID YOU FINISH YOUR CAKE, PING-CHAN?>
<YES, I DID! IT WAS VERY GOOD! THANK YOU, MIHO-CHAN!>
<SHALL WE GO?>
<SURE! WHERE ARE WE GOING?>
UH... LARGO, IS IT ME, OR IS THIS GIRL REALLY CREEPY?
T3H 3VIL IS SO STRONG, EVEN YOUR DULL SENSES CAN DETECT IT.
L4T3NCY
D3D
<I'D LIKE TO DO SOME SHOPPING. YOU NEED SOME THINGS TOO, PING-CHAN.>
YOU BOYS ARE WELCOME TO JOIN US, IF YOU LIKE.
<KAY>
<YOU WERE REALLY HUNGRY, MIHO-CHAN. DID YOU ENJOY YOUR CAKE?>
BUILD IT
D3D BOX
BREAK IT
<YES, PING, I DID. I'M QUITE FULL NOW.>

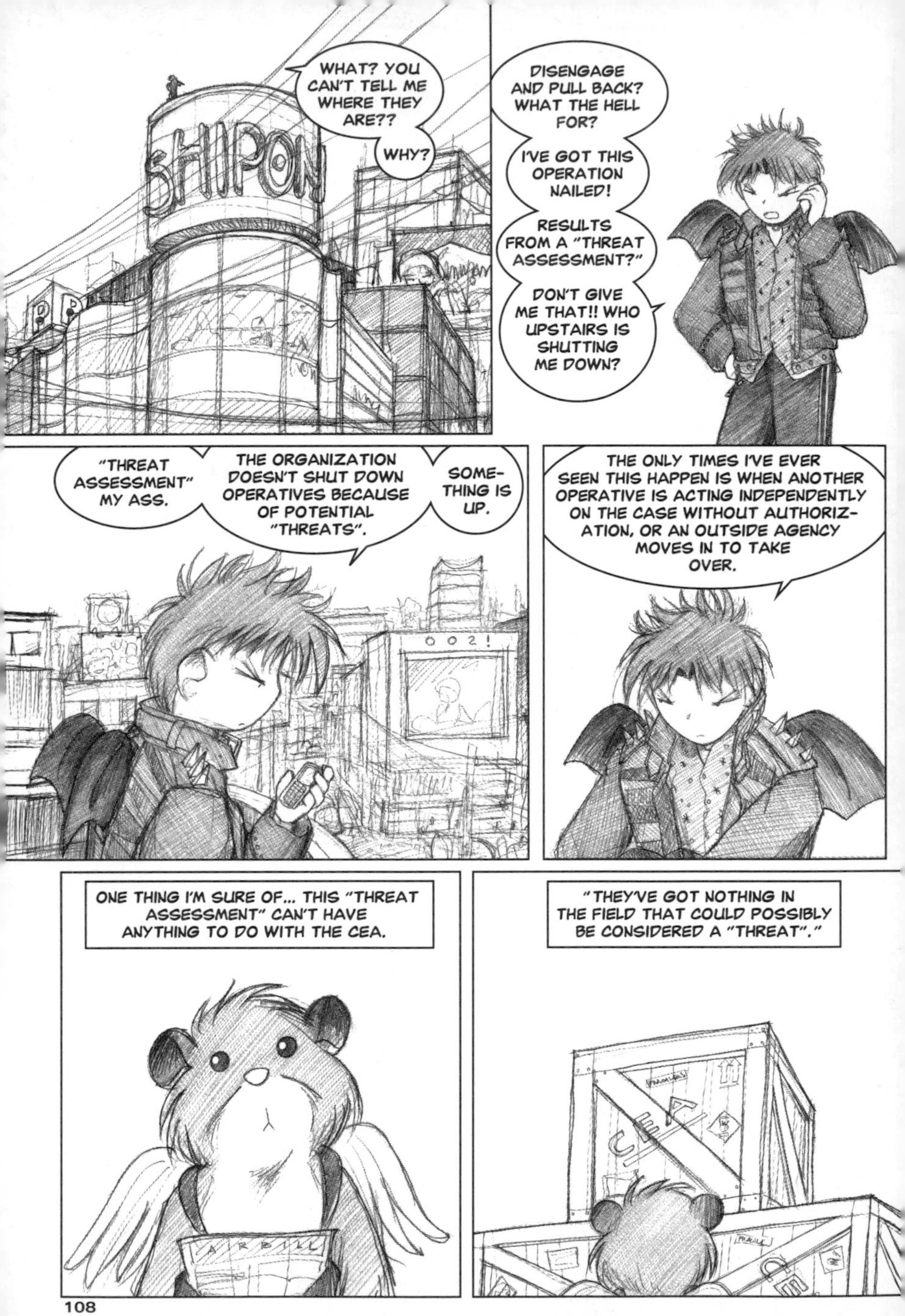
WHAT? YOU CAN'T TELL ME WHERE THEY ARE??
WHY?
SHIPON
DISENGAGE AND PULL BACK? WHAT THE HELL FOR?
I'VE GOT THIS OPERATION NAILED!
RESULTS FROM A "THREAT ASSESSMENT?"
DON'T GIVE ME THAT!! WHO UPSTAIRS IS SHUTTING ME DOWN?
"THREAT ASSESSMENT" MY ASS.
THE ORGANIZATION DOESN'T SHUT DOWN OPERATIVES BECAUSE OF POTENTIAL "THREATS".
SOME-THING IS UP.
002!
THE ONLY TIMES I'VE EVER SEEN THIS HAPPEN IS WHEN ANOTHER OPERATIVE IS ACTING INDEPENDENTLY ON THE CASE WITHOUT AUTHORIZ-ATION, OR AN OUTSIDE AGENCY MOVES IN TO TAKE OVER.
ONE THING I'M SURE OF... THIS "THREAT ASSESSMENT" CAN'T HAVE ANYTHING TO DO WITH THE CEA.
"THEY'VE GOT NOTHING IN THE FIELD THAT COULD POSSIBLY BE CONSIDERED A "THREAT"."

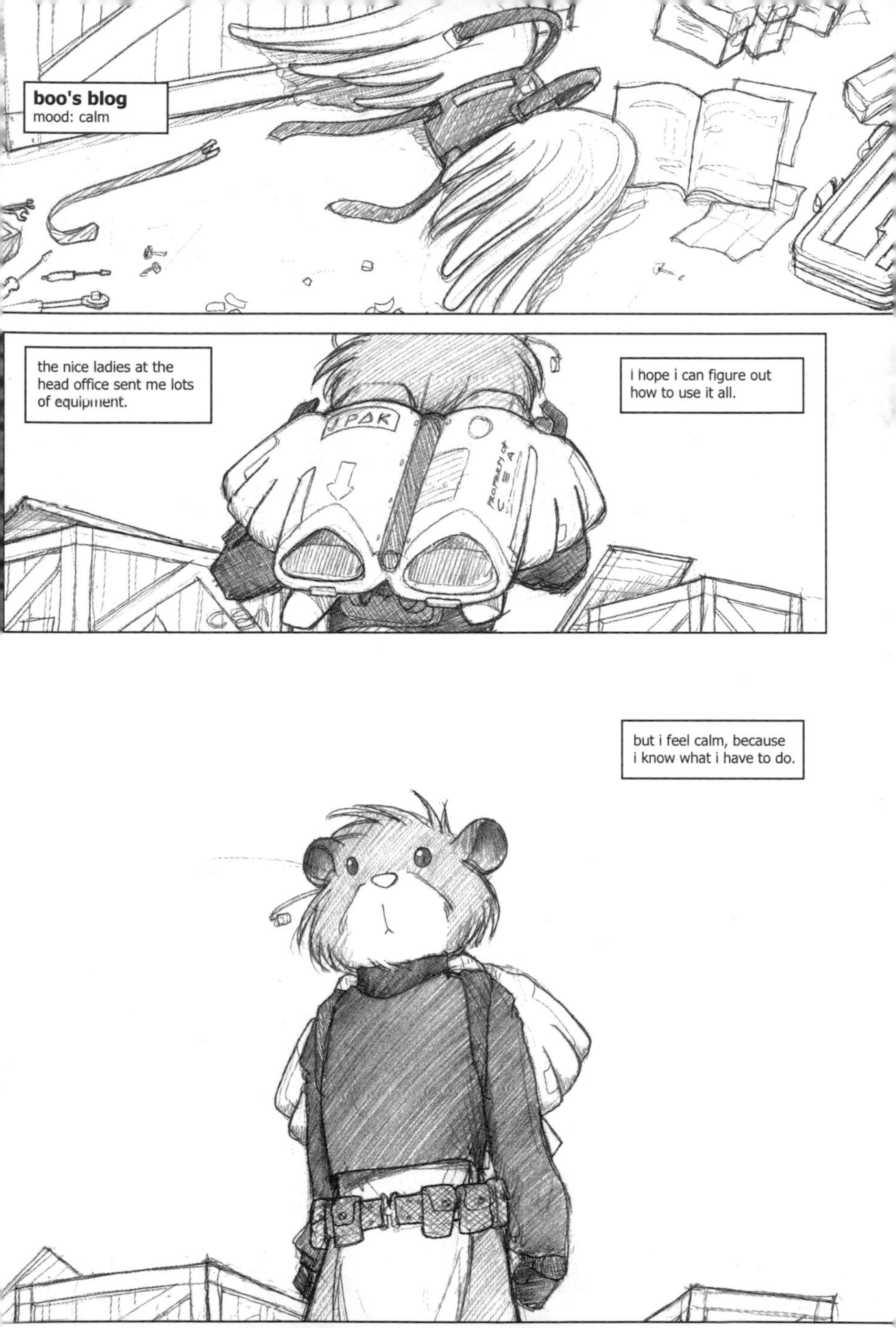
boo's blog
mood: calm
the nice ladies at the head office sent me lots of equipment.
JPAK
i hope i can figure out how to use it all.
but i feel calm, because i know what i have to do.

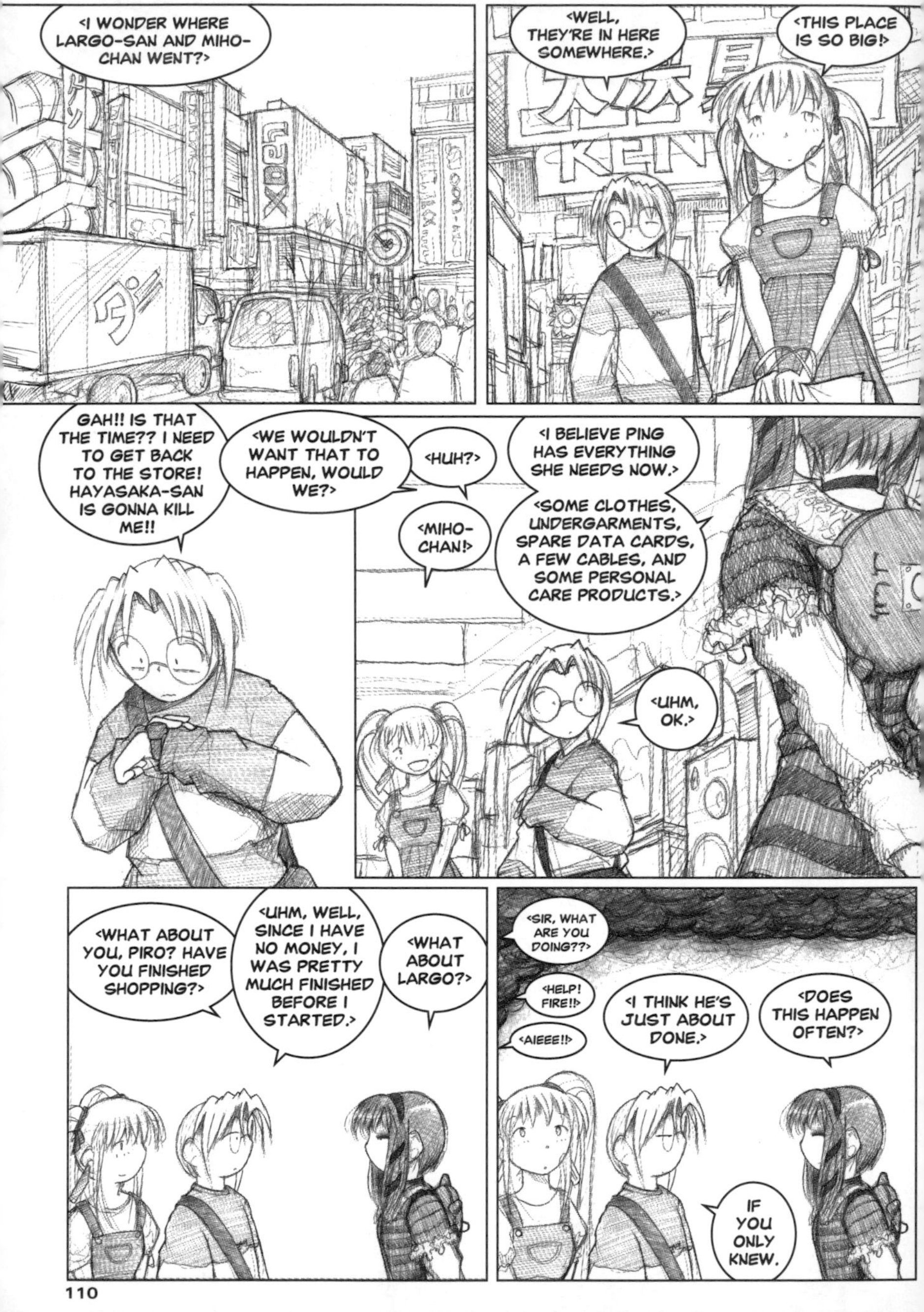
<I WONDER WHERE LARGO-SAN AND MIHO-CHAN WENT?>
<WELL, THEY'RE IN HERE SOMEWHERE.>
<THIS PLACE IS SO BIG!>
KEN
GAH!! IS THAT THE TIME?? I NEED TO GET BACK TO THE STORE! HAYASAKA-SAN IS GONNA KILL ME!!
<WE WOULDN'T WANT THAT TO HAPPEN, WOULD WE?>
<HUH?>
<MIHO-CHAN!>
<I BELIEVE PING HAS EVERYTHING SHE NEEDS NOW.>
<SOME CLOTHES, UNDERGARMENTS, SPARE DATA CARDS, A FEW CABLES, AND SOME PERSONAL CARE PRODUCTS.>
<UHM, OK.>
<WHAT ABOUT YOU, PIRO? HAVE YOU FINISHED SHOPPING?>
<UHM, WELL, SINCE I HAVE NO MONEY, I WAS PRETTY MUCH FINISHED BEFORE I STARTED.>
<WHAT ABOUT LARGO?>
<SIR, WHAT ARE YOU DOING??>
<HELP! FIRE!!>
<AIEEE!!>
<I THINK HE'S JUST ABOUT DONE.>
<DOES THIS HAPPEN OFTEN?>
IF YOU ONLY KNEW.

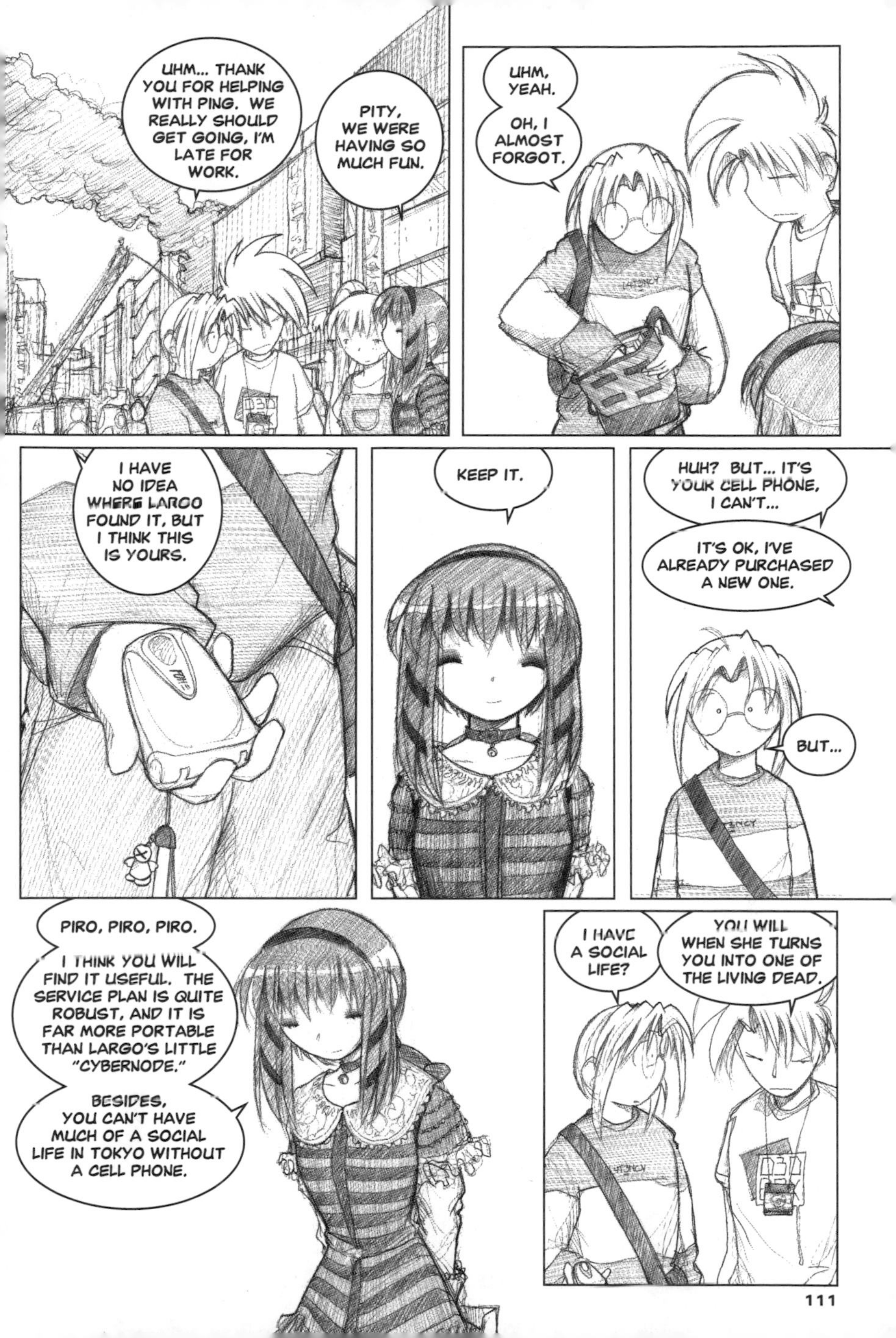

UHM... THANK YOU FOR HELPING WITH PING. WE REALLY SHOULD GET GOING, I'M LATE FOR WORK.
PITY, WE WERE HAVING SO MUCH FUN.
UHM, YEAH.
OH, I ALMOST FORGOT.
I HAVE NO IDEA WHERE LARGO FOUND IT, BUT I THINK THIS IS YOURS.
KEEP IT.
HUH? BUT... IT'S YOUR CELL PHONE, I CAN'T...
IT'S OK, I'VE ALREADY PURCHASED A NEW ONE.
BUT...
PIRO, PIRO, PIRO.
I THINK YOU WILL FIND IT USEFUL. THE SERVICE PLAN IS QUITE ROBUST, AND IT IS FAR MORE PORTABLE THAN LARGO'S LITTLE "CYBERNODE."
BESIDES, YOU CAN'T HAVE MUCH OF A SOCIAL LIFE IN TOKYO WITHOUT A CELL PHONE.
I HAVE A SOCIAL LIFE?
YOU WILL WHEN SHE TURNS YOU INTO ONE OF THE LIVING DEAD.

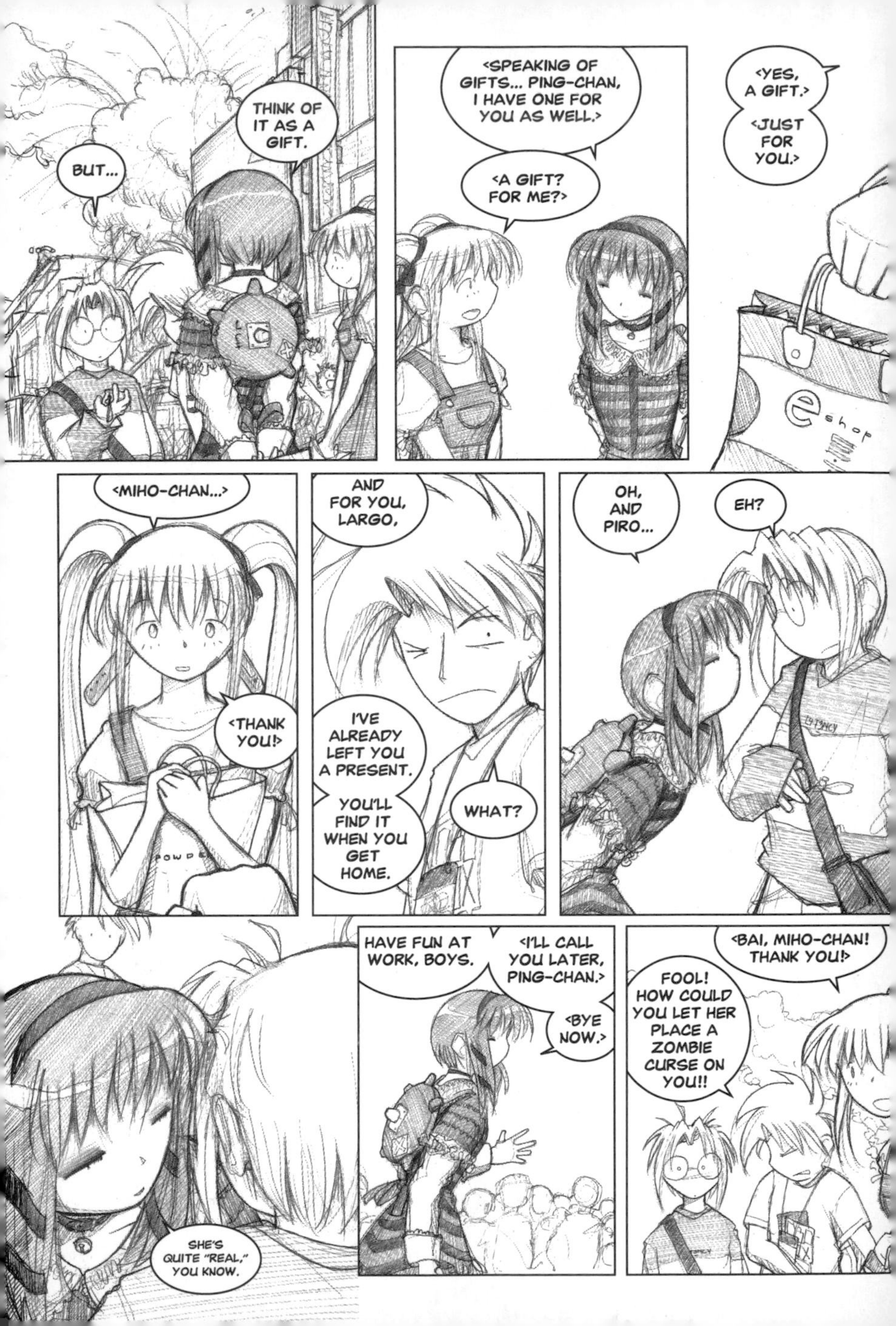
BUT...
THINK OF IT AS A GIFT.
<SPEAKING OF GIFTS... PING-CHAN, I HAVE ONE FOR YOU AS WELL.>
<A GIFT? FOR ME?>
<YES, A GIFT.>
<JUST FOR YOU.>
eshop
<MIHO-CHAN...>
<THANK YOU!>
AND FOR YOU, LARGO,
I'VE ALREADY LEFT YOU A PRESENT.
YOU'LL FIND IT WHEN YOU GET HOME.
WHAT?
OH, AND PIRO...
EH?
SHE'S QUITE "REAL," YOU KNOW.
HAVE FUN AT WORK, BOYS.
<I'LL CALL YOU LATER, PING-CHAN.>
<BYE NOW.>
<BAI, MIHO-CHAN! THANK YOU!>
FOOL! HOW COULD YOU LET HER PLACE A ZOMBIE CURSE ON YOU!!

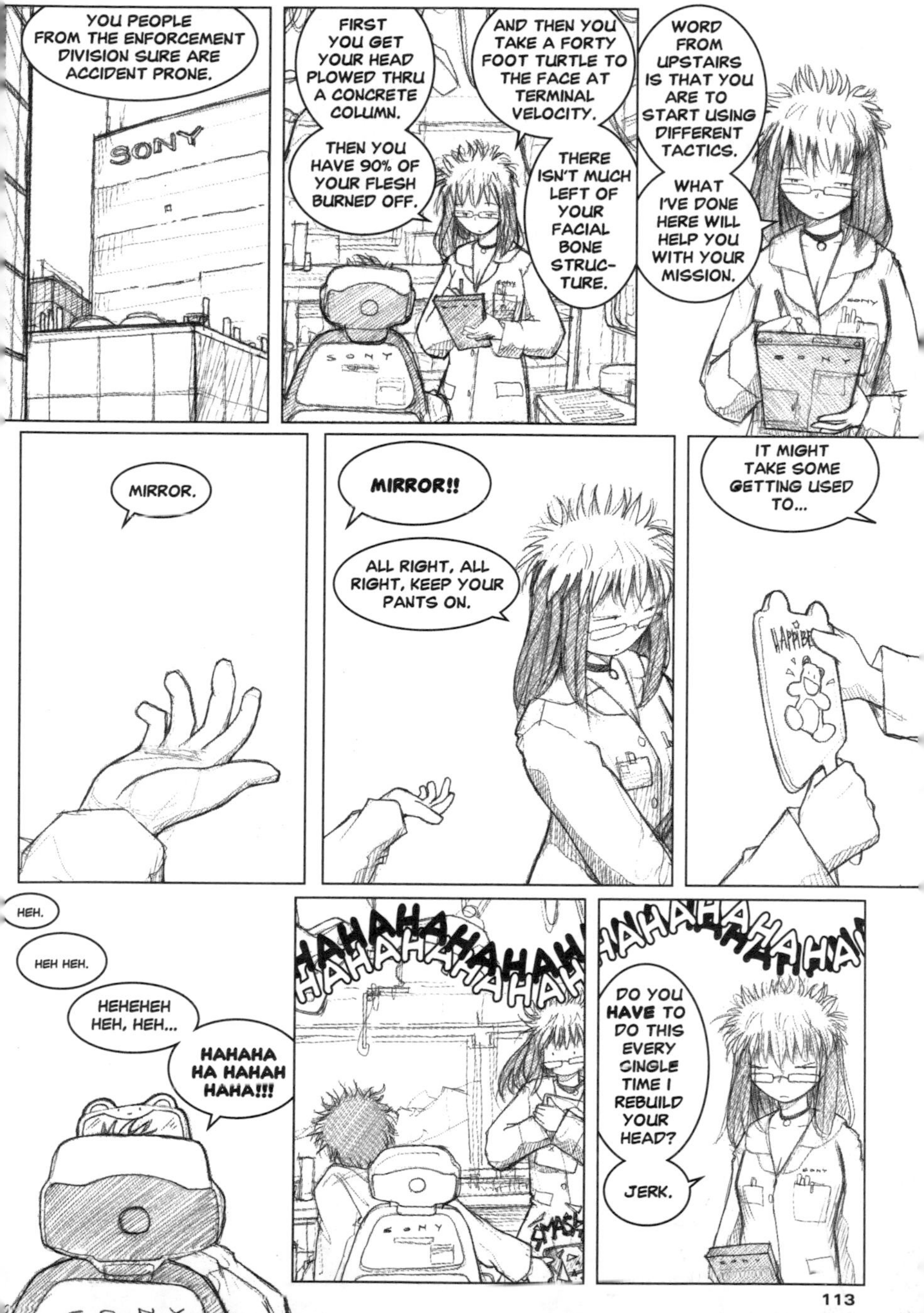
YOU PEOPLE FROM THE ENFORCEMENT DIVISION SURE ARE ACCIDENT PRONE.
SONY
FIRST YOU GET YOUR HEAD PLOWED THRU A CONCRETE COLUMN.
THEN YOU HAVE 90% OF YOUR FLESH BURNED OFF.
AND THEN YOU TAKE A FORTY FOOT TURTLE TO THE FACE AT TERMINAL VELOCITY.
THERE ISN'T MUCH LEFT OF YOUR FACIAL BONE STRUC-TURE.
SONY
WORD FROM UPSTAIRS IS THAT YOU ARE TO START USING DIFFERENT TACTICS.
WHAT I'VE DONE HERE WILL HELP YOU WITH YOUR MISSION.
MIRROR.
MIRROR!!
ALL RIGHT, ALL RIGHT, KEEP YOUR PANTS ON.
IT MIGHT TAKE SOME GETTING USED TO...
HEH.
HEH HEH.
HEHEHEH HEH, HEH...
HAHAHA HA HAHAH HAHA!!!
SONY
HAHAHAHAHAH HAHAHAHAHAHAH
SONY
HAHAHAHAHAHAHAHA!
DO YOU HAVE TO DO THIS EVERY SINGLE TIME I REBUILD YOUR HEAD?
JERK.

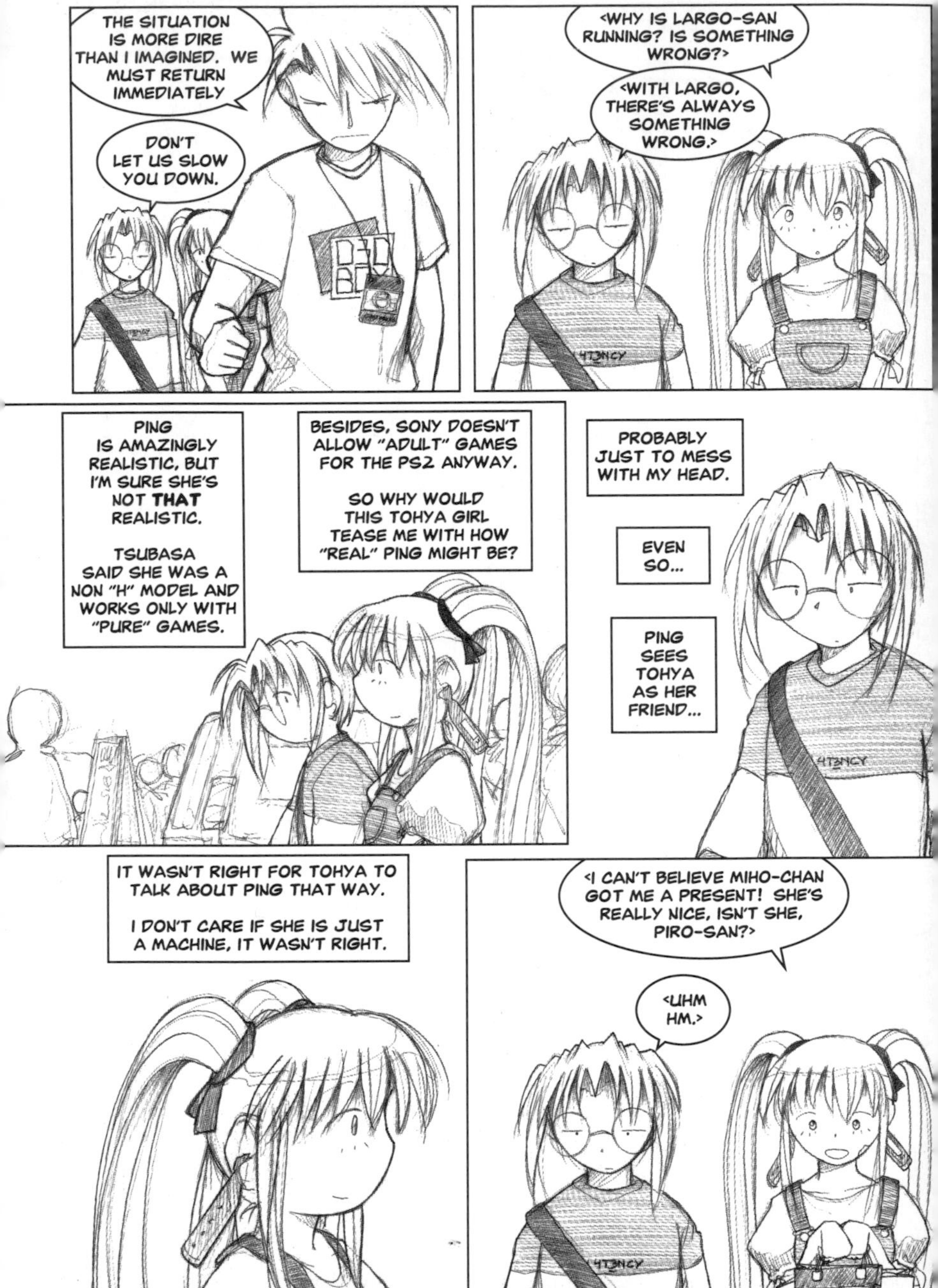
THE SITUATION IS MORE DIRE THAN I IMAGINED. WE MUST RETURN IMMEDIATELY
DON'T LET US SLOW YOU DOWN.
<WHY IS LARGO-SAN RUNNING? IS SOMETHING WRONG?>
<WITH LARGO, THERE'S ALWAYS SOMETHING WRONG.>
PING IS AMAZINGLY REALISTIC, BUT I'M SURE SHE'S NOT **THAT** REALISTIC.
TSUBASA SAID SHE WAS A NON "H" MODEL AND WORKS ONLY WITH "PURE" GAMES.
BESIDES, SONY DOESN'T ALLOW "ADULT" GAMES FOR THE PS2 ANYWAY.
SO WHY WOULD THIS TOHYA GIRL TEASE ME WITH HOW "REAL" PING MIGHT BE?
PROBABLY JUST TO MESS WITH MY HEAD.
EVEN SO...
PING SEES TOHYA AS HER FRIEND...
IT WASN'T RIGHT FOR TOHYA TO TALK ABOUT PING THAT WAY.
I DON'T CARE IF SHE IS JUST A MACHINE, IT WASN'T RIGHT.
<I CAN'T BELIEVE MIHO-CHAN GOT ME A PRESENT! SHE'S REALLY NICE, ISN'T SHE, PIRO-SAN?>
<UHM HM.>

あいだに。。。

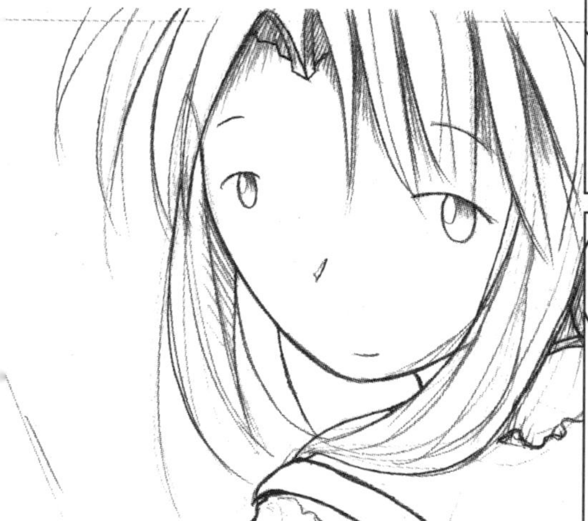

a megatokyo moment...

"A LITTLE MORE SAD"

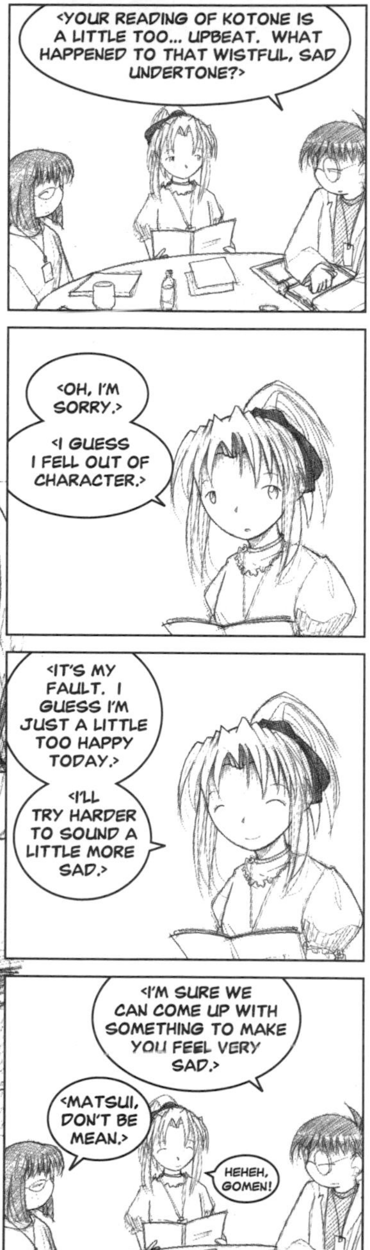
<YOUR READING OF KOTONE IS A LITTLE TOO... UPBEAT. WHAT HAPPENED TO THAT WISTFUL, SAD UNDERTONE?>
<OH, I'M SORRY.>
<I GUESS I FELL OUT OF CHARACTER.>
<IT'S MY FAULT. I GUESS I'M JUST A LITTLE TOO HAPPY TODAY.>
<I'LL TRY HARDER TO SOUND A LITTLE MORE SAD.>
<I'M SURE WE CAN COME UP WITH SOMETHING TO MAKE YOU FEEL VERY SAD.>
<MATSUI, DON'T BE MEAN.>
HEHEH, GOMEN!

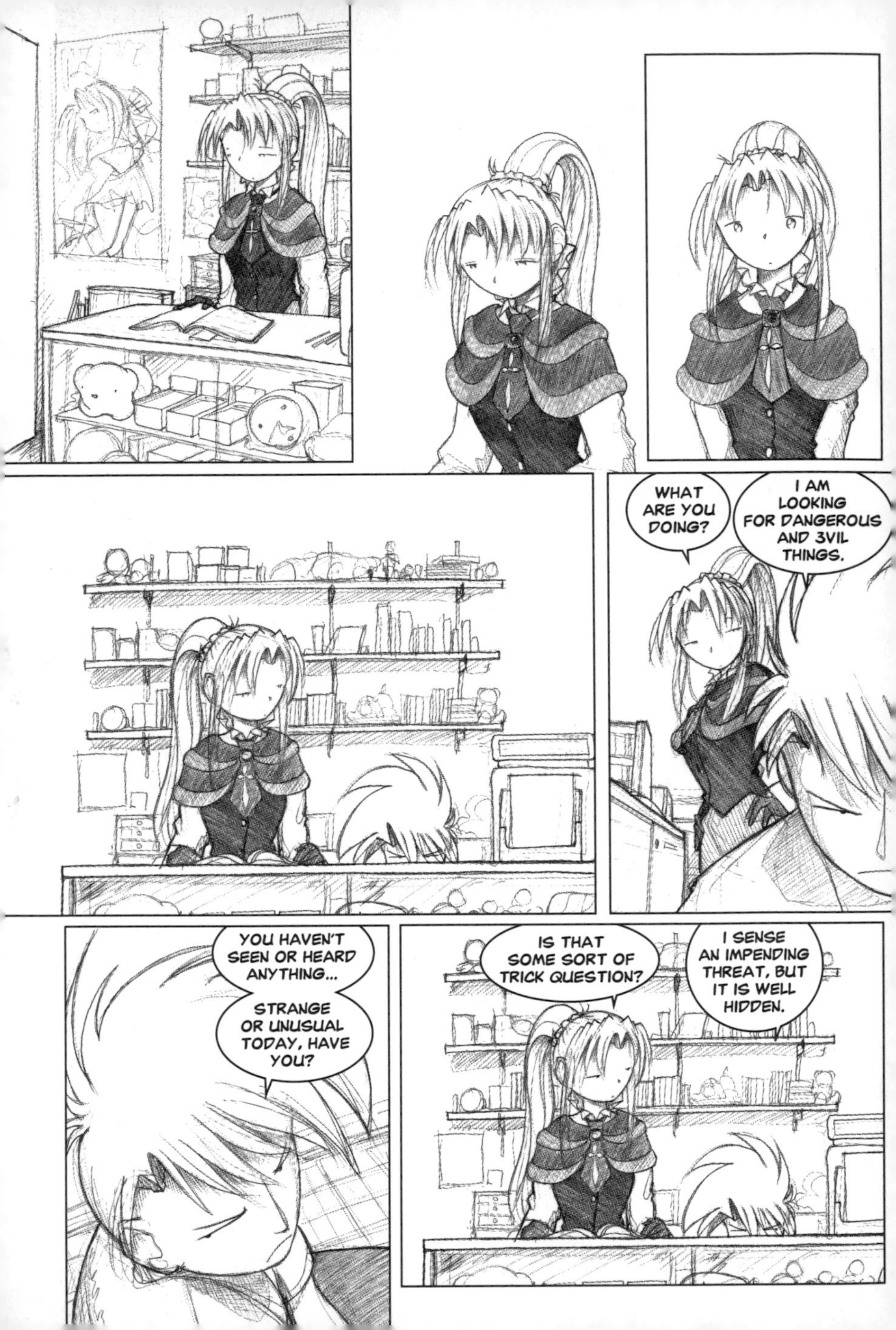
WHAT ARE YOU DOING?
I AM LOOKING FOR DANGEROUS AND 3VIL THINGS.
YOU HAVEN'T SEEN OR HEARD ANYTHING...
STRANGE OR UNUSUAL TODAY, HAVE YOU?
IS THAT SOME SORT OF TRICK QUESTION?
I SENSE AN IMPENDING THREAT, BUT IT IS WELL HIDDEN.

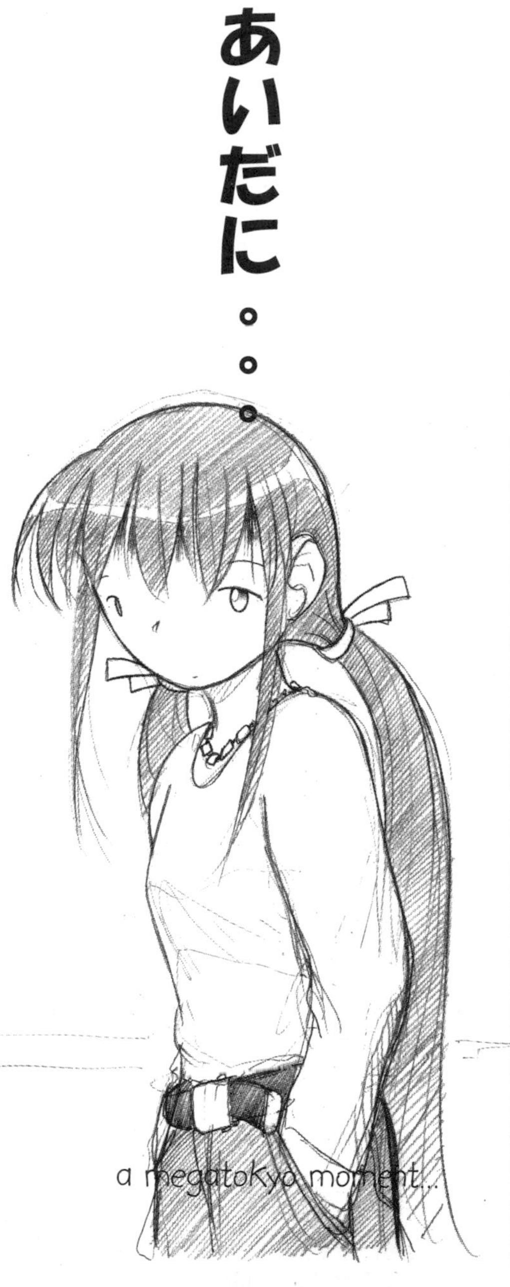
あいだに。。。
a megatokyo moment...

"PULL HERE FOR CHEER"

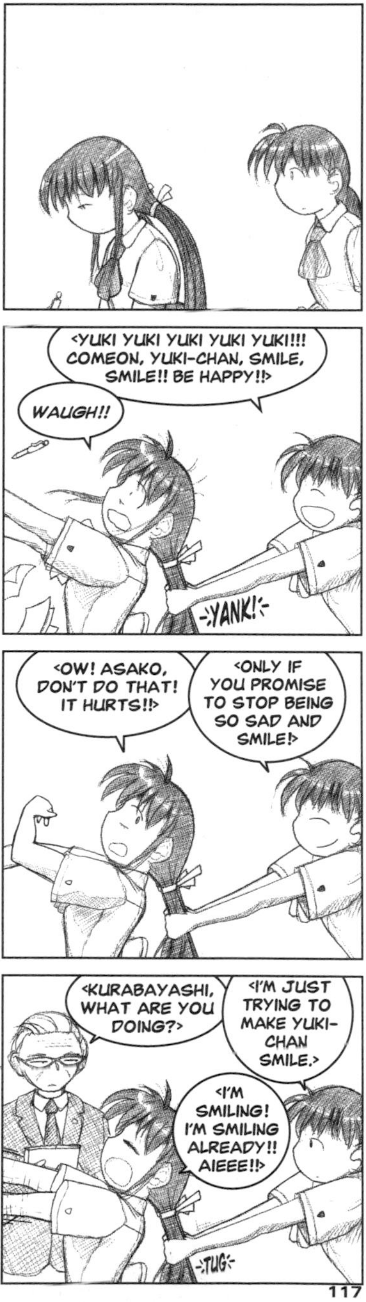
<YUKI YUKI YUKI YUKI YUKI!!! COMEON, YUKI-CHAN, SMILE, SMILE!! BE HAPPY!!>
WAUGH!!
YANK!
<OW! ASAKO, DON'T DO THAT! IT HURTS!!>
<ONLY IF YOU PROMISE TO STOP BEING SO SAD AND SMILE!>
<KURABAYASHI, WHAT ARE YOU DOING?>
<I'M JUST TRYING TO MAKE YUKI-CHAN SMILE.>
<I'M SMILING! I'M SMILING ALREADY!! AIEEE!!>
TUG

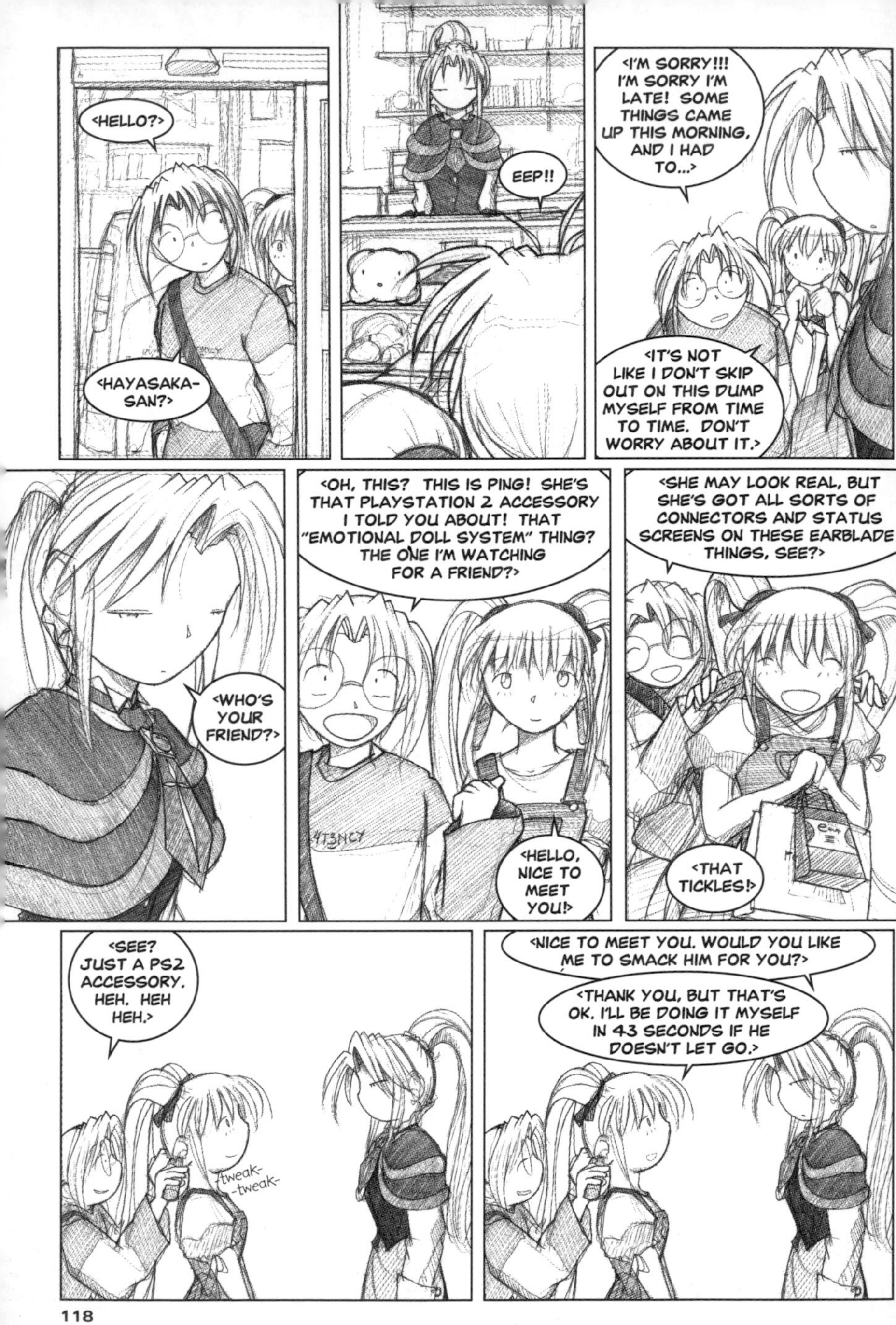
<HELLO?>
<HAYASAKA-SAN?>
EEP!!
<I'M SORRY!!! I'M SORRY I'M LATE! SOME THINGS CAME UP THIS MORNING, AND I HAD TO...>
<IT'S NOT LIKE I DON'T SKIP OUT ON THIS DUMP MYSELF FROM TIME TO TIME. DON'T WORRY ABOUT IT.>
<WHO'S YOUR FRIEND?>
<OH, THIS? THIS IS PING! SHE'S THAT PLAYSTATION 2 ACCESSORY I TOLD YOU ABOUT! THAT "EMOTIONAL DOLL SYSTEM" THING? THE ONE I'M WATCHING FOR A FRIEND?>
<HELLO, NICE TO MEET YOU!>
<SHE MAY LOOK REAL, BUT SHE'S GOT ALL SORTS OF CONNECTORS AND STATUS SCREENS ON THESE EARBLADE THINGS, SEE?>
<THAT TICKLES!>
<SEE? JUST A PS2 ACCESSORY. HEH. HEH HEH.>
-tweak-tweak-
<NICE TO MEET YOU. WOULD YOU LIKE ME TO SMACK HIM FOR YOU?>
<THANK YOU, BUT THAT'S OK. I'LL BE DOING IT MYSELF IN 43 SECONDS IF HE DOESN'T LET GO.>

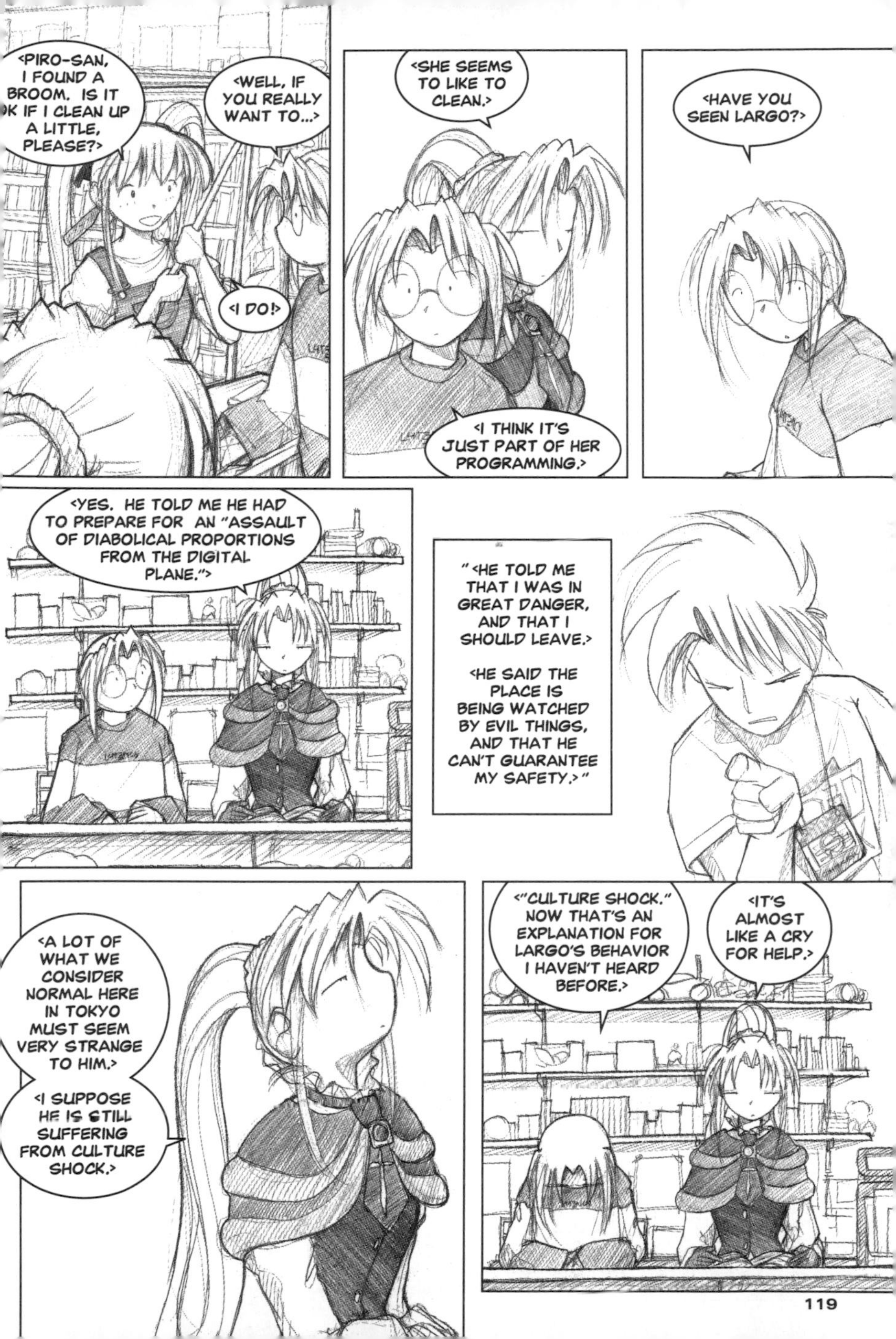
<PIRO-SAN, I FOUND A BROOM. IS IT OK IF I CLEAN UP A LITTLE, PLEASE?>
<WELL, IF YOU REALLY WANT TO...>
<I DO!>
<SHE SEEMS TO LIKE TO CLEAN.>
<I THINK IT'S JUST PART OF HER PROGRAMMING.>
<HAVE YOU SEEN LARGO?>
<YES. HE TOLD ME HE HAD TO PREPARE FOR AN "ASSAULT OF DIABOLICAL PROPORTIONS FROM THE DIGITAL PLANE.">
"<HE TOLD ME THAT I WAS IN GREAT DANGER, AND THAT I SHOULD LEAVE.>
<HE SAID THE PLACE IS BEING WATCHED BY EVIL THINGS, AND THAT HE CAN'T GUARANTEE MY SAFETY.>"
<A LOT OF WHAT WE CONSIDER NORMAL HERE IN TOKYO MUST SEEM VERY STRANGE TO HIM.>
<I SUPPOSE HE IS STILL SUFFERING FROM CULTURE SHOCK.>
<"CULTURE SHOCK." NOW THAT'S AN EXPLANATION FOR LARGO'S BEHAVIOR I HAVEN'T HEARD BEFORE.>
<IT'S ALMOST LIKE A CRY FOR HELP.>

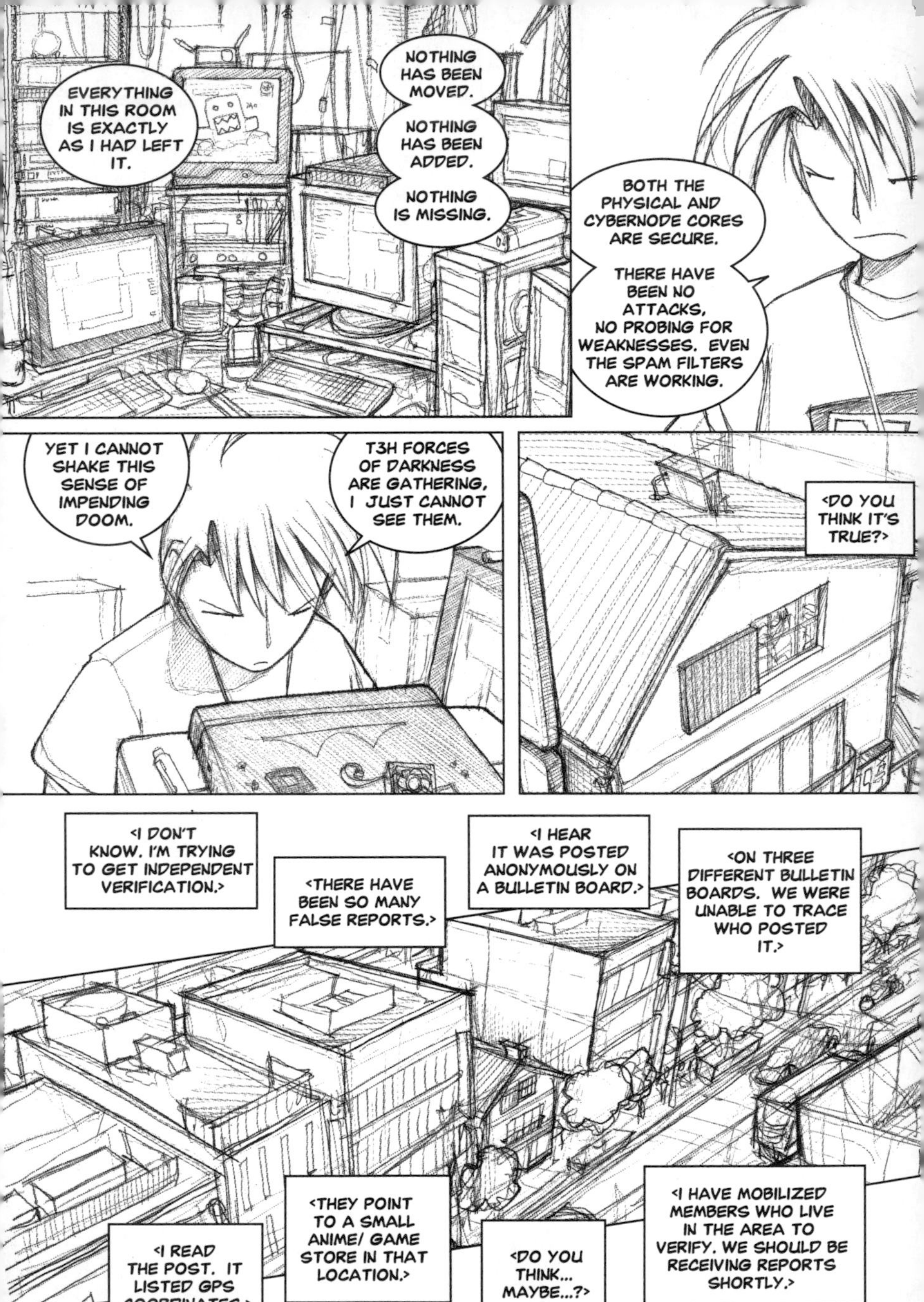
EVERYTHING IN THIS ROOM IS EXACTLY AS I HAD LEFT IT.
NOTHING HAS BEEN MOVED.
NOTHING HAS BEEN ADDED.
NOTHING IS MISSING.
BOTH THE PHYSICAL AND CYBERNODE CORES ARE SECURE.
THERE HAVE BEEN NO ATTACKS, NO PROBING FOR WEAKNESSES. EVEN THE SPAM FILTERS ARE WORKING.
YET I CANNOT SHAKE THIS SENSE OF IMPENDING DOOM.
T3H FORCES OF DARKNESS ARE GATHERING, I JUST CANNOT SEE THEM.
<DO YOU THINK IT'S TRUE?>
<I DON'T KNOW. I'M TRYING TO GET INDEPENDENT VERIFICATION.>
<THERE HAVE BEEN SO MANY FALSE REPORTS.>
<I HEAR IT WAS POSTED ANONYMOUSLY ON A BULLETIN BOARD.>
<ON THREE DIFFERENT BULLETIN BOARDS. WE WERE UNABLE TO TRACE WHO POSTED IT.>
<I READ THE POST. IT LISTED GPS COORDINATES.>
<THEY POINT TO A SMALL ANIME/ GAME STORE IN THAT LOCATION.>
<DO YOU THINK... MAYBE...?>
<I HAVE MOBILIZED MEMBERS WHO LIVE IN THE AREA TO VERIFY. WE SHOULD BE RECEIVING REPORTS SHORTLY.>

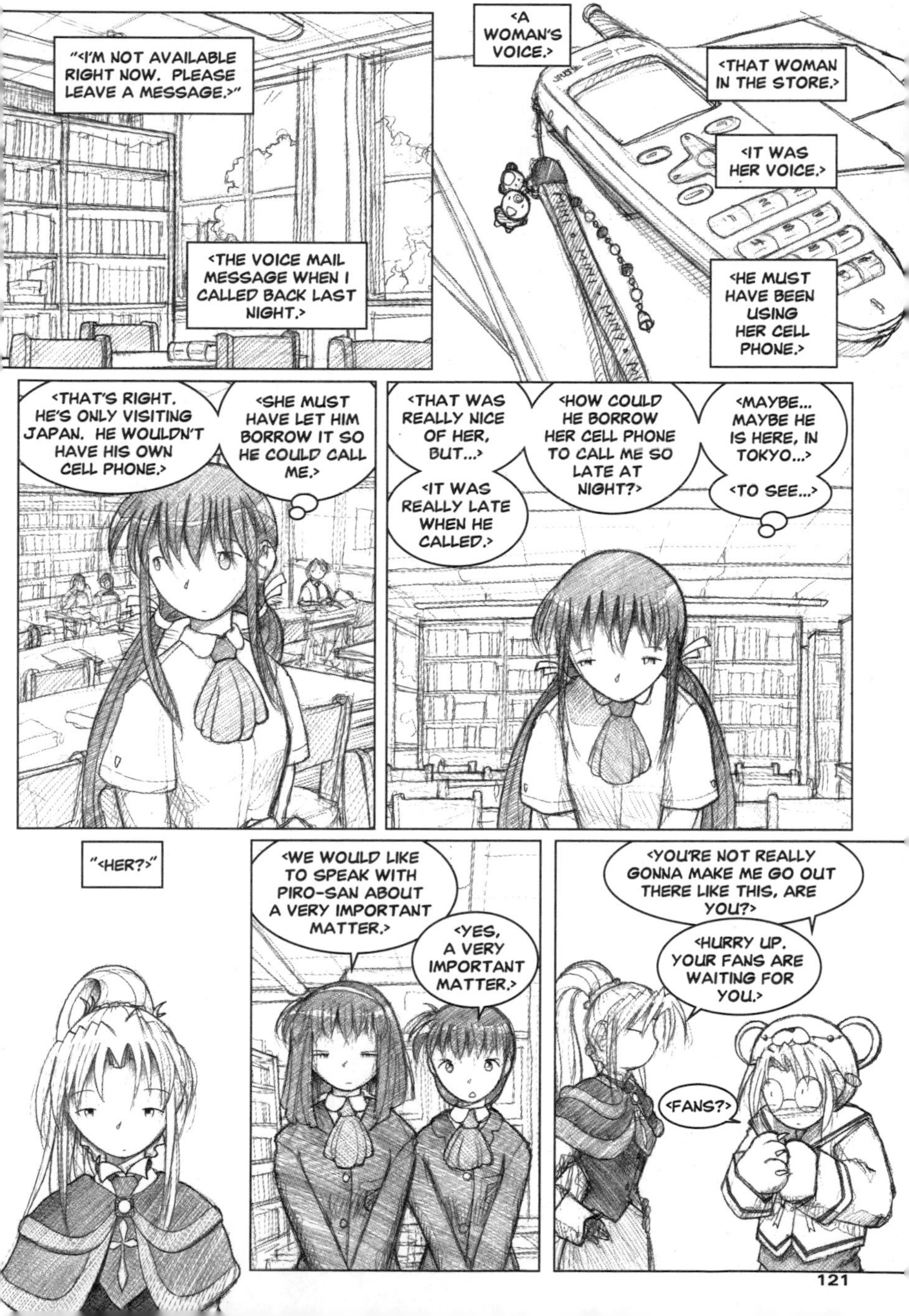
"<I'M NOT AVAILABLE RIGHT NOW. PLEASE LEAVE A MESSAGE.>"
<THE VOICE MAIL MESSAGE WHEN I CALLED BACK LAST NIGHT.>
<A WOMAN'S VOICE.>
<THAT WOMAN IN THE STORE.>
<IT WAS HER VOICE.>
<HE MUST HAVE BEEN USING HER CELL PHONE.>
<THAT'S RIGHT. HE'S ONLY VISITING JAPAN. HE WOULDN'T HAVE HIS OWN CELL PHONE.>
<SHE MUST HAVE LET HIM BORROW IT SO HE COULD CALL ME.>
<THAT WAS REALLY NICE OF HER, BUT...>
<IT WAS REALLY LATE WHEN HE CALLED.>
<HOW COULD HE BORROW HER CELL PHONE TO CALL ME SO LATE AT NIGHT?>
<MAYBE... MAYBE HE IS HERE, IN TOKYO...>
<TO SEE...>
"<HER?>"
<WE WOULD LIKE TO SPEAK WITH PIRO-SAN ABOUT A VERY IMPORTANT MATTER.>
<YES, A VERY IMPORTANT MATTER.>
<YOU'RE NOT REALLY GONNA MAKE ME GO OUT THERE LIKE THIS, ARE YOU?>
<HURRY UP. YOUR FANS ARE WAITING FOR YOU.>
<FANS?>

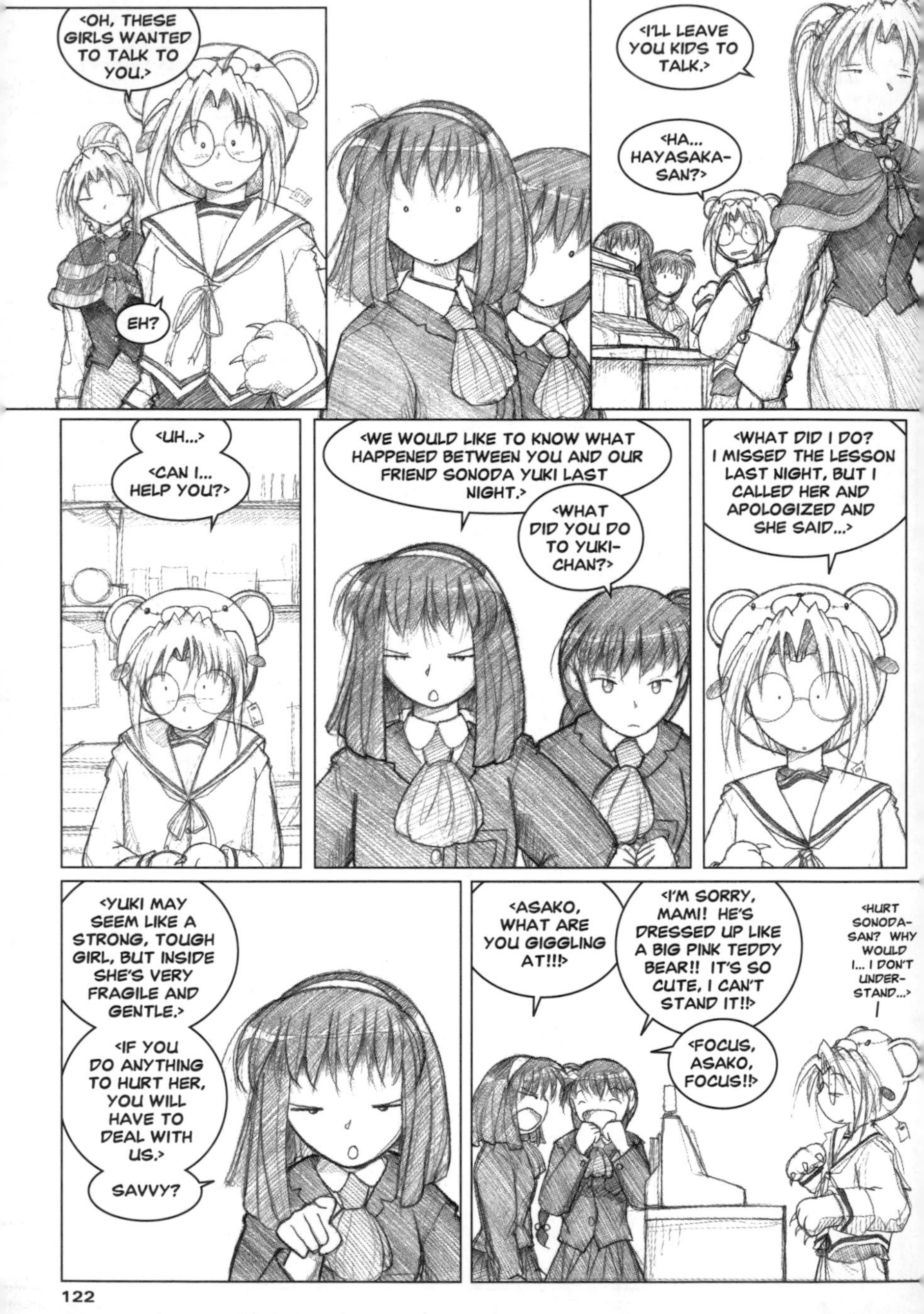
<OH, THESE GIRLS WANTED TO TALK TO YOU.>
EH?
<I'LL LEAVE YOU KIDS TO TALK.>
<HA... HAYASAKA-SAN?>
<UH...>
<CAN I... HELP YOU?>
<WE WOULD LIKE TO KNOW WHAT HAPPENED BETWEEN YOU AND OUR FRIEND SONODA YUKI LAST NIGHT.>
<WHAT DID YOU DO TO YUKI-CHAN?>
<WHAT DID I DO? I MISSED THE LESSON LAST NIGHT, BUT I CALLED HER AND APOLOGIZED AND SHE SAID...>
<YUKI MAY SEEM LIKE A STRONG, TOUGH GIRL, BUT INSIDE SHE'S VERY FRAGILE AND GENTLE.>
<IF YOU DO ANYTHING TO HURT HER, YOU WILL HAVE TO DEAL WITH US.>
SAVVY?
<ASAKO, WHAT ARE YOU GIGGLING AT!!!>
<I'M SORRY, MAMI! HE'S DRESSED UP LIKE A BIG PINK TEDDY BEAR!! IT'S SO CUTE, I CAN'T STAND IT!!>
<FOCUS, ASAKO, FOCUS!!>
<HURT SONODA-SAN? WHY WOULD I... I DON'T UNDERSTAND...>

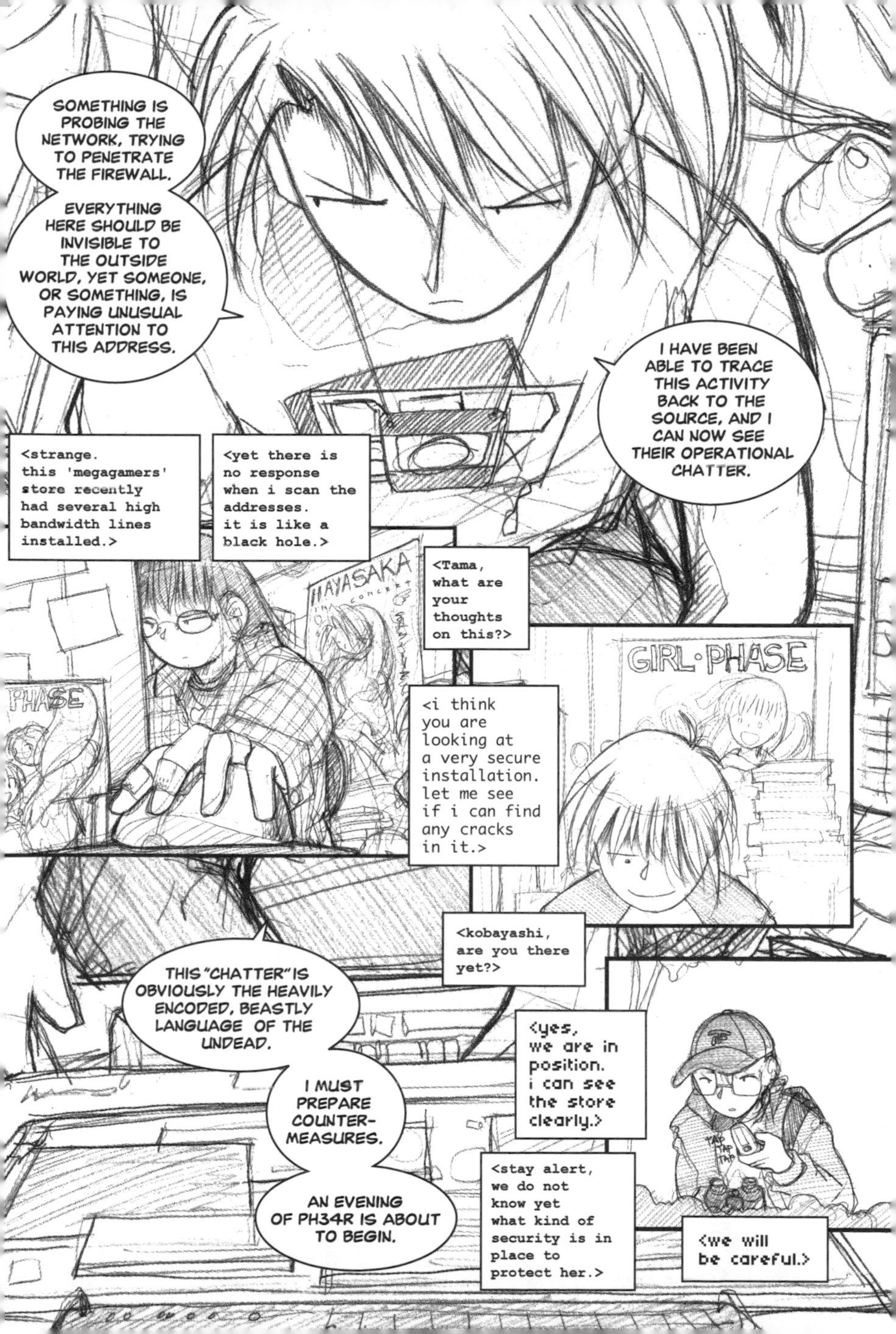
SOMETHING IS PROBING THE NETWORK, TRYING TO PENETRATE THE FIREWALL.
EVERYTHING HERE SHOULD BE INVISIBLE TO THE OUTSIDE WORLD, YET SOMEONE, OR SOMETHING, IS PAYING UNUSUAL ATTENTION TO THIS ADDRESS.
I HAVE BEEN ABLE TO TRACE THIS ACTIVITY BACK TO THE SOURCE, AND I CAN NOW SEE THEIR OPERATIONAL CHATTER.
<strange. this 'megagamers' store recently had several high bandwidth lines installed.>
<yet there is no response when i scan the addresses. it is like a black hole.>
HAYASAKA
<Tama, what are your thoughts on this?>
GIRL·PHASE
<i think you are looking at a very secure installation. let me see if i can find any cracks in it.>
<kobayashi, are you there yet?>
THIS "CHATTER" IS OBVIOUSLY THE HEAVILY ENCODED, BEASTLY LANGUAGE OF THE UNDEAD.
I MUST PREPARE COUNTER-MEASURES.
AN EVENING OF PH34R IS ABOUT TO BEGIN.
<yes, we are in position. i can see the store clearly.>
TAP TAP TAP
<stay alert, we do not know yet what kind of security is in place to protect her.>
<we will be careful.>

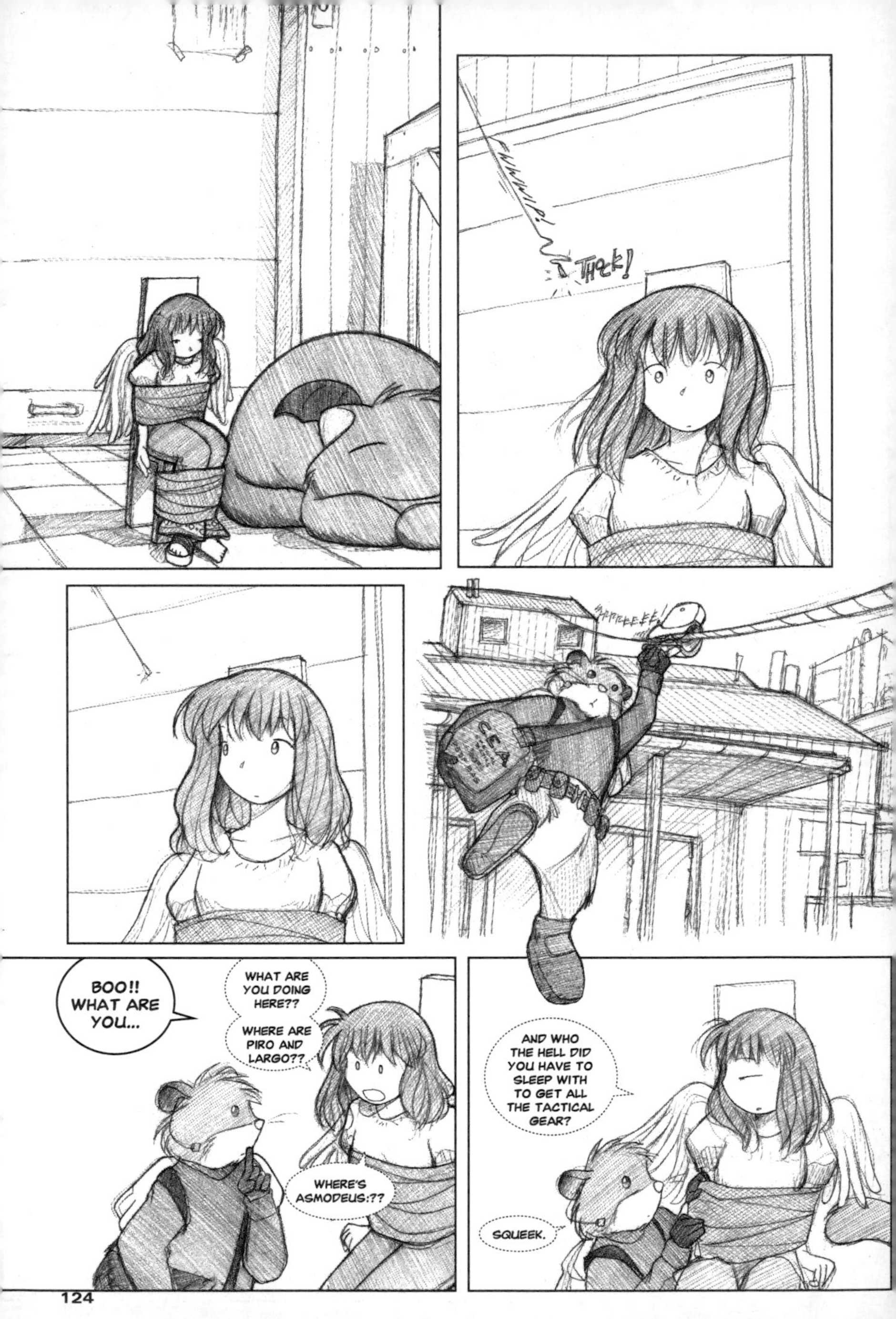
THOCK!
BOO!! WHAT ARE YOU...
WHAT ARE YOU DOING HERE??
WHERE ARE PIRO AND LARGO??
WHERE'S ASMODEUS:??
AND WHO THE HELL DID YOU HAVE TO SLEEP WITH TO GET ALL THE TACTICAL GEAR?
SQUEEK.

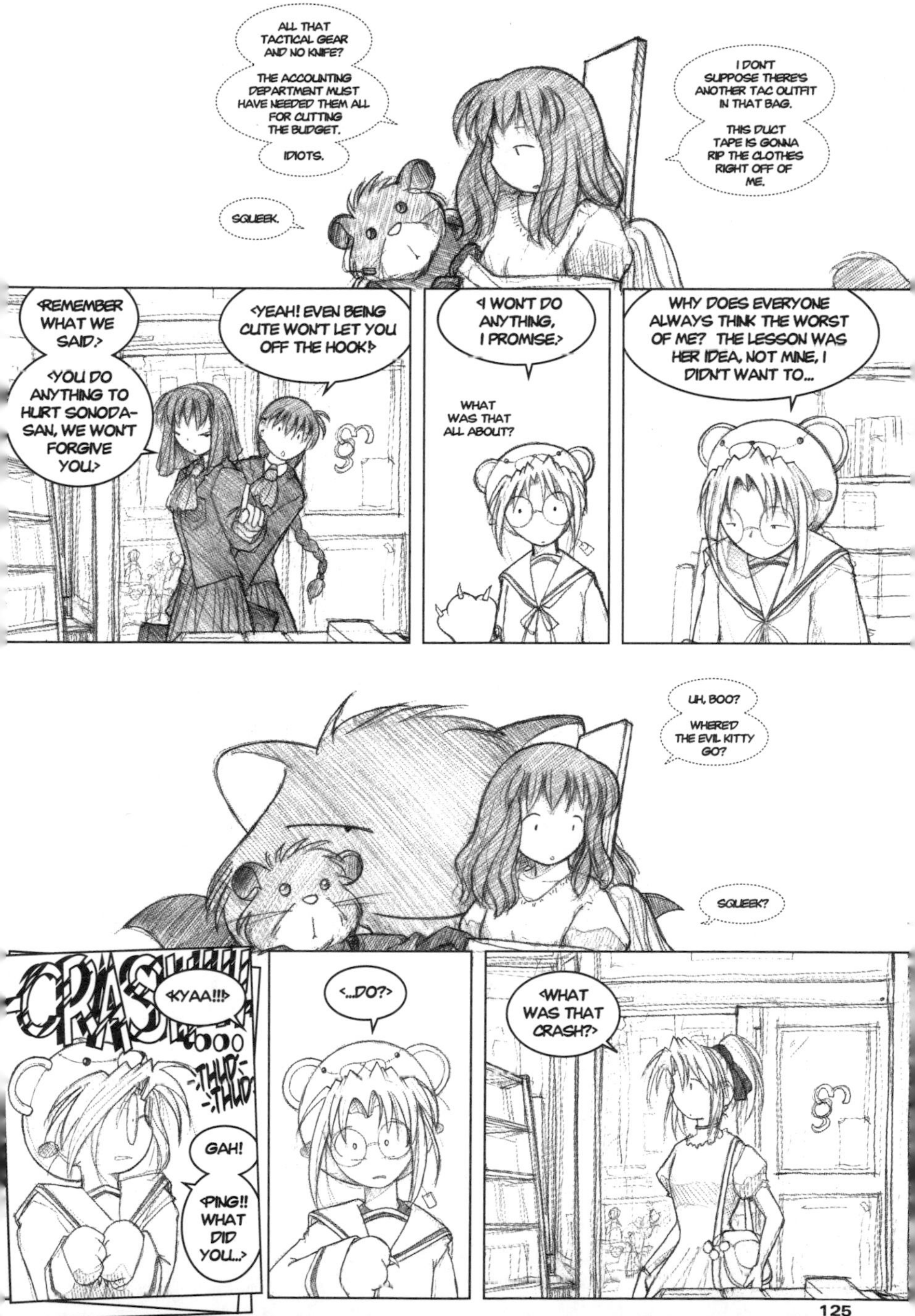
ALL THAT TACTICAL GEAR AND NO KNIFE?
THE ACCOUNTING DEPARTMENT MUST HAVE NEEDED THEM ALL FOR CUTTING THE BUDGET.
IDIOTS.
I DON'T SUPPOSE THERE'S ANOTHER TAC OUTFIT IN THAT BAG.
THIS DUCT TAPE IS GONNA RIP THE CLOTHES RIGHT OFF OF ME.
SQUEEK.
<REMEMBER WHAT WE SAID.>
<YEAH! EVEN BEING CUTE WON'T LET YOU OFF THE HOOK!>
<YOU DO ANYTHING TO HURT SONODA-SAN, WE WON'T FORGIVE YOU.>
<I WON'T DO ANYTHING, I PROMISE.>
WHAT WAS THAT ALL ABOUT?
WHY DOES EVERYONE ALWAYS THINK THE WORST OF ME? THE LESSON WAS HER IDEA, NOT MINE, I DIDN'T WANT TO...
UH, BOO?
WHERE'D THE EVIL KITTY GO?
SQUEEK?
CRASH
<KYAA!!!>
OOO
THUD THUD
GAH!
<PING!! WHAT DID YOU...>
<...DO?>
<WHAT WAS THAT CRASH?>

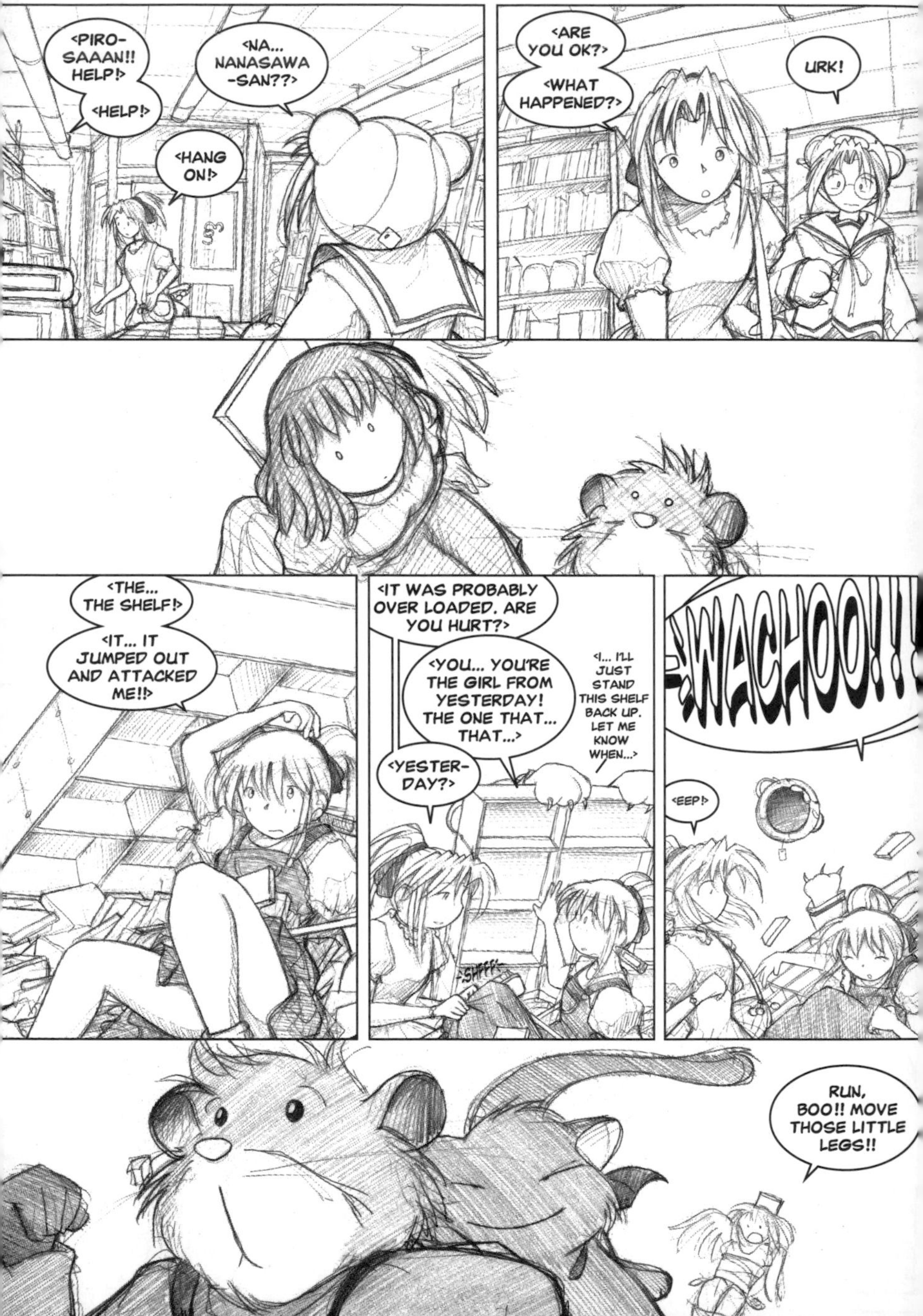

<PIRO-SAAAN!! HELP!>
<HELP!>
<NA... NANASAWA-SAN??>
<HANG ON!>
<ARE YOU OK?>
<WHAT HAPPENED?>
URK!
<THE... THE SHELF!>
<IT... IT JUMPED OUT AND ATTACKED ME!!>
<IT WAS PROBABLY OVER LOADED. ARE YOU HURT?>
<YOU... YOU'RE THE GIRL FROM YESTERDAY! THE ONE THAT... THAT...>
<I... I'LL JUST STAND THIS SHELF BACK UP. LET ME KNOW WHEN...>
<YESTER-DAY?>
WACHOO!!!
<EEP!>
RUN, BOO!! MOVE THOSE LITTLE LEGS!!

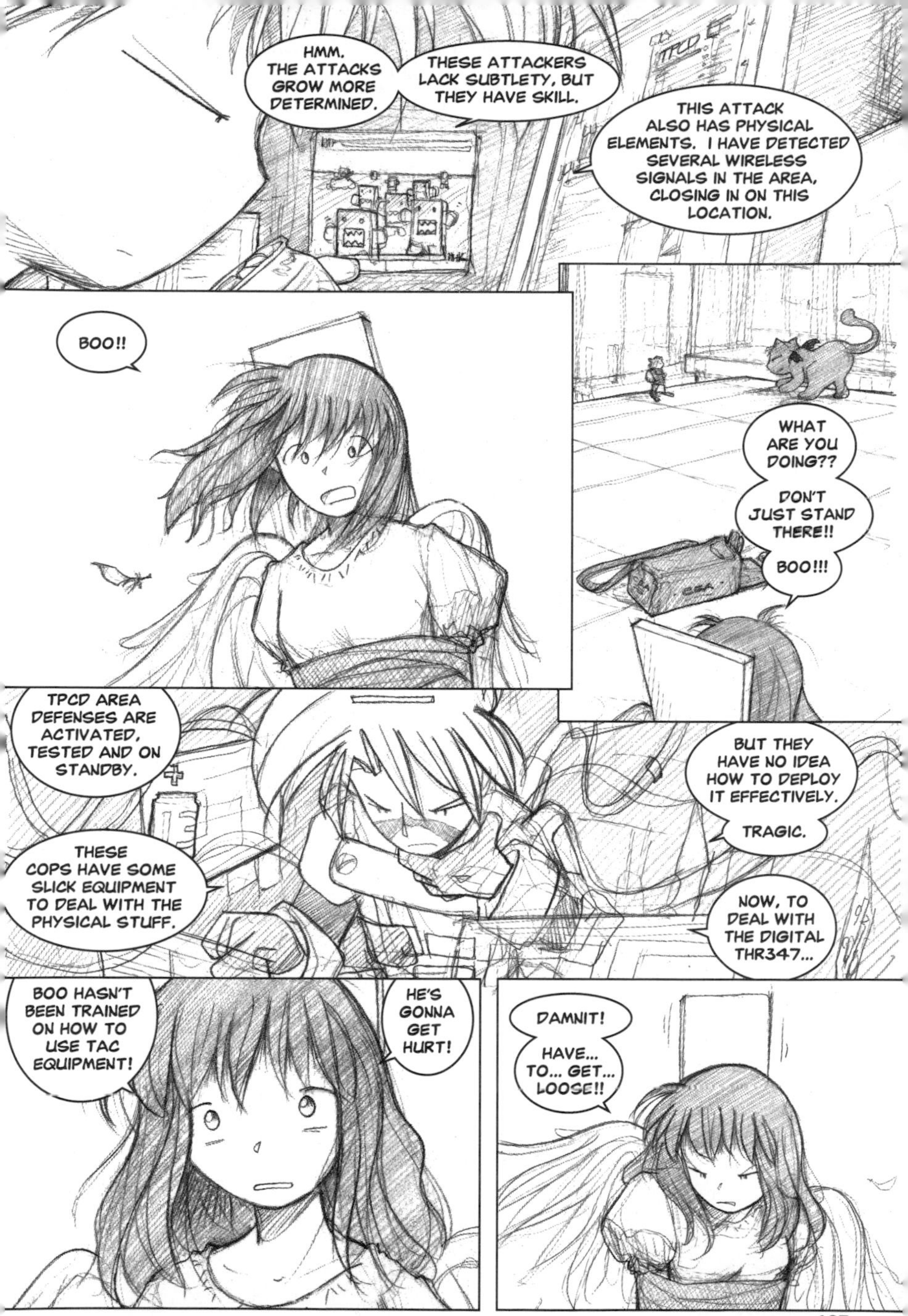

HMM. THE ATTACKS GROW MORE DETERMINED.
THESE ATTACKERS LACK SUBTLETY, BUT THEY HAVE SKILL.
THIS ATTACK ALSO HAS PHYSICAL ELEMENTS. I HAVE DETECTED SEVERAL WIRELESS SIGNALS IN THE AREA, CLOSING IN ON THIS LOCATION.
BOO!!
WHAT ARE YOU DOING??
DON'T JUST STAND THERE!!
BOO!!!
TPCD AREA DEFENSES ARE ACTIVATED, TESTED AND ON STANDBY.
THESE COPS HAVE SOME SLICK EQUIPMENT TO DEAL WITH THE PHYSICAL STUFF.
BUT THEY HAVE NO IDEA HOW TO DEPLOY IT EFFECTIVELY.
TRAGIC.
NOW, TO DEAL WITH THE DIGITAL THR347...
BOO HASN'T BEEN TRAINED ON HOW TO USE TAC EQUIPMENT!
HE'S GONNA GET HURT!
DAMNIT!
HAVE... TO... GET... LOOSE!!

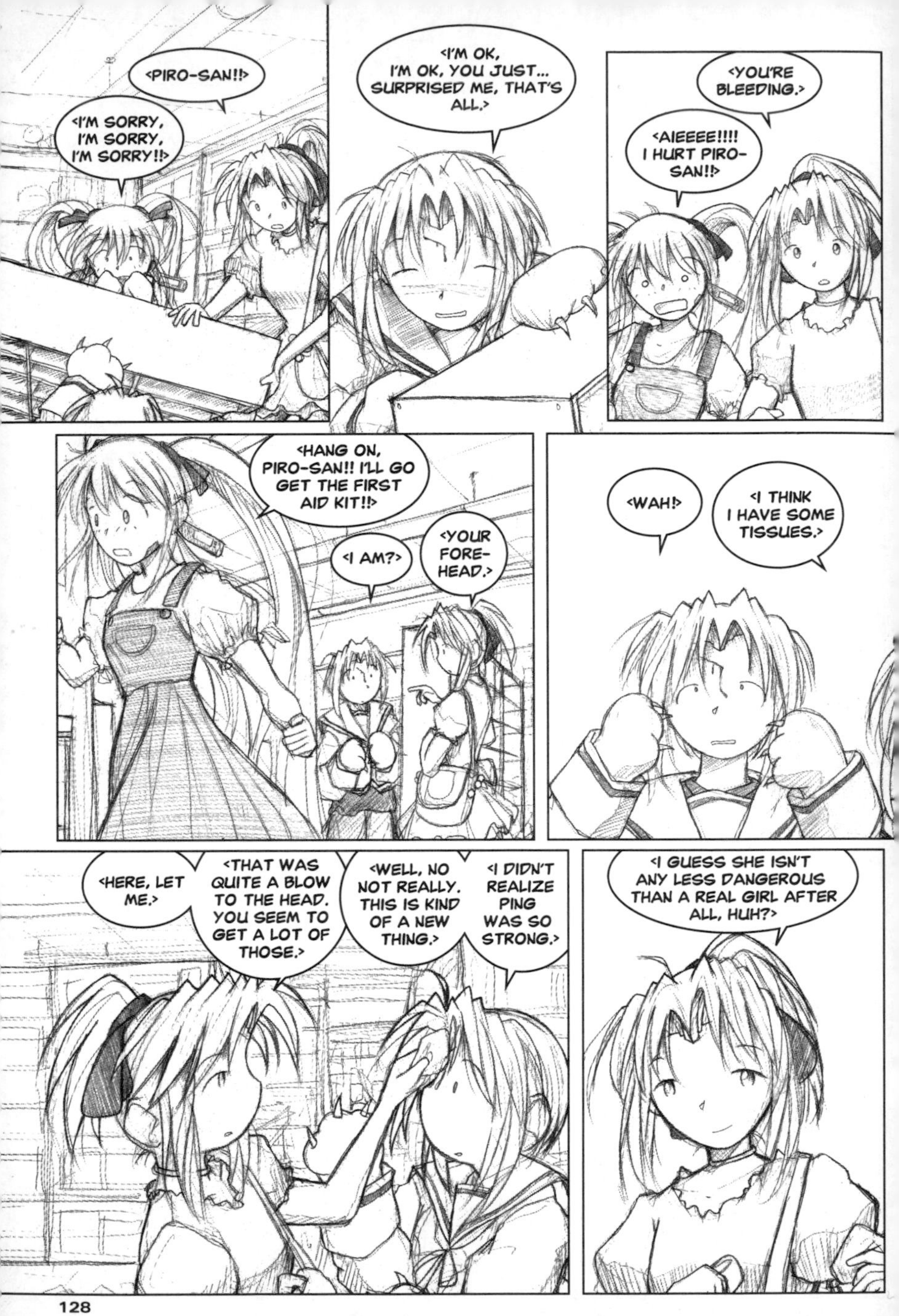
<PIRO-SAN!!>
<I'M SORRY, I'M SORRY, I'M SORRY!!>
<I'M OK, I'M OK, YOU JUST... SURPRISED ME, THAT'S ALL.>
<YOU'RE BLEEDING.>
<AIEEEE!!!! I HURT PIRO-SAN!!>
<HANG ON, PIRO-SAN!! I'LL GO GET THE FIRST AID KIT!!>
<I AM?>
<YOUR FORE-HEAD.>
<WAH!>
<I THINK I HAVE SOME TISSUES.>
<HERE, LET ME.>
<THAT WAS QUITE A BLOW TO THE HEAD. YOU SEEM TO GET A LOT OF THOSE.>
<WELL, NO NOT REALLY. THIS IS KIND OF A NEW THING.>
<I DIDN'T REALIZE PING WAS SO STRONG.>
<I GUESS SHE ISN'T ANY LESS DANGEROUS THAN A REAL GIRL AFTER ALL, HUH?>

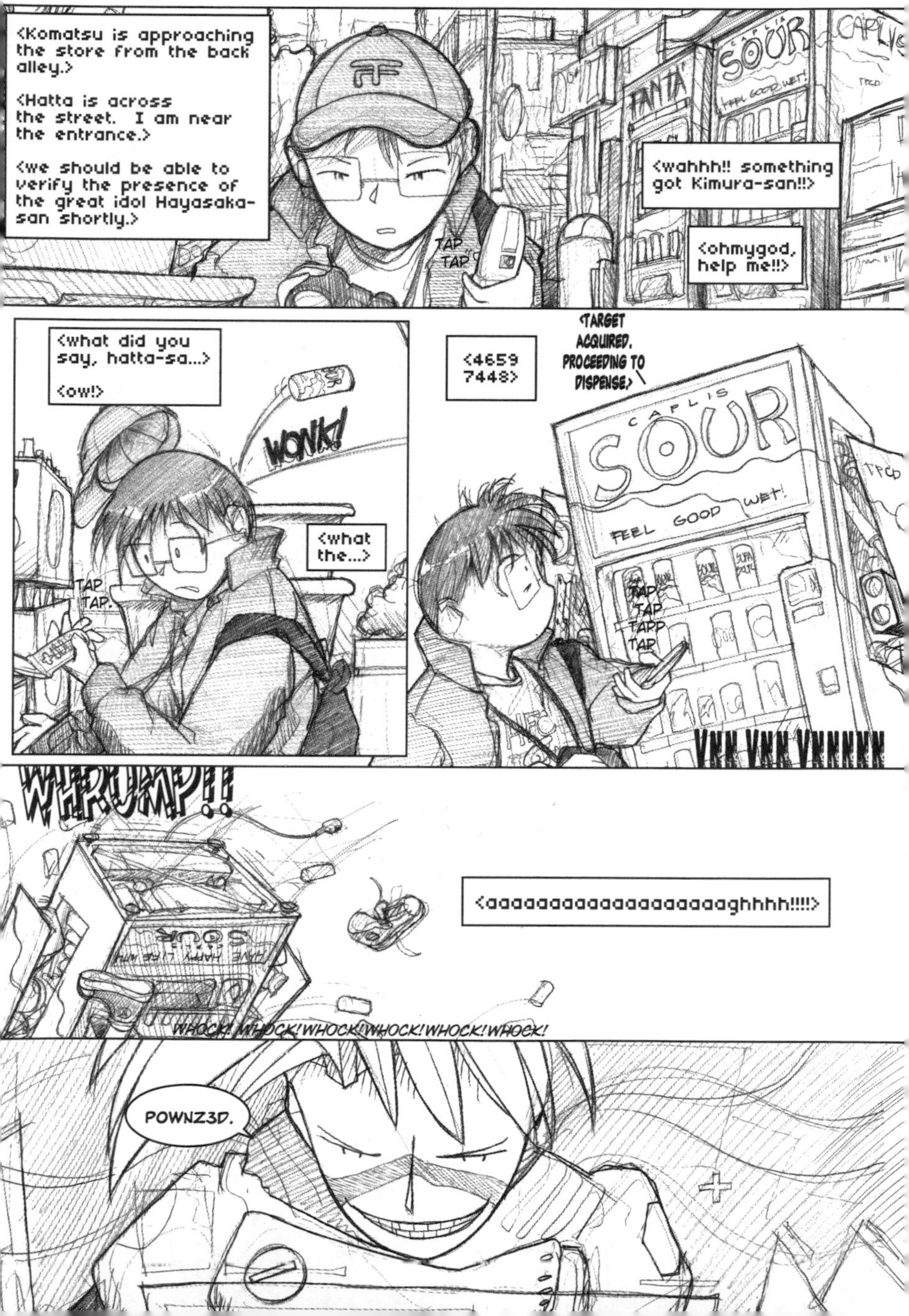

<Komatsu is approaching the store from the back alley.>
<Hatta is across the street. I am near the entrance.>
<we should be able to verify the presence of the great idol Hayasaka-san shortly.>
<wahhh!! something got Kimura-san!!>
TAP, TAP
<ohmygod, help me!!>
<what did you say, hatta-sa...>
<ow!>
WONK!
<what the...>
TAP TAP.
<4659 7448>
<TARGET ACQUIRED. PROCEEDING TO DISPENSE.>
CAPLIS SOUR
FEEL GOOD WET!
TAP TAP TAPP TAP
VNN VNN VNNNNN
WHROMP!!
<aaaaaaaaaaaaaaaaaaaghhhh!!!!>
WHOCK! WHOCK! WHOCK! WHOCK! WHOCK! WHOCK!
POWNZ3D.

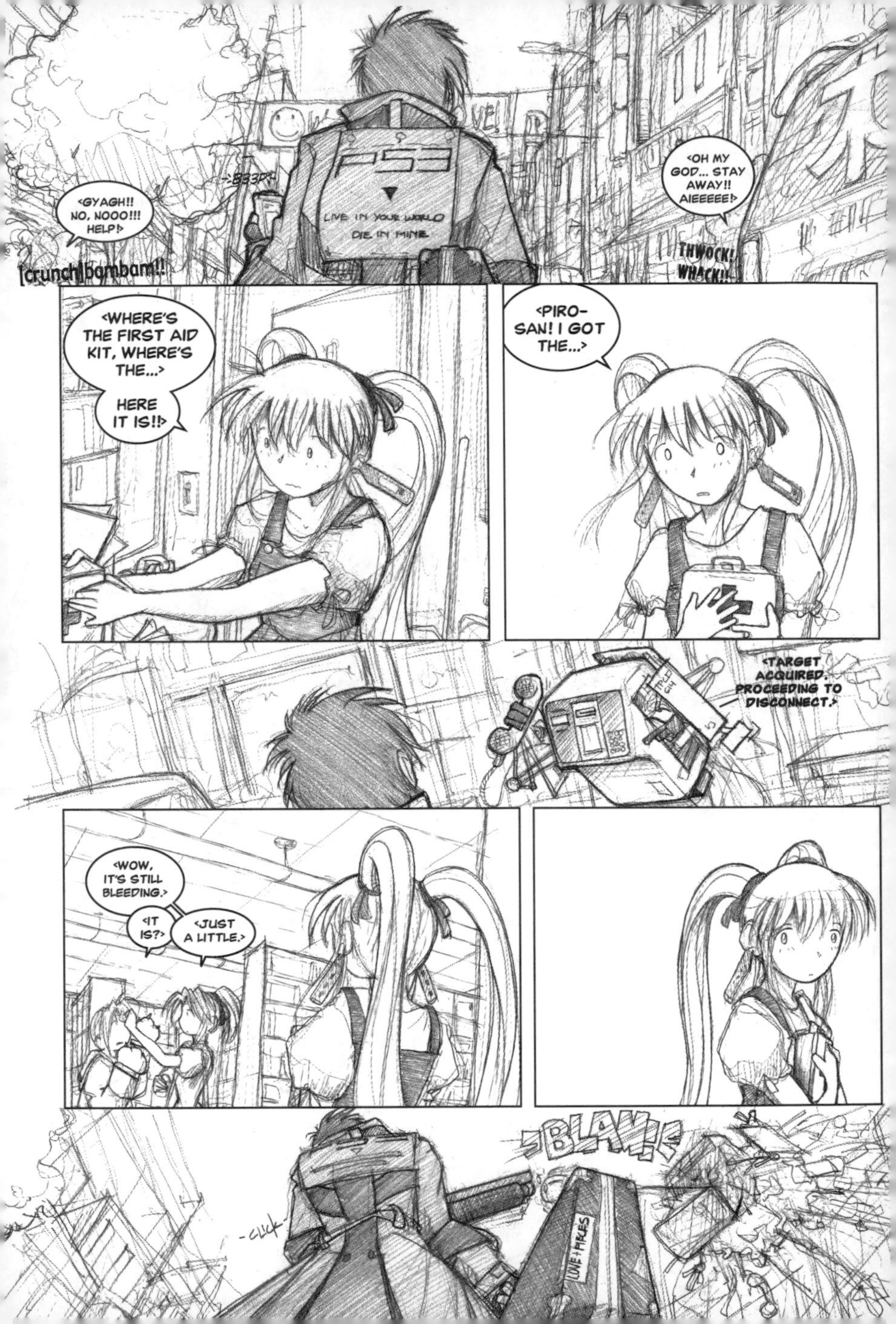
~B33P~
<GYAGH!! NO, NOOO!!! HELP!>
LIVE IN YOUR WORLD DIE IN MINE
<OH MY GOD... STAY AWAY!! AIEEEEE!>
[crunch]bambam!!
THWOCK! WHACK!!
<WHERE'S THE FIRST AID KIT, WHERE'S THE...>
HERE IT IS!!>
<PIRO-SAN! I GOT THE...>
<TARGET ACQUIRED. PROCEEDING TO DISCONNECT.>
<WOW, IT'S STILL BLEEDING.>
<IT IS?>
<JUST A LITTLE.>
-CLICK-
BLAM!
LOVE+PIECES

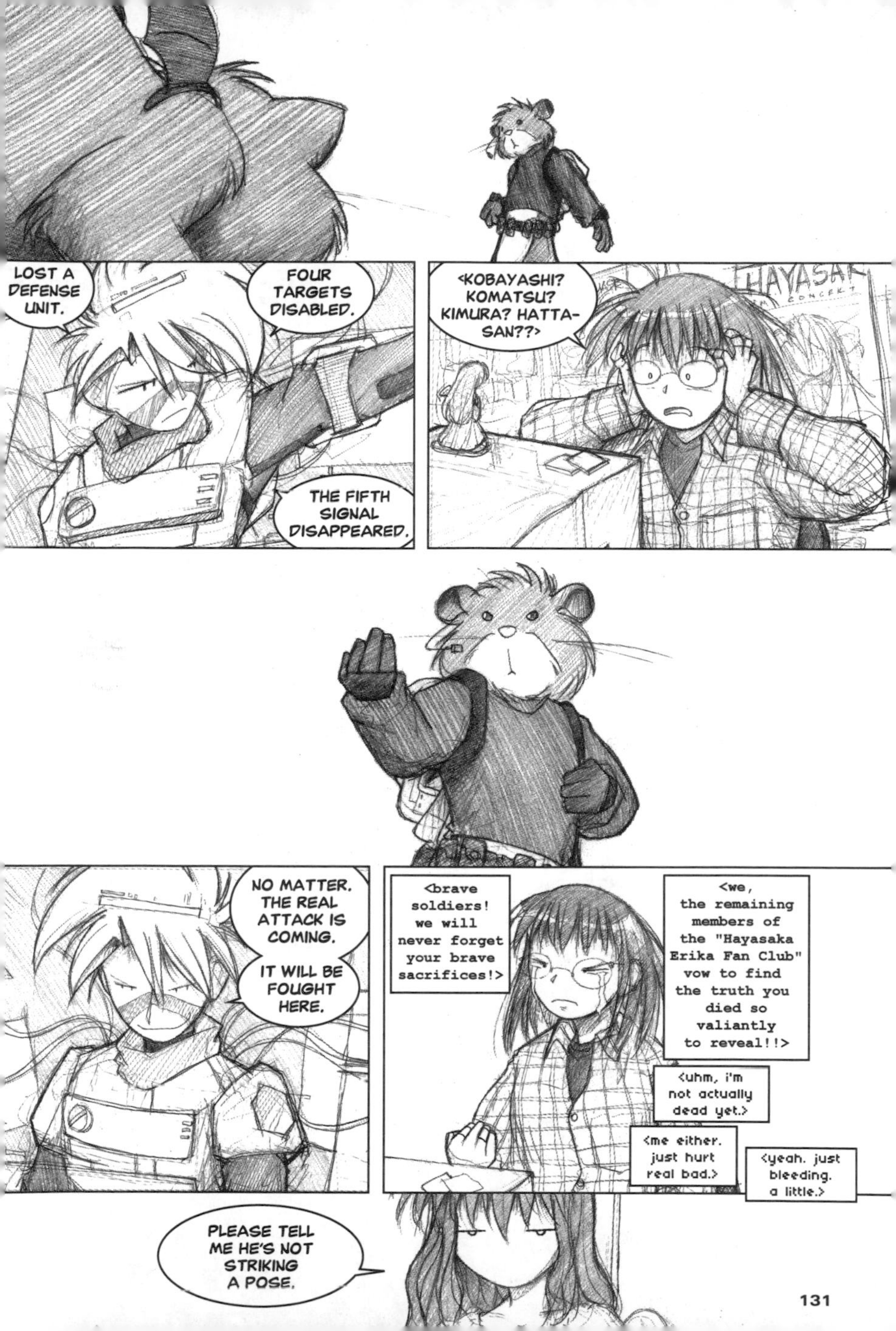
LOST A DEFENSE UNIT.
FOUR TARGETS DISABLED.
THE FIFTH SIGNAL DISAPPEARED.
<KOBAYASHI? KOMATSU? KIMURA? HATTA-SAN??>
HAYASAK
CONCERT
NO MATTER. THE REAL ATTACK IS COMING.
IT WILL BE FOUGHT HERE.
<brave soldiers! we will never forget your brave sacrifices!>
<we, the remaining members of the "Hayasaka Erika Fan Club" vow to find the truth you died so valiantly to reveal!!>
<uhm, i'm not actually dead yet.>
<me either. just hurt real bad.>
<yeah. just bleeding. a little.>
PLEASE TELL ME HE'S NOT STRIKING A POSE.

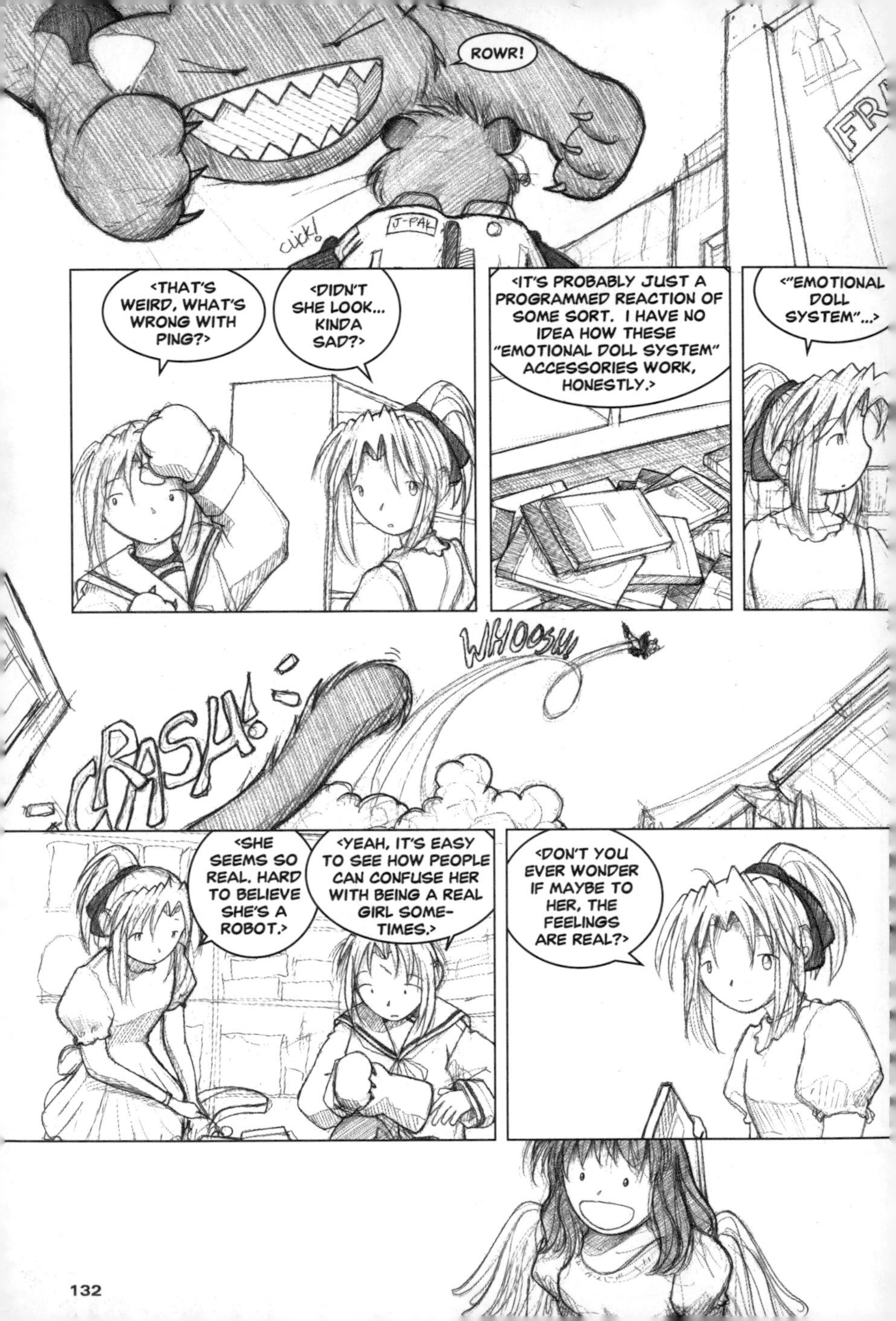
ROWR!
click!
J-PAK
<THAT'S WEIRD, WHAT'S WRONG WITH PING?>
<DIDN'T SHE LOOK... KINDA SAD?>
<IT'S PROBABLY JUST A PROGRAMMED REACTION OF SOME SORT. I HAVE NO IDEA HOW THESE "EMOTIONAL DOLL SYSTEM" ACCESSORIES WORK, HONESTLY.>
<"EMOTIONAL DOLL SYSTEM"...>
CRASH!
WHOOSH!
<SHE SEEMS SO REAL. HARD TO BELIEVE SHE'S A ROBOT.>
<YEAH, IT'S EASY TO SEE HOW PEOPLE CAN CONFUSE HER WITH BEING A REAL GIRL SOMETIMES.>
<DON'T YOU EVER WONDER IF MAYBE TO HER, THE FEELINGS ARE REAL?>

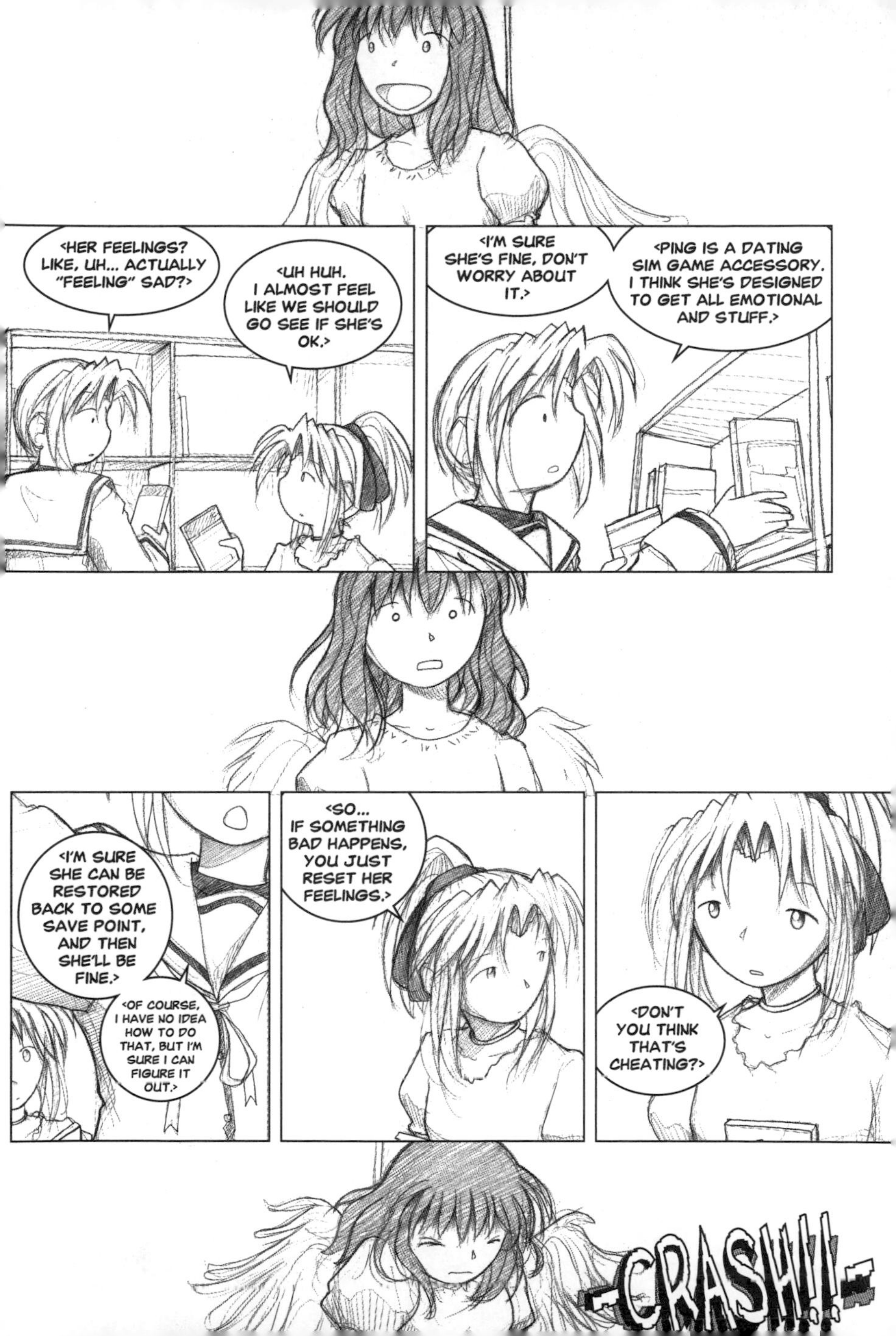
<HER FEELINGS? LIKE, UH... ACTUALLY "FEELING" SAD?>
<UH HUH. I ALMOST FEEL LIKE WE SHOULD GO SEE IF SHE'S OK.>
<I'M SURE SHE'S FINE, DON'T WORRY ABOUT IT.>
<PING IS A DATING SIM GAME ACCESSORY. I THINK SHE'S DESIGNED TO GET ALL EMOTIONAL AND STUFF.>
<I'M SURE SHE CAN BE RESTORED BACK TO SOME SAVE POINT, AND THEN SHE'LL BE FINE.>
<OF COURSE, I HAVE NO IDEA HOW TO DO THAT, BUT I'M SURE I CAN FIGURE IT OUT.>
<SO... IF SOMETHING BAD HAPPENS, YOU JUST RESET HER FEELINGS.>
<DON'T YOU THINK THAT'S CHEATING?>
-CRASH!!-

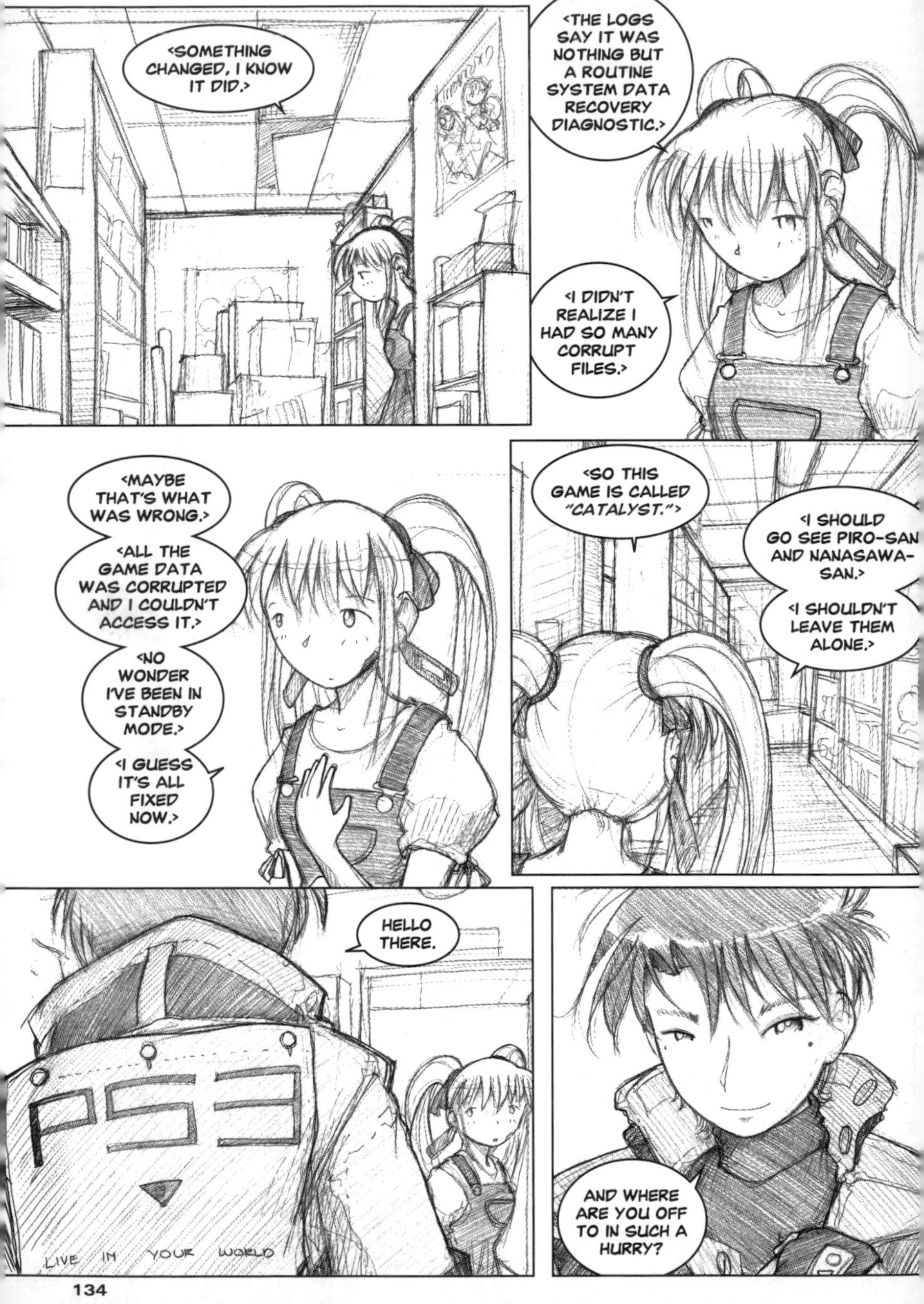
<SOMETHING CHANGED, I KNOW IT DID.>
<THE LOGS SAY IT WAS NOTHING BUT A ROUTINE SYSTEM DATA RECOVERY DIAGNOSTIC.>
<I DIDN'T REALIZE I HAD SO MANY CORRUPT FILES.>
<MAYBE THAT'S WHAT WAS WRONG.>
<ALL THE GAME DATA WAS CORRUPTED AND I COULDN'T ACCESS IT.>
<NO WONDER I'VE BEEN IN STANDBY MODE.>
<I GUESS IT'S ALL FIXED NOW.>
<SO THIS GAME IS CALLED *"CATALYST."*>
<I SHOULD GO SEE PIRO-SAN AND NANASAWA-SAN.>
<I SHOULDN'T LEAVE THEM ALONE.>
HELLO THERE.
LIVE IN YOUR WORLD
AND WHERE ARE YOU OFF TO IN SUCH A HURRY?

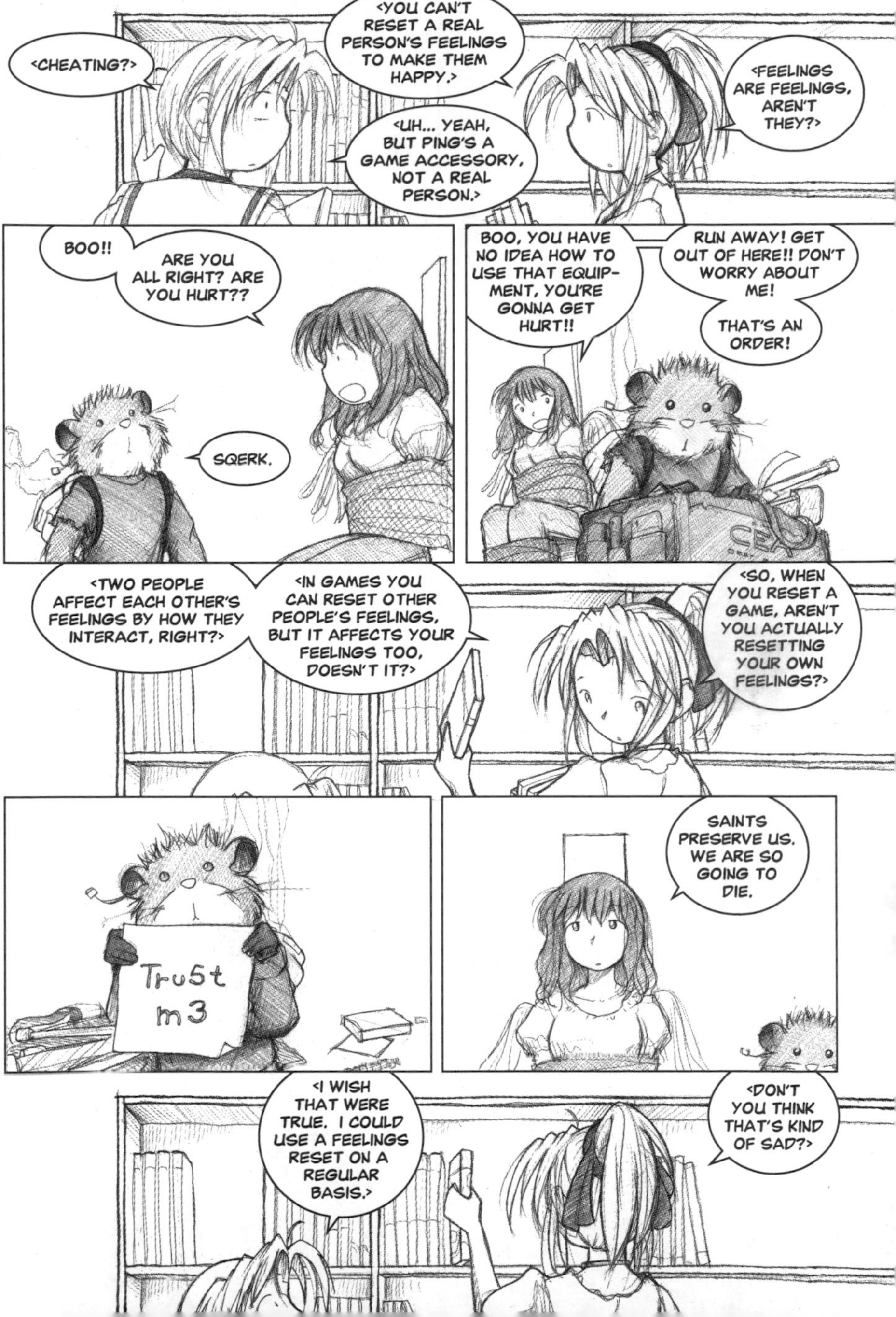

<CHEATING?>
<YOU CAN'T RESET A REAL PERSON'S FEELINGS TO MAKE THEM HAPPY.>
<UH... YEAH, BUT PING'S A GAME ACCESSORY, NOT A REAL PERSON.>
<FEELINGS ARE FEELINGS, AREN'T THEY?>
BOO!!
ARE YOU ALL RIGHT? ARE YOU HURT??
SQERK.
BOO, YOU HAVE NO IDEA HOW TO USE THAT EQUIP-MENT, YOU'RE GONNA GET HURT!!
RUN AWAY! GET OUT OF HERE!! DON'T WORRY ABOUT ME!
THAT'S AN ORDER!
<TWO PEOPLE AFFECT EACH OTHER'S FEELINGS BY HOW THEY INTERACT, RIGHT?>
<IN GAMES YOU CAN RESET OTHER PEOPLE'S FEELINGS, BUT IT AFFECTS YOUR FEELINGS TOO, DOESN'T IT?>
<SO, WHEN YOU RESET A GAME, AREN'T YOU ACTUALLY RESETTING YOUR OWN FEELINGS?>
Tru5t m3
SAINTS PRESERVE US. WE ARE SO GOING TO DIE.
<I WISH THAT WERE TRUE. I COULD USE A FEELINGS RESET ON A REGULAR BASIS.>
<DON'T YOU THINK THAT'S KIND OF SAD?>

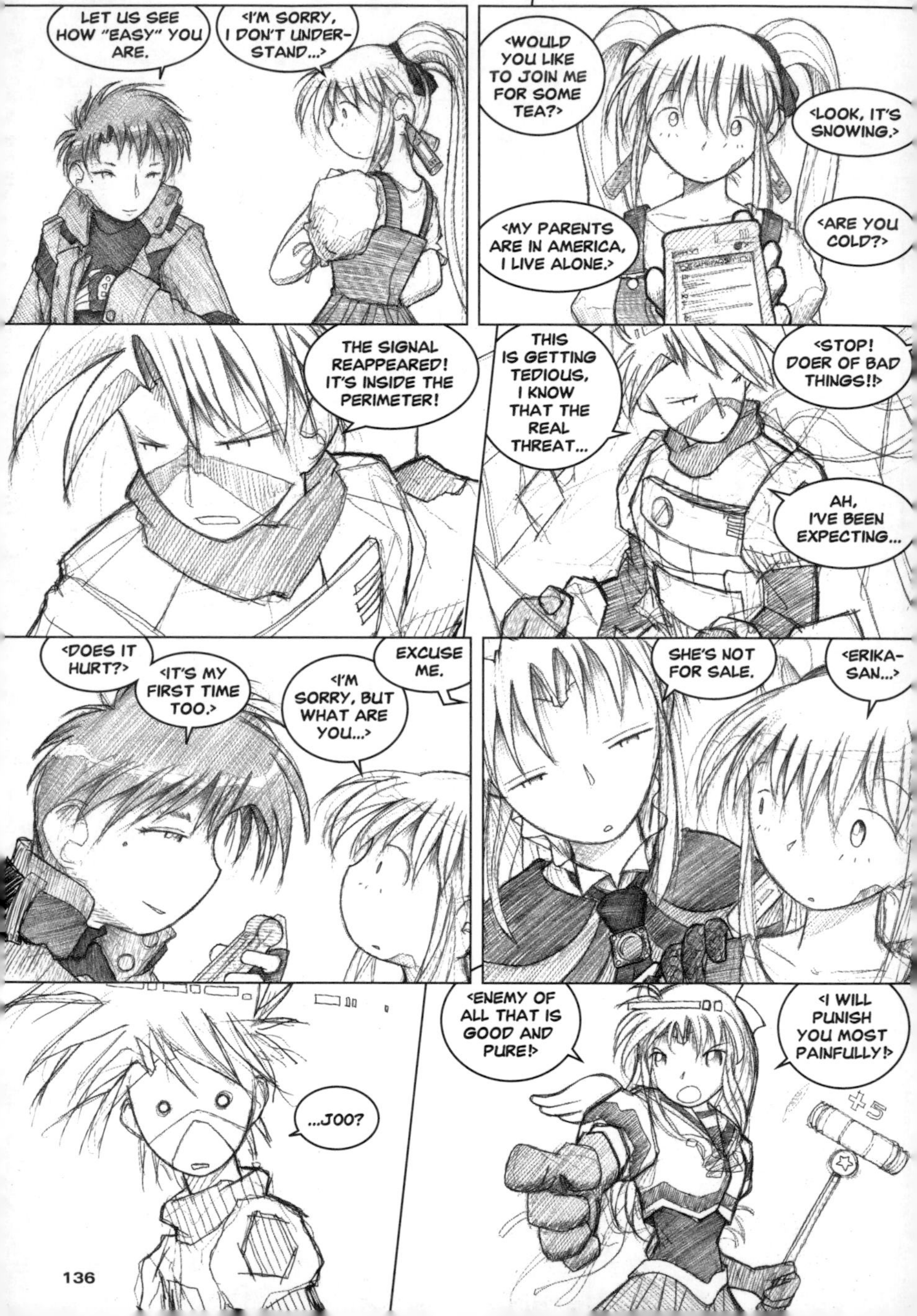

LET US SEE HOW "EASY" YOU ARE.
<I'M SORRY, I DON'T UNDER-STAND...>
<WOULD YOU LIKE TO JOIN ME FOR SOME TEA?>
<LOOK, IT'S SNOWING.>
<MY PARENTS ARE IN AMERICA, I LIVE ALONE.>
<ARE YOU COLD?>
THE SIGNAL REAPPEARED! IT'S INSIDE THE PERIMETER!
THIS IS GETTING TEDIOUS, I KNOW THAT THE REAL THREAT...
<STOP! DOER OF BAD THINGS!!>
AH, I'VE BEEN EXPECTING...
<DOES IT HURT?>
<IT'S MY FIRST TIME TOO.>
EXCUSE ME.
<I'M SORRY, BUT WHAT ARE YOU...>
SHE'S NOT FOR SALE.
<ERIKA-SAN...>
...JOO?
<ENEMY OF ALL THAT IS GOOD AND PURE!>
<I WILL PUNISH YOU MOST PAINFULLY!>
+5

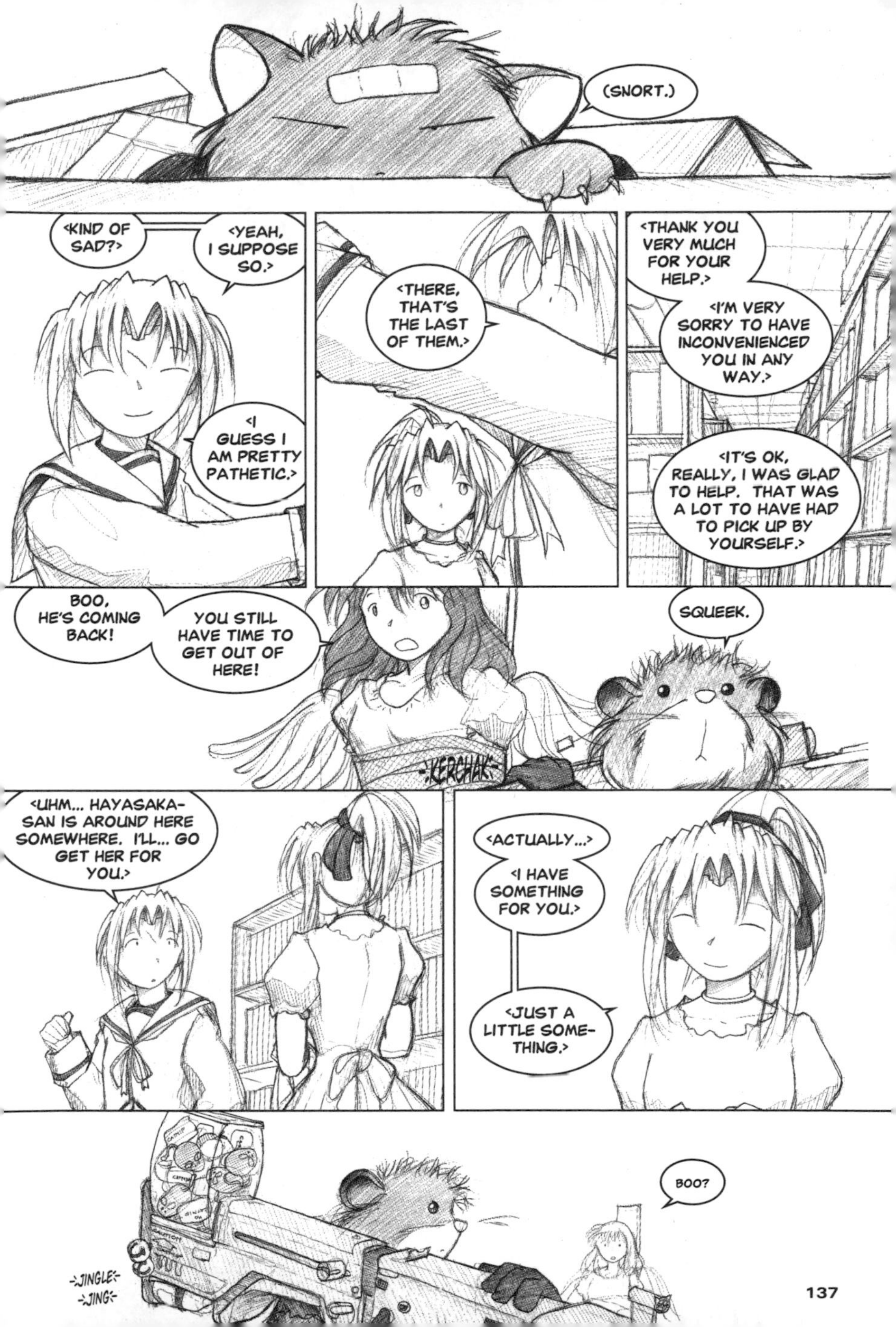
(SNORT.)
<KIND OF SAD?>
<YEAH, I SUPPOSE SO.>
<I GUESS I AM PRETTY PATHETIC.>
<THERE, THAT'S THE LAST OF THEM.>
<THANK YOU VERY MUCH FOR YOUR HELP.>
<I'M VERY SORRY TO HAVE INCONVENIENCED YOU IN ANY WAY.>
<IT'S OK, REALLY, I WAS GLAD TO HELP. THAT WAS A LOT TO HAVE HAD TO PICK UP BY YOURSELF.>
BOO, HE'S COMING BACK!
YOU STILL HAVE TIME TO GET OUT OF HERE!
KERCHAK
SQUEEK.
<UHM... HAYASAKA-SAN IS AROUND HERE SOMEWHERE. I'LL... GO GET HER FOR YOU.>
<ACTUALLY...>
<I HAVE SOMETHING FOR YOU.>
<JUST A LITTLE SOME-THING.>
BOO?
JINGLE
JING

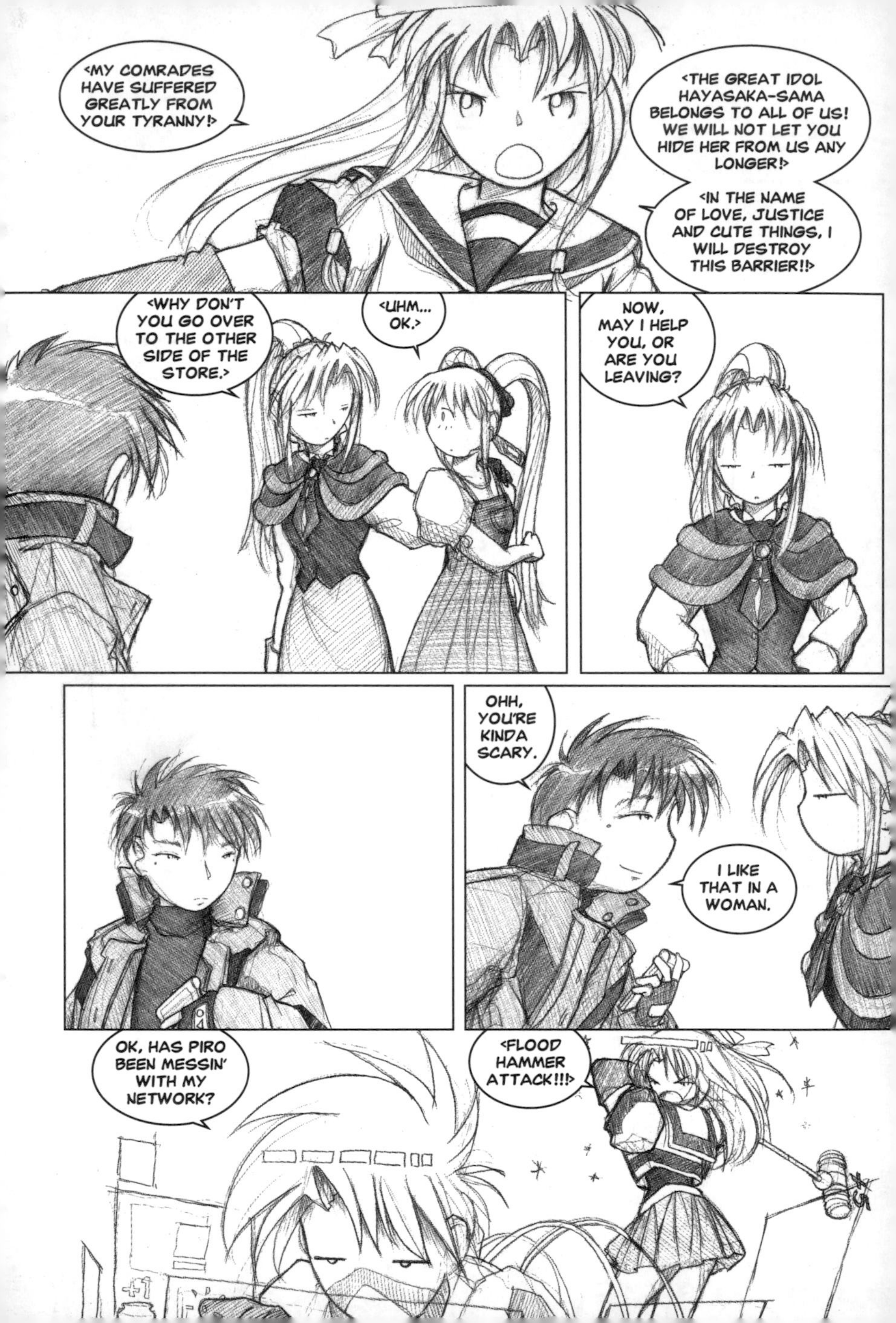

<MY COMRADES HAVE SUFFERED GREATLY FROM YOUR TYRANNY!>
<THE GREAT IDOL HAYASAKA-SAMA BELONGS TO ALL OF US! WE WILL NOT LET YOU HIDE HER FROM US ANY LONGER!>
<IN THE NAME OF LOVE, JUSTICE AND CUTE THINGS, I WILL DESTROY THIS BARRIER!!>
<WHY DON'T YOU GO OVER TO THE OTHER SIDE OF THE STORE.>
<UHM... OK.>
NOW, MAY I HELP YOU, OR ARE YOU LEAVING?
OHH, YOU'RE KINDA SCARY.
I LIKE THAT IN A WOMAN.
OK, HAS PIRO BEEN MESSIN' WITH MY NETWORK?
<FLOOD HAMMER ATTACK!!!>

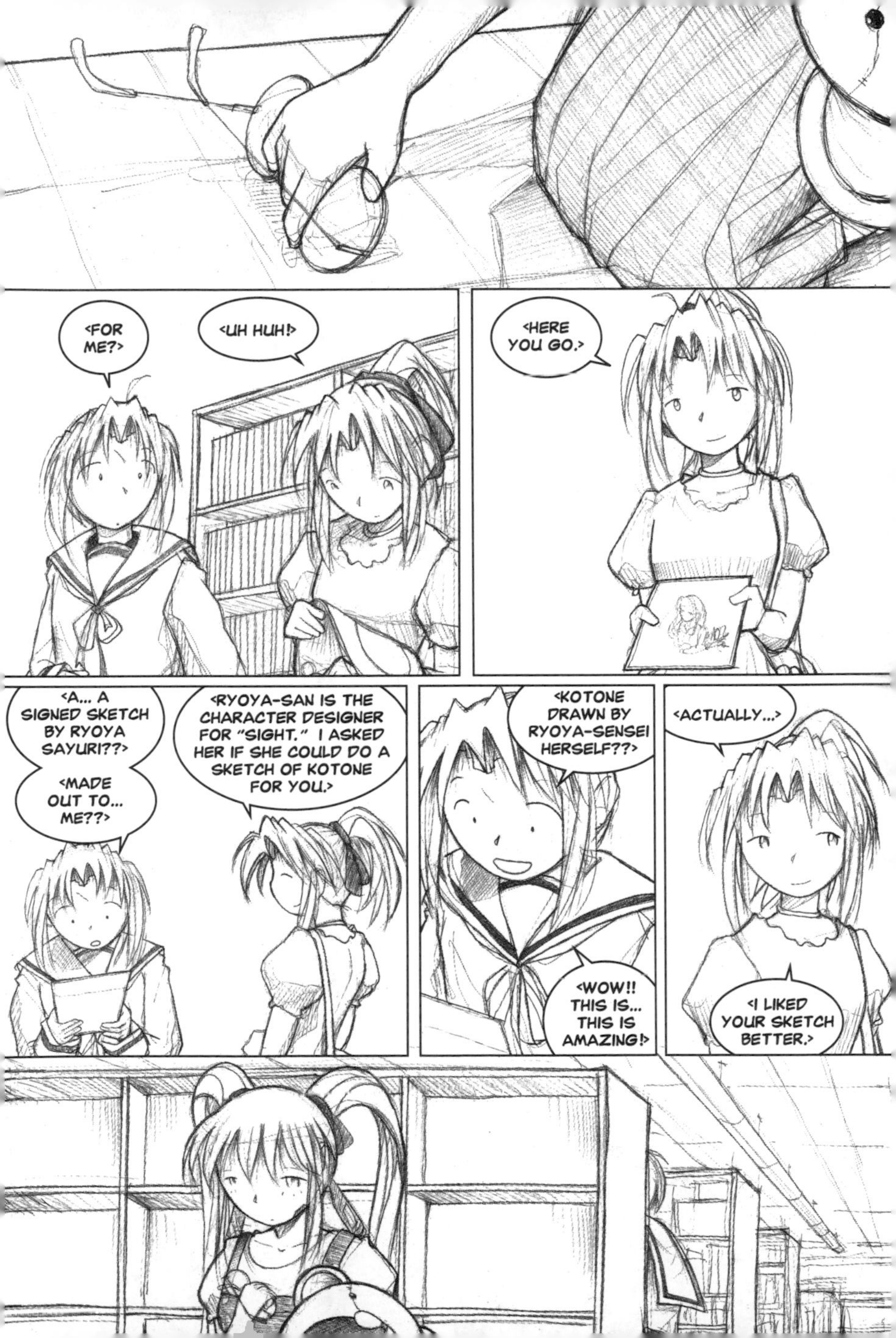

<FOR ME?>
<UH HUH!>
<HERE YOU GO.>
<A... A SIGNED SKETCH BY RYOYA SAYURI??>
<MADE OUT TO... ME??>
<RYOYA-SAN IS THE CHARACTER DESIGNER FOR "SIGHT." I ASKED HER IF SHE COULD DO A SKETCH OF KOTONE FOR YOU.>
<KOTONE DRAWN BY RYOYA-SENSEI HERSELF??>
<WOW!! THIS IS... THIS IS AMAZING!>
<ACTUALLY...>
<I LIKED YOUR SKETCH BETTER.>

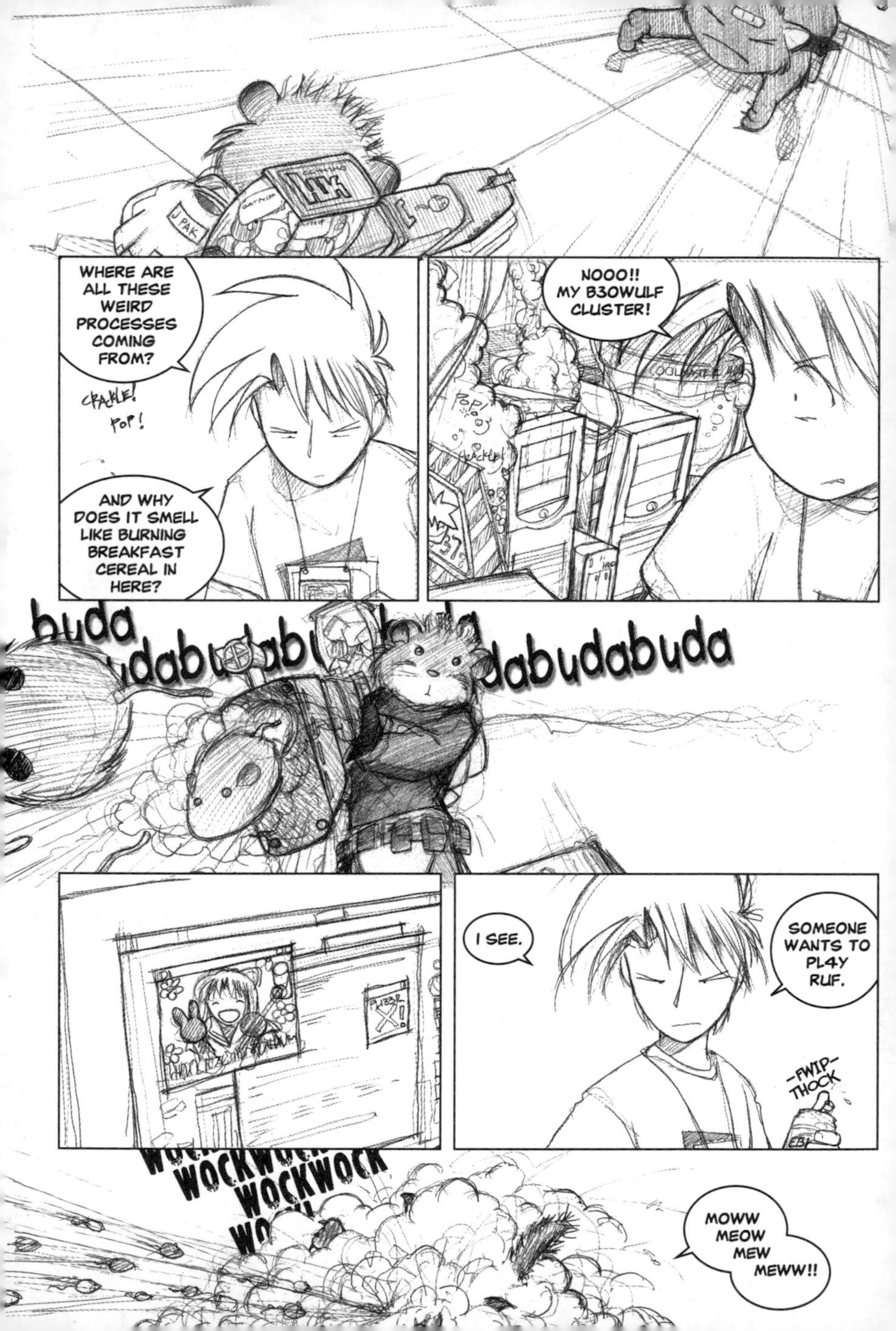
WHERE ARE ALL THESE WEIRD PROCESSES COMING FROM?
CRACKLE!
POP!
AND WHY DOES IT SMELL LIKE BURNING BREAKFAST CEREAL IN HERE?
NOOO!! MY B3OWULF CLUSTER!
POP!
CRACKLE!
buda
dabudabuda
I SEE.
SOMEONE WANTS TO PL4Y RUF.
-FWIP-
THOCK
WOCKWOCK
WOCKWOCK
MOWW MEOW MEW MEWW!!

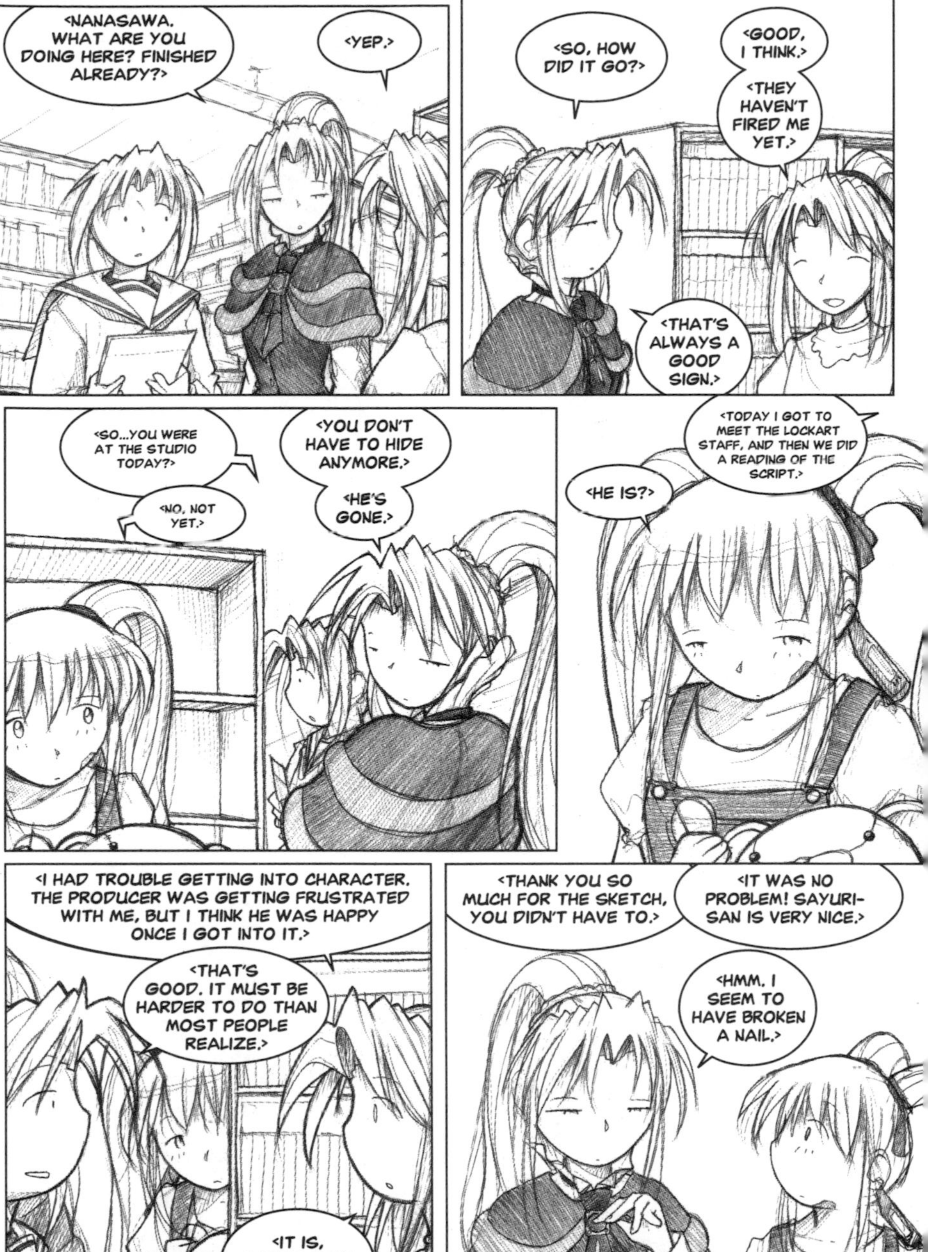
<NANASAWA. WHAT ARE YOU DOING HERE? FINISHED ALREADY?>
<YEP.>
<SO, HOW DID IT GO?>
<GOOD, I THINK.>
<THEY HAVEN'T FIRED ME YET.>
<THAT'S ALWAYS A GOOD SIGN.>
<SO...YOU WERE AT THE STUDIO TODAY?>
<NO, NOT YET.>
<YOU DON'T HAVE TO HIDE ANYMORE.>
<HE'S GONE.>
<HE IS?>
<TODAY I GOT TO MEET THE LOCKART STAFF, AND THEN WE DID A READING OF THE SCRIPT.>
<I HAD TROUBLE GETTING INTO CHARACTER. THE PRODUCER WAS GETTING FRUSTRATED WITH ME, BUT I THINK HE WAS HAPPY ONCE I GOT INTO IT.>
<THAT'S GOOD. IT MUST BE HARDER TO DO THAN MOST PEOPLE REALIZE.>
<IT IS, ACTING ISN'T EASY.>
<THANK YOU SO MUCH FOR THE SKETCH, YOU DIDN'T HAVE TO.>
<IT WAS NO PROBLEM! SAYURI-SAN IS VERY NICE.>
<HMM. I SEEM TO HAVE BROKEN A NAIL.>

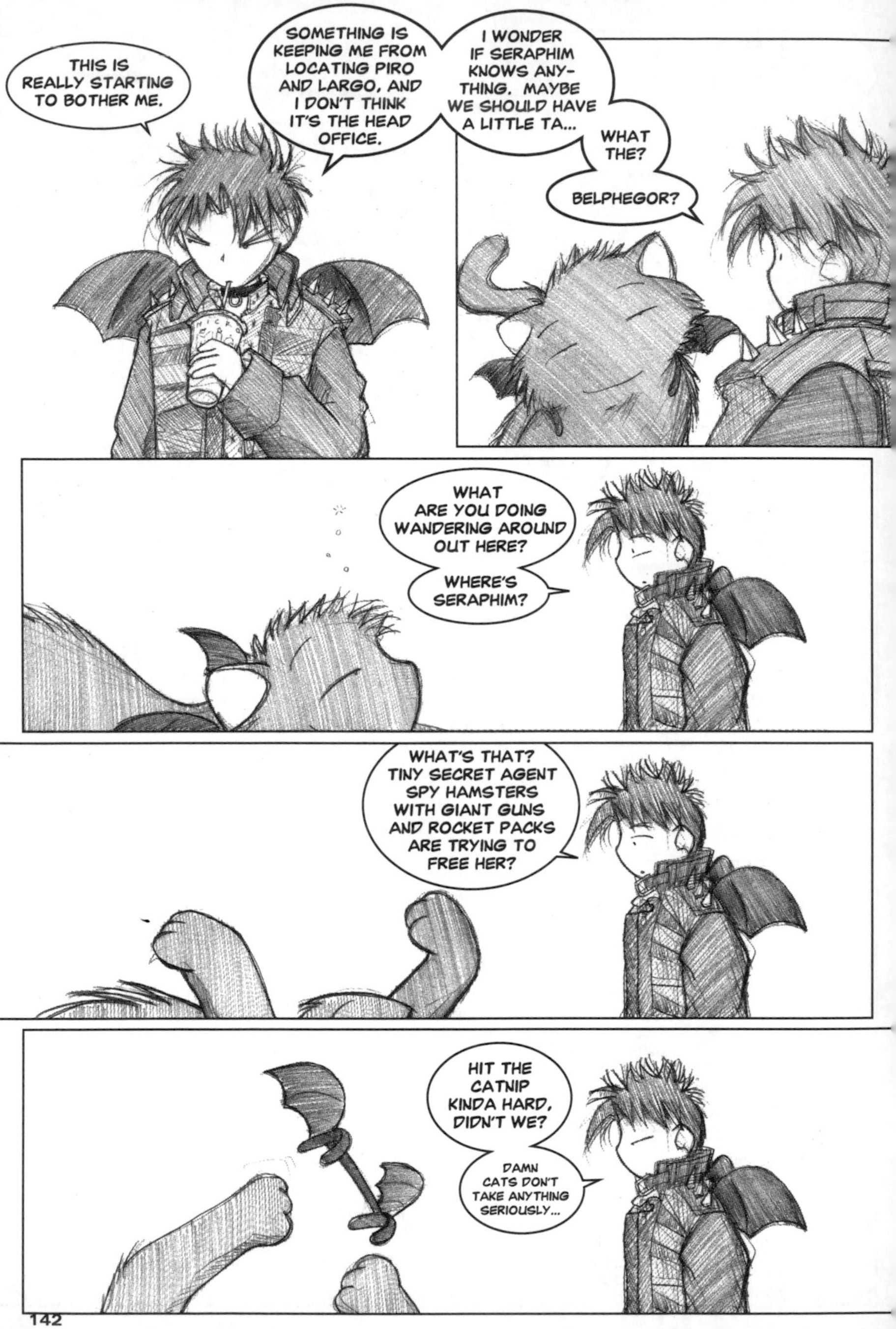

THIS IS REALLY STARTING TO BOTHER ME.
SOMETHING IS KEEPING ME FROM LOCATING PIRO AND LARGO, AND I DON'T THINK IT'S THE HEAD OFFICE.
I WONDER IF SERAPHIM KNOWS ANY-THING. MAYBE WE SHOULD HAVE A LITTLE TA...
WHAT THE?
BELPHEGOR?
WHAT ARE YOU DOING WANDERING AROUND OUT HERE?
WHERE'S SERAPHIM?
WHAT'S THAT? TINY SECRET AGENT SPY HAMSTERS WITH GIANT GUNS AND ROCKET PACKS ARE TRYING TO FREE HER?
HIT THE CATNIP KINDA HARD, DIDN'T WE?
DAMN CATS DON'T TAKE ANYTHING SERIOUSLY...

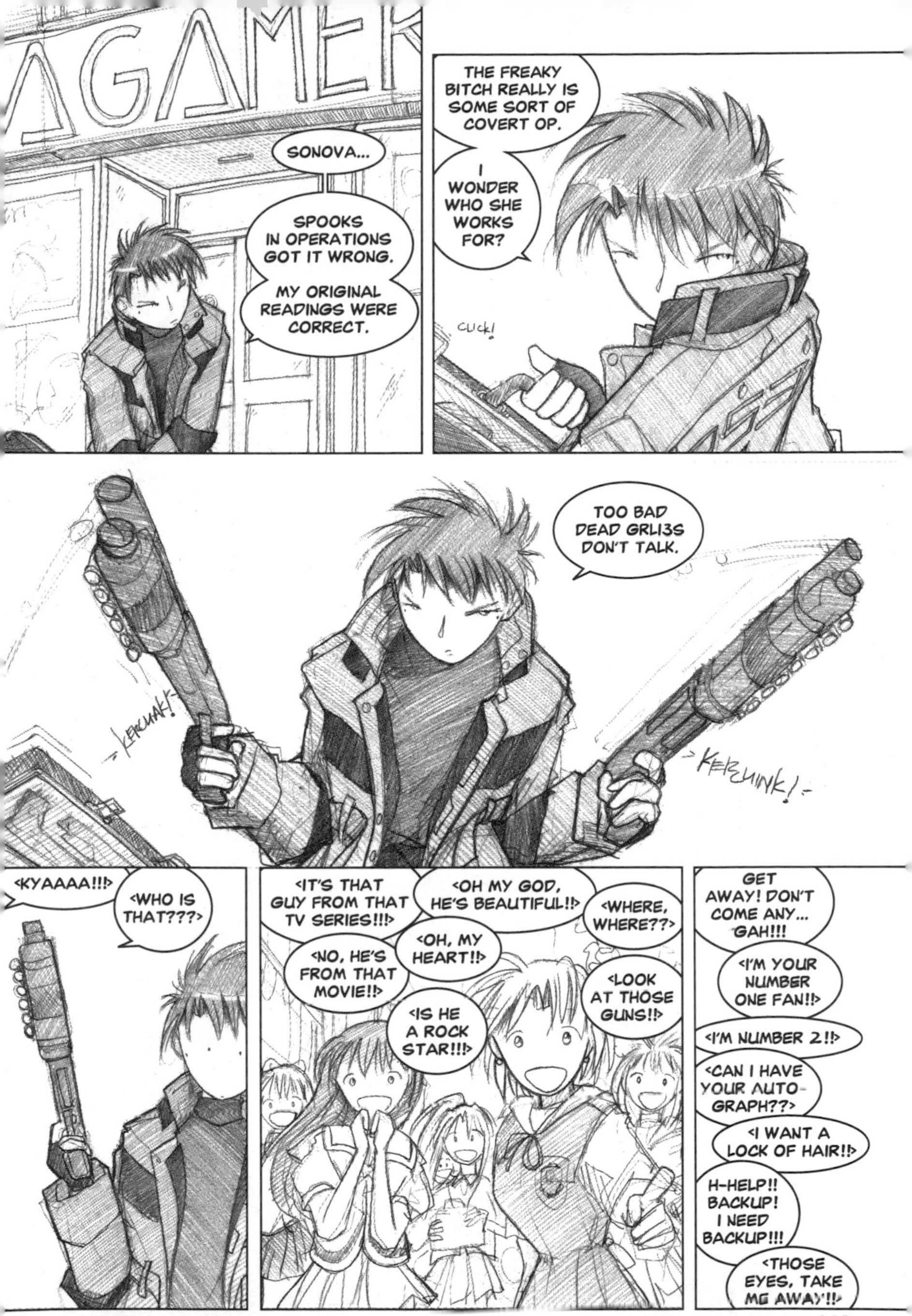
AGAMER
SONOVA...
SPOOKS IN OPERATIONS GOT IT WRONG.
MY ORIGINAL READINGS WERE CORRECT.
THE FREAKY BITCH REALLY IS SOME SORT OF COVERT OP.
I WONDER WHO SHE WORKS FOR?
CLICK!
TOO BAD DEAD GRLI3S DON'T TALK.
KERCHAK!
KERCHINK!
<KYAAAA!!!>
<WHO IS THAT???>
<IT'S THAT GUY FROM THAT TV SERIES!!!>
<OH MY GOD, HE'S BEAUTIFUL!!>
<WHERE, WHERE??>
<OH, MY HEART!!>
<NO, HE'S FROM THAT MOVIE!!>
<LOOK AT THOSE GUNS!!>
<IS HE A ROCK STAR!!!>
GET AWAY! DON'T COME ANY... GAH!!!
<I'M YOUR NUMBER ONE FAN!!>
<I'M NUMBER 2!!>
<CAN I HAVE YOUR AUTO-GRAPH??>
<I WANT A LOCK OF HAIR!!>
H-HELP!! BACKUP! I NEED BACKUP!!!
<THOSE EYES, TAKE ME AWAY!!>

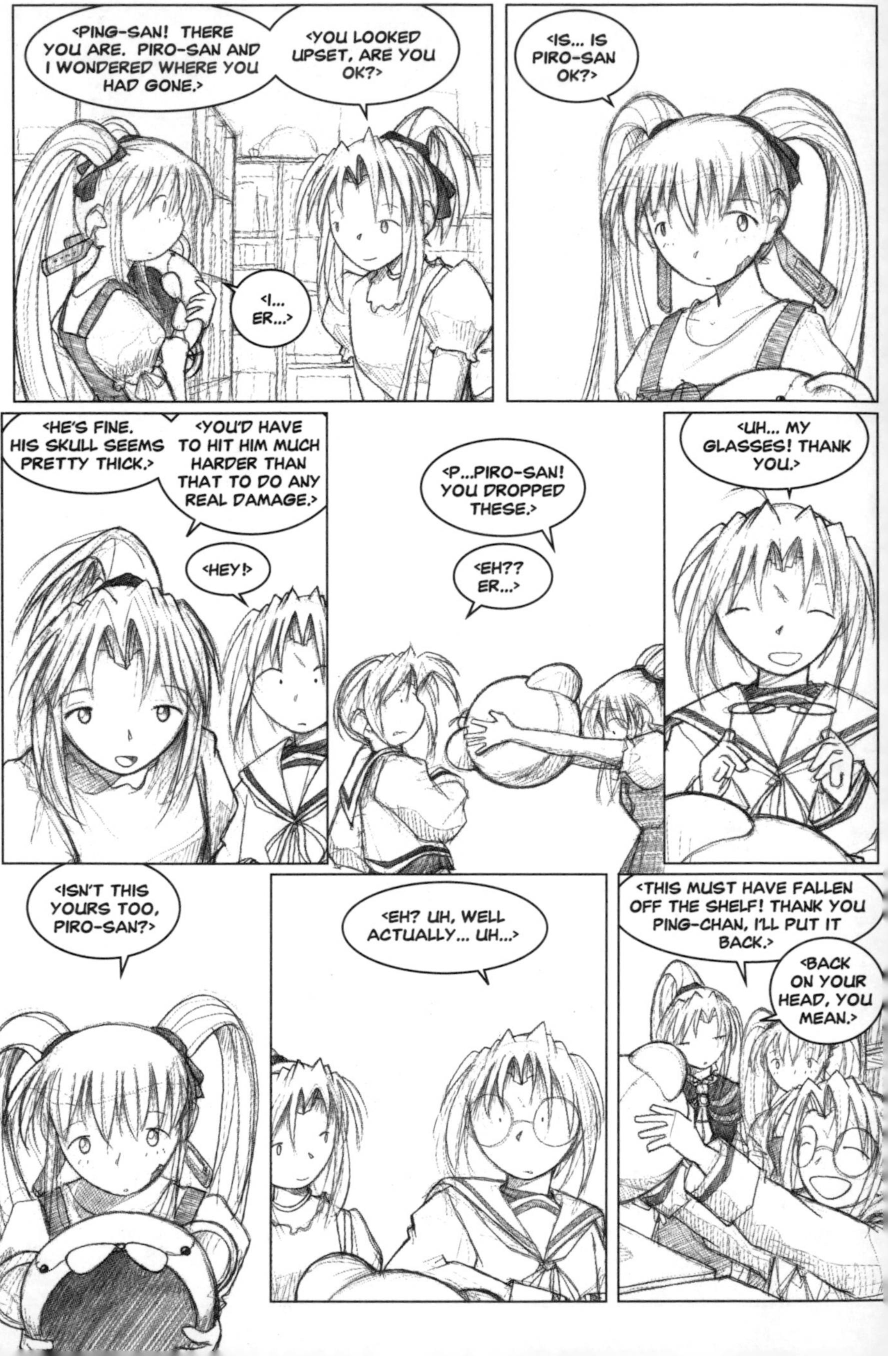
<PING-SAN! THERE YOU ARE. PIRO-SAN AND I WONDERED WHERE YOU HAD GONE.>
<YOU LOOKED UPSET, ARE YOU OK?>
<I... ER...>
<IS... IS PIRO-SAN OK?>
<HE'S FINE. HIS SKULL SEEMS PRETTY THICK.>
<YOU'D HAVE TO HIT HIM MUCH HARDER THAN THAT TO DO ANY REAL DAMAGE.>
<HEY!>
<P...PIRO-SAN! YOU DROPPED THESE.>
<EH?? ER...>
<UH... MY GLASSES! THANK YOU.>
<ISN'T THIS YOURS TOO, PIRO-SAN?>
<EH? UH, WELL ACTUALLY... UH...>
<THIS MUST HAVE FALLEN OFF THE SHELF! THANK YOU PING-CHAN, I'LL PUT IT BACK.>
<BACK ON YOUR HEAD, YOU MEAN.>

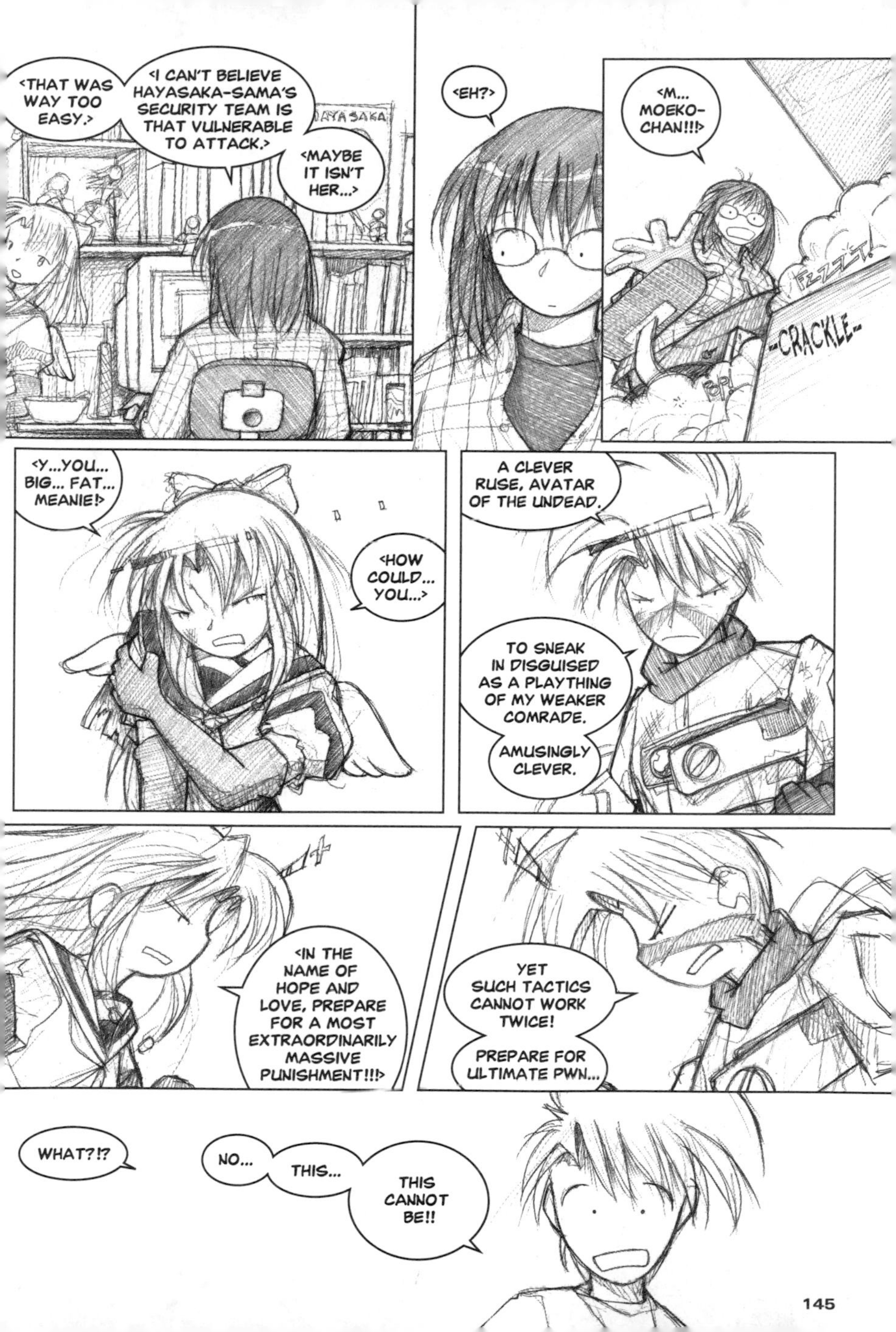
<THAT WAS WAY TOO EASY.>
<I CAN'T BELIEVE HAYASAKA-SAMA'S SECURITY TEAM IS THAT VULNERABLE TO ATTACK.>
HAYASAKA
<MAYBE IT ISN'T HER...>
<EH?>
<M... MOEKO-CHAN!!!>
FZZZT!
CRACKLE
<Y...YOU... BIG... FAT... MEANIE!>
<HOW COULD... YOU...>
A CLEVER RUSE, AVATAR OF THE UNDEAD.
TO SNEAK IN DISGUISED AS A PLAYTHING OF MY WEAKER COMRADE.
AMUSINGLY CLEVER.
<IN THE NAME OF HOPE AND LOVE, PREPARE FOR A MOST EXTRAORDINARILY MASSIVE PUNISHMENT!!!>
YET SUCH TACTICS CANNOT WORK TWICE!
PREPARE FOR ULTIMATE PWN...
WHAT?!?
NO...
THIS...
THIS CANNOT BE!!

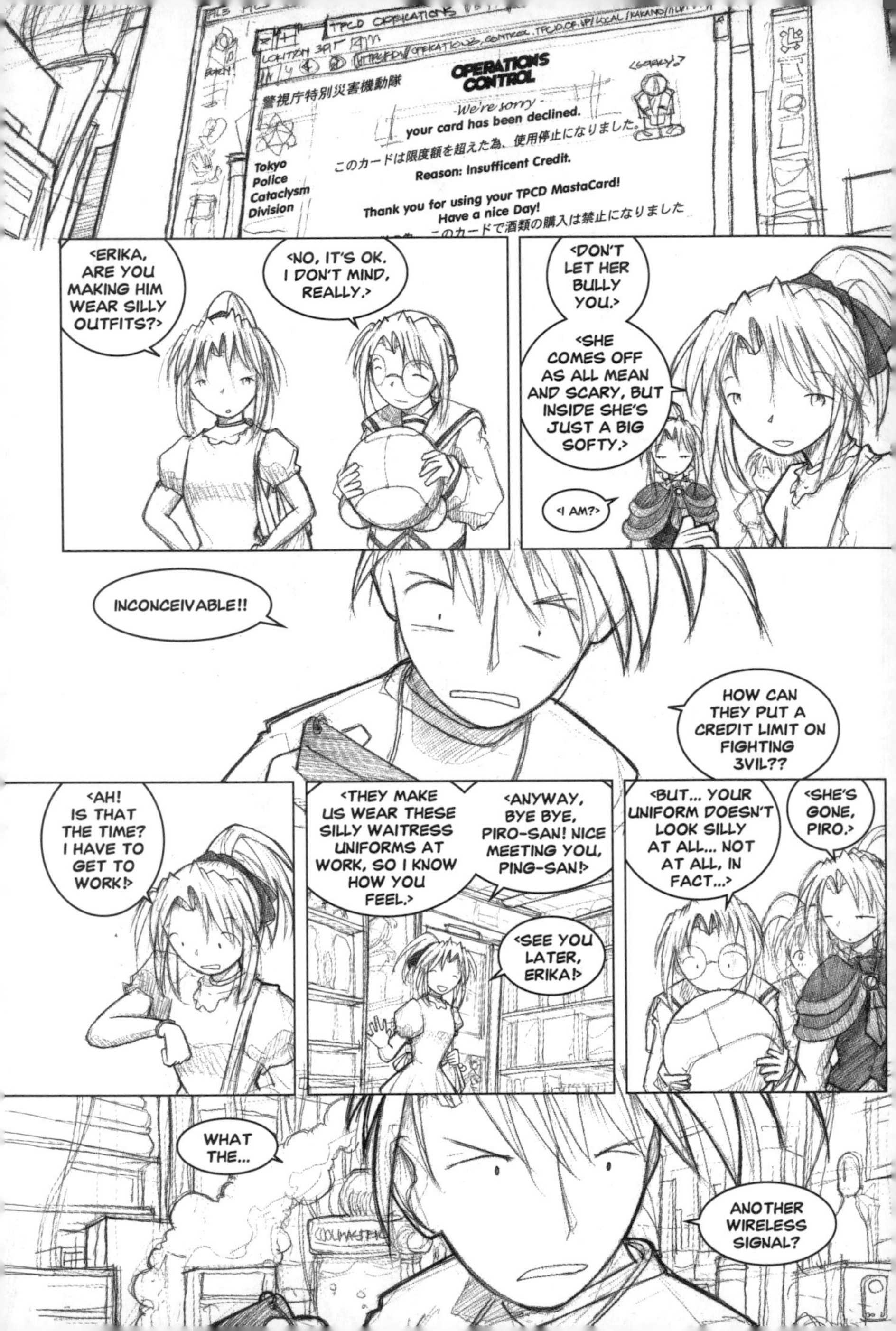
TPCD OPERATIONS
OPERATIONS CONTROL
警視庁特別災害機動隊
Tokyo Police Cataclysm Division
-We're sorry -
your card has been declined.
このカードは限度額を超えた為、使用停止になりました。
Reason: Insufficent Credit.
Thank you for using your TPCD MastaCard!
Have a nice Day!
このカードで酒類の購入は禁止になりました
<ERIKA, ARE YOU MAKING HIM WEAR SILLY OUTFITS?>
<NO, IT'S OK. I DON'T MIND, REALLY.>
<DON'T LET HER BULLY YOU.>
<SHE COMES OFF AS ALL MEAN AND SCARY, BUT INSIDE SHE'S JUST A BIG SOFTY.>
<I AM?>
INCONCEIVABLE!!
HOW CAN THEY PUT A CREDIT LIMIT ON FIGHTING 3VIL??
<AH! IS THAT THE TIME? I HAVE TO GET TO WORK!>
<THEY MAKE US WEAR THESE SILLY WAITRESS UNIFORMS AT WORK, SO I KNOW HOW YOU FEEL.>
<ANYWAY, BYE BYE, PIRO-SAN! NICE MEETING YOU, PING-SAN!>
<SEE YOU LATER, ERIKA!>
<BUT... YOUR UNIFORM DOESN'T LOOK SILLY AT ALL... NOT AT ALL, IN FACT...>
<SHE'S GONE, PIRO.>
WHAT THE...
ANOTHER WIRELESS SIGNAL?

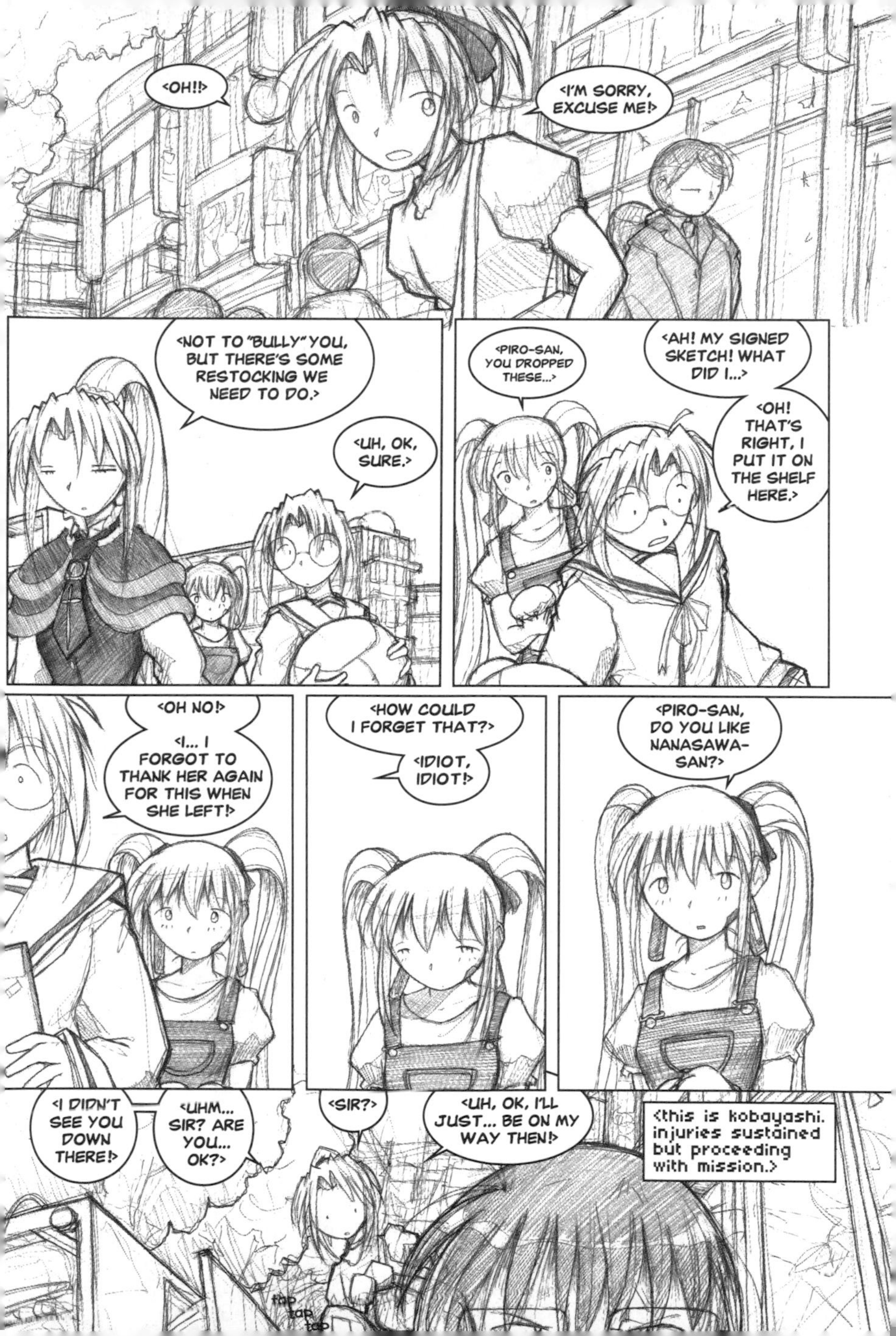
<OH!!>
<I'M SORRY, EXCUSE ME!>
<NOT TO "BULLY" YOU, BUT THERE'S SOME RESTOCKING WE NEED TO DO.>
<UH, OK, SURE.>
<PIRO-SAN, YOU DROPPED THESE...>
<AH! MY SIGNED SKETCH! WHAT DID I...>
<OH! THAT'S RIGHT, I PUT IT ON THE SHELF HERE.>
<OH NO!>
<I... I FORGOT TO THANK HER AGAIN FOR THIS WHEN SHE LEFT!>
<HOW COULD I FORGET THAT?>
<IDIOT, IDIOT!>
<PIRO-SAN, DO YOU LIKE NANASAWA-SAN?>
<I DIDN'T SEE YOU DOWN THERE!>
<UHM... SIR? ARE YOU... OK?>
<SIR?>
<UH, OK, I'LL JUST... BE ON MY WAY THEN!>
<this is kobayashi. injuries sustained but proceeding with mission.>
tap tap tap

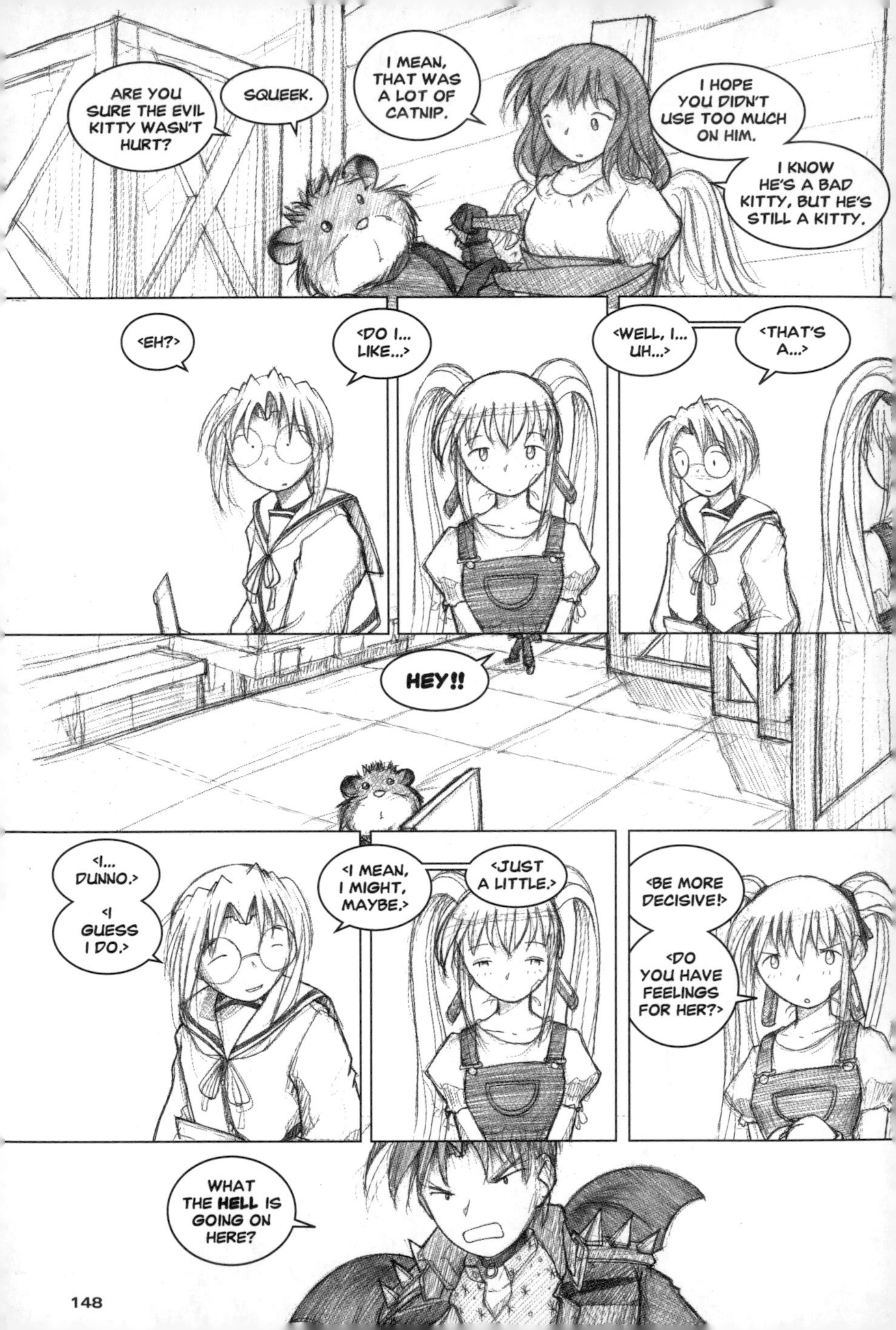
ARE YOU SURE THE EVIL KITTY WASN'T HURT?
SQUEEK.
I MEAN, THAT WAS A LOT OF CATNIP.
I HOPE YOU DIDN'T USE TOO MUCH ON HIM.
I KNOW HE'S A BAD KITTY, BUT HE'S STILL A KITTY.
<EH?>
<DO I... LIKE...>
<WELL, I... UH...>
<THAT'S A...>
HEY!!
<I... DUNNO.>
<I GUESS I DO.>
<I MEAN, I MIGHT, MAYBE.>
<JUST A LITTLE.>
<BE MORE DECISIVE!>
<DO YOU HAVE FEELINGS FOR HER?>
WHAT THE **HELL** IS GOING ON HERE?

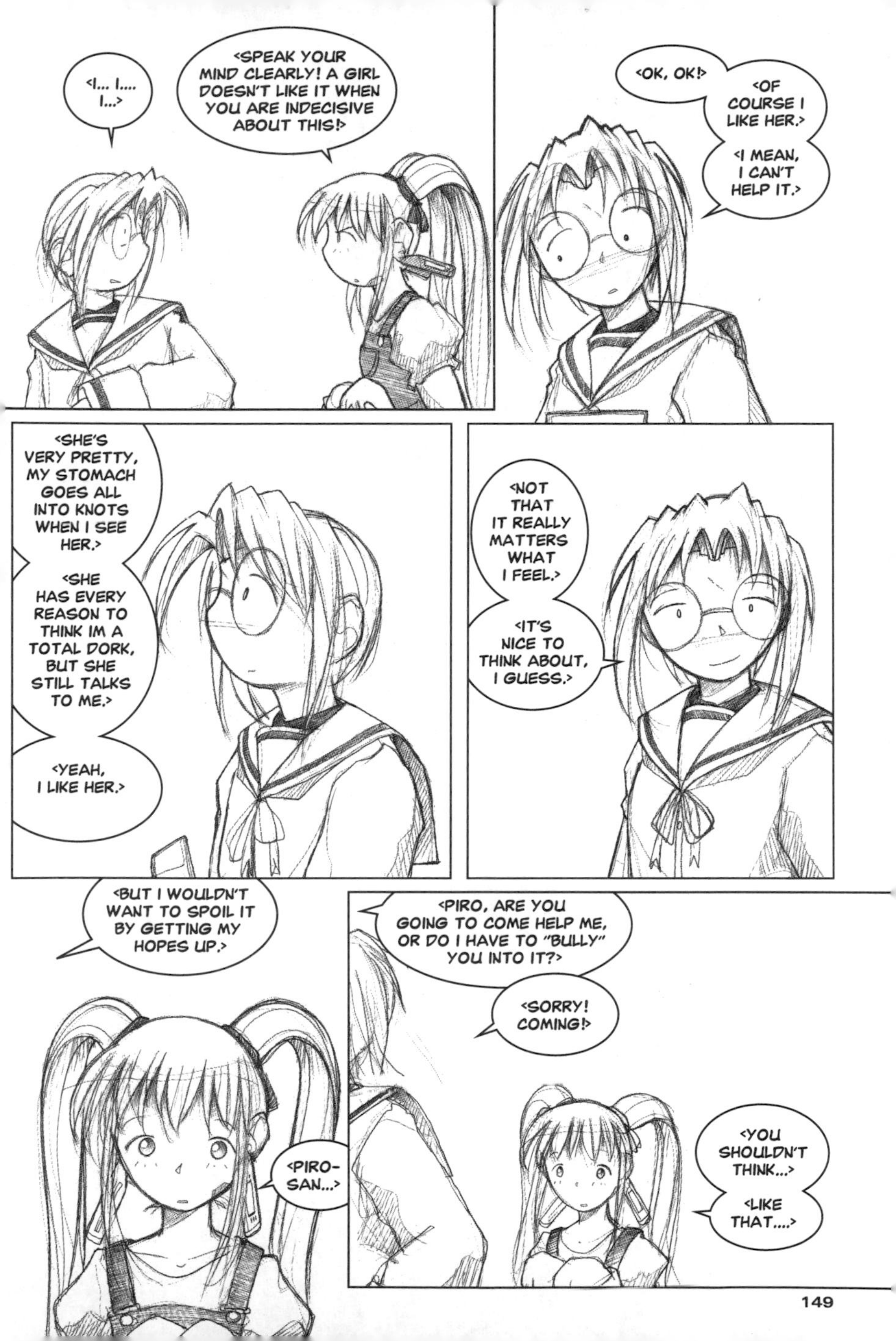
<I... I.... I...>
<SPEAK YOUR MIND CLEARLY! A GIRL DOESN'T LIKE IT WHEN YOU ARE INDECISIVE ABOUT THIS!>
<OK, OK!>
<OF COURSE I LIKE HER.>
<I MEAN, I CAN'T HELP IT.>
<SHE'S VERY PRETTY, MY STOMACH GOES ALL INTO KNOTS WHEN I SEE HER.>
<SHE HAS EVERY REASON TO THINK IM A TOTAL DORK, BUT SHE STILL TALKS TO ME.>
<YEAH, I LIKE HER.>
<NOT THAT IT REALLY MATTERS WHAT I FEEL.>
<IT'S NICE TO THINK ABOUT, I GUESS.>
<BUT I WOULDN'T WANT TO SPOIL IT BY GETTING MY HOPES UP.>
<PIRO-SAN...>
<PIRO, ARE YOU GOING TO COME HELP ME, OR DO I HAVE TO "BULLY" YOU INTO IT?>
<SORRY! COMING!>
<YOU SHOULDN'T THINK...>
<LIKE THAT....>

150

<NOW APPROACHING MAIN ENTRY OF "MEGAGAMERS" STORE. DOORS APPEAR TO BE AUTOMATIC.>

<I AM WORKING WITH LIMITED RESOURCES, BUT WILL ATTEMPT TO CAPTURE VISUAL OF HAYASAKA-SAMA.>

<YOU SORT AND PUT PRICE TAGS ON THEM. I'LL PUT THEM ON THE SHELVES.>

<OK.>

UGH, THESE AREN'T IN ANY KIND OF ORDER...

<PIRO-SAN... IS THERE ANYTHING I CAN DO TO HELP?>

<NAH, I GOT IT.>

<Y'KNOW YOU DON'T ALWAYS HAVE TO BE HELPING, PING-CHAN.>

<JUST RELAX A LITTLE, OK?>

<SO, PING, DID YOU EVER CHECK TO SEE WHAT TOHYA-SAN GOT YOU-->

<OH! NO, I HAVEN'T! NOT YET!>

<PIRO? ARE YOU HELPING ME OR NOT?>

<SORRY!>

<DOORS OPENED UPON APPROACH.>

<VISUAL OF STORE INTERIOR ESTABLISHED.>

<PROCEEDING TO ENTER STORE.>

<WILL CONTINUE LIVE VIDEO FEED AS LONG AS POSSIBLE.>

<FEMALE BEHIND COUNTER CUTE BUT NOT HAYASAKA-SAMA.>

<NOW LOOKING TO THE RIGHT.>

<WAIT! SEXY FIGURE AHEAD! STYLISH SKIRT, COMBAT BOOTS, TALL FEMALE.>

<COULD THIS BE HAYASAKA-SAMA???>

<MY HEART IS BEATING FAST. NOW MOVING CLOSER TO VERIFY...>

<SORRY ABOUT THAT.>

<THAT'S OK, PIRO-SAN.>

<SO... SHOULD I OPEN MIHO-CHAN'S PRESENT?>

<SURE, GO FOR IT.>

<WAI!>

<IT'S... IT'S A CELL PHONE!>

<AND A DATA CABLE!>

<WOW. THAT'S A REALLY NICE ONE TOO.>

<IT'S EVEN THE RIGHT KIND OF CABLE! I CAN USE THIS TO GET ONLINE!>

<I WON'T HAVE TO TRY TO USE LARGO-SAN'S SUPER SCARY NETWORK ANY MORE!>

<I HAVE TO ADMIT, THAT'S PROBABLY THE BEST GIFT YOU CAN GIVE A COMPUTER.>

<MIHO-CHAN IS THE BEST FRIEND EVER!>

6264?

<!!!>

153

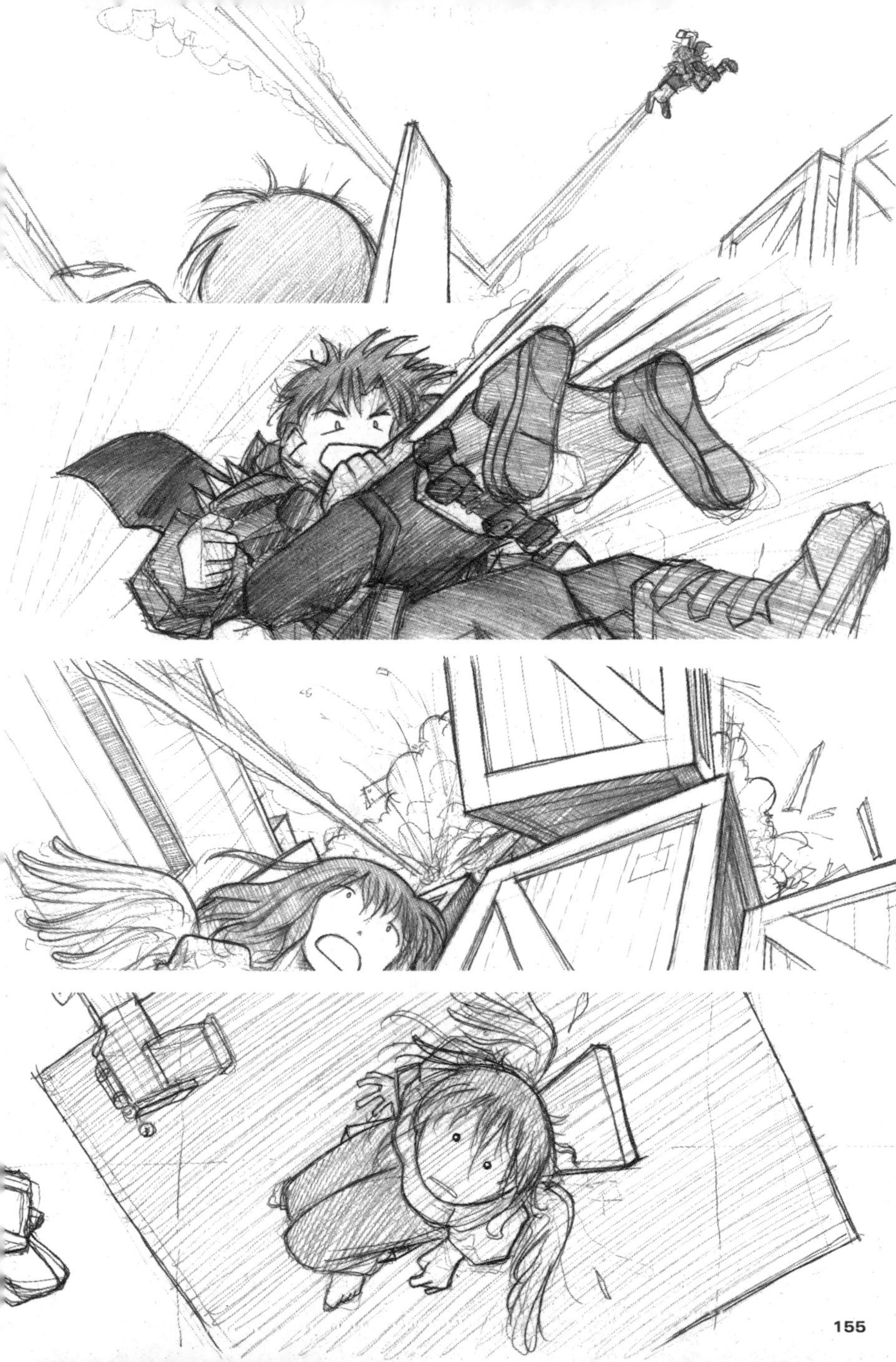

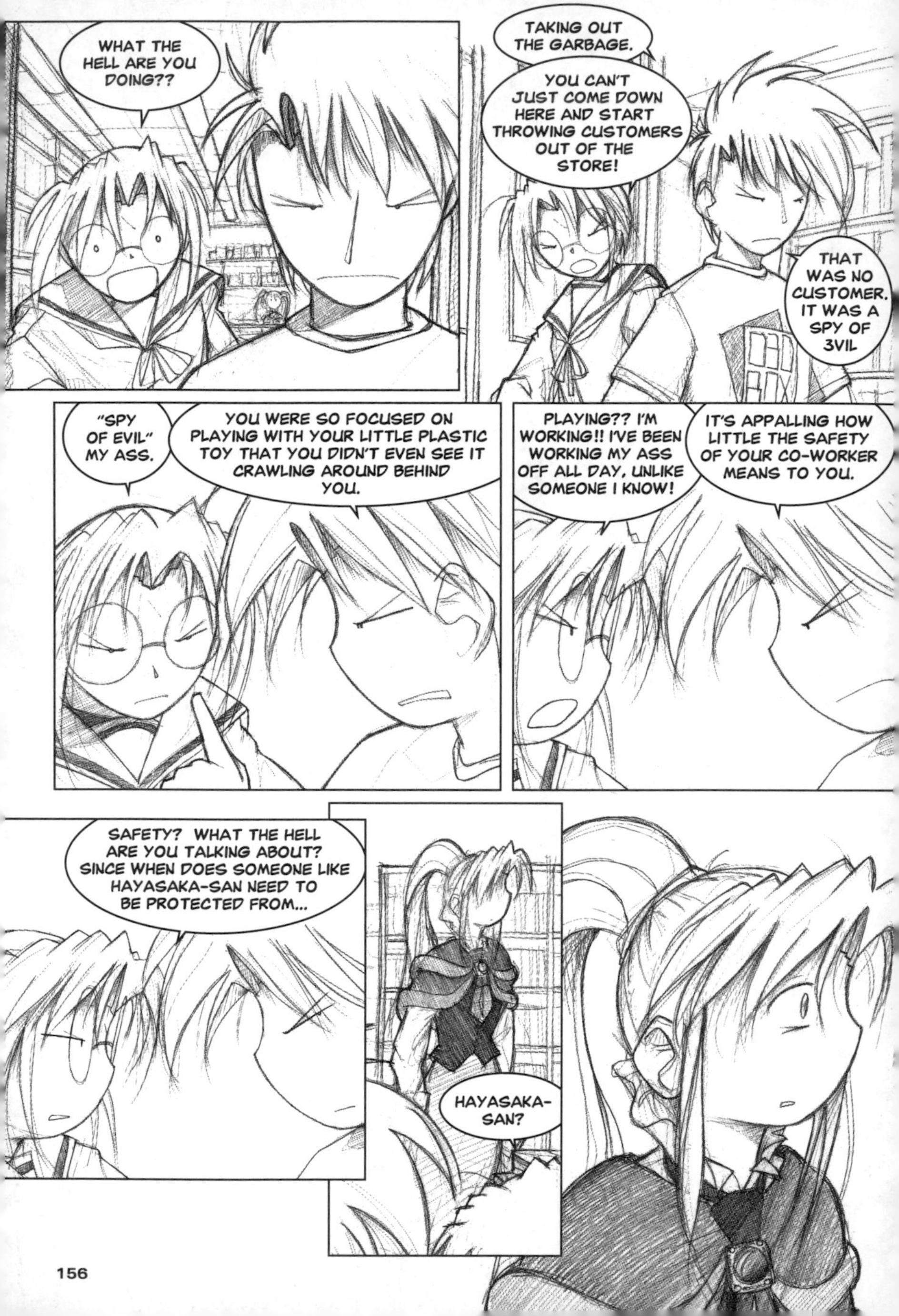
WHAT THE HELL ARE YOU DOING??
TAKING OUT THE GARBAGE.
YOU CAN'T JUST COME DOWN HERE AND START THROWING CUSTOMERS OUT OF THE STORE!
THAT WAS NO CUSTOMER. IT WAS A SPY OF 3VIL
"SPY OF EVIL" MY ASS.
YOU WERE SO FOCUSED ON PLAYING WITH YOUR LITTLE PLASTIC TOY THAT YOU DIDN'T EVEN SEE IT CRAWLING AROUND BEHIND YOU.
PLAYING?? I'M WORKING!! I'VE BEEN WORKING MY ASS OFF ALL DAY, UNLIKE SOMEONE I KNOW!
IT'S APPALLING HOW LITTLE THE SAFETY OF YOUR CO-WORKER MEANS TO YOU.
SAFETY? WHAT THE HELL ARE YOU TALKING ABOUT? SINCE WHEN DOES SOMEONE LIKE HAYASAKA-SAN NEED TO BE PROTECTED FROM...
HAYASAKA-SAN?

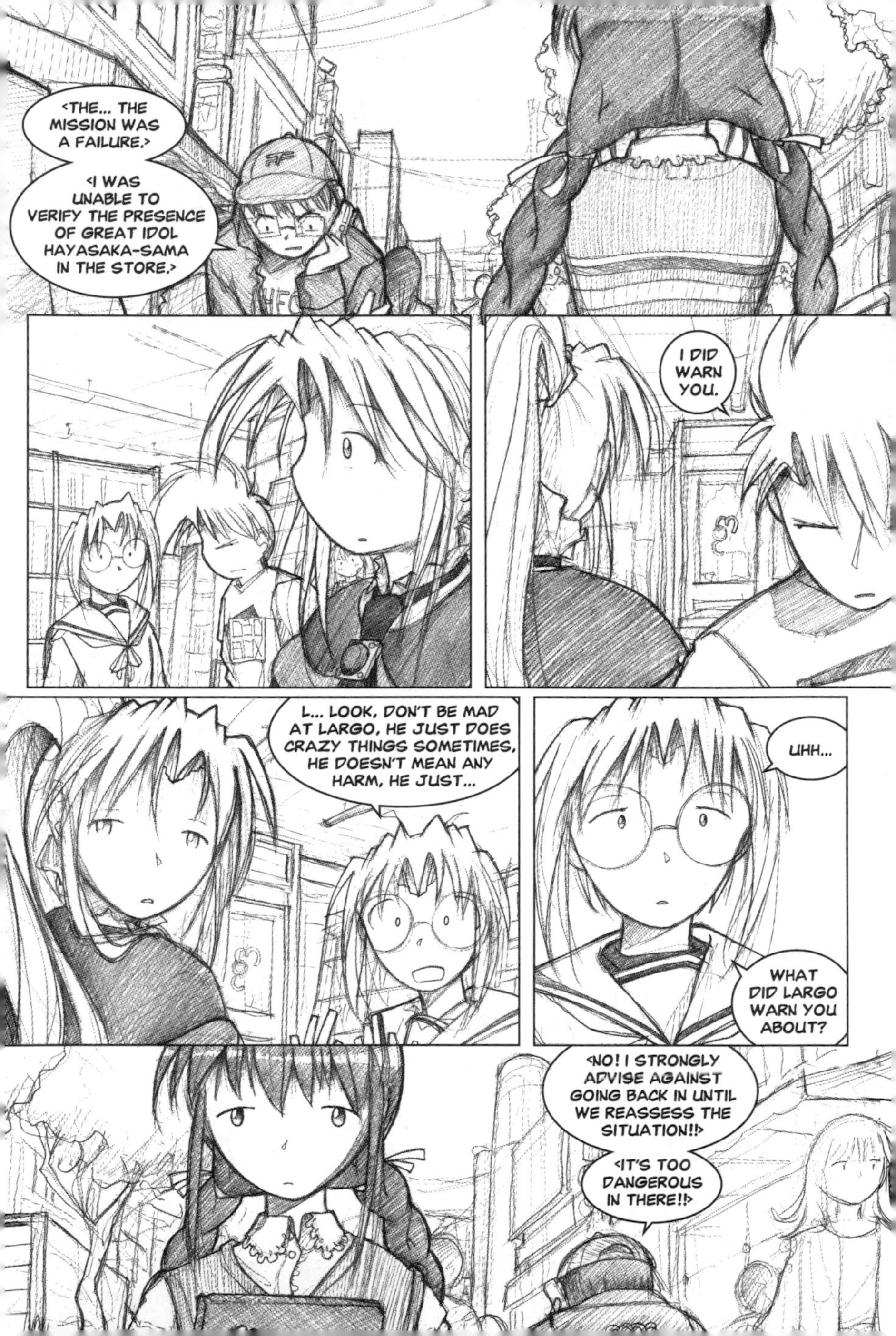

<THE... THE MISSION WAS A FAILURE.>
<I WAS UNABLE TO VERIFY THE PRESENCE OF GREAT IDOL HAYASAKA-SAMA IN THE STORE.>
I DID WARN YOU.
L... LOOK, DON'T BE MAD AT LARGO, HE JUST DOES CRAZY THINGS SOMETIMES, HE DOESN'T MEAN ANY HARM, HE JUST...
UHH...
WHAT DID LARGO WARN YOU ABOUT?
<NO! I STRONGLY ADVISE AGAINST GOING BACK IN UNTIL WE REASSESS THE SITUATION!!>
<IT'S TOO DANGEROUS IN THERE!!>

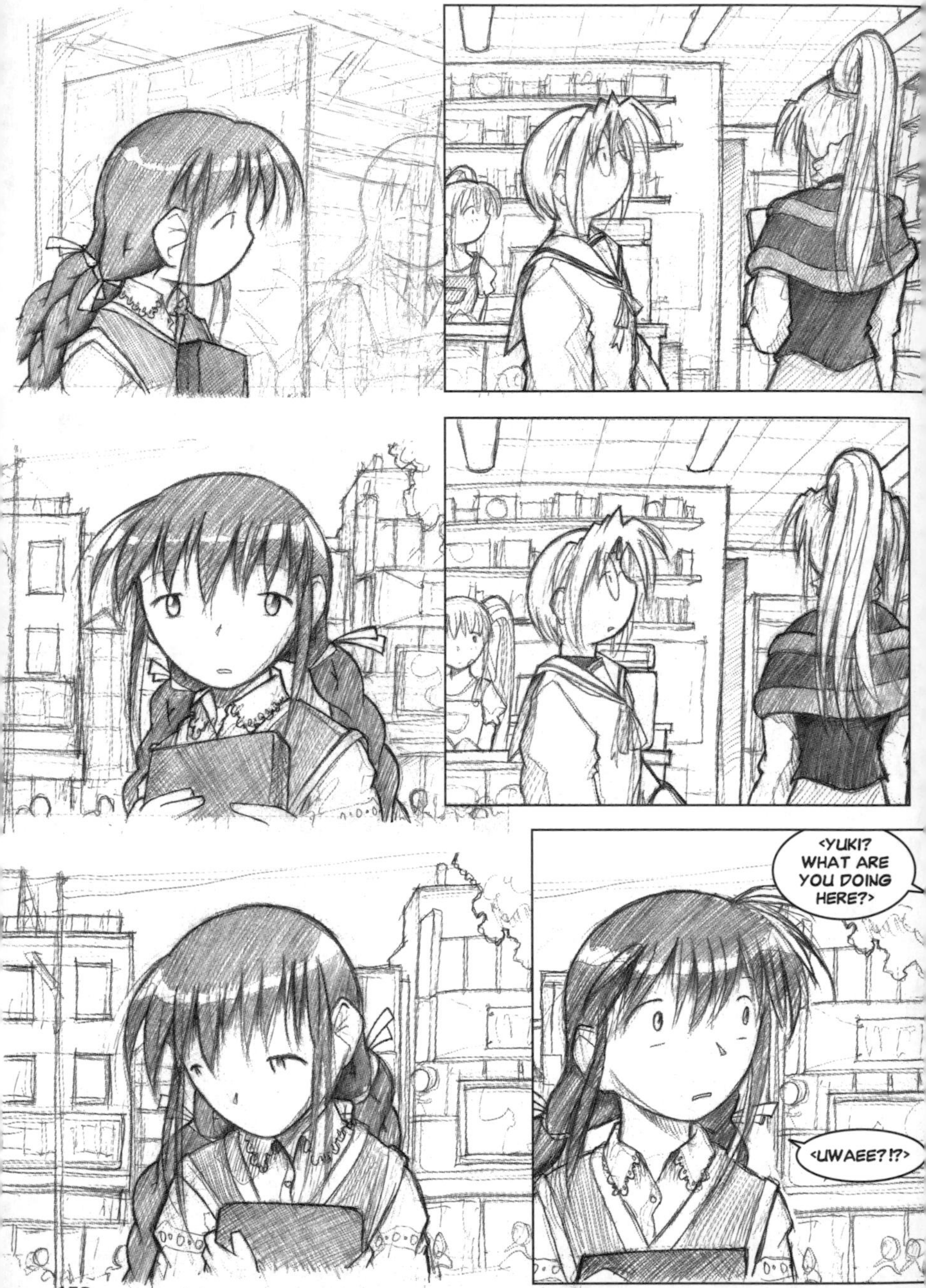

<YUKI? WHAT ARE YOU DOING HERE?>
<UWAEE?!?>

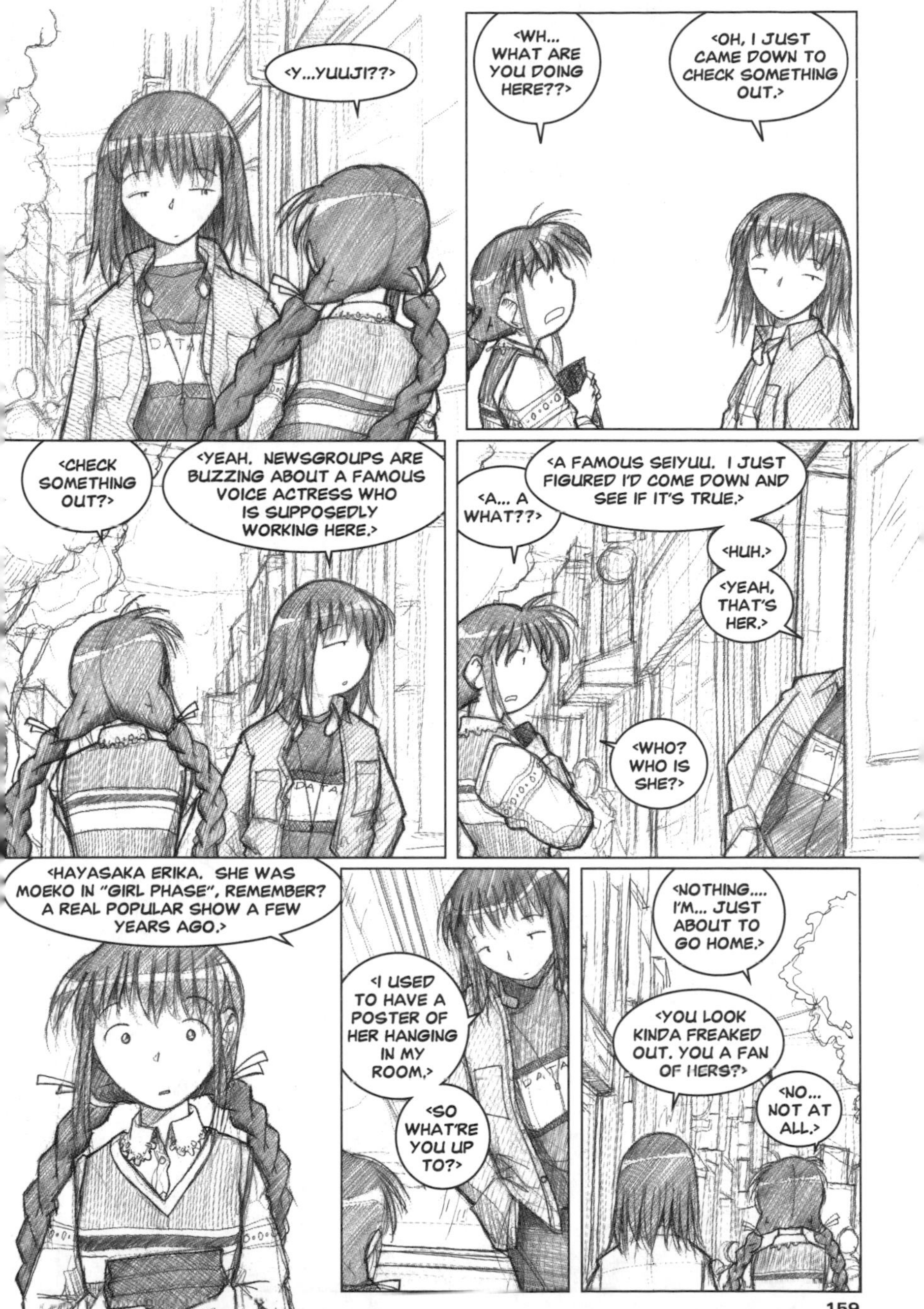
<Y...YUUJI??>
<WH... WHAT ARE YOU DOING HERE??>
<OH, I JUST CAME DOWN TO CHECK SOMETHING OUT.>
<CHECK SOMETHING OUT?>
<YEAH. NEWSGROUPS ARE BUZZING ABOUT A FAMOUS VOICE ACTRESS WHO IS SUPPOSEDLY WORKING HERE.>
<A... A WHAT??>
<A FAMOUS SEIYUU. I JUST FIGURED I'D COME DOWN AND SEE IF IT'S TRUE.>
<HUH.>
<YEAH, THAT'S HER.>
<WHO? WHO IS SHE?>
<HAYASAKA ERIKA. SHE WAS MOEKO IN "GIRL PHASE", REMEMBER? A REAL POPULAR SHOW A FEW YEARS AGO.>
<I USED TO HAVE A POSTER OF HER HANGING IN MY ROOM.>
<SO WHAT'RE YOU UP TO?>
<NOTHING.... I'M... JUST ABOUT TO GO HOME.>
<YOU LOOK KINDA FREAKED OUT. YOU A FAN OF HERS?>
<NO... NOT AT ALL.>

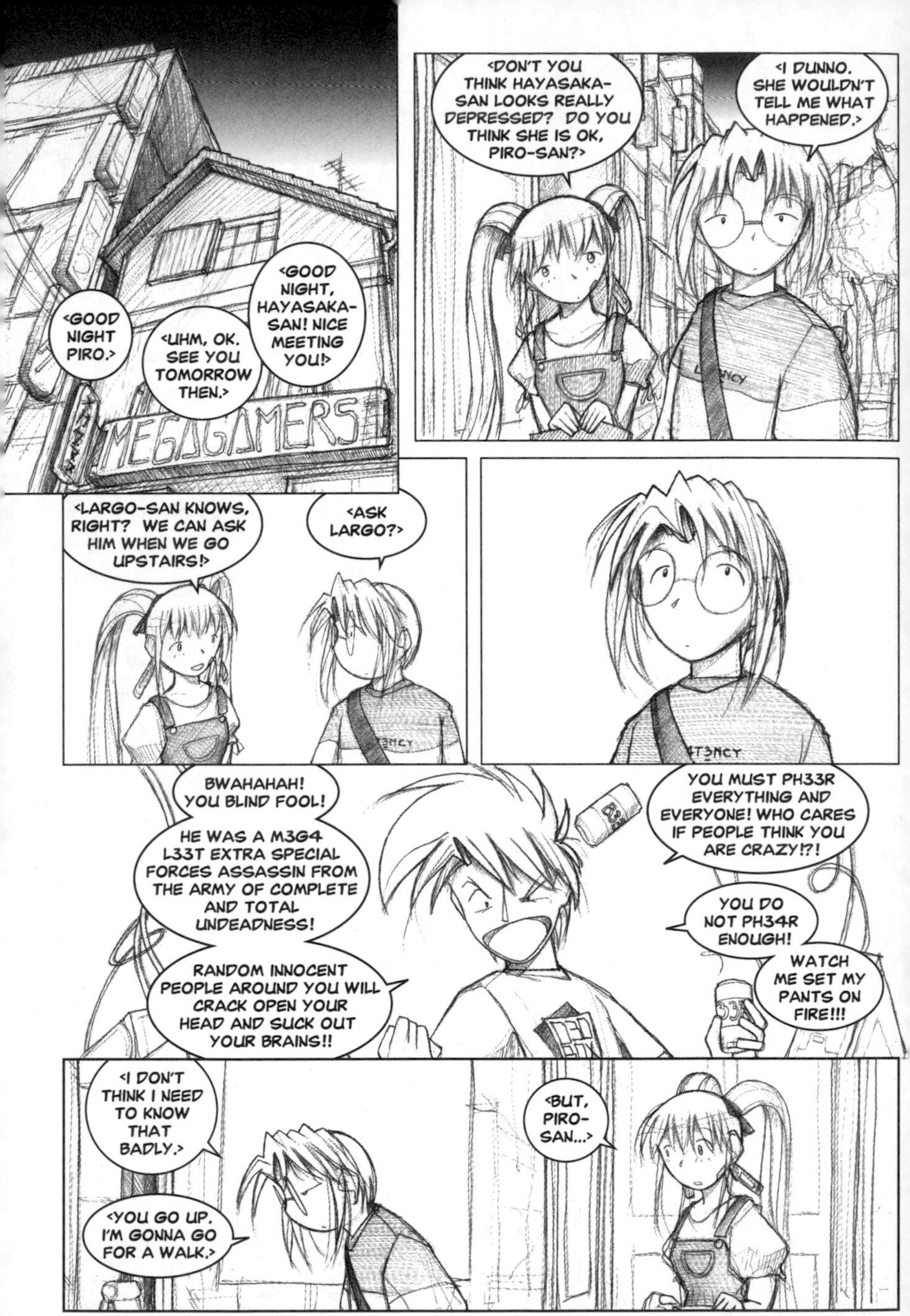

<GOOD NIGHT PIRO.>
<UHM, OK. SEE YOU TOMORROW THEN.>
<GOOD NIGHT, HAYASAKA-SAN! NICE MEETING YOU!>
MEGAGAMERS
<DON'T YOU THINK HAYASAKA-SAN LOOKS REALLY DEPRESSED? DO YOU THINK SHE IS OK, PIRO-SAN?>
<I DUNNO. SHE WOULDN'T TELL ME WHAT HAPPENED.>
<LARGO-SAN KNOWS, RIGHT? WE CAN ASK HIM WHEN WE GO UPSTAIRS!>
<ASK LARGO?>
BWAHAHAH! YOU BLIND FOOL!
HE WAS A M3G4 L33T EXTRA SPECIAL FORCES ASSASSIN FROM THE ARMY OF COMPLETE AND TOTAL UNDEADNESS!
RANDOM INNOCENT PEOPLE AROUND YOU WILL CRACK OPEN YOUR HEAD AND SUCK OUT YOUR BRAINS!!
YOU MUST PH33R EVERYTHING AND EVERYONE! WHO CARES IF PEOPLE THINK YOU ARE CRAZY!?!
YOU DO NOT PH34R ENOUGH!
WATCH ME SET MY PANTS ON FIRE!!!
<I DON'T THINK I NEED TO KNOW THAT BADLY.>
<YOU GO UP. I'M GONNA GO FOR A WALK.>
<BUT, PIRO-SAN...>

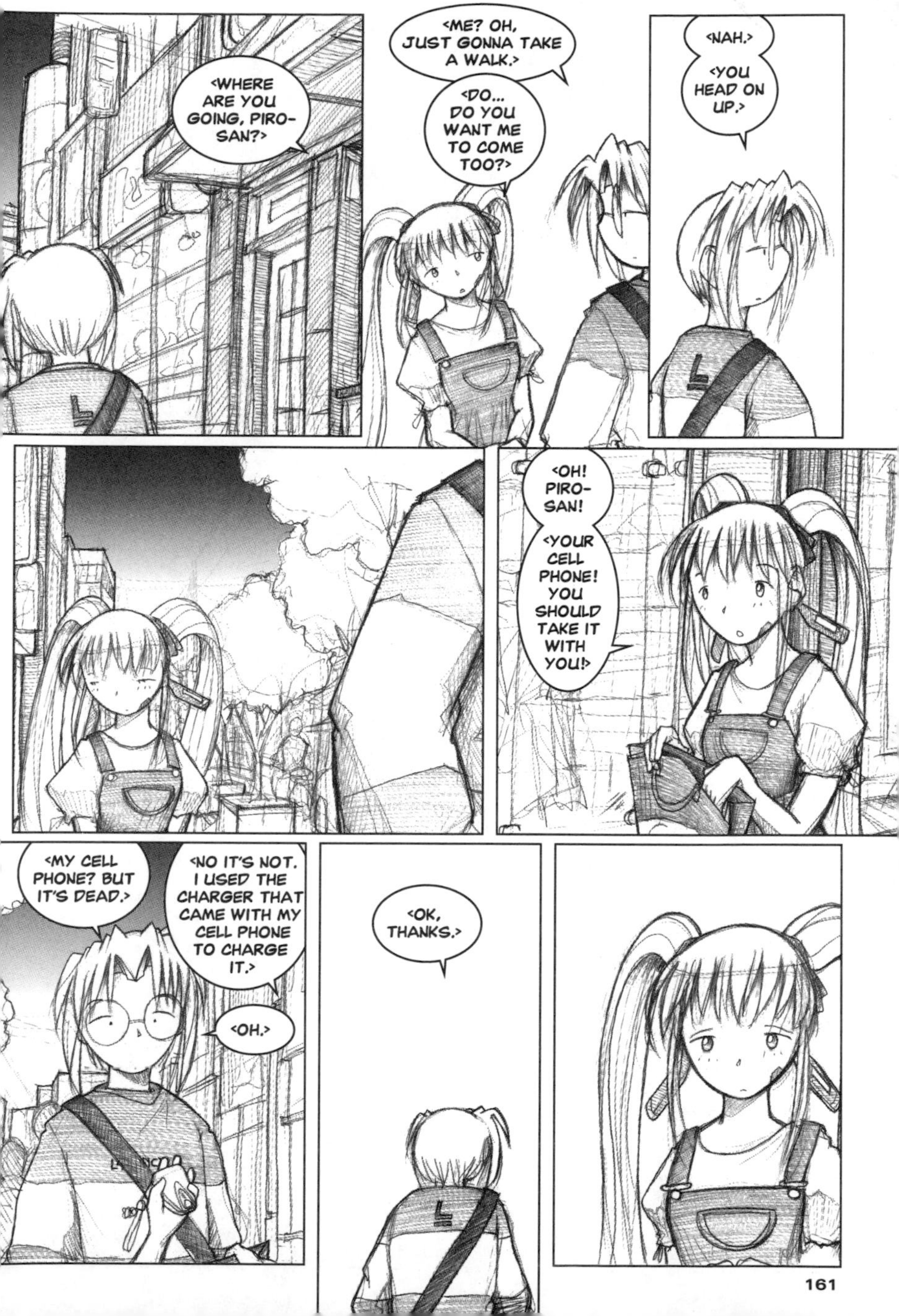

<WHERE ARE YOU GOING, PIRO-SAN?>
<ME? OH, JUST GONNA TAKE A WALK.>
<DO... DO YOU WANT ME TO COME TOO?>
<NAH.>
<YOU HEAD ON UP.>
<OH! PIRO-SAN!
<YOUR CELL PHONE! YOU SHOULD TAKE IT WITH YOU!>
<MY CELL PHONE? BUT IT'S DEAD.>
<NO IT'S NOT. I USED THE CHARGER THAT CAME WITH MY CELL PHONE TO CHARGE IT.>
<OH.>
<OK, THANKS.>

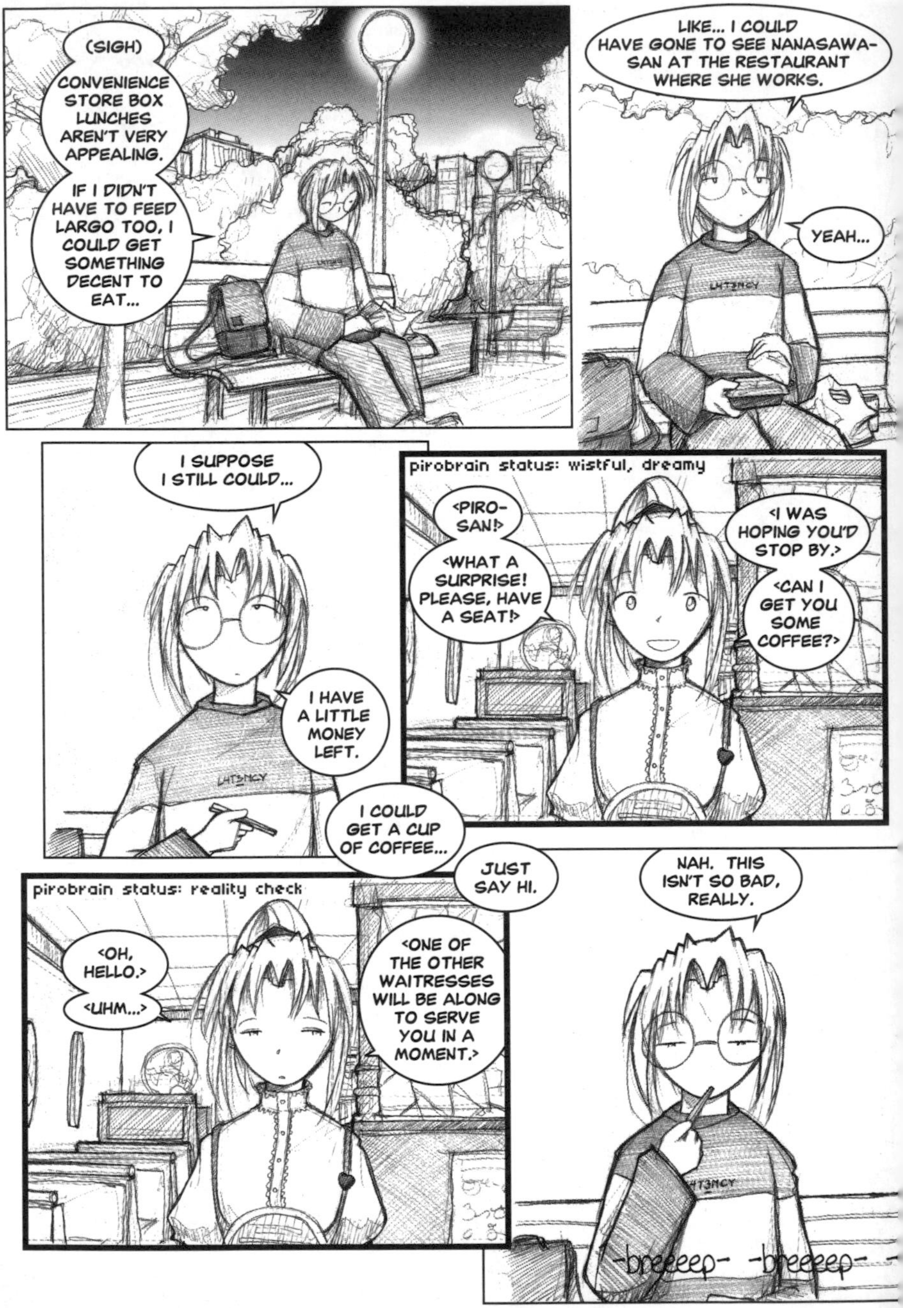
(SIGH)
CONVENIENCE STORE BOX LUNCHES AREN'T VERY APPEALING.
IF I DIDN'T HAVE TO FEED LARGO TOO, I COULD GET SOMETHING DECENT TO EAT...
LIKE... I COULD HAVE GONE TO SEE NANASAWA-SAN AT THE RESTAURANT WHERE SHE WORKS.
YEAH...
I SUPPOSE I STILL COULD...
I HAVE A LITTLE MONEY LEFT.
pirobrain status: wistful, dreamy
<PIRO-SAN!>
<WHAT A SURPRISE! PLEASE, HAVE A SEAT!>
<I WAS HOPING YOU'D STOP BY.>
<CAN I GET YOU SOME COFFEE?>
I COULD GET A CUP OF COFFEE...
JUST SAY HI.
pirobrain status: reality check
<OH, HELLO.>
<UHM...>
<ONE OF THE OTHER WAITRESSES WILL BE ALONG TO SERVE YOU IN A MOMENT.>
NAH. THIS ISN'T SO BAD, REALLY.
-breeeep- -breeeep-

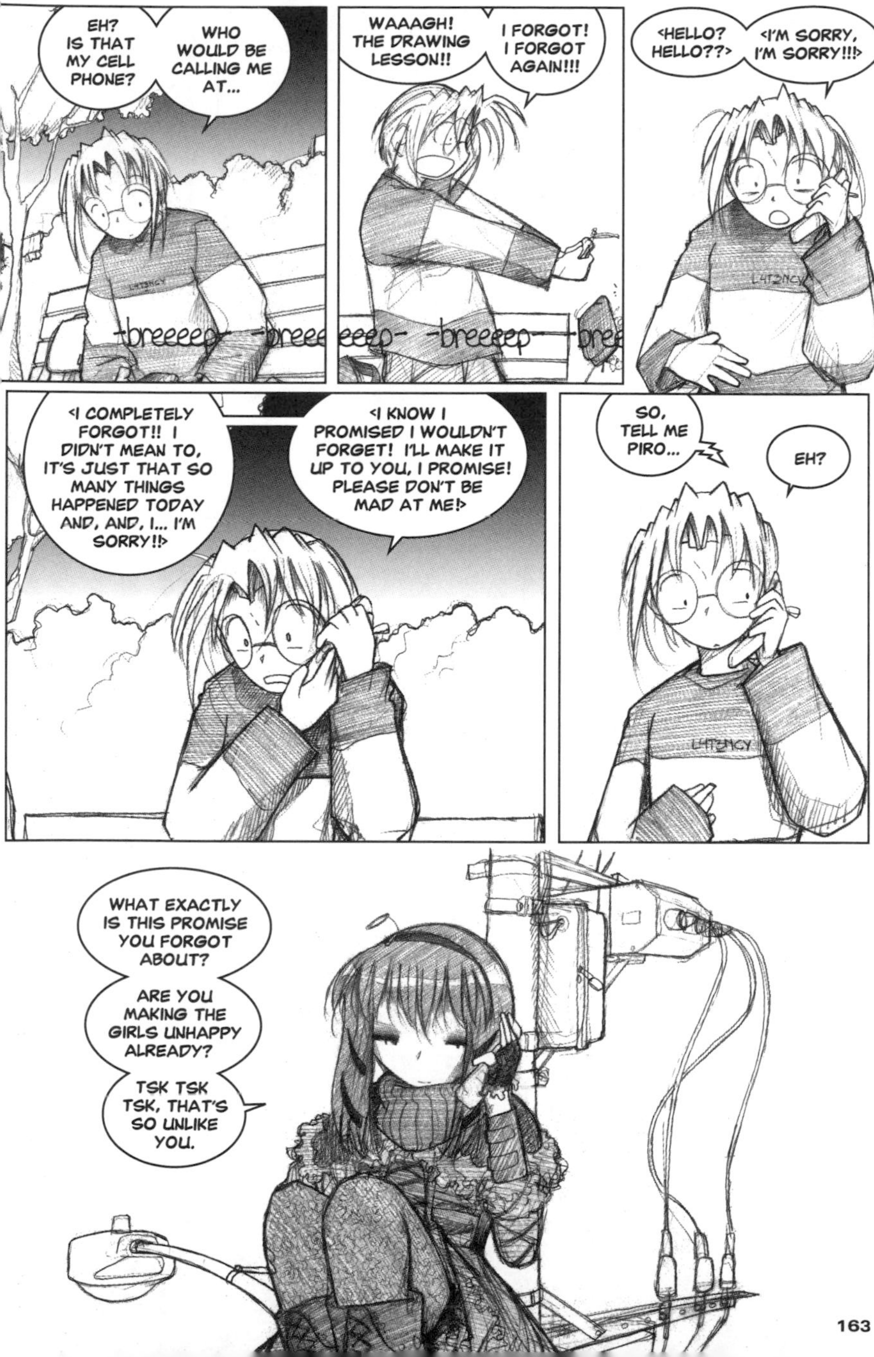
EH? IS THAT MY CELL PHONE?
WHO WOULD BE CALLING ME AT...
-breeeep- -breeeeeep- -breeeep- -bree
WAAAGH! THE DRAWING LESSON!!
I FORGOT! I FORGOT AGAIN!!!
<HELLO? HELLO??>
<I'M SORRY, I'M SORRY!!!>
<I COMPLETELY FORGOT!! I DIDN'T MEAN TO, IT'S JUST THAT SO MANY THINGS HAPPENED TODAY AND, AND, I... I'M SORRY!!>
<I KNOW I PROMISED I WOULDN'T FORGET! I'LL MAKE IT UP TO YOU, I PROMISE! PLEASE DON'T BE MAD AT ME!>
SO, TELL ME PIRO...
EH?
WHAT EXACTLY IS THIS PROMISE YOU FORGOT ABOUT?
ARE YOU MAKING THE GIRLS UNHAPPY ALREADY?
TSK TSK TSK, THAT'S SO UNLIKE YOU.

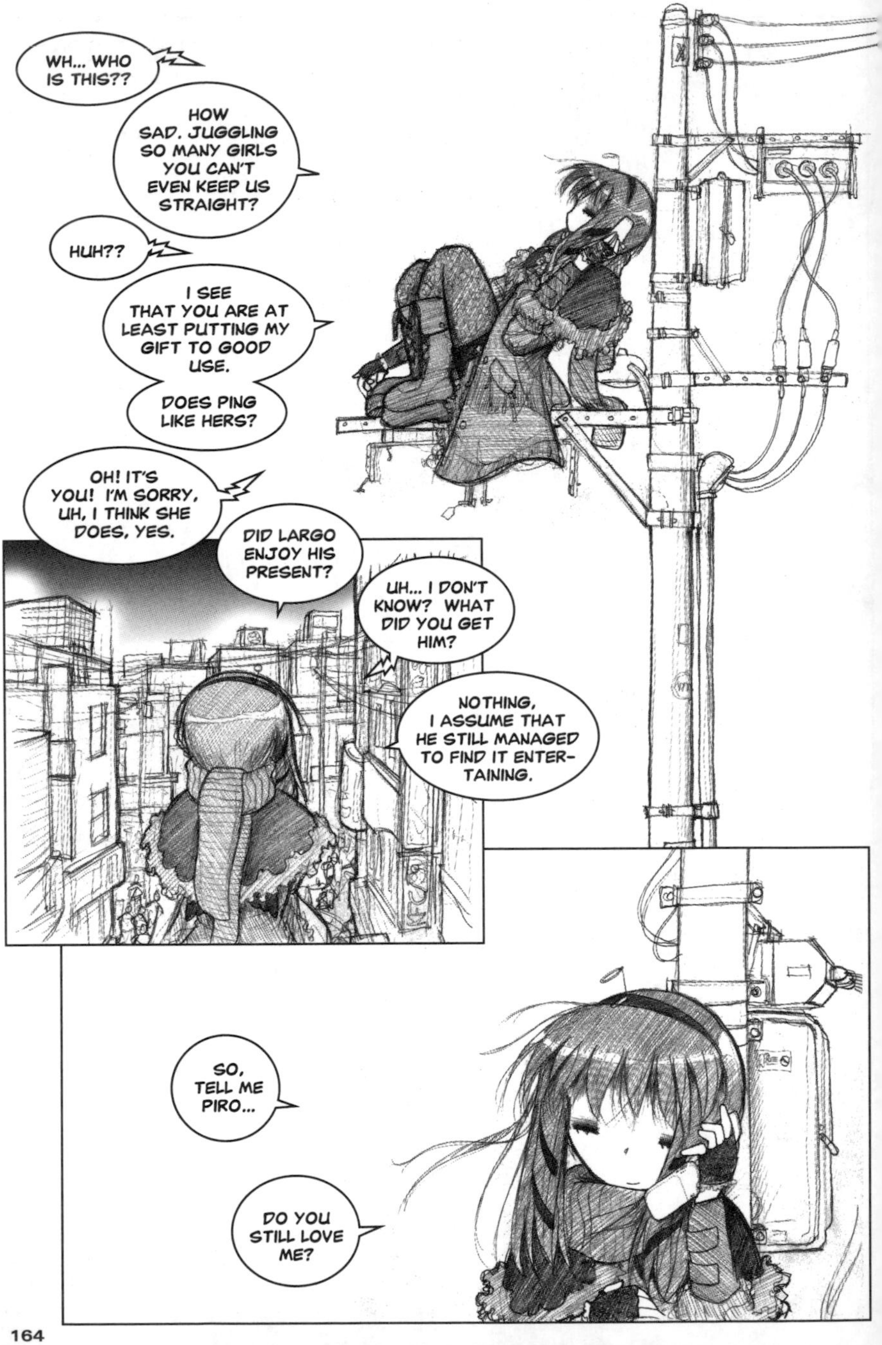
WH... WHO IS THIS??
HOW SAD. JUGGLING SO MANY GIRLS YOU CAN'T EVEN KEEP US STRAIGHT?
HUH??
I SEE THAT YOU ARE AT LEAST PUTTING MY GIFT TO GOOD USE.
DOES PING LIKE HERS?
OH! IT'S YOU! I'M SORRY, UH, I THINK SHE DOES, YES.
DID LARGO ENJOY HIS PRESENT?
UH... I DON'T KNOW? WHAT DID YOU GET HIM?
NOTHING, I ASSUME THAT HE STILL MANAGED TO FIND IT ENTER-TAINING.
SO, TELL ME PIRO...
DO YOU STILL LOVE ME?

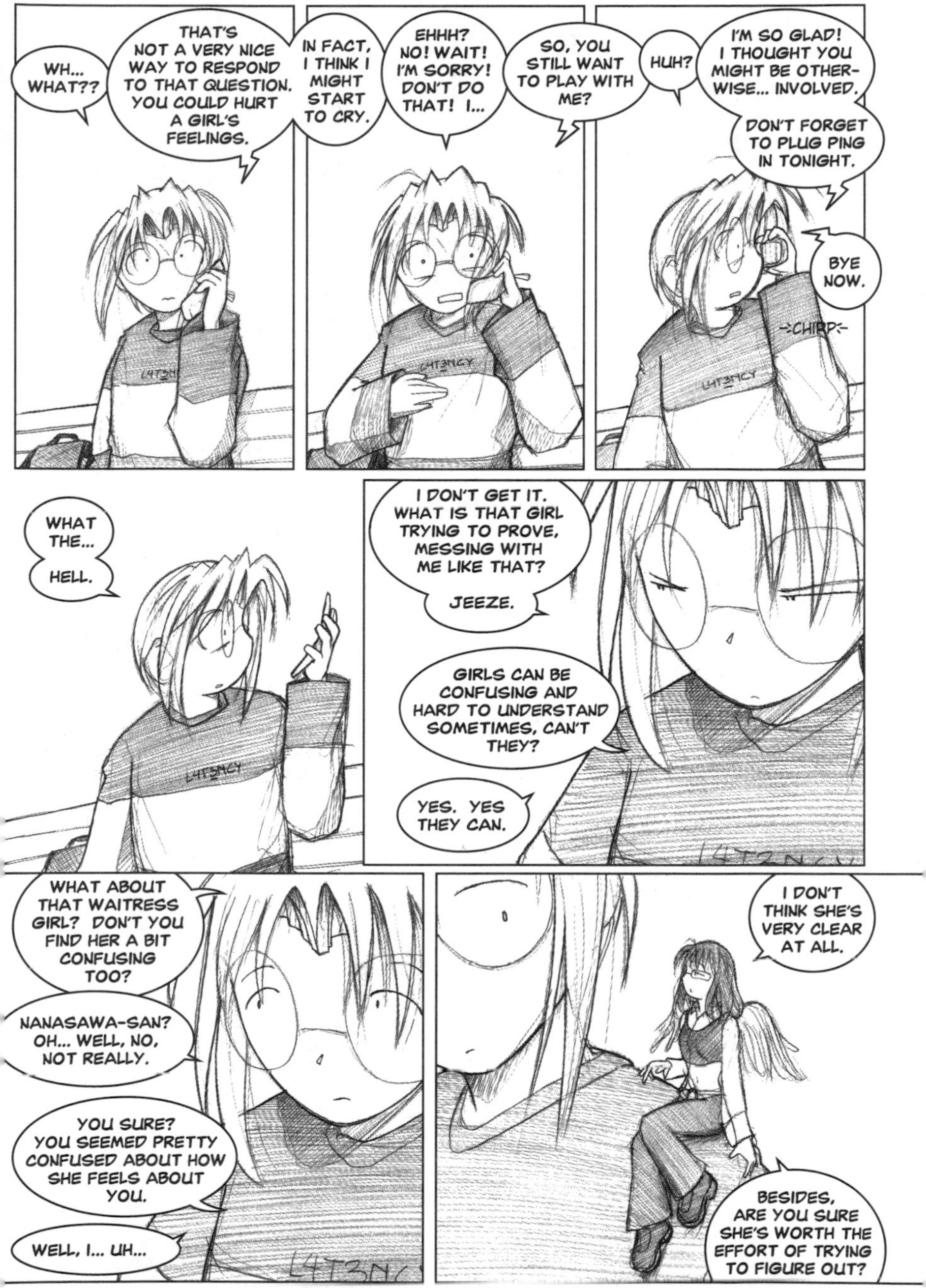
WH... WHAT??
THAT'S NOT A VERY NICE WAY TO RESPOND TO THAT QUESTION. YOU COULD HURT A GIRL'S FEELINGS.
IN FACT, I THINK I MIGHT START TO CRY.
EHHH? NO! WAIT! I'M SORRY! DON'T DO THAT! I...
L4T3NCY
SO, YOU STILL WANT TO PLAY WITH ME?
HUH?
I'M SO GLAD! I THOUGHT YOU MIGHT BE OTHER-WISE... INVOLVED.
DON'T FORGET TO PLUG PING IN TONIGHT.
BYE NOW.
-CHIRP-
WHAT THE...
HELL.
I DON'T GET IT. WHAT IS THAT GIRL TRYING TO PROVE, MESSING WITH ME LIKE THAT?
JEEZE.
GIRLS CAN BE CONFUSING AND HARD TO UNDERSTAND SOMETIMES, CAN'T THEY?
YES. YES THEY CAN.
WHAT ABOUT THAT WAITRESS GIRL? DON'T YOU FIND HER A BIT CONFUSING TOO?
NANASAWA-SAN? OH... WELL, NO, NOT REALLY.
YOU SURE? YOU SEEMED PRETTY CONFUSED ABOUT HOW SHE FEELS ABOUT YOU.
WELL, I... UH...
I DON'T THINK SHE'S VERY CLEAR AT ALL.
BESIDES, ARE YOU SURE SHE'S WORTH THE EFFORT OF TRYING TO FIGURE OUT?

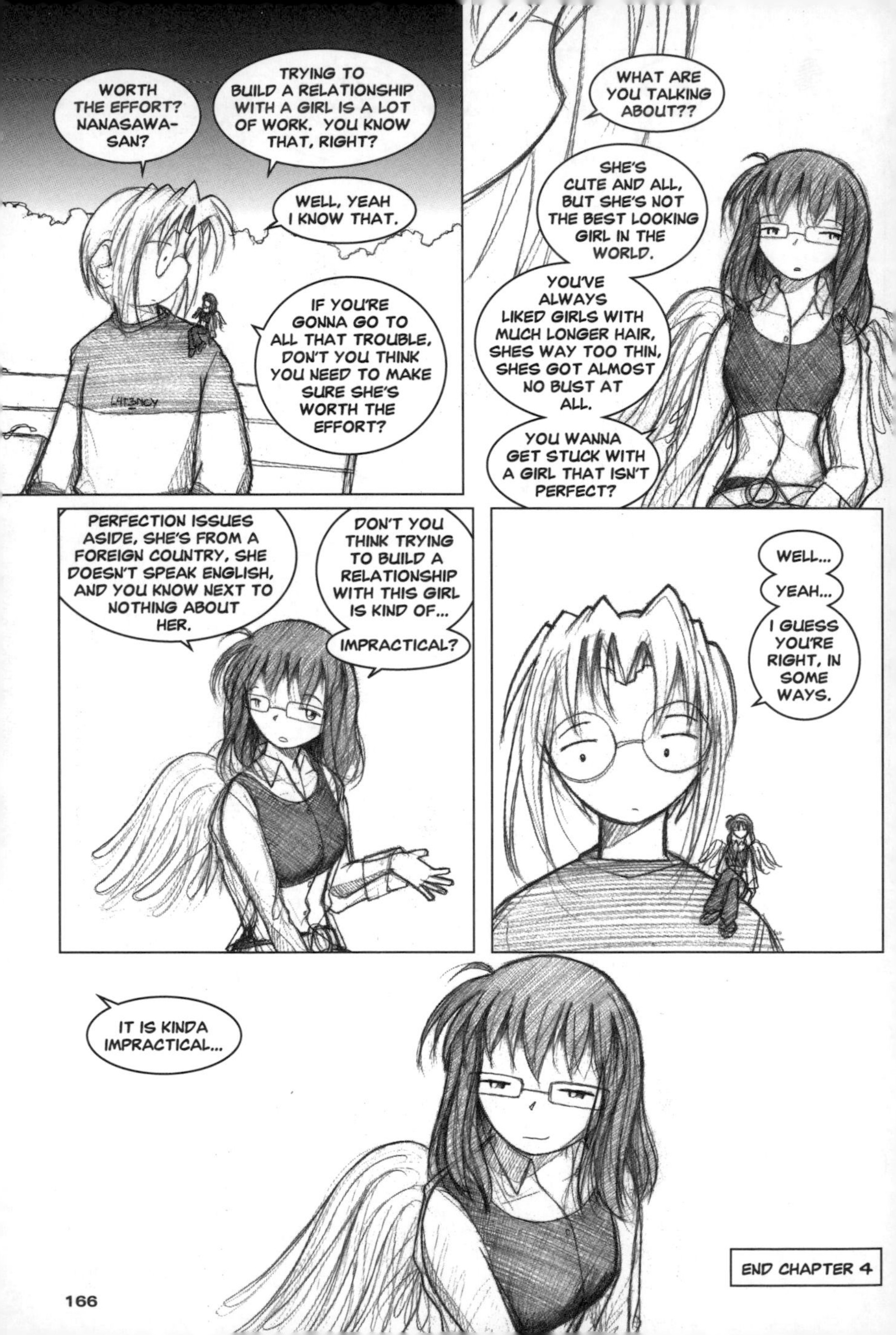
WORTH THE EFFORT? NANASAWA-SAN?
TRYING TO BUILD A RELATIONSHIP WITH A GIRL IS A LOT OF WORK. YOU KNOW THAT, RIGHT?
WELL, YEAH I KNOW THAT.
IF YOU'RE GONNA GO TO ALL THAT TROUBLE, DON'T YOU THINK YOU NEED TO MAKE SURE SHE'S WORTH THE EFFORT?
WHAT ARE YOU TALKING ABOUT??
SHE'S CUTE AND ALL, BUT SHE'S NOT THE BEST LOOKING GIRL IN THE WORLD.
YOU'VE ALWAYS LIKED GIRLS WITH MUCH LONGER HAIR, SHES WAY TOO THIN, SHES GOT ALMOST NO BUST AT ALL.
YOU WANNA GET STUCK WITH A GIRL THAT ISN'T PERFECT?
PERFECTION ISSUES ASIDE, SHE'S FROM A FOREIGN COUNTRY, SHE DOESN'T SPEAK ENGLISH, AND YOU KNOW NEXT TO NOTHING ABOUT HER.
DON'T YOU THINK TRYING TO BUILD A RELATIONSHIP WITH THIS GIRL IS KIND OF...
IMPRACTICAL?
WELL...
YEAH...
I GUESS YOU'RE RIGHT, IN SOME WAYS.
IT IS KINDA IMPRACTICAL...
END CHAPTER 4

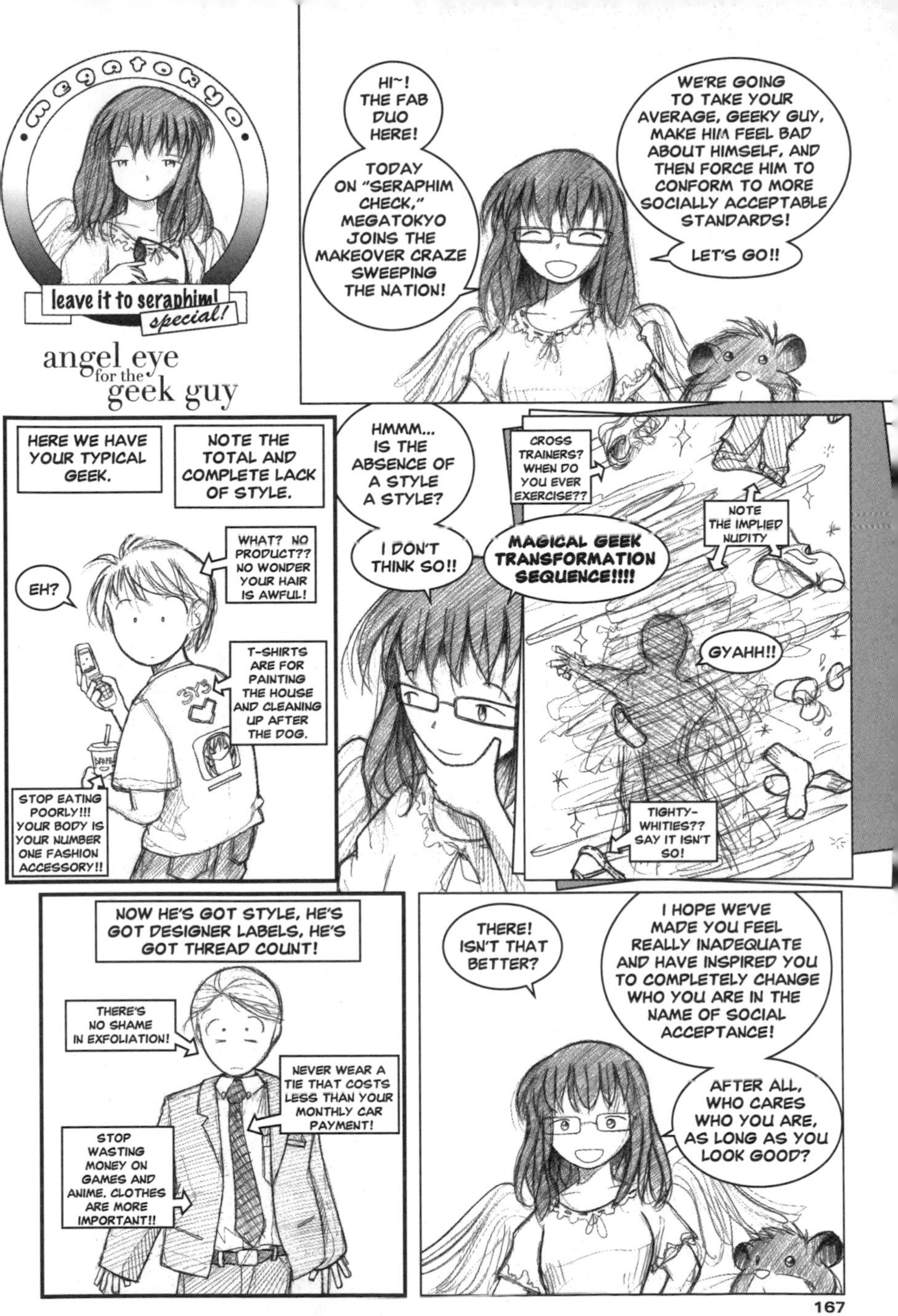
megatokyo
leave it to seraphim! special!
angel eye for the geek guy
HI~! THE FAB DUO HERE!
TODAY ON "SERAPHIM CHECK," MEGATOKYO JOINS THE MAKEOVER CRAZE SWEEPING THE NATION!
WE'RE GOING TO TAKE YOUR AVERAGE, GEEKY GUY, MAKE HIM FEEL BAD ABOUT HIMSELF, AND THEN FORCE HIM TO CONFORM TO MORE SOCIALLY ACCEPTABLE STANDARDS!
LET'S GO!!
HERE WE HAVE YOUR TYPICAL GEEK.
NOTE THE TOTAL AND COMPLETE LACK OF STYLE.
EH?
WHAT? NO PRODUCT?? NO WONDER YOUR HAIR IS AWFUL!
T-SHIRTS ARE FOR PAINTING THE HOUSE AND CLEANING UP AFTER THE DOG.
STOP EATING POORLY!!! YOUR BODY IS YOUR NUMBER ONE FASHION ACCESSORY!!
HMMM... IS THE ABSENCE OF A STYLE A STYLE?
I DON'T THINK SO!!
MAGICAL GEEK TRANSFORMATION SEQUENCE!!!!
CROSS TRAINERS? WHEN DO YOU EVER EXERCISE??
NOTE THE IMPLIED NUDITY
GYAHH!!
TIGHTY-WHITIES?? SAY IT ISN'T SO!
NOW HE'S GOT STYLE, HE'S GOT DESIGNER LABELS, HE'S GOT THREAD COUNT!
THERE'S NO SHAME IN EXFOLIATION!
NEVER WEAR A TIE THAT COSTS LESS THAN YOUR MONTHLY CAR PAYMENT!
STOP WASTING MONEY ON GAMES AND ANIME. CLOTHES ARE MORE IMPORTANT!!
THERE! ISN'T THAT BETTER?
I HOPE WE'VE MADE YOU FEEL REALLY INADEQUATE AND HAVE INSPIRED YOU TO COMPLETELY CHANGE WHO YOU ARE IN THE NAME OF SOCIAL ACCEPTANCE!
AFTER ALL, WHO CARES WHO YOU ARE, AS LONG AS YOU LOOK GOOD?

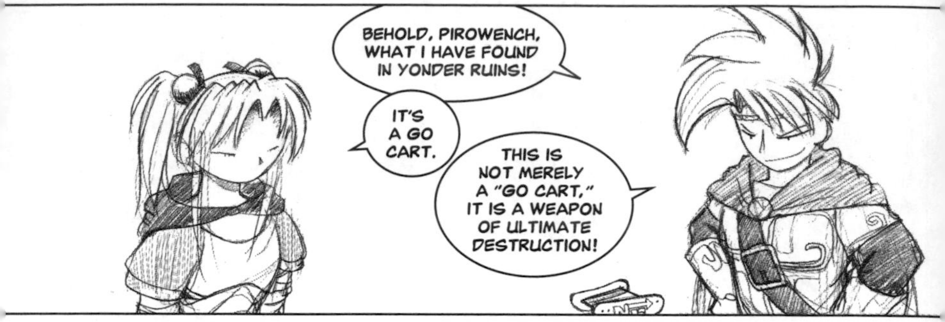
BEHOLD, PIROWENCH, WHAT I HAVE FOUND IN YONDER RUINS!
IT'S A GO CART.
THIS IS NOT MERELY A "GO CART," IT IS A WEAPON OF ULTIMATE DESTRUCTION!

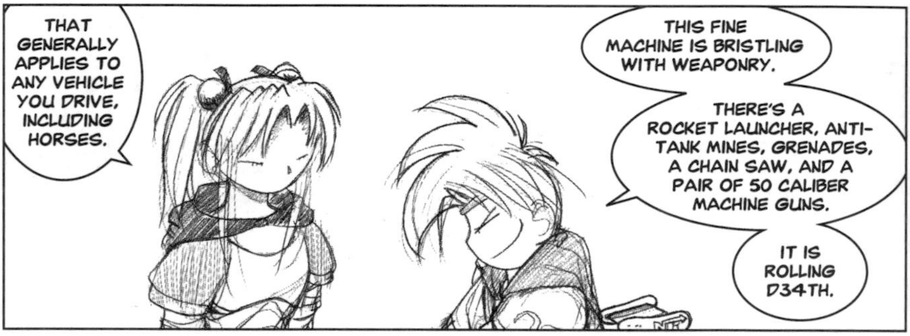
THAT GENERALLY APPLIES TO ANY VEHICLE YOU DRIVE, INCLUDING HORSES.
THIS FINE MACHINE IS BRISTLING WITH WEAPONRY.
THERE'S A ROCKET LAUNCHER, ANTI-TANK MINES, GRENADES, A CHAIN SAW, AND A PAIR OF 50 CALIBER MACHINE GUNS.
IT IS ROLLING D34TH.

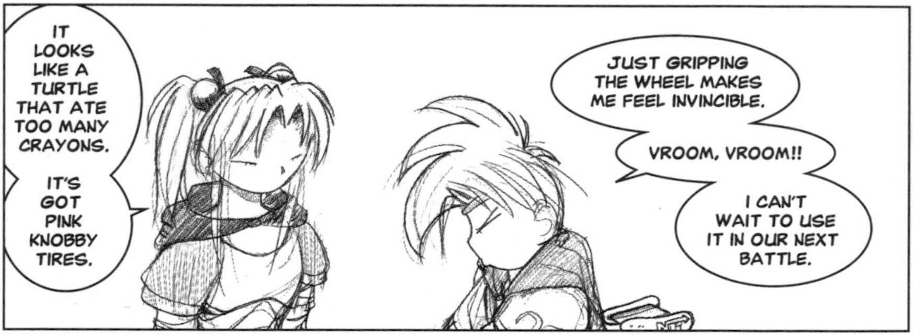
IT LOOKS LIKE A TURTLE THAT ATE TOO MANY CRAYONS.
IT'S GOT PINK KNOBBY TIRES.
JUST GRIPPING THE WHEEL MAKES ME FEEL INVINCIBLE.
VROOM, VROOM!!
I CAN'T WAIT TO USE IT IN OUR NEXT BATTLE.

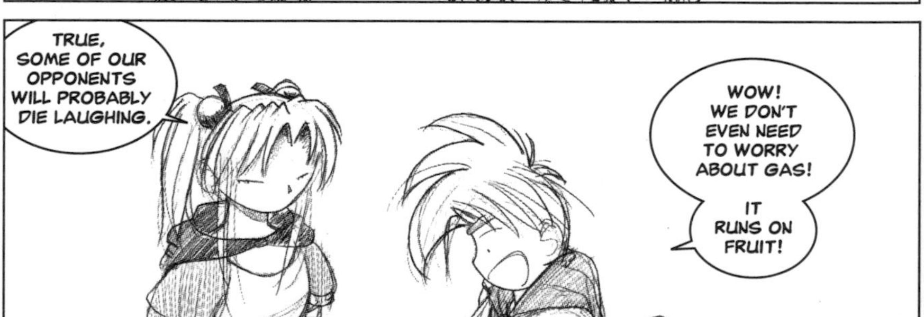
TRUE, SOME OF OUR OPPONENTS WILL PROBABLY DIE LAUGHING.
WOW! WE DON'T EVEN NEED TO WORRY ABOUT GAS!
IT RUNS ON FRUIT!

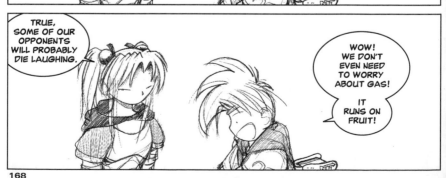

"naze nani 'gameworld' megatokyo"

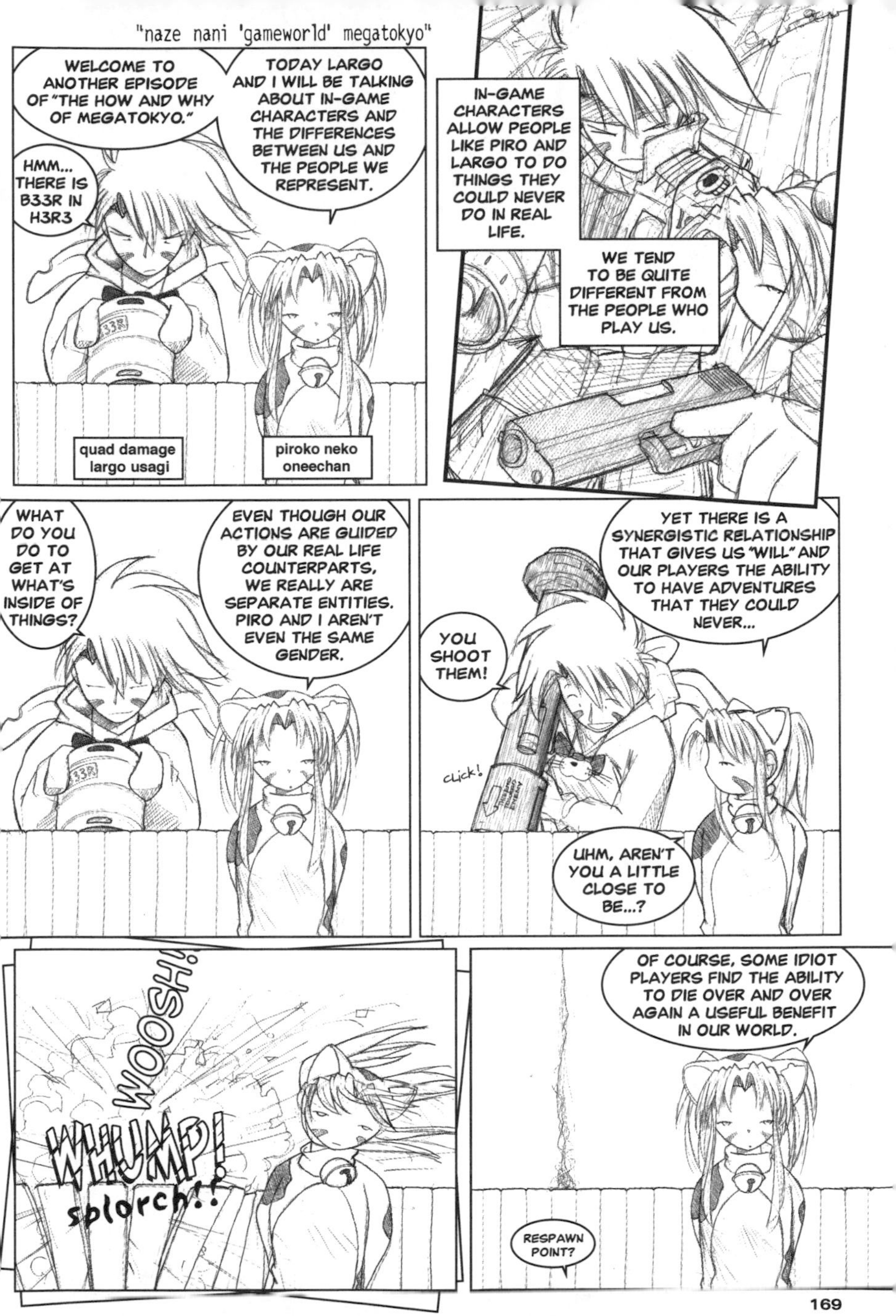
WELCOME TO ANOTHER EPISODE OF "THE HOW AND WHY OF MEGATOKYO."
TODAY LARGO AND I WILL BE TALKING ABOUT IN-GAME CHARACTERS AND THE DIFFERENCES BETWEEN US AND THE PEOPLE WE REPRESENT.
HMM... THERE IS B33R IN H3R3
B33R
quad damage largo usagi
piroko neko oneechan
IN-GAME CHARACTERS ALLOW PEOPLE LIKE PIRO AND LARGO TO DO THINGS THEY COULD NEVER DO IN REAL LIFE.
WE TEND TO BE QUITE DIFFERENT FROM THE PEOPLE WHO PLAY US.
WHAT DO YOU DO TO GET AT WHAT'S INSIDE OF THINGS?
EVEN THOUGH OUR ACTIONS ARE GUIDED BY OUR REAL LIFE COUNTERPARTS, WE REALLY ARE SEPARATE ENTITIES. PIRO AND I AREN'T EVEN THE SAME GENDER.
B33R
YET THERE IS A SYNERGISTIC RELATIONSHIP THAT GIVES US "WILL" AND OUR PLAYERS THE ABILITY TO HAVE ADVENTURES THAT THEY COULD NEVER...
YOU SHOOT THEM!
click!
UHM, AREN'T YOU A LITTLE CLOSE TO BE...?
WOOSH!
WHUMP!
splorch!!
OF COURSE, SOME IDIOT PLAYERS FIND THE ABILITY TO DIE OVER AND OVER AGAIN A USEFUL BENEFIT IN OUR WORLD.
RESPAWN POINT?

Shirt_Guy_Dom.txt

I'm sure by now most of you are (unfortunately) aware of what a "Shirt Guy Dom" strip is. Shirt Guy Dom strips are stick figure comics that Dom creates using dreaded trackball technology™ coupled with the reckless abandon of his somewhat demented mind (did I say "somewhat?"). On days that these travesties of the digital world are released, shrieks of terror and cries of horror can be heard as these abominations slowly materialize in browsers around the world.

Needless to say, the more comics I do on time and the less Shirt Guy Dom strips there are, the happier the world will be.

I wish I could say that these two SGD strips were the only ones to escape from captivity during chapter three and four...sadly, they are not. The others were, well...the horror was too much for print.

As always, please note that the following page is perforated for easy removal.

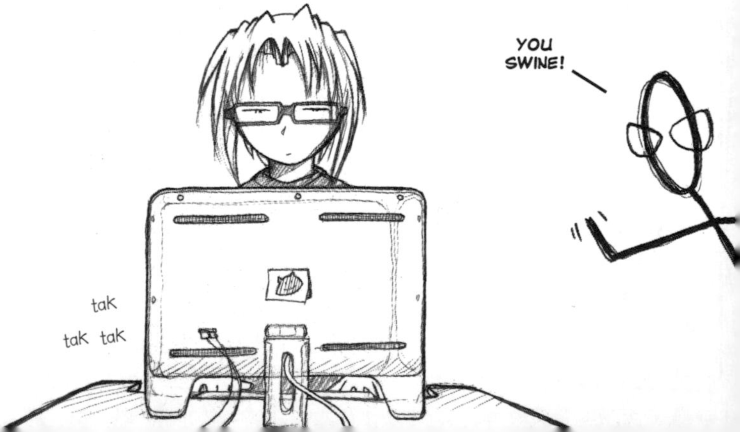

YOU SWINE!
tak
tak tak

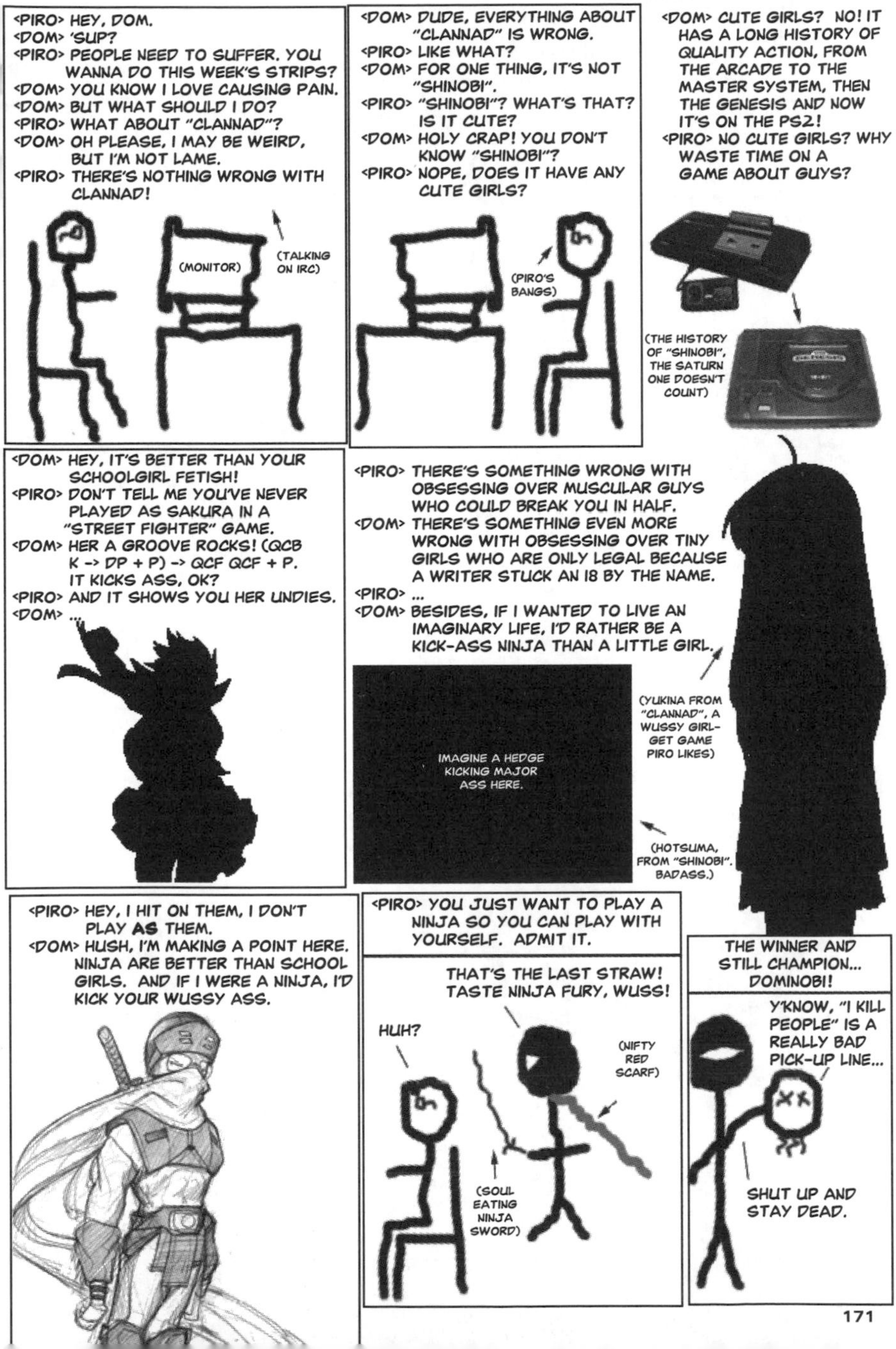

<PIRO> HEY, DOM.
<DOM> 'SUP?
<PIRO> PEOPLE NEED TO SUFFER. YOU WANNA DO THIS WEEK'S STRIPS?
<DOM> YOU KNOW I LOVE CAUSING PAIN.
<DOM> BUT WHAT SHOULD I DO?
<PIRO> WHAT ABOUT "CLANNAD"?
<DOM> OH PLEASE, I MAY BE WEIRD, BUT I'M NOT LAME.
<PIRO> THERE'S NOTHING WRONG WITH CLANNAD!
(MONITOR)
(TALKING ON IRC)
<DOM> DUDE, EVERYTHING ABOUT "CLANNAD" IS WRONG.
<PIRO> LIKE WHAT?
<DOM> FOR ONE THING, IT'S NOT "SHINOBI".
<PIRO> "SHINOBI"? WHAT'S THAT? IS IT CUTE?
<DOM> HOLY CRAP! YOU DON'T KNOW "SHINOBI"?
<PIRO> NOPE, DOES IT HAVE ANY CUTE GIRLS?
(PIRO'S BANGS)
<DOM> CUTE GIRLS? NO! IT HAS A LONG HISTORY OF QUALITY ACTION, FROM THE ARCADE TO THE MASTER SYSTEM, THEN THE GENESIS AND NOW IT'S ON THE PS2!
<PIRO> NO CUTE GIRLS? WHY WASTE TIME ON A GAME ABOUT GUYS?
(THE HISTORY OF "SHINOBI", THE SATURN ONE DOESN'T COUNT)
<DOM> HEY, IT'S BETTER THAN YOUR SCHOOLGIRL FETISH!
<PIRO> DON'T TELL ME YOU'VE NEVER PLAYED AS SAKURA IN A "STREET FIGHTER" GAME.
<DOM> HER A GROOVE ROCKS! (QCB K -> DP + P) -> QCF QCF + P. IT KICKS ASS, OK?
<PIRO> AND IT SHOWS YOU HER UNDIES.
<DOM> ...
<PIRO> THERE'S SOMETHING WRONG WITH OBSESSING OVER MUSCULAR GUYS WHO COULD BREAK YOU IN HALF.
<DOM> THERE'S SOMETHING EVEN MORE WRONG WITH OBSESSING OVER TINY GIRLS WHO ARE ONLY LEGAL BECAUSE A WRITER STUCK AN 18 BY THE NAME.
<PIRO> ...
<DOM> BESIDES, IF I WANTED TO LIVE AN IMAGINARY LIFE, I'D RATHER BE A KICK-ASS NINJA THAN A LITTLE GIRL.
IMAGINE A HEDGE KICKING MAJOR ASS HERE.
(YUKINA FROM "CLANNAD", A WUSSY GIRL-GET GAME PIRO LIKES)
(HOTSUMA, FROM "SHINOBI". BADASS.)
<PIRO> HEY, I HIT ON THEM, I DON'T PLAY **AS** THEM.
<DOM> HUSH, I'M MAKING A POINT HERE. NINJA ARE BETTER THAN SCHOOL GIRLS. AND IF I WERE A NINJA, I'D KICK YOUR WUSSY ASS.
<PIRO> YOU JUST WANT TO PLAY A NINJA SO YOU CAN PLAY WITH YOURSELF. ADMIT IT.
THAT'S THE LAST STRAW! TASTE NINJA FURY, WUSS!
HUH?
(NIFTY RED SCARF)
(SOUL EATING NINJA SWORD)
THE WINNER AND STILL CHAMPION... DOMINOBI!
Y'KNOW, "I KILL PEOPLE" IS A REALLY BAD PICK-UP LINE...
SHUT UP AND STAY DEAD.

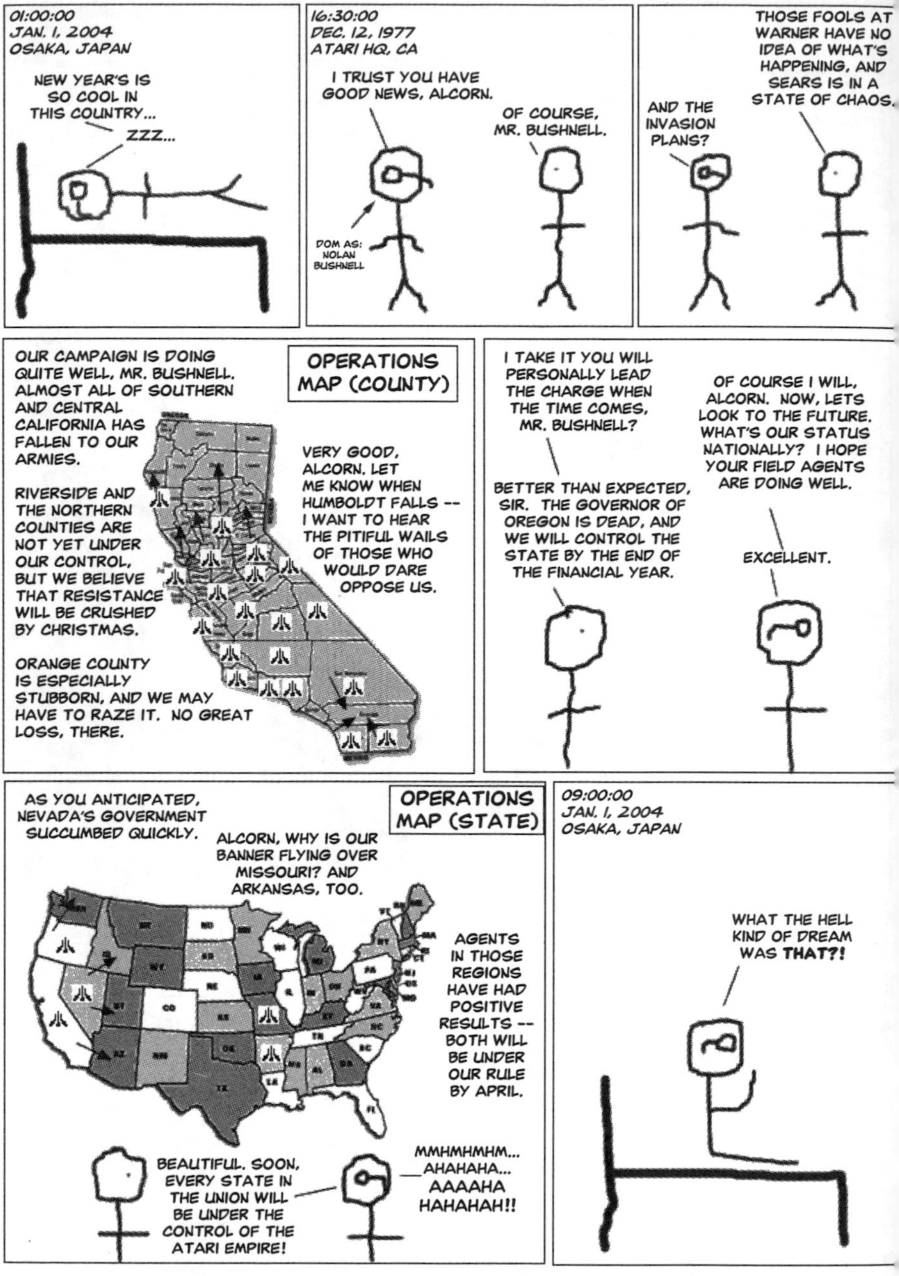
01:00:00
JAN. 1, 2004
OSAKA, JAPAN
NEW YEAR'S IS SO COOL IN THIS COUNTRY...
ZZZ...
16:30:00
DEC. 12, 1977
ATARI HQ, CA
I TRUST YOU HAVE GOOD NEWS, ALCORN.
DOM AS: NOLAN BUSHNELL
OF COURSE, MR. BUSHNELL.
AND THE INVASION PLANS?
THOSE FOOLS AT WARNER HAVE NO IDEA OF WHAT'S HAPPENING, AND SEARS IS IN A STATE OF CHAOS.
OPERATIONS MAP (COUNTY)
OUR CAMPAIGN IS DOING QUITE WELL, MR. BUSHNELL. ALMOST ALL OF SOUTHERN AND CENTRAL CALIFORNIA HAS FALLEN TO OUR ARMIES.
RIVERSIDE AND THE NORTHERN COUNTIES ARE NOT YET UNDER OUR CONTROL, BUT WE BELIEVE THAT RESISTANCE WILL BE CRUSHED BY CHRISTMAS.
ORANGE COUNTY IS ESPECIALLY STUBBORN, AND WE MAY HAVE TO RAZE IT. NO GREAT LOSS, THERE.
VERY GOOD, ALCORN. LET ME KNOW WHEN HUMBOLDT FALLS -- I WANT TO HEAR THE PITIFUL WAILS OF THOSE WHO WOULD DARE OPPOSE US.
I TAKE IT YOU WILL PERSONALLY LEAD THE CHARGE WHEN THE TIME COMES, MR. BUSHNELL?
OF COURSE I WILL, ALCORN. NOW, LETS LOOK TO THE FUTURE. WHAT'S OUR STATUS NATIONALLY? I HOPE YOUR FIELD AGENTS ARE DOING WELL.
BETTER THAN EXPECTED, SIR. THE GOVERNOR OF OREGON IS DEAD, AND WE WILL CONTROL THE STATE BY THE END OF THE FINANCIAL YEAR.
EXCELLENT.
AS YOU ANTICIPATED, NEVADA'S GOVERNMENT SUCCUMBED QUICKLY.
OPERATIONS MAP (STATE)
ALCORN, WHY IS OUR BANNER FLYING OVER MISSOURI? AND ARKANSAS, TOO.
AGENTS IN THOSE REGIONS HAVE HAD POSITIVE RESULTS -- BOTH WILL BE UNDER OUR RULE BY APRIL.
BEAUTIFUL. SOON, EVERY STATE IN THE UNION WILL BE UNDER THE CONTROL OF THE ATARI EMPIRE!
MMHMHMHM... AHAHAHA... AAAAHA HAHAHAH!!
09:00:00
JAN. 1, 2004
OSAKA, JAPAN
WHAT THE HELL KIND OF DREAM WAS THAT?!

pipe cleaner dom theater

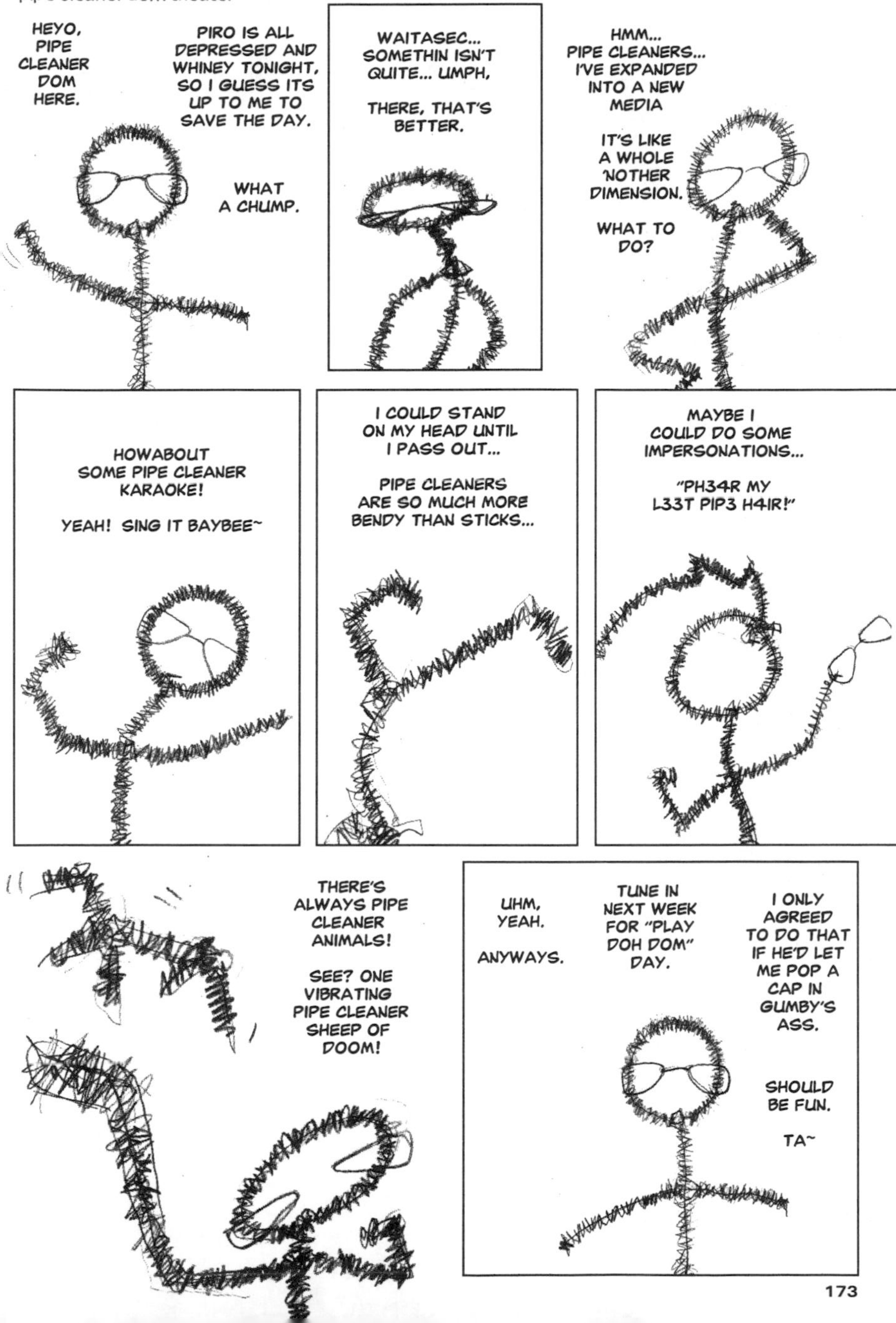

HEYO, PIPE CLEANER DOM HERE.
PIRO IS ALL DEPRESSED AND WHINEY TONIGHT, SO I GUESS ITS UP TO ME TO SAVE THE DAY.
WHAT A CHUMP.
WAITASEC... SOMETHIN ISN'T QUITE... UMPH,
THERE, THAT'S BETTER.
HMM... PIPE CLEANERS... I'VE EXPANDED INTO A NEW MEDIA
IT'S LIKE A WHOLE 'NOTHER DIMENSION.
WHAT TO DO?
HOWABOUT SOME PIPE CLEANER KARAOKE!
YEAH! SING IT BAYBEE~
I COULD STAND ON MY HEAD UNTIL I PASS OUT...
PIPE CLEANERS ARE SO MUCH MORE BENDY THAN STICKS...
MAYBE I COULD DO SOME IMPERSONATIONS...
"PH34R MY L33T PIP3 H4IR!"
THERE'S ALWAYS PIPE CLEANER ANIMALS!
SEE? ONE VIBRATING PIPE CLEANER SHEEP OF DOOM!
UHM, YEAH.
ANYWAYS.
TUNE IN NEXT WEEK FOR "PLAY DOH DOM" DAY.
I ONLY AGREED TO DO THAT IF HE'D LET ME POP A CAP IN GUMBY'S ASS.
SHOULD BE FUN.
TA~

I posted this drawing of Boo with an olive branch on September 11, 2002.

It just felt like the right thing to say, on that day, one year later. Sometimes it's ok to say things in a simple, quiet way.

september 11, 2001- just remembering...

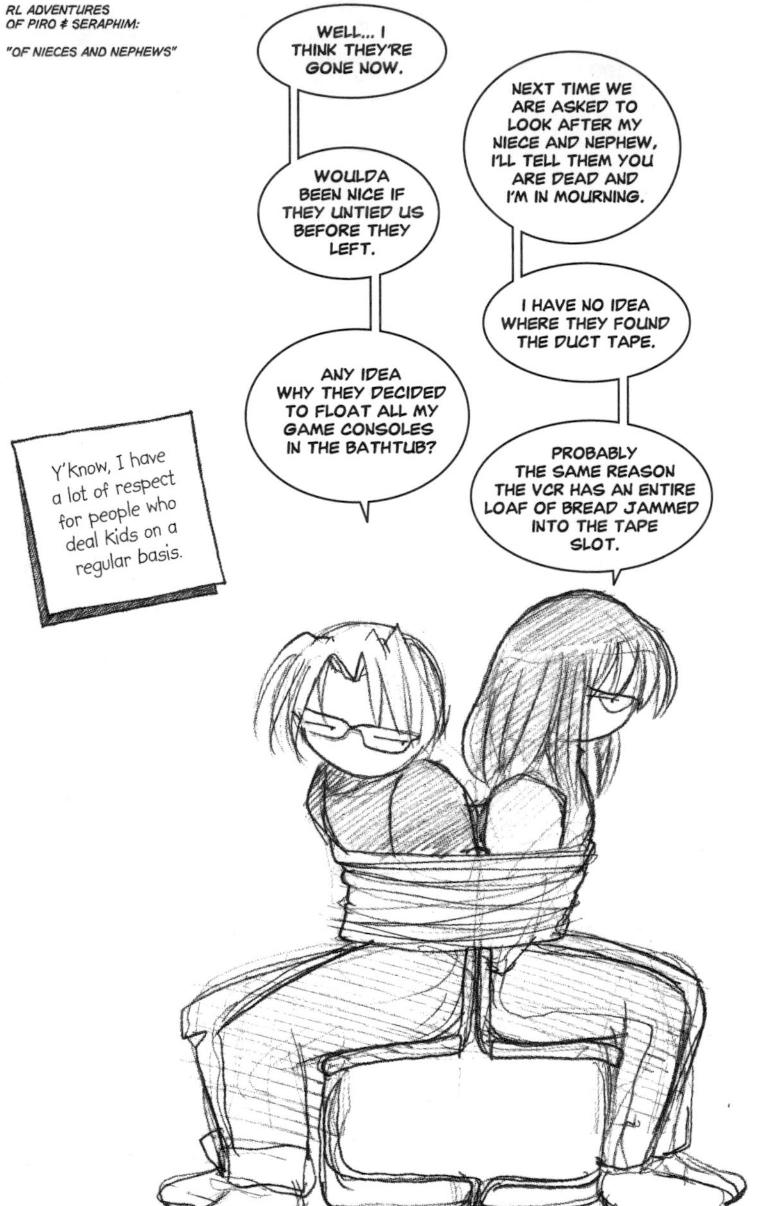
RL ADVENTURES OF PIRO & SERAPHIM:
"OF NIECES AND NEPHEWS"
WELL... I THINK THEY'RE GONE NOW.
NEXT TIME WE ARE ASKED TO LOOK AFTER MY NIECE AND NEPHEW, I'LL TELL THEM YOU ARE DEAD AND I'M IN MOURNING.
WOULDA BEEN NICE IF THEY UNTIED US BEFORE THEY LEFT.
I HAVE NO IDEA WHERE THEY FOUND THE DUCT TAPE.
ANY IDEA WHY THEY DECIDED TO FLOAT ALL MY GAME CONSOLES IN THE BATHTUB?
PROBABLY THE SAME REASON THE VCR HAS AN ENTIRE LOAF OF BREAD JAMMED INTO THE TAPE SLOT.
Y'Know, I have a lot of respect for people who deal kids on a regular basis.
(NOTE: SERAPHIM AND I BARELY SURVIVED LOOKING AFTER HER LITTLE NIECE AND NEPHEW OVER THE WEEKEND.)

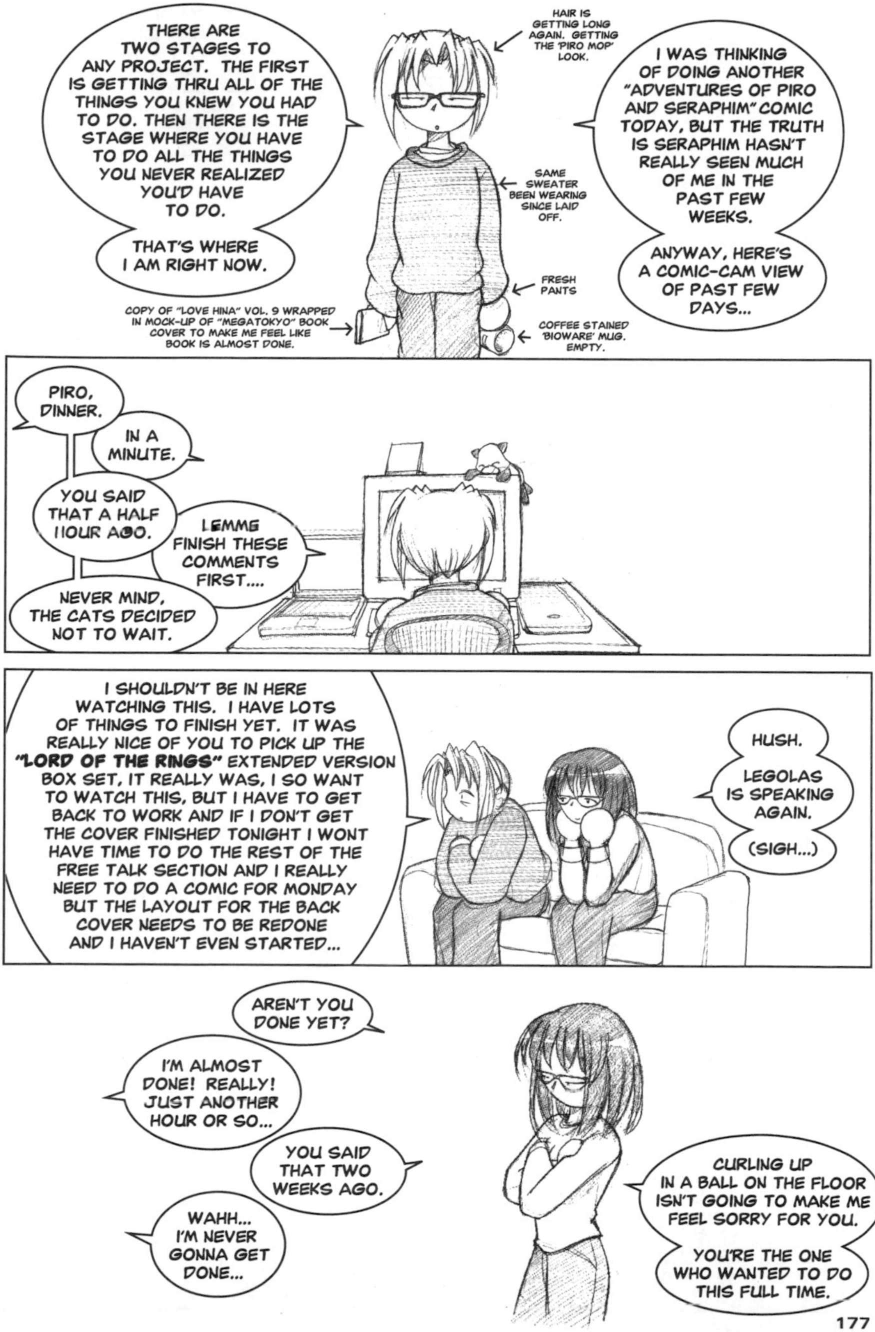
THERE ARE TWO STAGES TO ANY PROJECT. THE FIRST IS GETTING THRU ALL OF THE THINGS YOU KNEW YOU HAD TO DO. THEN THERE IS THE STAGE WHERE YOU HAVE TO DO ALL THE THINGS YOU NEVER REALIZED YOU'D HAVE TO DO.
THAT'S WHERE I AM RIGHT NOW.
HAIR IS GETTING LONG AGAIN. GETTING THE 'PIRO MOP' LOOK.
SAME SWEATER BEEN WEARING SINCE LAID OFF.
FRESH PANTS
COPY OF "LOVE HINA" VOL. 9 WRAPPED IN MOCK-UP OF "MEGATOKYO" BOOK COVER TO MAKE ME FEEL LIKE BOOK IS ALMOST DONE.
COFFEE STAINED 'BIOWARE' MUG. EMPTY.
I WAS THINKING OF DOING ANOTHER "ADVENTURES OF PIRO AND SERAPHIM" COMIC TODAY, BUT THE TRUTH IS SERAPHIM HASN'T REALLY SEEN MUCH OF ME IN THE PAST FEW WEEKS.
ANYWAY, HERE'S A COMIC-CAM VIEW OF PAST FEW DAYS...
PIRO, DINNER.
IN A MINUTE.
YOU SAID THAT A HALF HOUR AGO.
LEMME FINISH THESE COMMENTS FIRST....
NEVER MIND, THE CATS DECIDED NOT TO WAIT.
I SHOULDN'T BE IN HERE WATCHING THIS. I HAVE LOTS OF THINGS TO FINISH YET. IT WAS REALLY NICE OF YOU TO PICK UP THE "LORD OF THE RINGS" EXTENDED VERSION BOX SET, IT REALLY WAS, I SO WANT TO WATCH THIS, BUT I HAVE TO GET BACK TO WORK AND IF I DON'T GET THE COVER FINISHED TONIGHT I WONT HAVE TIME TO DO THE REST OF THE FREE TALK SECTION AND I REALLY NEED TO DO A COMIC FOR MONDAY BUT THE LAYOUT FOR THE BACK COVER NEEDS TO BE REDONE AND I HAVEN'T EVEN STARTED...
HUSH.
LEGOLAS IS SPEAKING AGAIN.
(SIGH...)
AREN'T YOU DONE YET?
I'M ALMOST DONE! REALLY! JUST ANOTHER HOUR OR SO...
YOU SAID THAT TWO WEEKS AGO.
WAHH... I'M NEVER GONNA GET DONE...
CURLING UP IN A BALL ON THE FLOOR ISN'T GOING TO MAKE ME FEEL SORRY FOR YOU.
YOU'RE THE ONE WHO WANTED TO DO THIS FULL TIME.

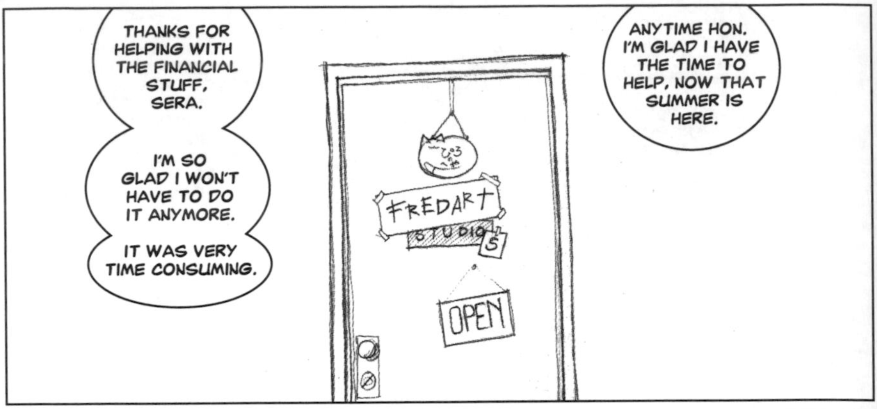
THANKS FOR HELPING WITH THE FINANCIAL STUFF, SERA.
I'M SO GLAD I WON'T HAVE TO DO IT ANYMORE.
IT WAS VERY TIME CONSUMING.
FREDART STUDIO 5
OPEN
ANYTIME HON. I'M GLAD I HAVE THE TIME TO HELP, NOW THAT SUMMER IS HERE.

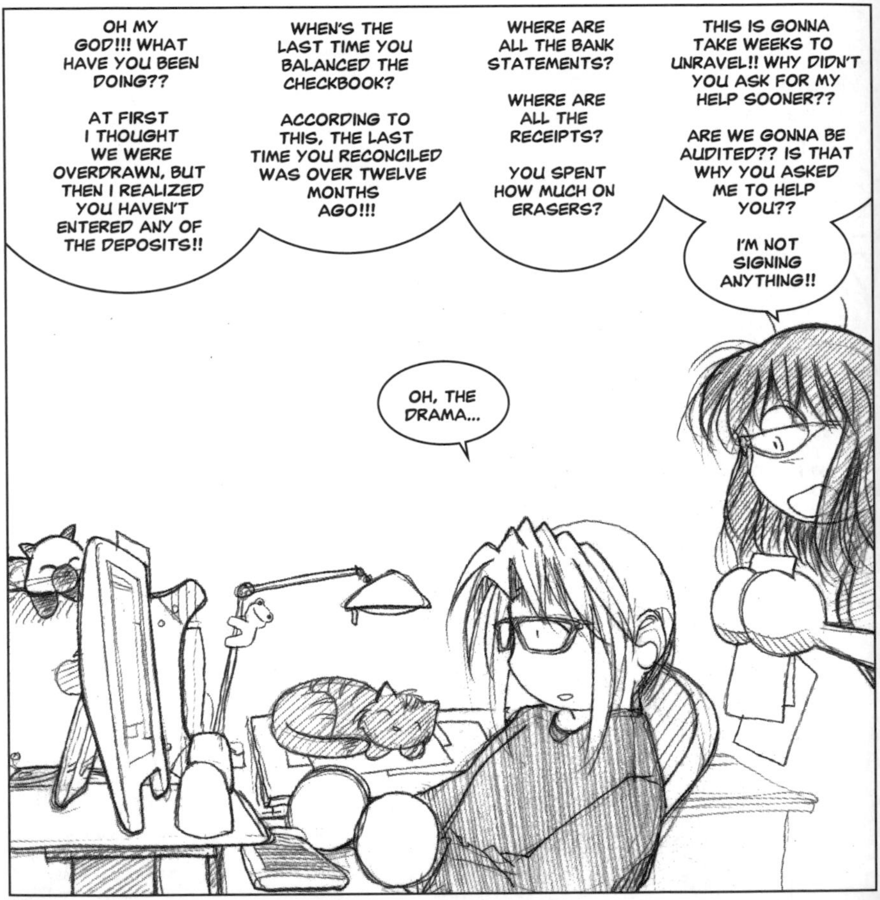
OH MY GOD!!! WHAT HAVE YOU BEEN DOING??
AT FIRST I THOUGHT WE WERE OVERDRAWN, BUT THEN I REALIZED YOU HAVEN'T ENTERED ANY OF THE DEPOSITS!!
WHEN'S THE LAST TIME YOU BALANCED THE CHECKBOOK?
ACCORDING TO THIS, THE LAST TIME YOU RECONCILED WAS OVER TWELVE MONTHS AGO!!!
WHERE ARE ALL THE BANK STATEMENTS?
WHERE ARE ALL THE RECEIPTS?
YOU SPENT HOW MUCH ON ERASERS?
THIS IS GONNA TAKE WEEKS TO UNRAVEL!! WHY DIDN'T YOU ASK FOR MY HELP SOONER??
ARE WE GONNA BE AUDITED?? IS THAT WHY YOU ASKED ME TO HELP YOU??
I'M NOT SIGNING ANYTHING!!
OH, THE DRAMA...

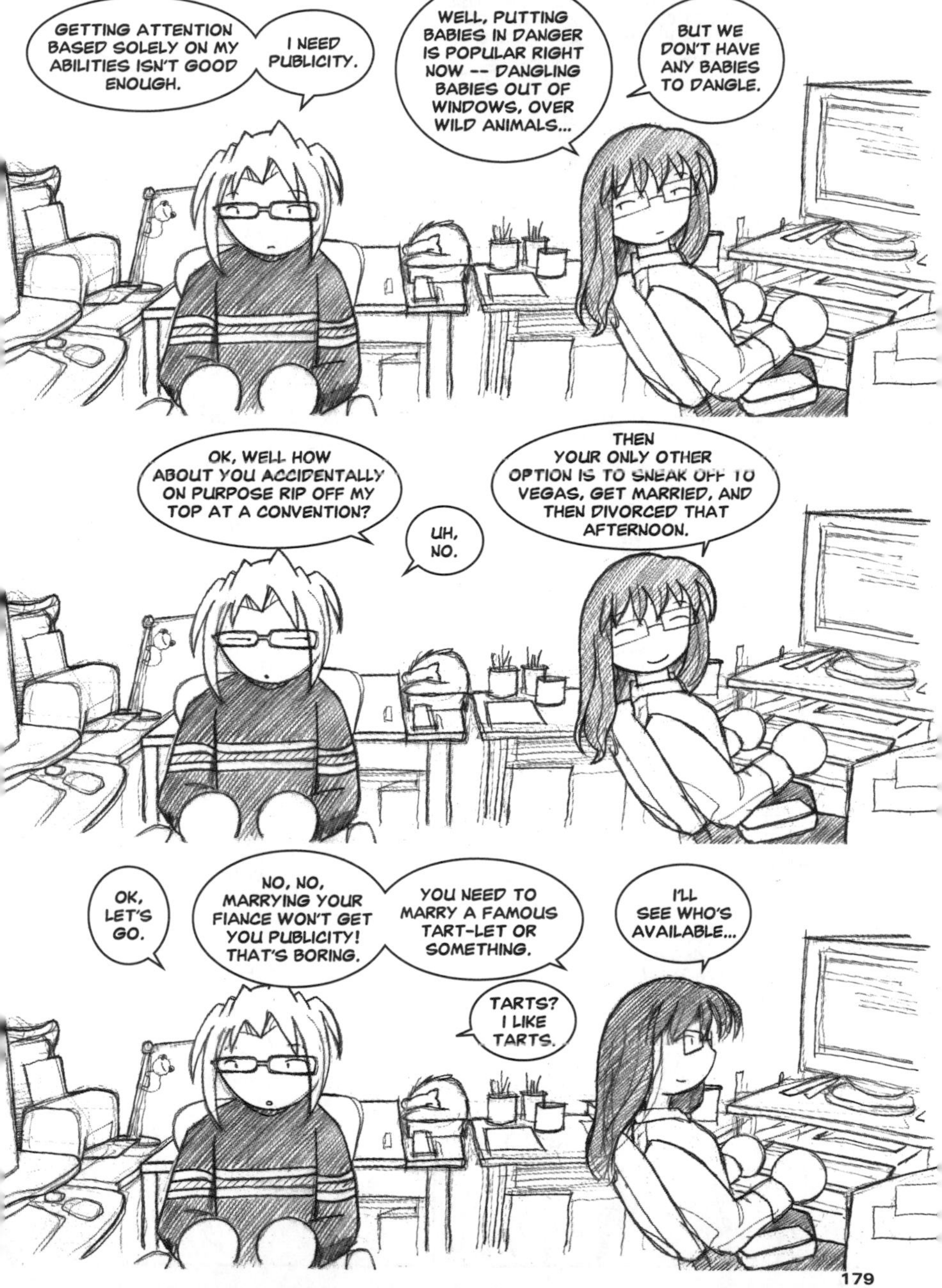
GETTING ATTENTION BASED SOLELY ON MY ABILITIES ISN'T GOOD ENOUGH.
I NEED PUBLICITY.
WELL, PUTTING BABIES IN DANGER IS POPULAR RIGHT NOW -- DANGLING BABIES OUT OF WINDOWS, OVER WILD ANIMALS...
BUT WE DON'T HAVE ANY BABIES TO DANGLE.
OK, WELL HOW ABOUT YOU ACCIDENTALLY ON PURPOSE RIP OFF MY TOP AT A CONVENTION?
UH, NO.
THEN YOUR ONLY OTHER OPTION IS TO SNEAK OFF TO VEGAS, GET MARRIED, AND THEN DIVORCED THAT AFTERNOON.
OK, LET'S GO.
NO, NO, MARRYING YOUR FIANCE WON'T GET YOU PUBLICITY! THAT'S BORING.
YOU NEED TO MARRY A FAMOUS TART-LET OR SOMETHING.
TARTS? I LIKE TARTS.
I'LL SEE WHO'S AVAILABLE...

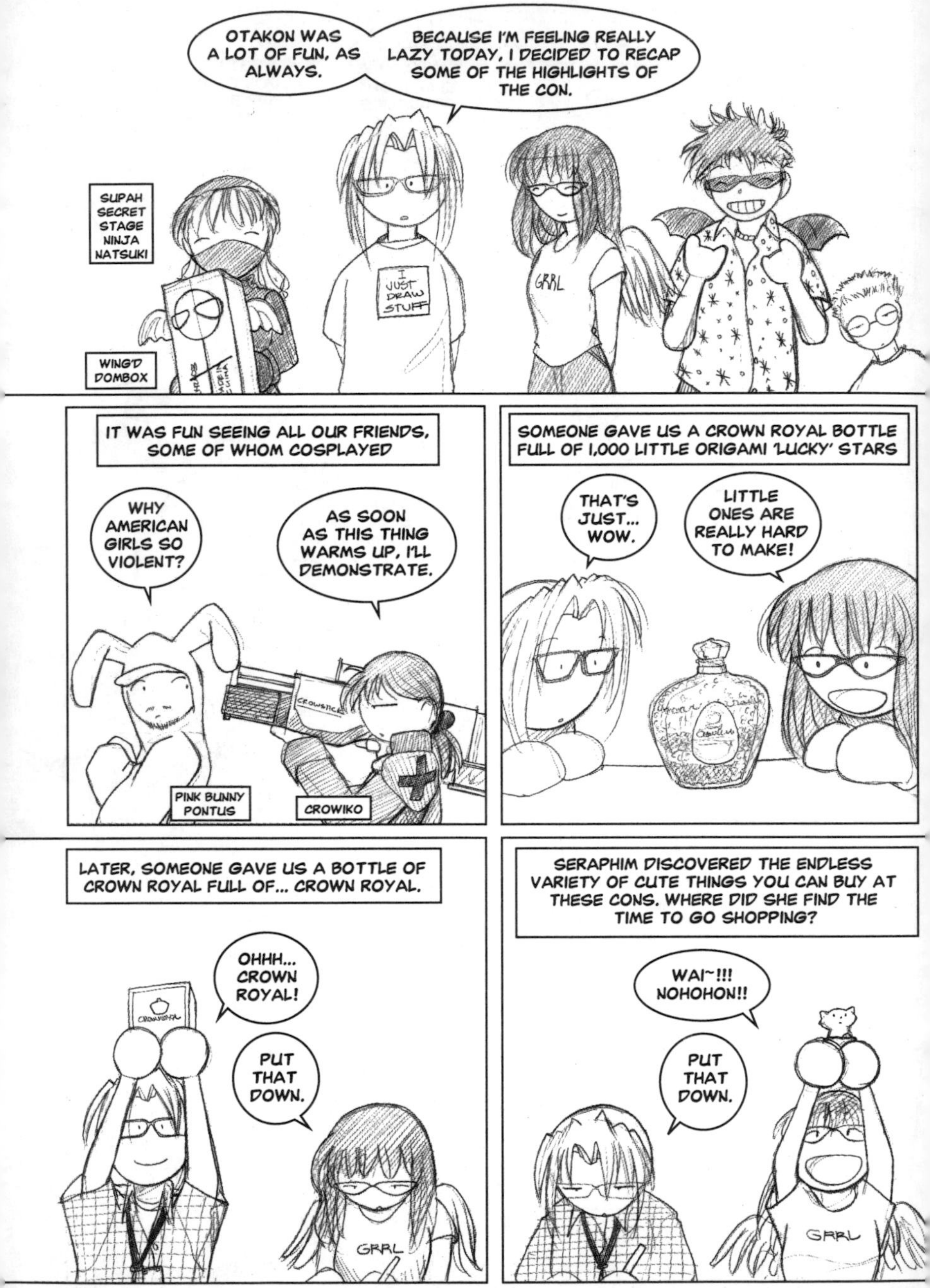
OTAKON WAS A LOT OF FUN, AS ALWAYS.
BECAUSE I'M FEELING REALLY LAZY TODAY, I DECIDED TO RECAP SOME OF THE HIGHLIGHTS OF THE CON.
SUPAH SECRET STAGE NINJA NATSUKI
I JUST DRAW STUFF
GRRL
WING'D DOMBOX
IT WAS FUN SEEING ALL OUR FRIENDS, SOME OF WHOM COSPLAYED
WHY AMERICAN GIRLS SO VIOLENT?
AS SOON AS THIS THING WARMS UP, I'LL DEMONSTRATE.
CROWSTICK
PINK BUNNY PONTUS
CROWIKO
SOMEONE GAVE US A CROWN ROYAL BOTTLE FULL OF 1,000 LITTLE ORIGAMI 'LUCKY' STARS
THAT'S JUST... WOW.
LITTLE ONES ARE REALLY HARD TO MAKE!
LATER, SOMEONE GAVE US A BOTTLE OF CROWN ROYAL FULL OF... CROWN ROYAL.
OHHH... CROWN ROYAL!
PUT THAT DOWN.
GRRL
SERAPHIM DISCOVERED THE ENDLESS VARIETY OF CUTE THINGS YOU CAN BUY AT THESE CONS. WHERE DID SHE FIND THE TIME TO GO SHOPPING?
WAI~!!! NOHOHON!!
PUT THAT DOWN.
GRRL

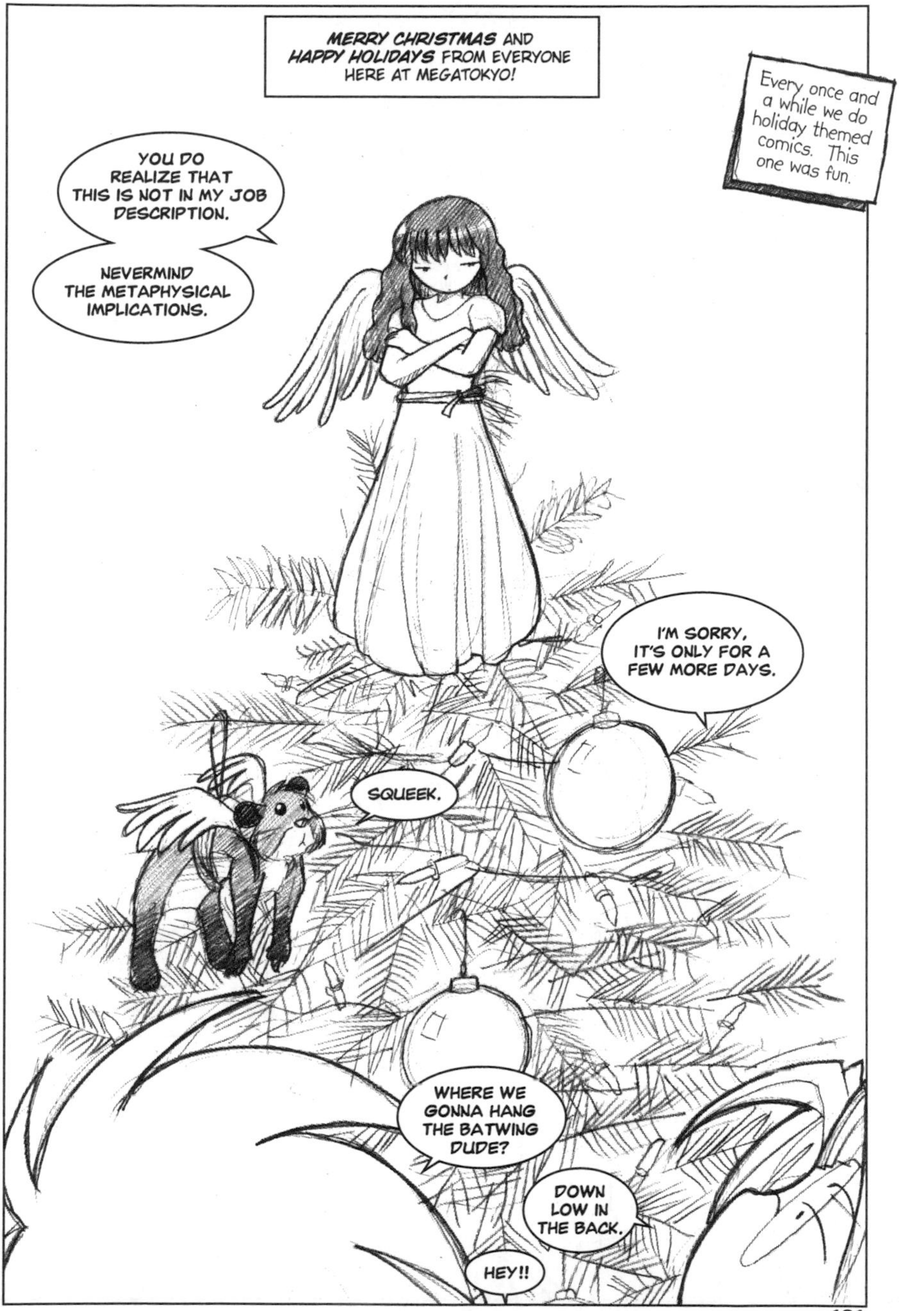
MERRY CHRISTMAS AND HAPPY HOLIDAYS FROM EVERYONE HERE AT MEGATOKYO!
Every once and a while we do holiday themed comics. This one was fun.
YOU DO REALIZE THAT THIS IS NOT IN MY JOB DESCRIPTION.
NEVERMIND THE METAPHYSICAL IMPLICATIONS.
I'M SORRY, IT'S ONLY FOR A FEW MORE DAYS.
SQUEEK.
WHERE WE GONNA HANG THE BATWING DUDE?
DOWN LOW IN THE BACK.
HEY!!

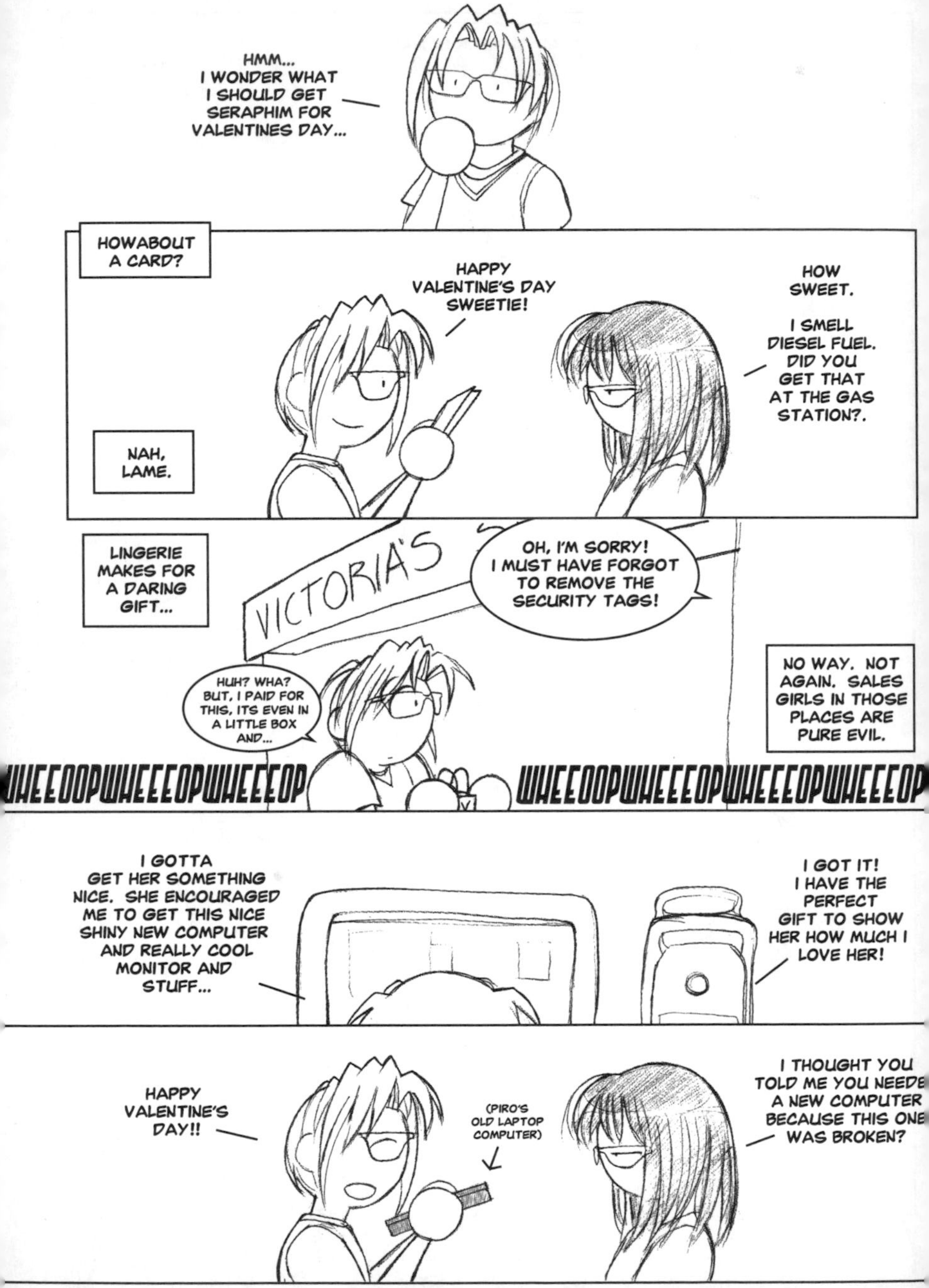
HMM... I WONDER WHAT I SHOULD GET SERAPHIM FOR VALENTINES DAY...
HOWABOUT A CARD?
HAPPY VALENTINE'S DAY SWEETIE!
HOW SWEET.
I SMELL DIESEL FUEL. DID YOU GET THAT AT THE GAS STATION?.
NAH, LAME.
LINGERIE MAKES FOR A DARING GIFT...
VICTORIA'S
OH, I'M SORRY! I MUST HAVE FORGOT TO REMOVE THE SECURITY TAGS!
HUH? WHA? BUT, I PAID FOR THIS, ITS EVEN IN A LITTLE BOX AND...
NO WAY. NOT AGAIN. SALES GIRLS IN THOSE PLACES ARE PURE EVIL.
WHEEOOPWHEEEOPWHEEEOP
WHEEOOPWHEEEOPWHEEEOP
I GOTTA GET HER SOMETHING NICE. SHE ENCOURAGED ME TO GET THIS NICE SHINY NEW COMPUTER AND REALLY COOL MONITOR AND STUFF...
I GOT IT! I HAVE THE PERFECT GIFT TO SHOW HER HOW MUCH I LOVE HER!
HAPPY VALENTINE'S DAY!!
(PIRO'S OLD LAPTOP COMPUTER)
I THOUGHT YOU TOLD ME YOU NEEDE A NEW COMPUTER BECAUSE THIS ONE WAS BROKEN?

OH, BY THE WAY,
REGARDING THAT SABBATICAL SARAH
AND I TOOK BACK IN DECEMBER...

WE ACTUALLY
GOT MARRIED ON
NEW YEARS EVE.

JUST THOUGHT
YOU MIGHT LIKE
TO KNOW.

On the last week of December 2003, Sarah and I snuck off and got married. We didn't tell anyone till February. :)

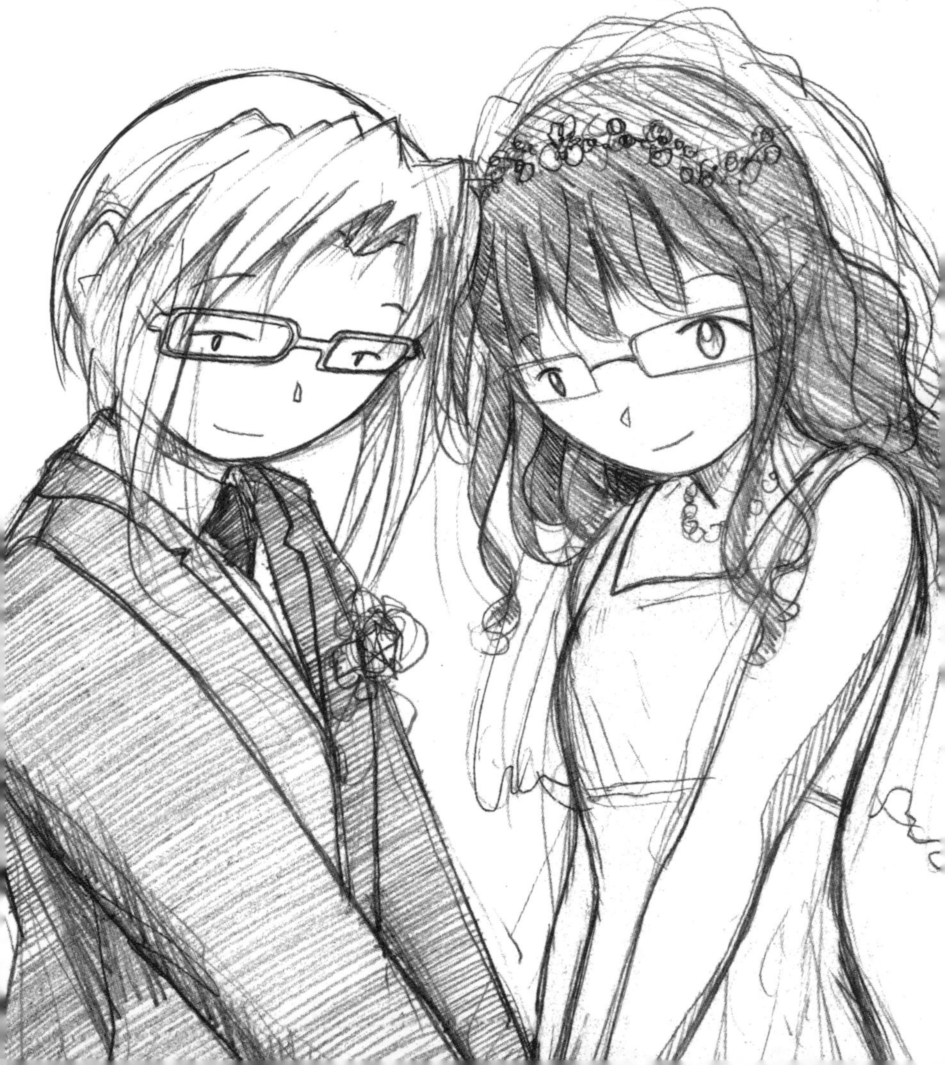

Grand_Theft_Colo.txt

One of the problems with doing a long running series like *Megatokyo*, with it's large cast of characters and it's many threaded storyline, is that sometimes you just want to break the boundaries a little and do something different. Stretch your legs. Get some air. Kill a few things.

The idea for Grand Theft Colo was vague at first. The first two episodes were done at the end of Chapter three and I didn't come back to it until Chapter four ended. I guess I just wanted to play a little and have all the Megatokyo characters act out of character...though I now wonder just how out of character they really are.

There are a lot of parodies and oddities in GTC, and many in-jokes that non-*MT* readers might not get. Makoto-rin really is the name of the main *Megatokyo* webserver, I've always wanted to put Largo in a 'fro, the metaphysical implications of having both Piro and Piroko in a comic at the same time, the idea of me channeling a certain homicidal maniac, and...uh...

Uhm, Yeah. Anyways, it was fun to do. Who said playing with your own characters can't be fun?

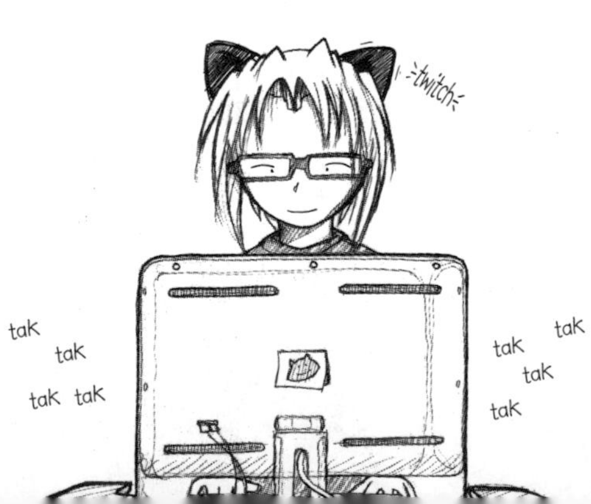
twitch
tak
tak
tak tak
tak
tak
tak
tak

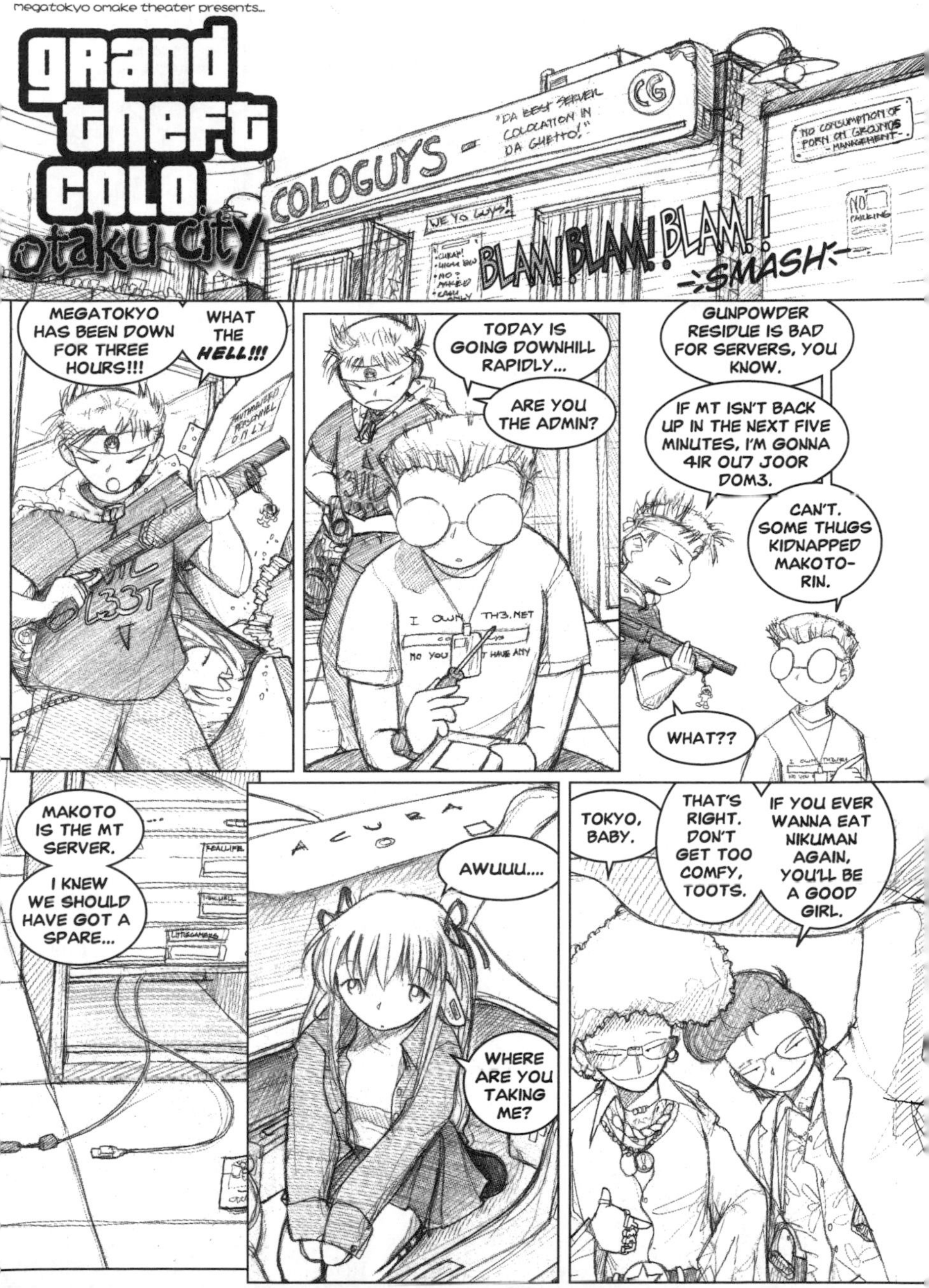
megatokyo omake theater presents...
grand theft colo
otaku city
COLOGUYS
"DA BEST SERVER COLOCATION IN DA GHETTO!"
NO CONSUMPTION OF PORN ON GROUNDS - MANAGEMENT -
WE YO GUYS!
BLAM! BLAM! BLAM!!
SMASH
MEGATOKYO HAS BEEN DOWN FOR THREE HOURS!!!
WHAT THE HELL!!!
TODAY IS GOING DOWNHILL RAPIDLY...
ARE YOU THE ADMIN?
I OWN TH3.NET
GUNPOWDER RESIDUE IS BAD FOR SERVERS, YOU KNOW.
IF MT ISN'T BACK UP IN THE NEXT FIVE MINUTES, I'M GONNA 4IR OU7 JOOR DOM3.
CAN'T. SOME THUGS KIDNAPPED MAKOTO-RIN.
WHAT??
MAKOTO IS THE MT SERVER.
I KNEW WE SHOULD HAVE GOT A SPARE...
AWUUU....
WHERE ARE YOU TAKING ME?
TOKYO, BABY.
THAT'S RIGHT. DON'T GET TOO COMFY, TOOTS.
IF YOU EVER WANNA EAT NIKUMAN AGAIN, YOU'LL BE A GOOD GIRL.

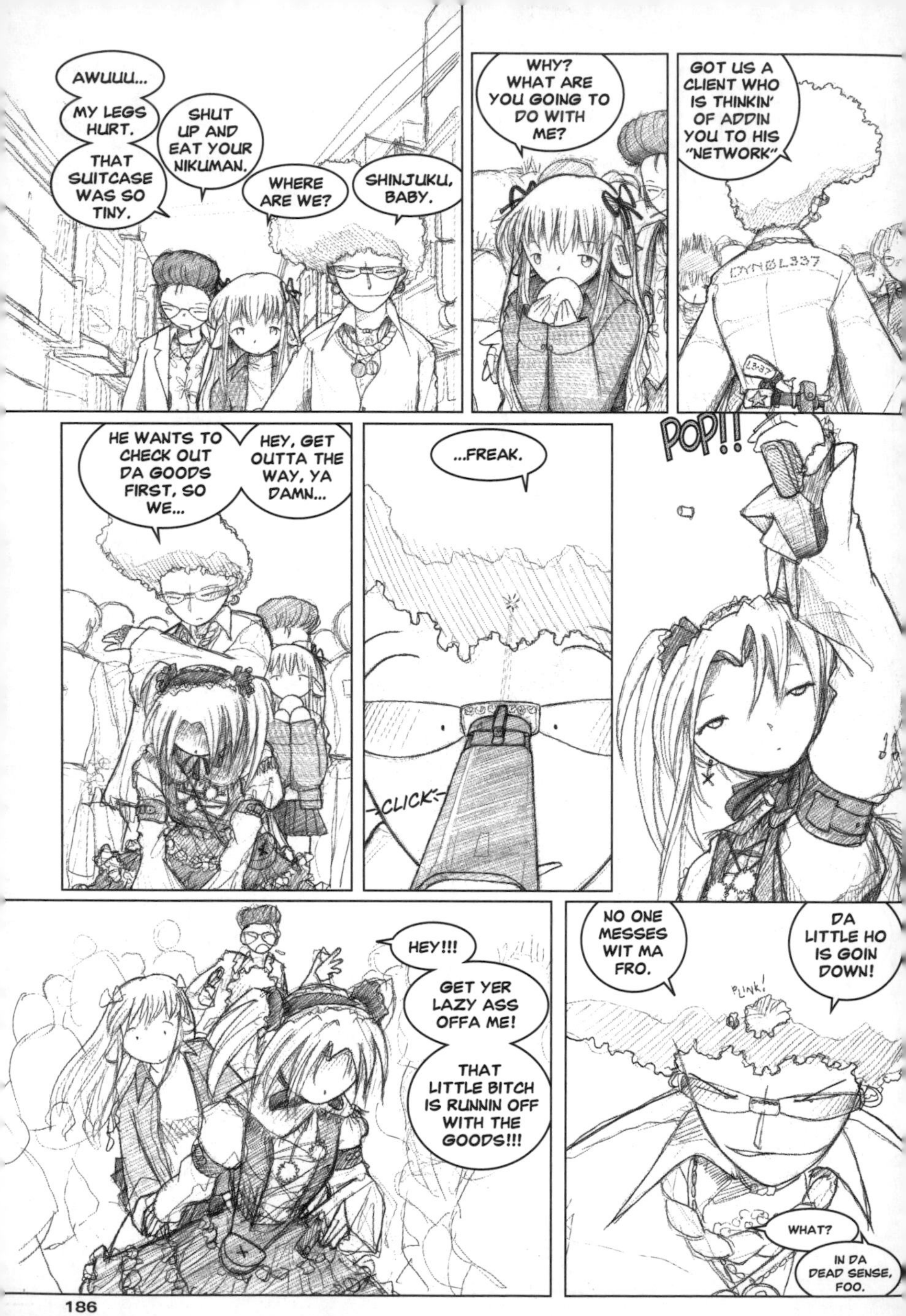

AWUUU...
MY LEGS HURT.
THAT SUITCASE WAS SO TINY.
SHUT UP AND EAT YOUR NIKUMAN.
WHERE ARE WE?
SHINJUKU, BABY.
WHY? WHAT ARE YOU GOING TO DO WITH ME?
GOT US A CLIENT WHO IS THINKIN' OF ADDIN YOU TO HIS "NETWORK"
DYNØL337
HE WANTS TO CHECK OUT DA GOODS FIRST, SO WE...
HEY, GET OUTTA THE WAY, YA DAMN...
...FREAK.
CLICK
POP!!
HEY!!!
GET YER LAZY ASS OFFA ME!
THAT LITTLE BITCH IS RUNNIN OFF WITH THE GOODS!!!
NO ONE MESSES WIT MA FRO.
DA LITTLE HO IS GOIN DOWN!
PLINK!
WHAT?
IN DA DEAD SENSE, FOO.

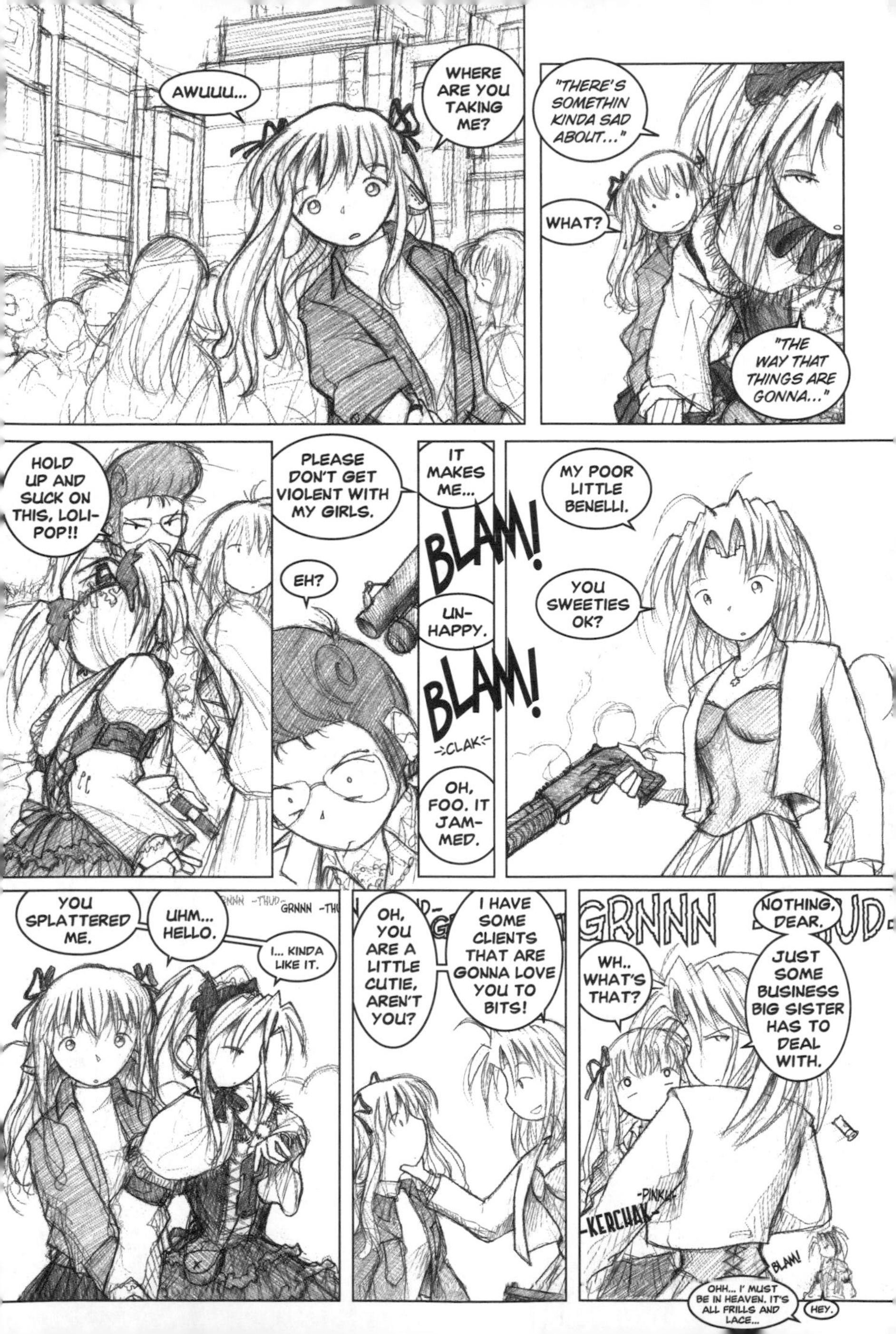
AWUUU...
WHERE ARE YOU TAKING ME?
"THERE'S SOMETHIN KINDA SAD ABOUT..."
WHAT?
"THE WAY THAT THINGS ARE GONNA..."
HOLD UP AND SUCK ON THIS, LOLI-POP!!
PLEASE DON'T GET VIOLENT WITH MY GIRLS.
EH?
IT MAKES ME...
BLAM!
UN-HAPPY.
BLAM!
-CLAK-
OH, FOO. IT JAM-MED.
MY POOR LITTLE BENELLI.
YOU SWEETIES OK?
YOU SPLATTERED ME.
UHM... HELLO.
GRNNN -THUD-
I... KINDA LIKE IT.
OH, YOU ARE A LITTLE CUTIE, AREN'T YOU?
I HAVE SOME CLIENTS THAT ARE GONNA LOVE YOU TO BITS!
GRNNN
NOTHING, DEAR.
WH.. WHAT'S THAT?
JUST SOME BUSINESS BIG SISTER HAS TO DEAL WITH.
-PINKU-
-KERCHAK-
BLAM!
OHH... I' MUST BE IN HEAVEN. IT'S ALL FRILLS AND LACE...
HEY.

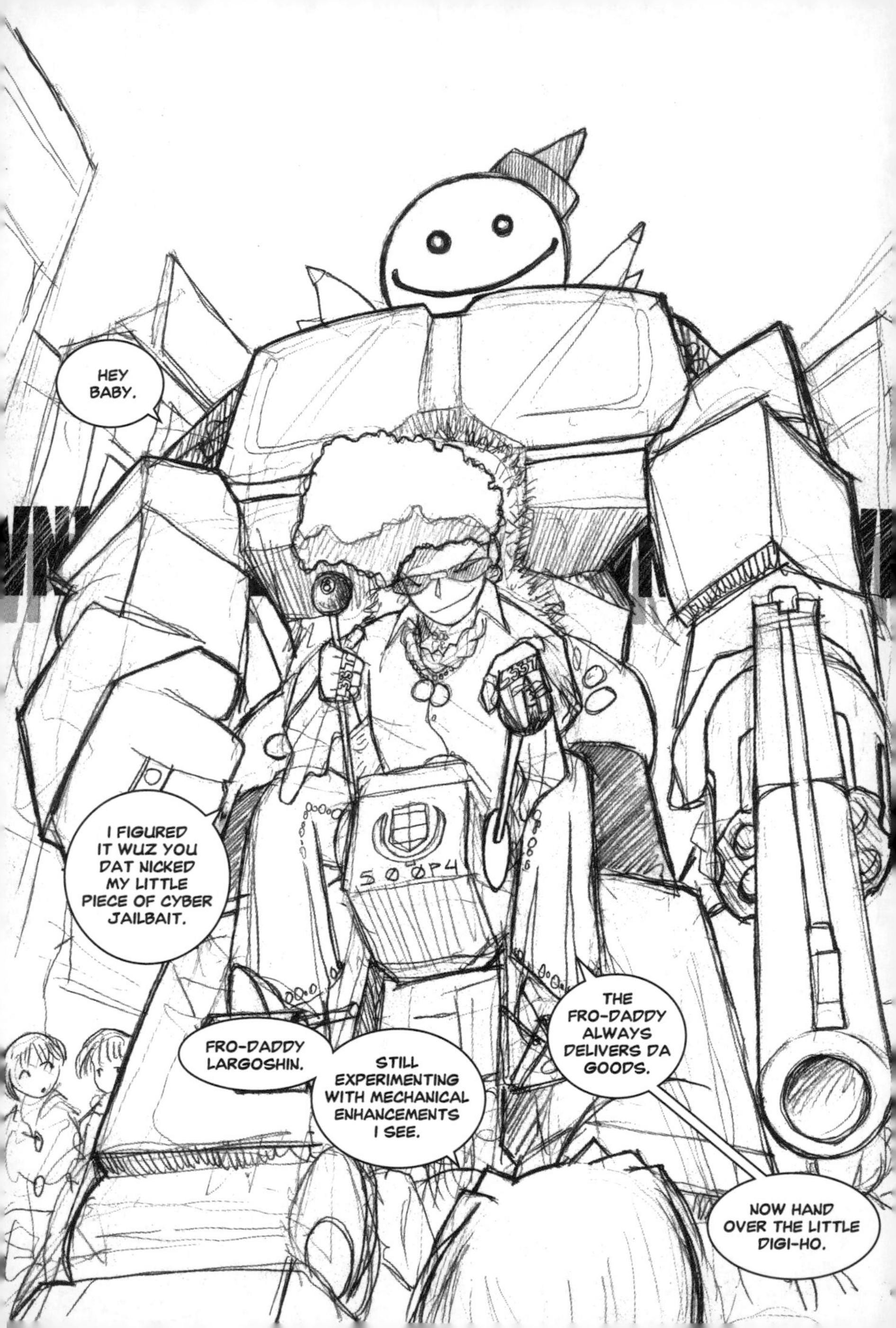

HEY BABY.
I FIGURED IT WUZ YOU DAT NICKED MY LITTLE PIECE OF CYBER JAILBAIT.
FRO-DADDY LARGOSHIN.
STILL EXPERIMENTING WITH MECHANICAL ENHANCEMENTS I SEE.
THE FRO-DADDY ALWAYS DELIVERS DA GOODS.
NOW HAND OVER THE LITTLE DIGI-HO.

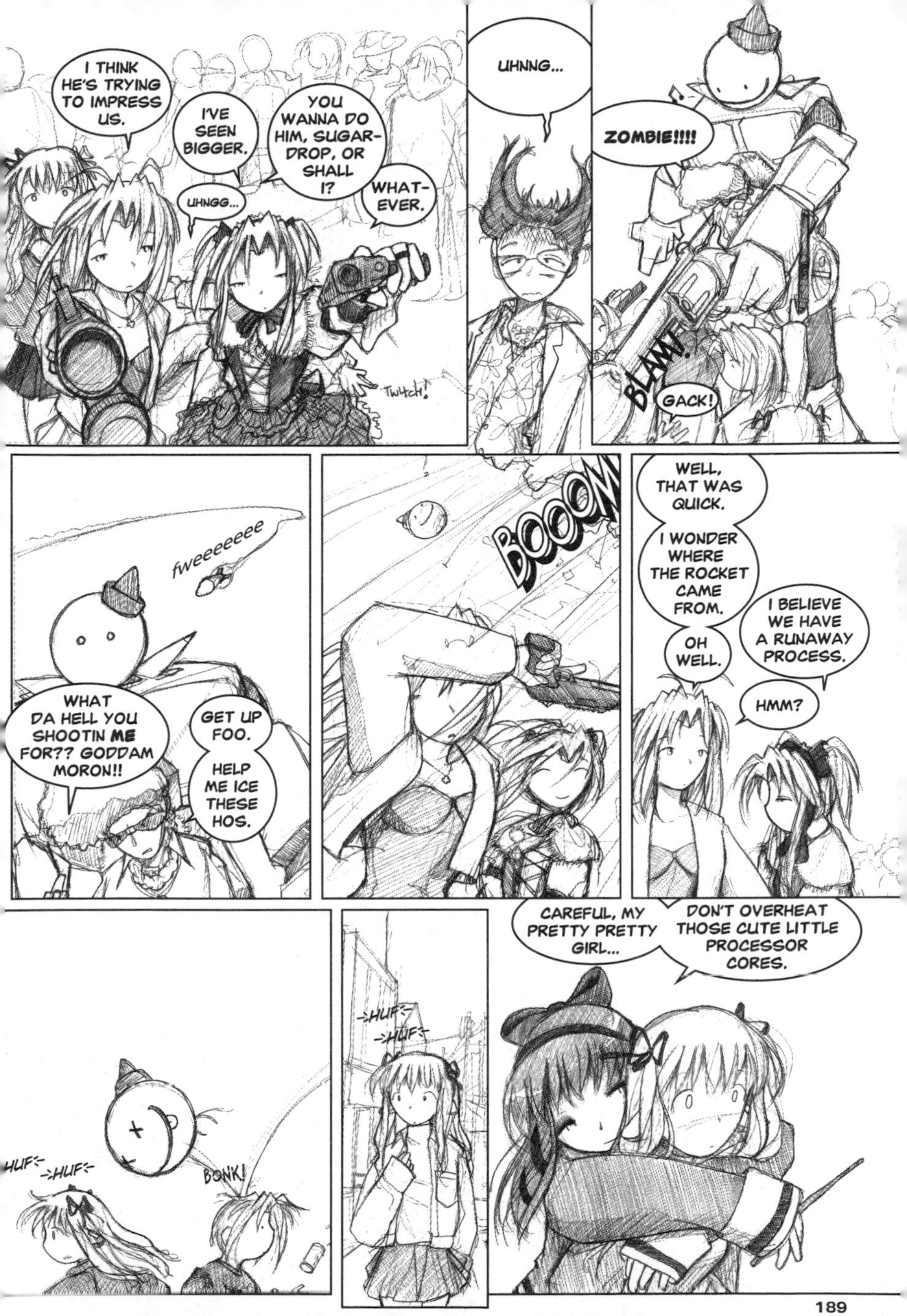
I THINK HE'S TRYING TO IMPRESS US.
I'VE SEEN BIGGER.
UHNGG...
YOU WANNA DO HIM, SUGAR-DROP, OR SHALL I?
WHAT-EVER.
TWITCH!
UHNNG...
ZOMBIE!!!!
BLAM!
GACK!
fweeeeeee
WHAT DA HELL YOU SHOOTIN **ME** FOR?? GODDAM MORON!!
GET UP FOO.
HELP ME ICE THESE HOS.
BOOOM
WELL, THAT WAS QUICK.
I WONDER WHERE THE ROCKET CAME FROM.
OH WELL.
I BELIEVE WE HAVE A RUNAWAY PROCESS.
HMM?
HUF
HUF
BONK!
HUF
HUF
CAREFUL, MY PRETTY PRETTY GIRL...
DON'T OVERHEAT THOSE CUTE LITTLE PROCESSOR CORES.

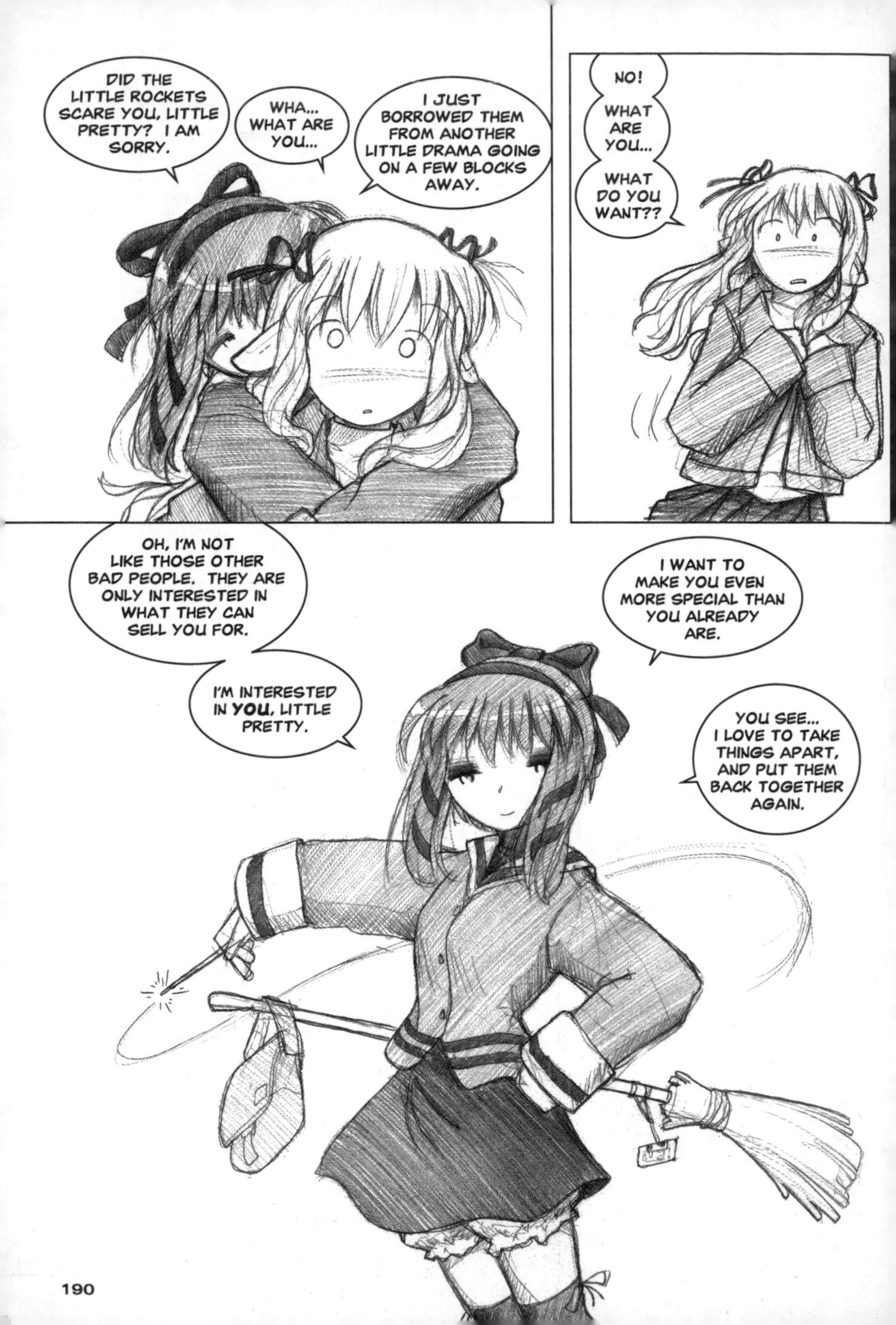
DID THE LITTLE ROCKETS SCARE YOU, LITTLE PRETTY? I AM SORRY.
WHA... WHAT ARE YOU...
I JUST BORROWED THEM FROM ANOTHER LITTLE DRAMA GOING ON A FEW BLOCKS AWAY.
NO!
WHAT ARE YOU...
WHAT DO YOU WANT??
OH, I'M NOT LIKE THOSE OTHER BAD PEOPLE. THEY ARE ONLY INTERESTED IN WHAT THEY CAN SELL YOU FOR.
I'M INTERESTED IN **YOU**, LITTLE PRETTY.
I WANT TO MAKE YOU EVEN MORE SPECIAL THAN YOU ALREADY ARE.
YOU SEE... I LOVE TO TAKE THINGS APART, AND PUT THEM BACK TOGETHER AGAIN.

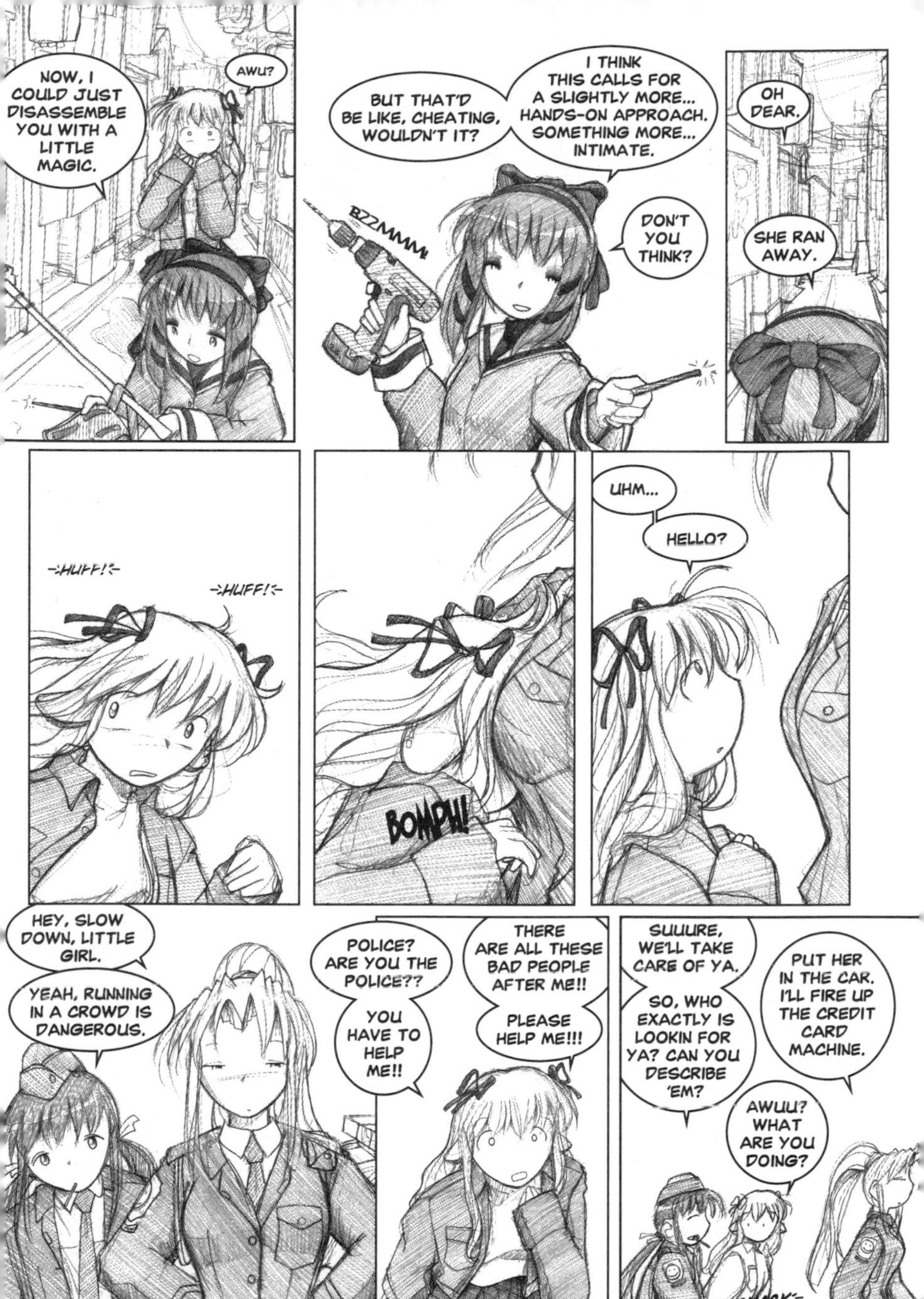

NOW, I COULD JUST DISASSEMBLE YOU WITH A LITTLE MAGIC.
AWU?
BUT THAT'D BE LIKE, CHEATING, WOULDN'T IT?
I THINK THIS CALLS FOR A SLIGHTLY MORE... HANDS-ON APPROACH. SOMETHING MORE... INTIMATE.
BZZMMM!
DON'T YOU THINK?
OH DEAR.
SHE RAN AWAY.
HUFF!
HUFF!
BOMPH!
UHM...
HELLO?
HEY, SLOW DOWN, LITTLE GIRL.
YEAH, RUNNING IN A CROWD IS DANGEROUS.
POLICE? ARE YOU THE POLICE??
YOU HAVE TO HELP ME!!
THERE ARE ALL THESE BAD PEOPLE AFTER ME!!
PLEASE HELP ME!!!
SUUURE, WE'LL TAKE CARE OF YA.
SO, WHO EXACTLY IS LOOKIN FOR YA? CAN YOU DESCRIBE 'EM?
PUT HER IN THE CAR. I'LL FIRE UP THE CREDIT CARD MACHINE.
AWUU? WHAT ARE YOU DOING?
KER-CHACK

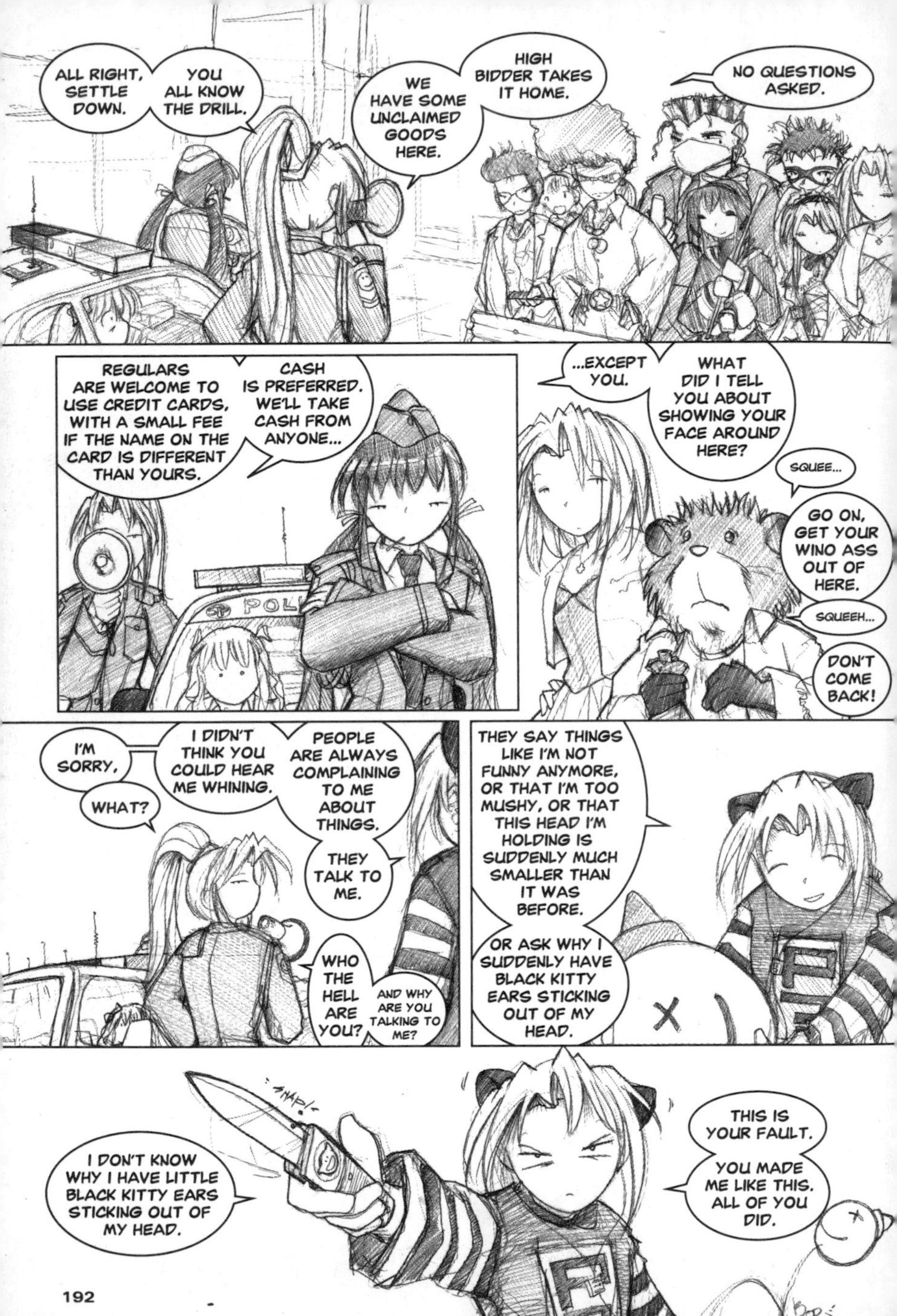

ALL RIGHT, SETTLE DOWN.
YOU ALL KNOW THE DRILL.
WE HAVE SOME UNCLAIMED GOODS HERE.
HIGH BIDDER TAKES IT HOME.
NO QUESTIONS ASKED.
REGULARS ARE WELCOME TO USE CREDIT CARDS, WITH A SMALL FEE IF THE NAME ON THE CARD IS DIFFERENT THAN YOURS.
CASH IS PREFERRED. WE'LL TAKE CASH FROM ANYONE...
...EXCEPT YOU.
WHAT DID I TELL YOU ABOUT SHOWING YOUR FACE AROUND HERE?
SQUEE...
GO ON, GET YOUR WINO ASS OUT OF HERE.
SQUEEH...
DON'T COME BACK!
I'M SORRY,
I DIDN'T THINK YOU COULD HEAR ME WHINING.
WHAT?
PEOPLE ARE ALWAYS COMPLAINING TO ME ABOUT THINGS.
THEY TALK TO ME.
WHO THE HELL ARE YOU?
AND WHY ARE YOU TALKING TO ME?
THEY SAY THINGS LIKE I'M NOT FUNNY ANYMORE, OR THAT I'M TOO MUSHY, OR THAT THIS HEAD I'M HOLDING IS SUDDENLY MUCH SMALLER THAN IT WAS BEFORE.
OR ASK WHY I SUDDENLY HAVE BLACK KITTY EARS STICKING OUT OF MY HEAD.
SNAP!
I DON'T KNOW WHY I HAVE LITTLE BLACK KITTY EARS STICKING OUT OF MY HEAD.
THIS IS YOUR FAULT.
YOU MADE ME LIKE THIS. ALL OF YOU DID.
Bop

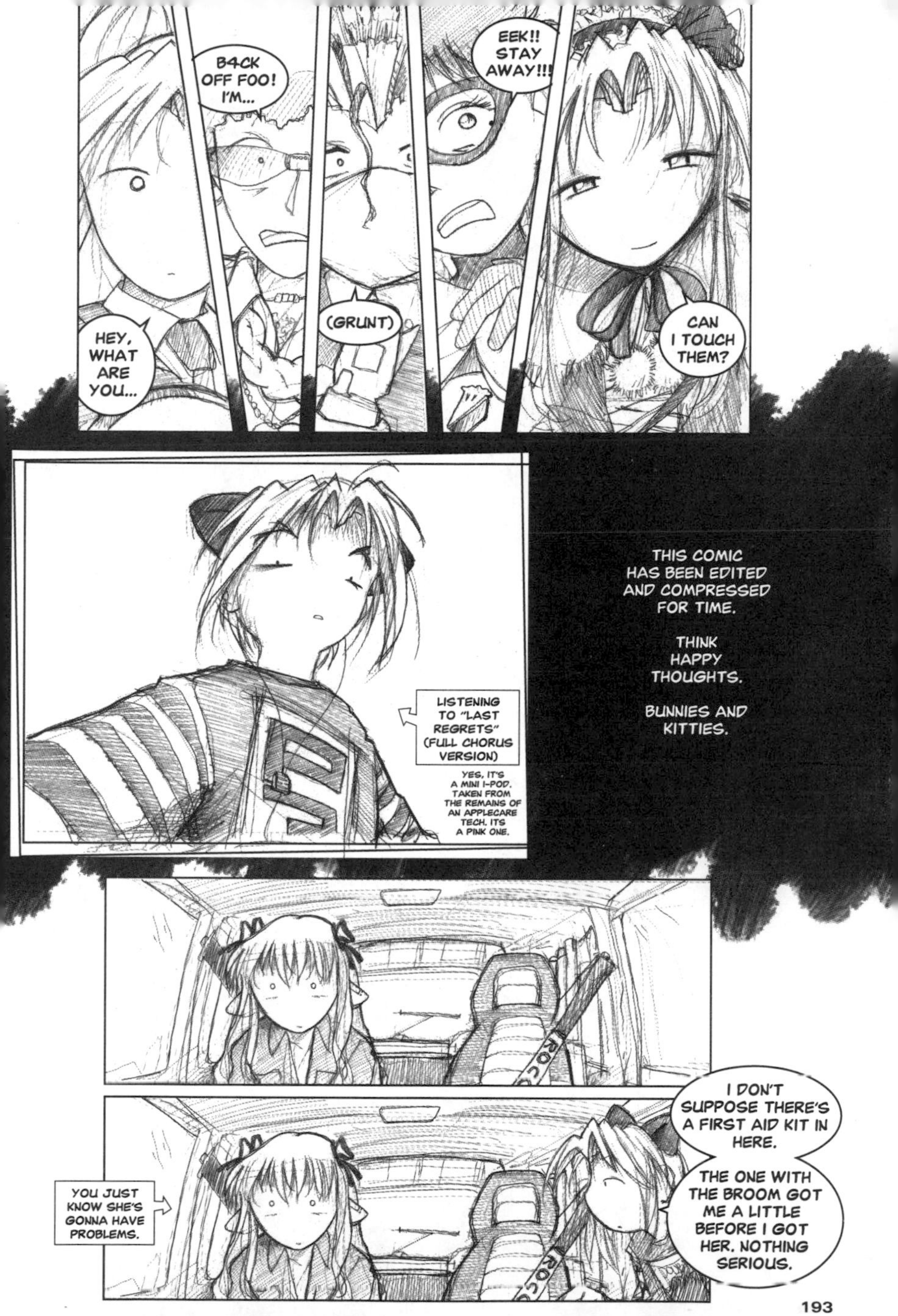

HEY, WHAT ARE YOU...
B4CK OFF FOO! I'M...
(GRUNT)
EEK!! STAY AWAY!!!
CAN I TOUCH THEM?
LISTENING TO "LAST REGRETS" (FULL CHORUS VERSION)
YES, IT'S A MINI I-POD, TAKEN FROM THE REMAINS OF AN APPLECARE TECH. ITS A PINK ONE.
THIS COMIC HAS BEEN EDITED AND COMPRESSED FOR TIME.
THINK HAPPY THOUGHTS.
BUNNIES AND KITTIES.
YOU JUST KNOW SHE'S GONNA HAVE PROBLEMS.
I DON'T SUPPOSE THERE'S A FIRST AID KIT IN HERE.
THE ONE WITH THE BROOM GOT ME A LITTLE BEFORE I GOT HER. NOTHING SERIOUS.

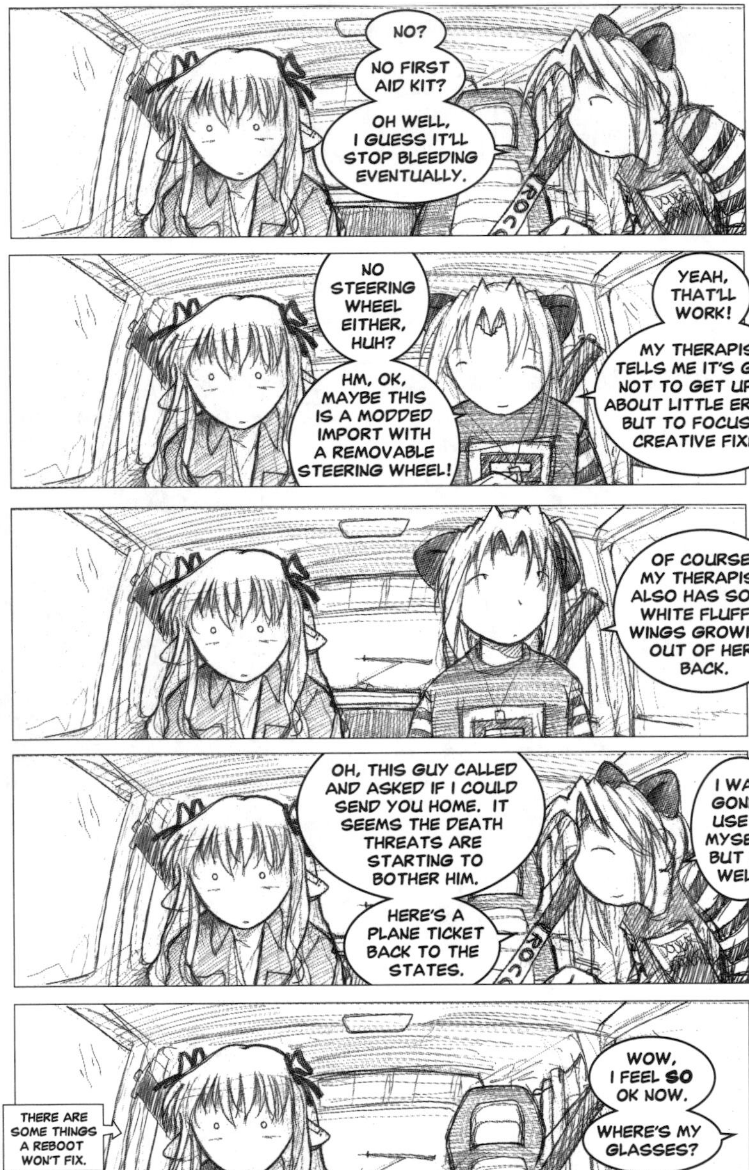
NO?
NO FIRST AID KIT?
OH WELL, I GUESS IT'LL STOP BLEEDING EVENTUALLY.
NO STEERING WHEEL EITHER, HUH?
HM, OK, MAYBE THIS IS A MODDED IMPORT WITH A REMOVABLE STEERING WHEEL!
YEAH, THAT'LL WORK!
MY THERAPIST TELLS ME IT'S GOOD NOT TO GET UPSET ABOUT LITTLE ERRORS BUT TO FOCUS ON CREATIVE FIXES.
OF COURSE, MY THERAPIST ALSO HAS SOFT, WHITE FLUFFY WINGS GROWING OUT OF HER BACK.
OH, THIS GUY CALLED AND ASKED IF I COULD SEND YOU HOME. IT SEEMS THE DEATH THREATS ARE STARTING TO BOTHER HIM.
HERE'S A PLANE TICKET BACK TO THE STATES.
I WAS GONNA USE IT MYSELF, BUT OH WELL.
THERE ARE SOME THINGS A REBOOT WON'T FIX.
WOW, I FEEL **SO** OK NOW.
WHERE'S MY GLASSES?

Dead_Piro_Art_Days.txt

Dead Piro Days are where I do a single illustration rather than a whole comic. Each *Megatokyo* comic takes about eight hours to complete, so doing a DPD illustration is one of the things I can do when I don't have the time to do a normal comic.

Unfortunately, you may notice that this section of the book is rather large. I did a lot of DPDs during the course of these two chapters. Too many--I missed a lot of comics.

One of the problems with DPDs is that people have high expectations of them. I swear there are times that I would have rather do a normal comic than try to figure out what to draw for a DPD. In the end I think that some of my best drawings have been DPDs, like the "In Search of Lost Wings" series you will find in this section. DPDs can say things about the characters that it's hard to do in normal *MT* comics.

Even if they are a cop-out of sorts, Dead Piro Days are an important part of *Megatokyo*. At least I keep telling myself that.

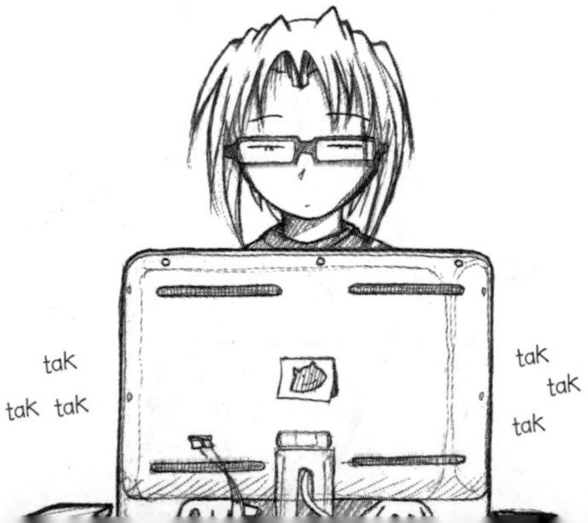
tak
tak tak
tak
tak
tak

megatokyo:gameworlds

fail condition

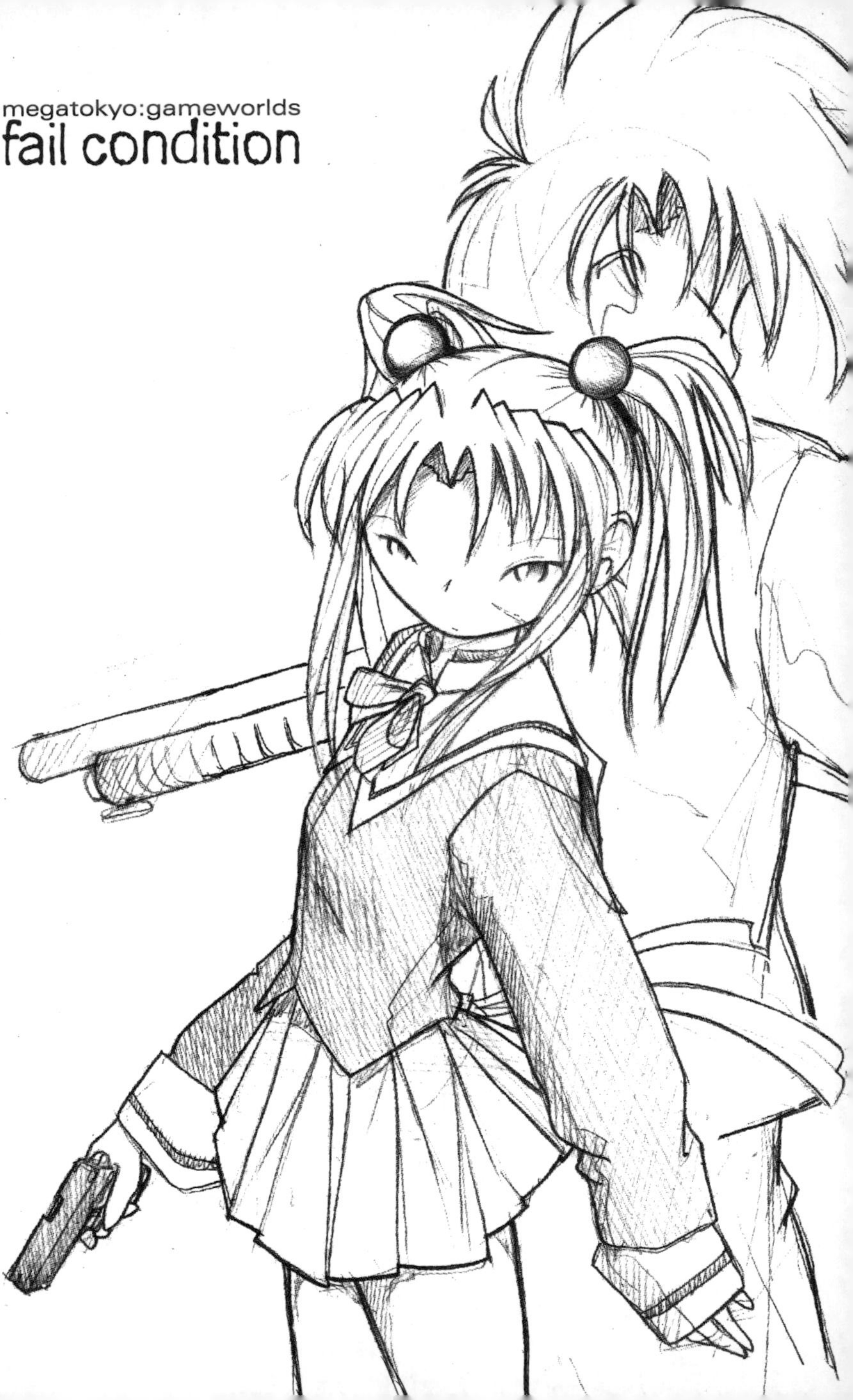

ph34r the kut3 ls

b4k4.md4 (alpha release 2.03)

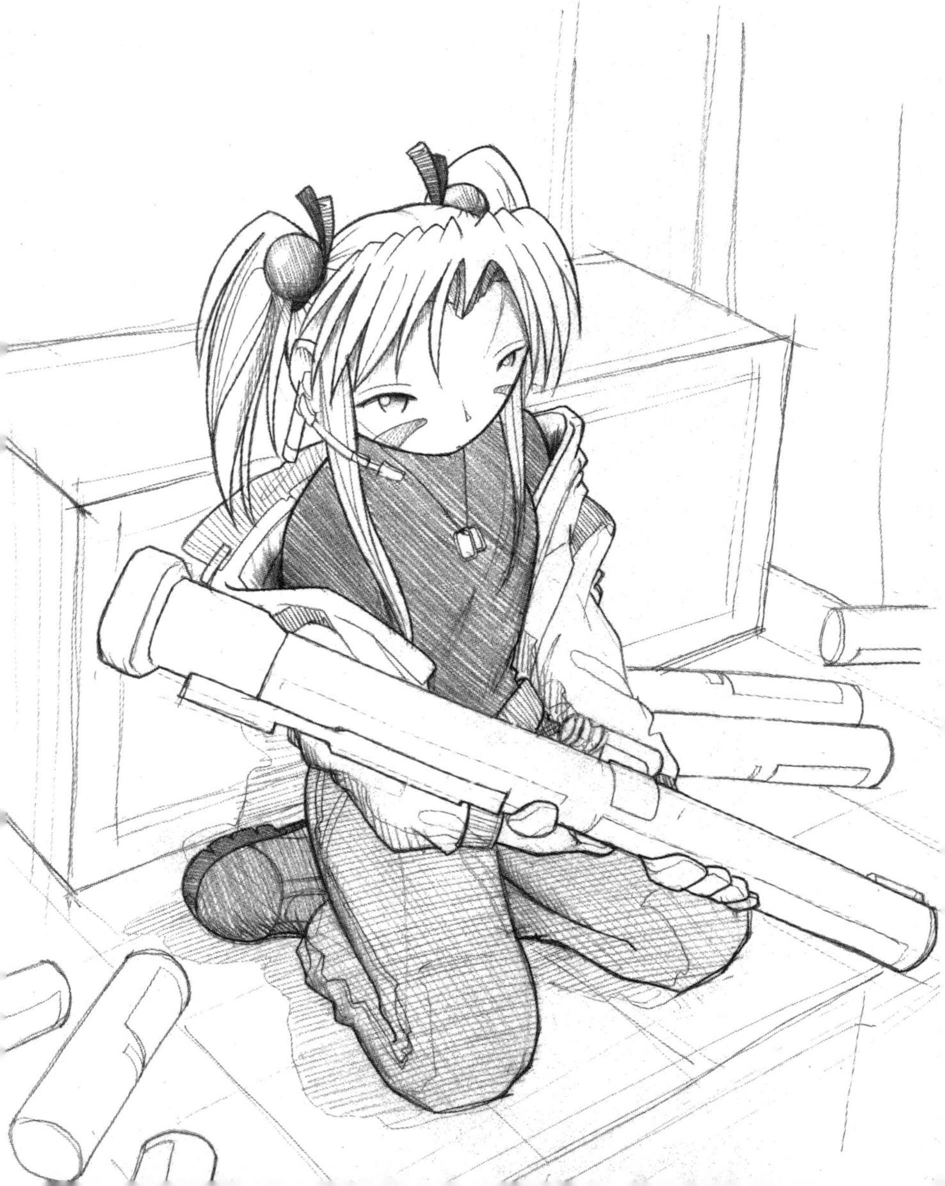

"ping & makoto"

time for a new server :) funds from the auction of this drawing at Anime Central 2003 next week will go towards the purchase of nayuki-chan, who will work with makoto to serve up the mt website and it's pages.

note that this is a direct scan of the drawing - i haven't cleaned up or adjusted levels.

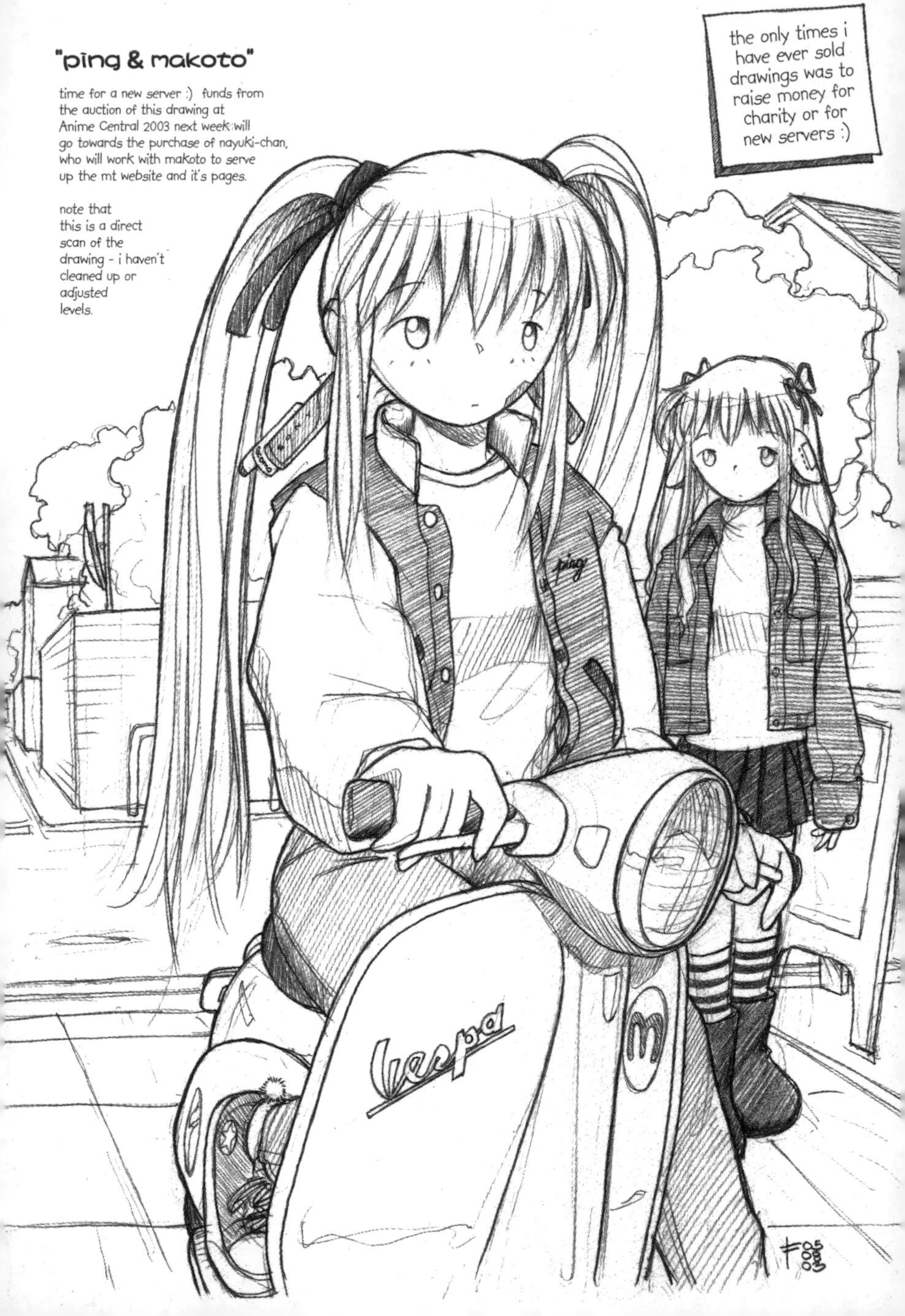

the only times i have ever sold drawings was to raise money for charity or for new servers :)
ping
vespa

"l33t folding skillz"

just a little something to tide you over 'till i get back from Anime Central. I kinda like these 'snapshot' style DPD drawings, they are a lot of fun.

Next MT comic will be wednesday next week.

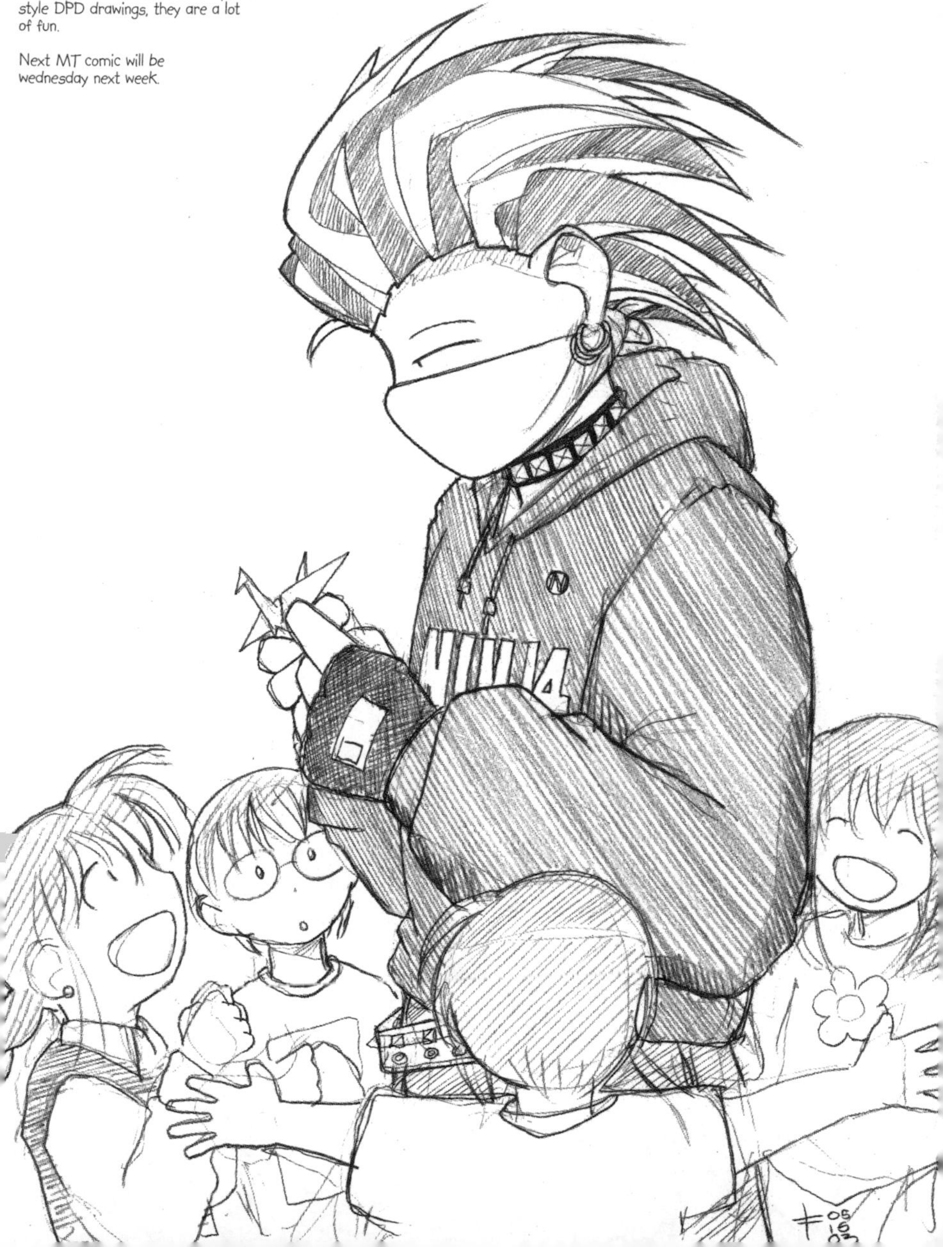

...MEGADUSTRIAL:R3M1><

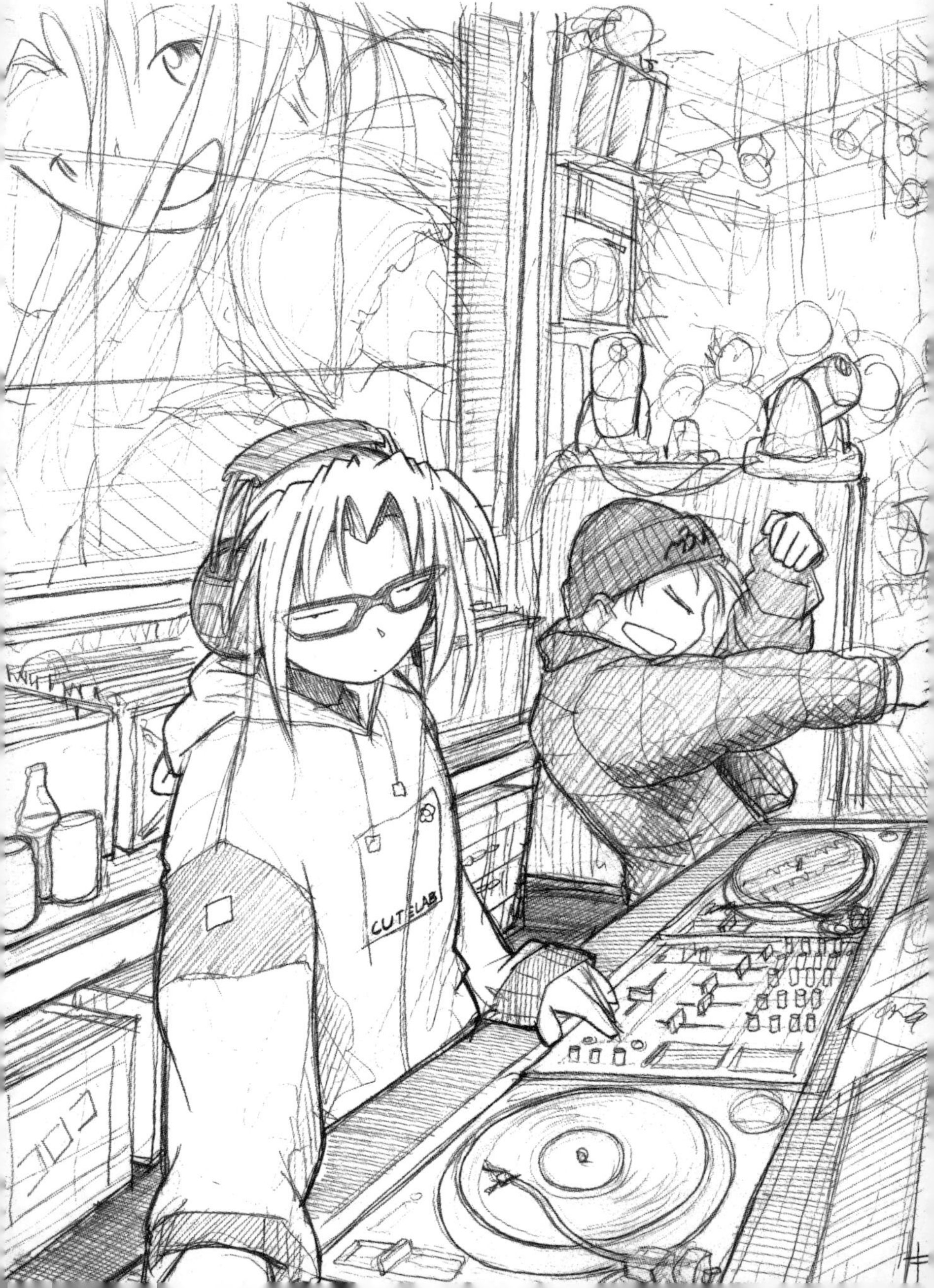
CUTELAB

motion stopped

hayasaka erika & nanasawa kimiko

artshow random sketching - otakon 2003

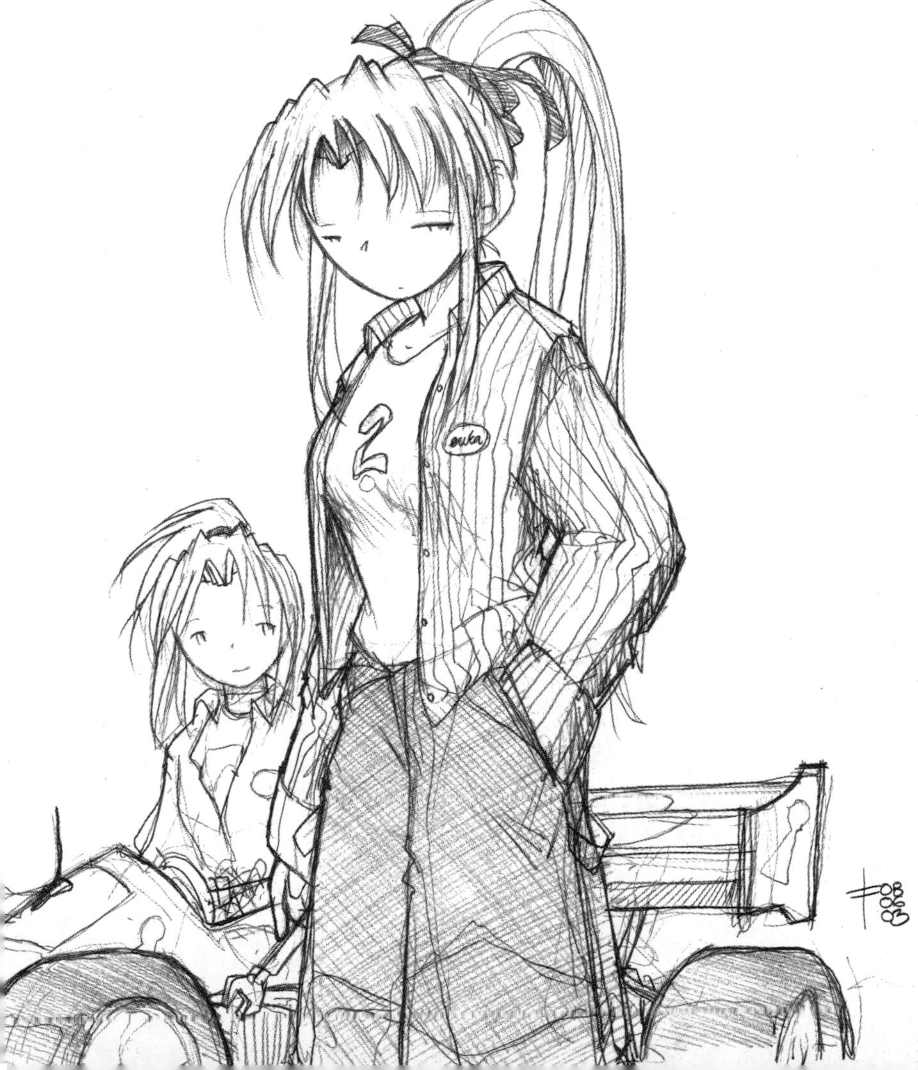
erika

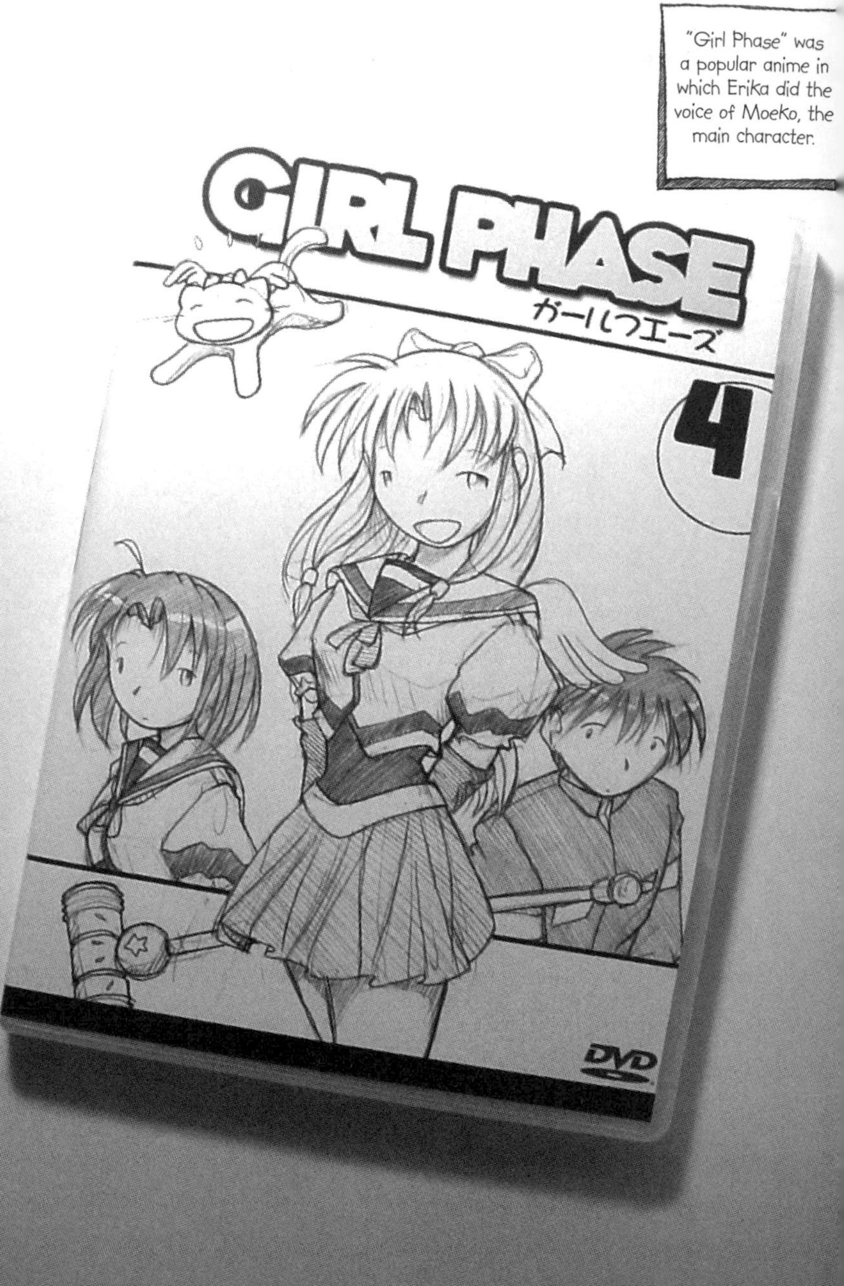
"Girl Phase" was a popular anime in which Erika did the voice of Moeko, the main character.
GIRL PHASE
ガールフエーズ
4
DVD

sight
サイト

"Sight" is a new game in which Kimiko is doing the voice of Kotone, shown here with her cat, Burn.

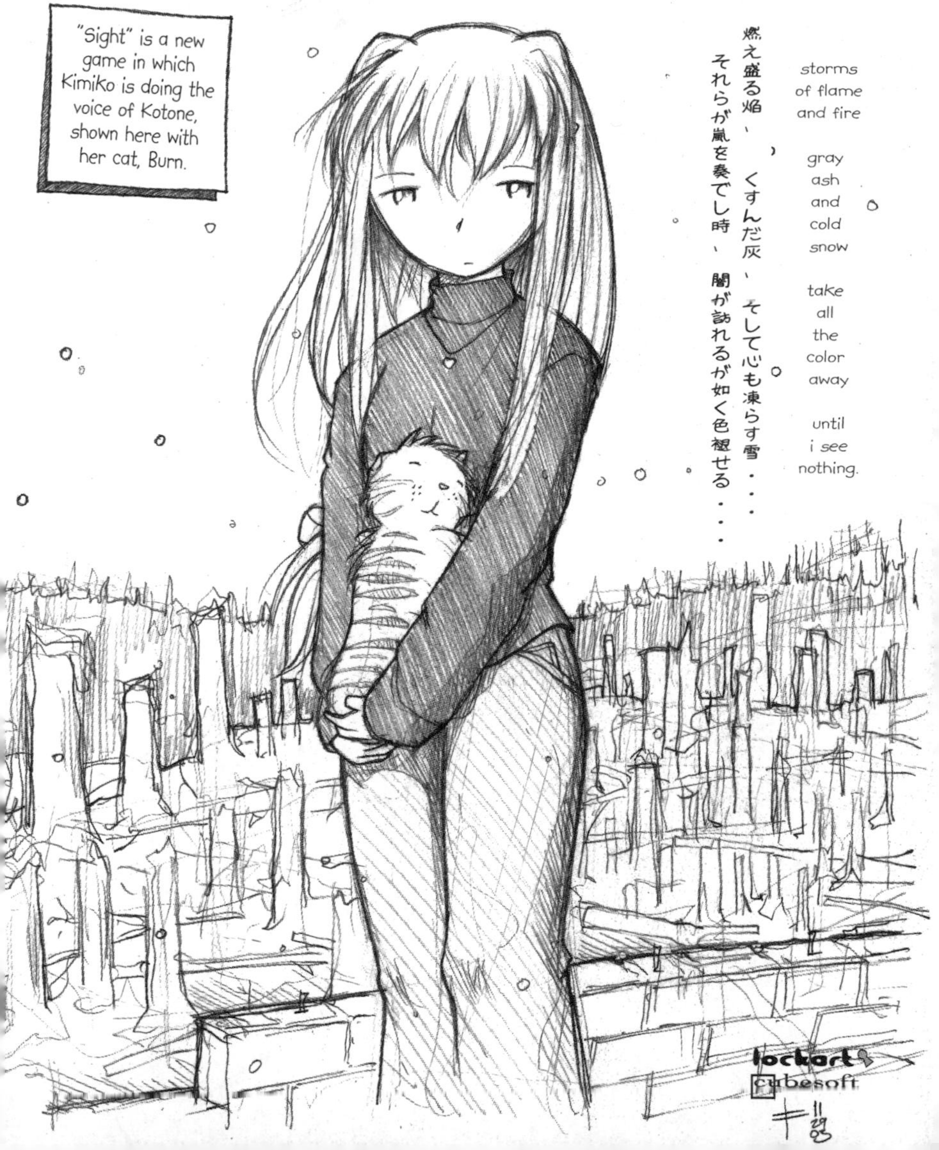

燃え盛る焔、くすんだ灰、そして心も凍らす雪・・・
それらが嵐を奏でし時、闇が訪れるが如く色褪せる・・・
storms of flame and fire
gray ash and cold snow
take all the color away
until i see nothing.
lockart
cubesoft

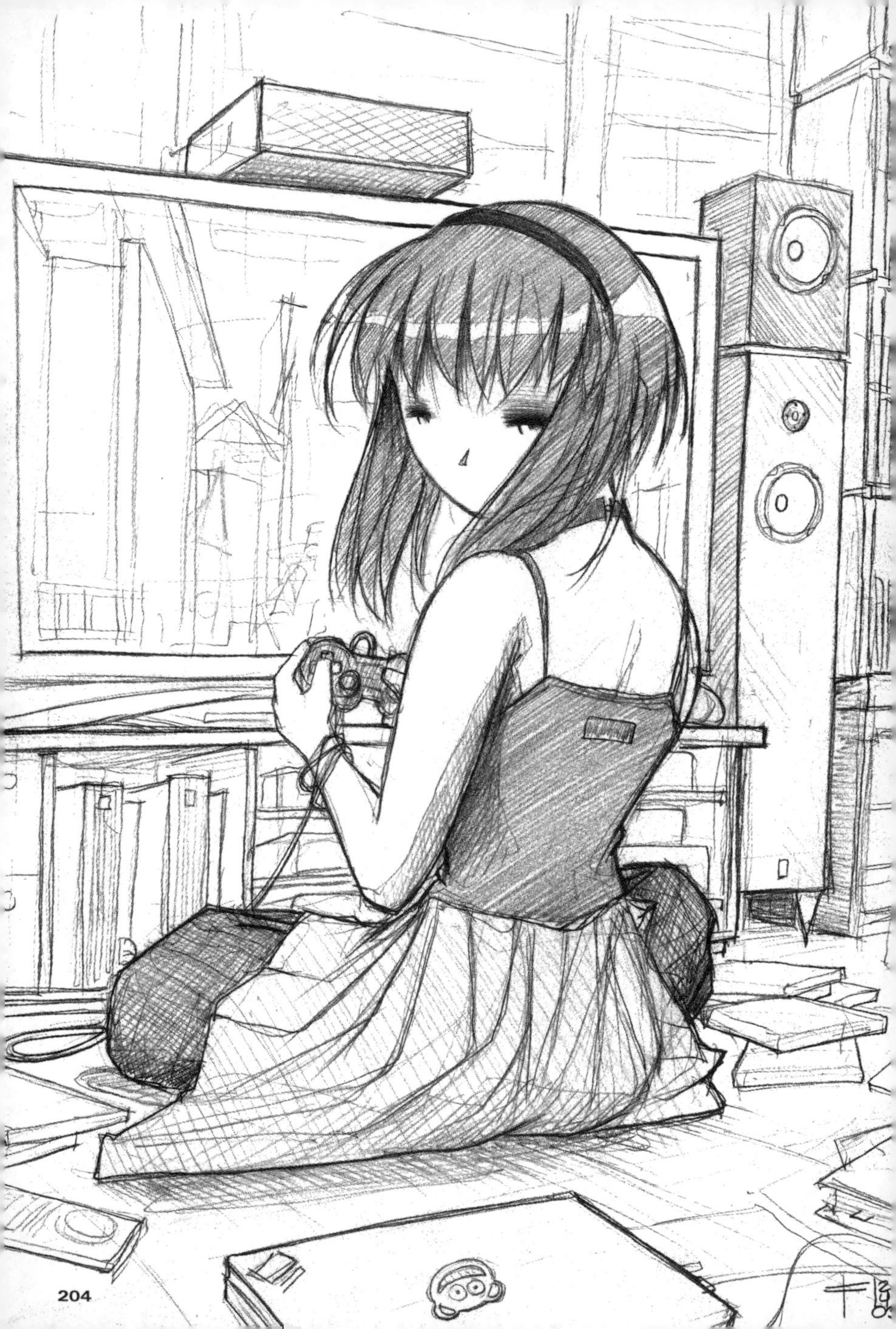

NOT-REALLY-DEAD-BUT-IN-JAPAN PIRO DAY

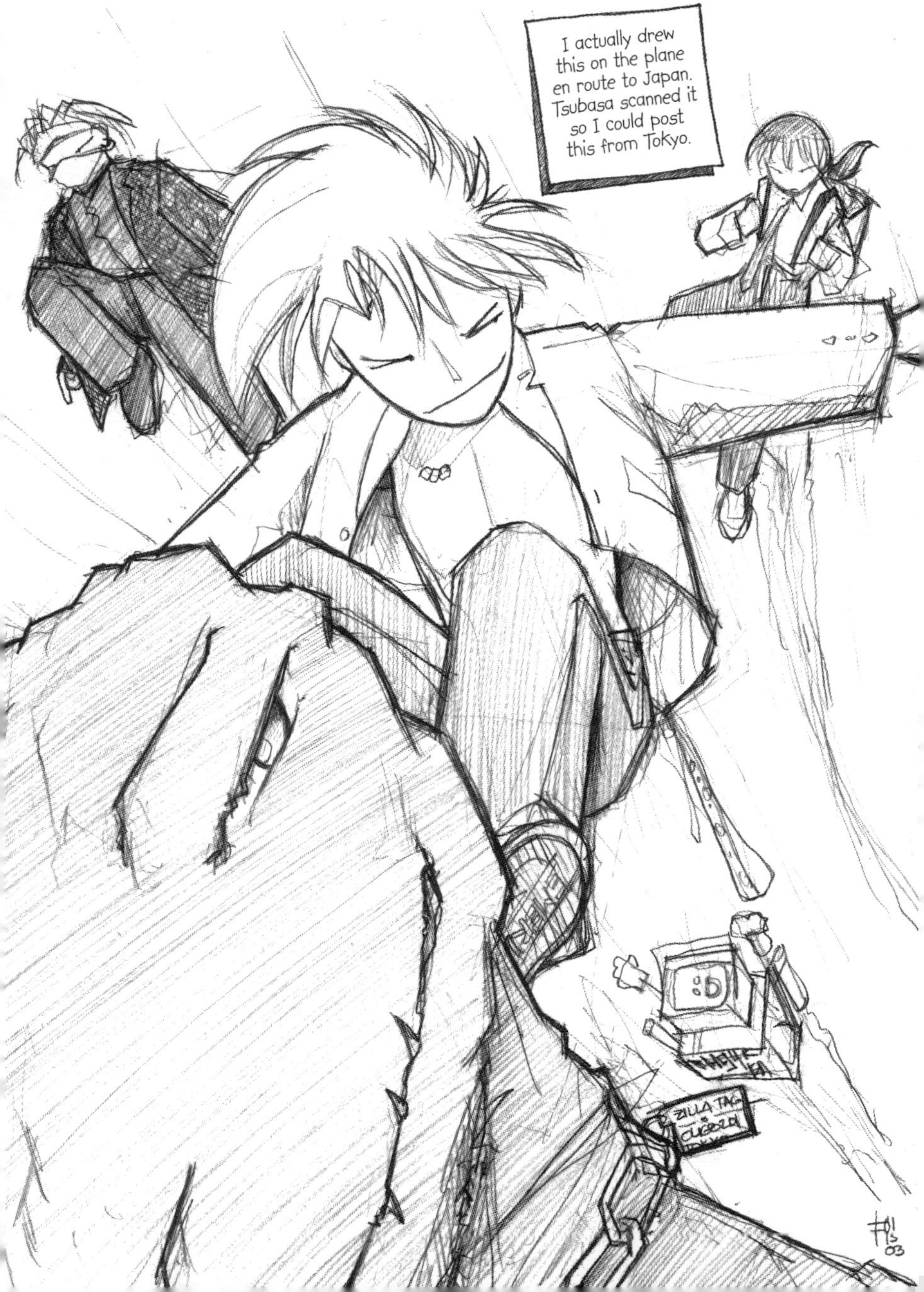
I actually drew this on the plane en route to Japan. Tsubasa scanned it so I could post this from Tokyo.

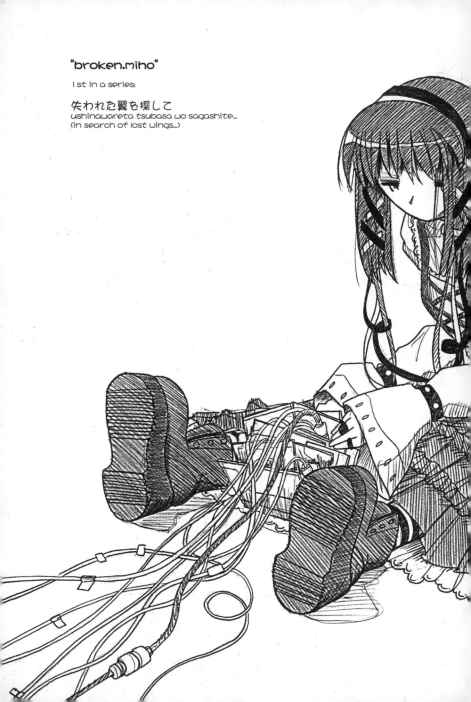

"broken.miho"

1st in a series:

失われた翼を探して
ushinawareta tsubasa wo sagashite...
(in search of lost wings...)

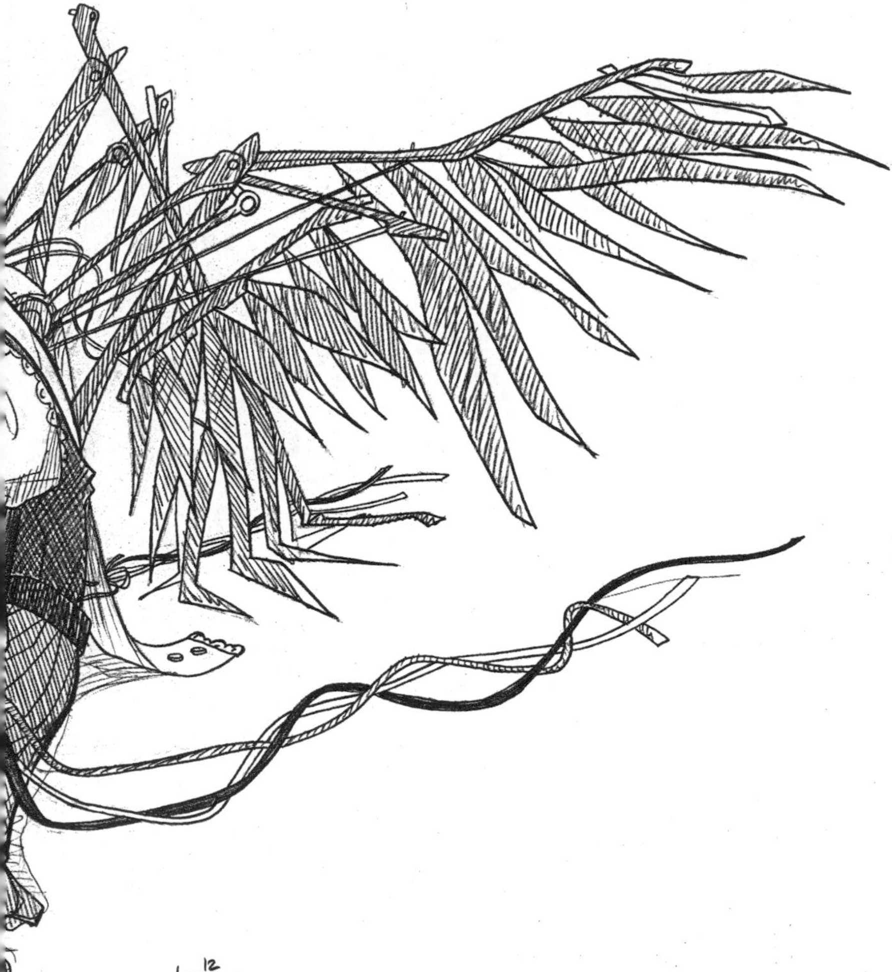

"Grey Erika"

2nd in a series:

失われた翼を探して
ushinawareta tsubasa wo sagashite...
(in search of lost wings...)

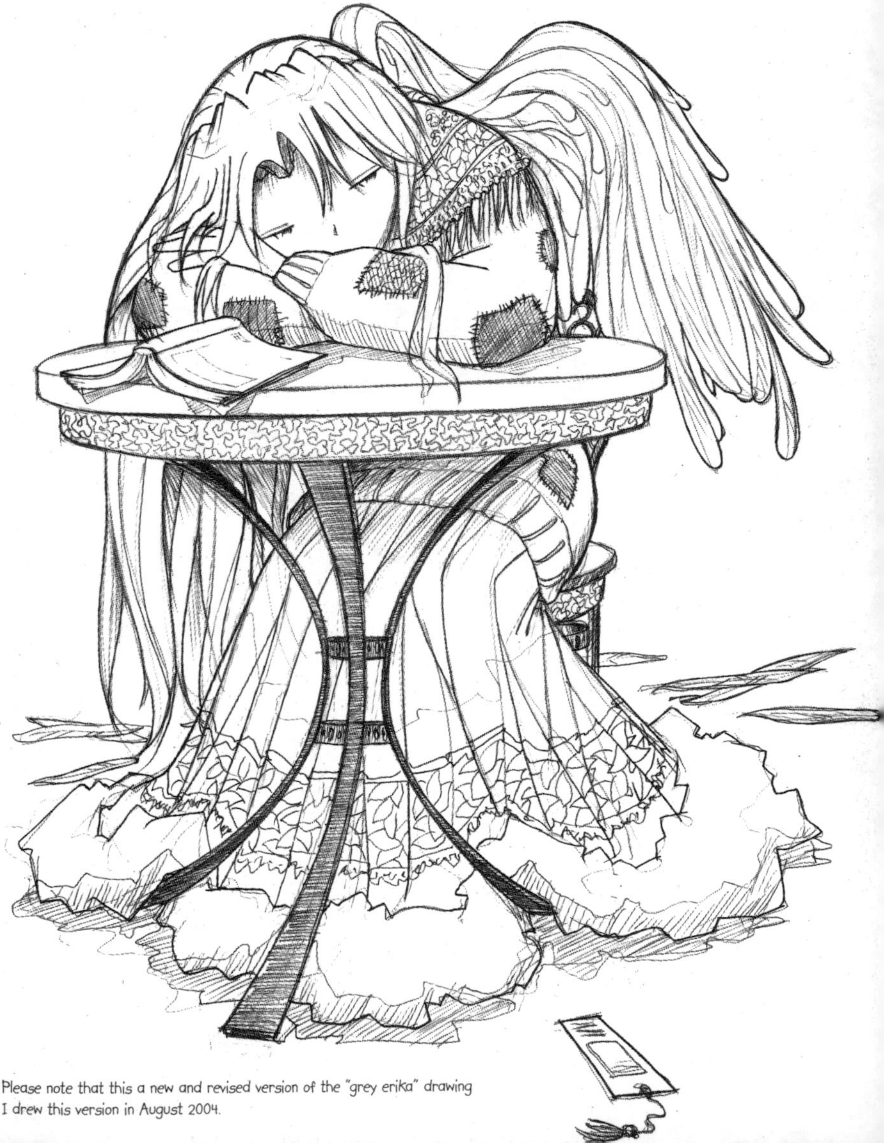

Please note that this a new and revised version of the "grey erika" drawing
I drew this version in August 2004.

"kimiko"

3rd in a series:

失われた翼を探して
ushinawareta tsubasa wo sagashite...
(in search of lost wings...)

"small feathers"

4th in a series:

失われた翼を探して
ushinawareta tsubasa wo sagashite...
(in search of lost wings...)

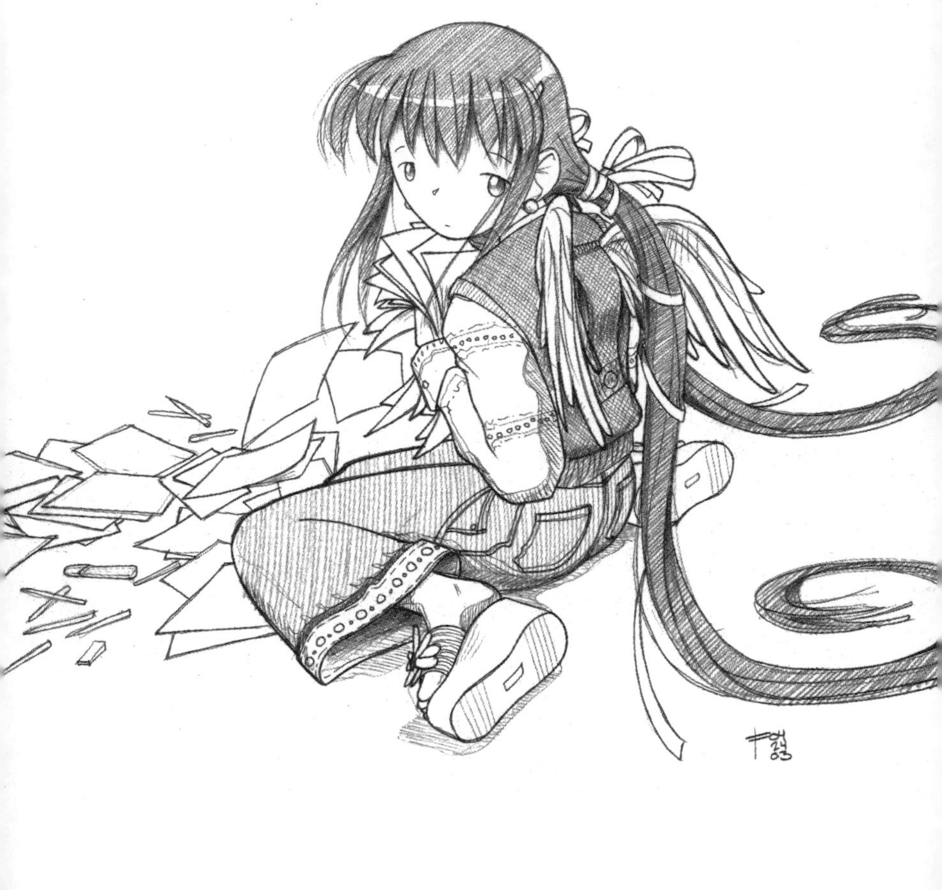

"glancing upwards"

5th in a series:

失われた翼を探して
ushinawareta tsubasa wo sagashite...
(in search of lost wings...)

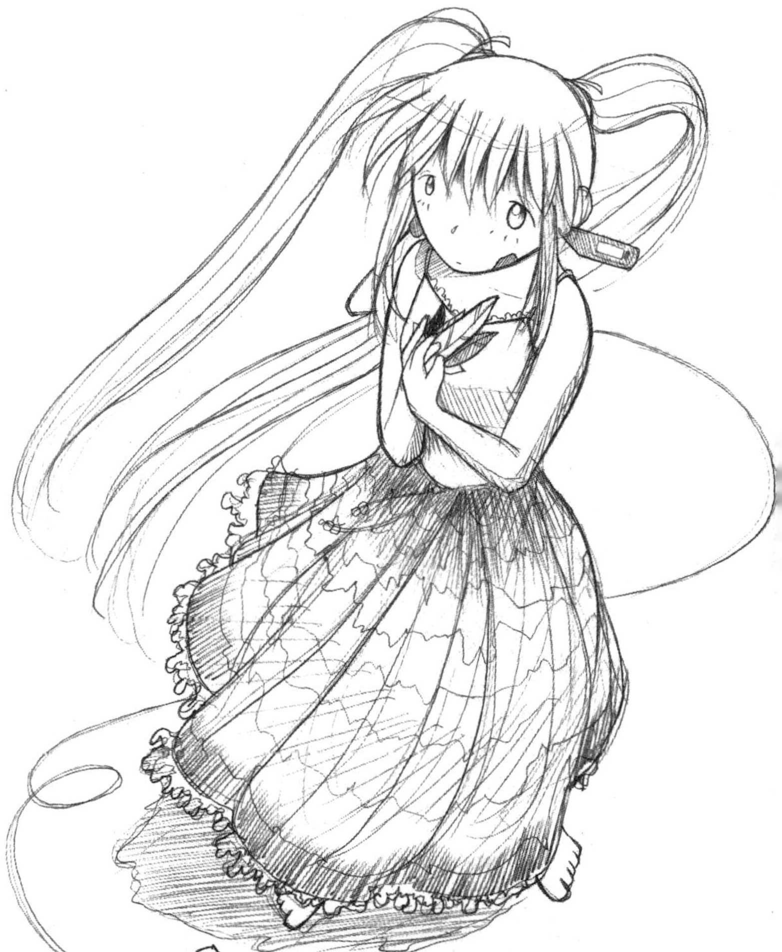

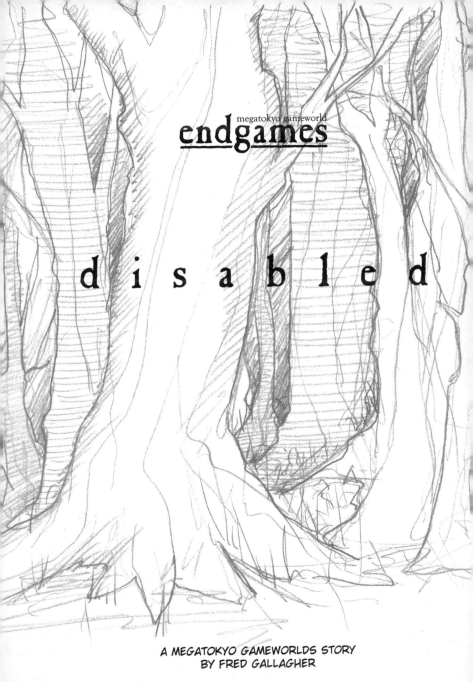

megatokyo gameworld

endgames

disabled

A MEGATOKYO GAMEWORLDS STORY
BY FRED GALLAGHER

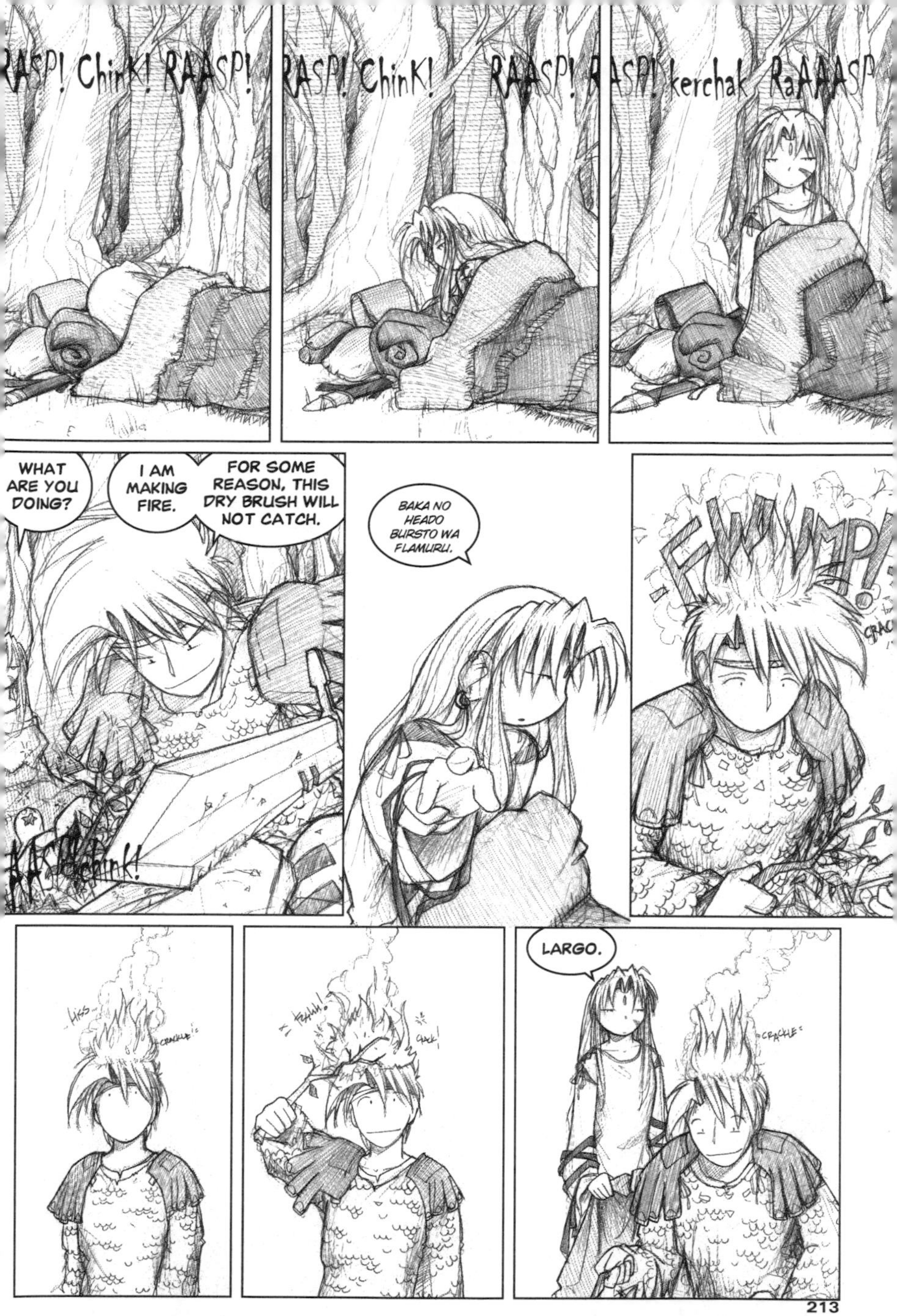
RASP! Chink! RAASP!
RASP! Chink!
RAASP! R
ASP! kerchak
RaAASP
WHAT ARE YOU DOING?
I AM MAKING FIRE.
FOR SOME REASON, THIS DRY BRUSH WILL NOT CATCH.
chink!
BAKA NO HEADO BURSTO WA FLAMURU.
FWUMP!
Hiss...
CRACKLE
CRACK!
LARGO.
CRACKLE

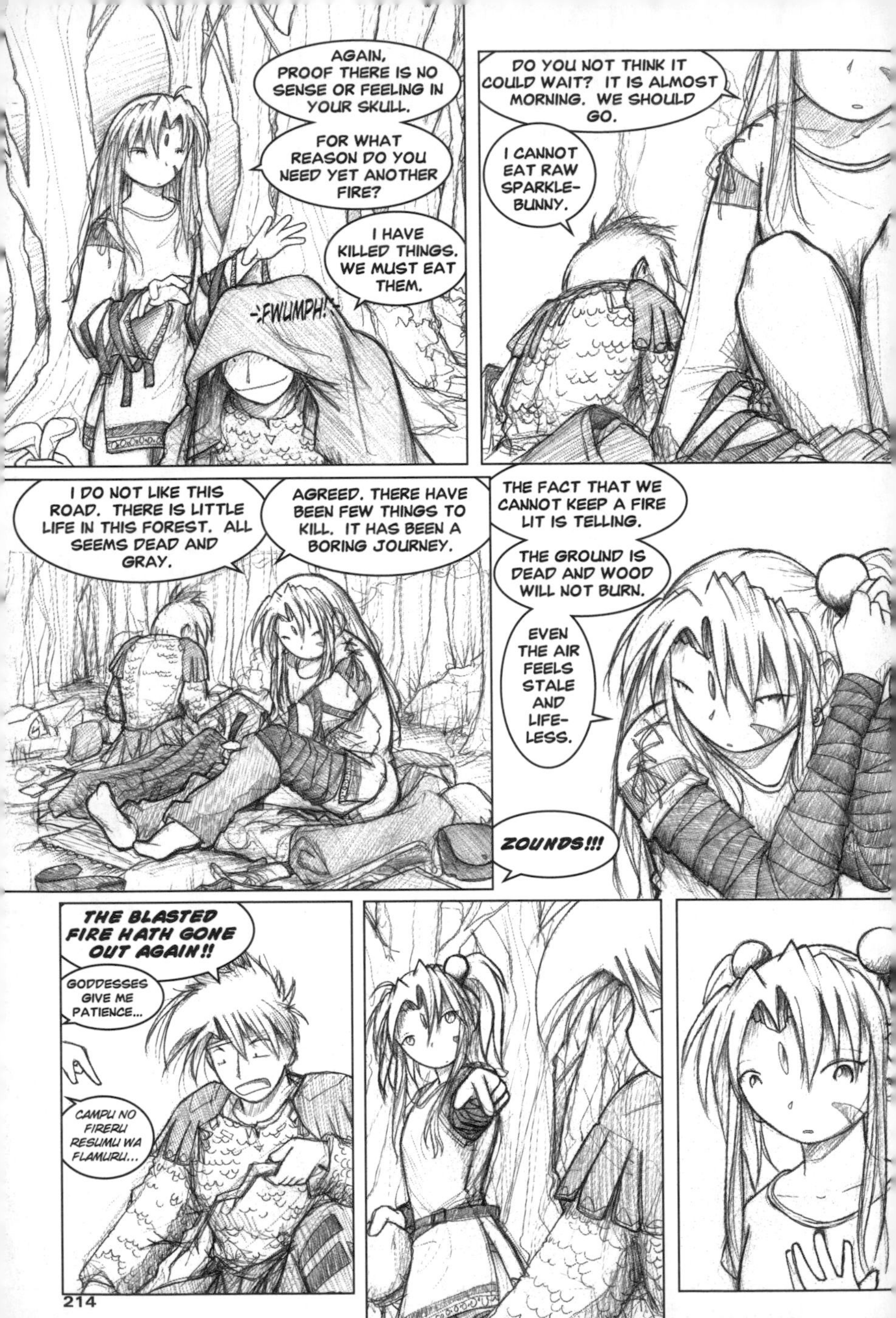
AGAIN, PROOF THERE IS NO SENSE OR FEELING IN YOUR SKULL.
FOR WHAT REASON DO YOU NEED YET ANOTHER FIRE?
I HAVE KILLED THINGS. WE MUST EAT THEM.
-FWUMPH!-
DO YOU NOT THINK IT COULD WAIT? IT IS ALMOST MORNING. WE SHOULD GO.
I CANNOT EAT RAW SPARKLE-BUNNY.
I DO NOT LIKE THIS ROAD. THERE IS LITTLE LIFE IN THIS FOREST. ALL SEEMS DEAD AND GRAY.
AGREED. THERE HAVE BEEN FEW THINGS TO KILL. IT HAS BEEN A BORING JOURNEY.
THE FACT THAT WE CANNOT KEEP A FIRE LIT IS TELLING.
THE GROUND IS DEAD AND WOOD WILL NOT BURN.
EVEN THE AIR FEELS STALE AND LIFE-LESS.
ZOUNDS!!!
THE BLASTED FIRE HATH GONE OUT AGAIN!!
GODDESSES GIVE ME PATIENCE...
CAMPU NO FIRERU RESUMU WA FLAMURU...

EXCESIVUS CRUSHURU NO EXSANGUINORU TOTO MAXIMUS SURO NYO!

EHM... WHAT BE YOU DOING, PIRO-GOETH?

THAT SPELL SHOULD HAVE CRUSHED YOU FROM HEAD TO FOOT, SQUEEZING THE FLUIDS FROM YOUR BODY AS YOU WRITHED IN AGONY, DYING A HORRIBLE DEATH.

(SIGH) BUT NOTHING HAP-PENED.

YOU SIGHETH AS IF THIS IS A BAD THING.

SO, YE CAN'NA DO MAGIC ANYMORE? IS IT THE DEAD AIR?

NO, THE AIR IS NOT DEAD. THERE ARE THREADS OF ENERGY AROUND US, BUT FOR SOME REASON I CANNOT DRAW UPON THEM.

I CAN NO LONGER DO EVEN THE SIMPLEST SPELL.

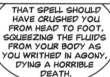

PERHAPS IT BE THE UNDEAD-NESS OF THE FOREST. THIS IS AN 3VIL WOOD.

THE LIVING CANNOT USE THE ENERGIES OF THE UNDEAD.

ONCE WE ARE CLEAR OF IT, I AM SURE YOUR POWERS WILL RETURN.

SEE? THERE BE THE GATES OF FOGOURETH.

WHY AM I NOT COMFORT-ED?

BECAUSE YE ARE A GRUMPY OLD WENCH.

COME, I AM IN NEED OF BREW.

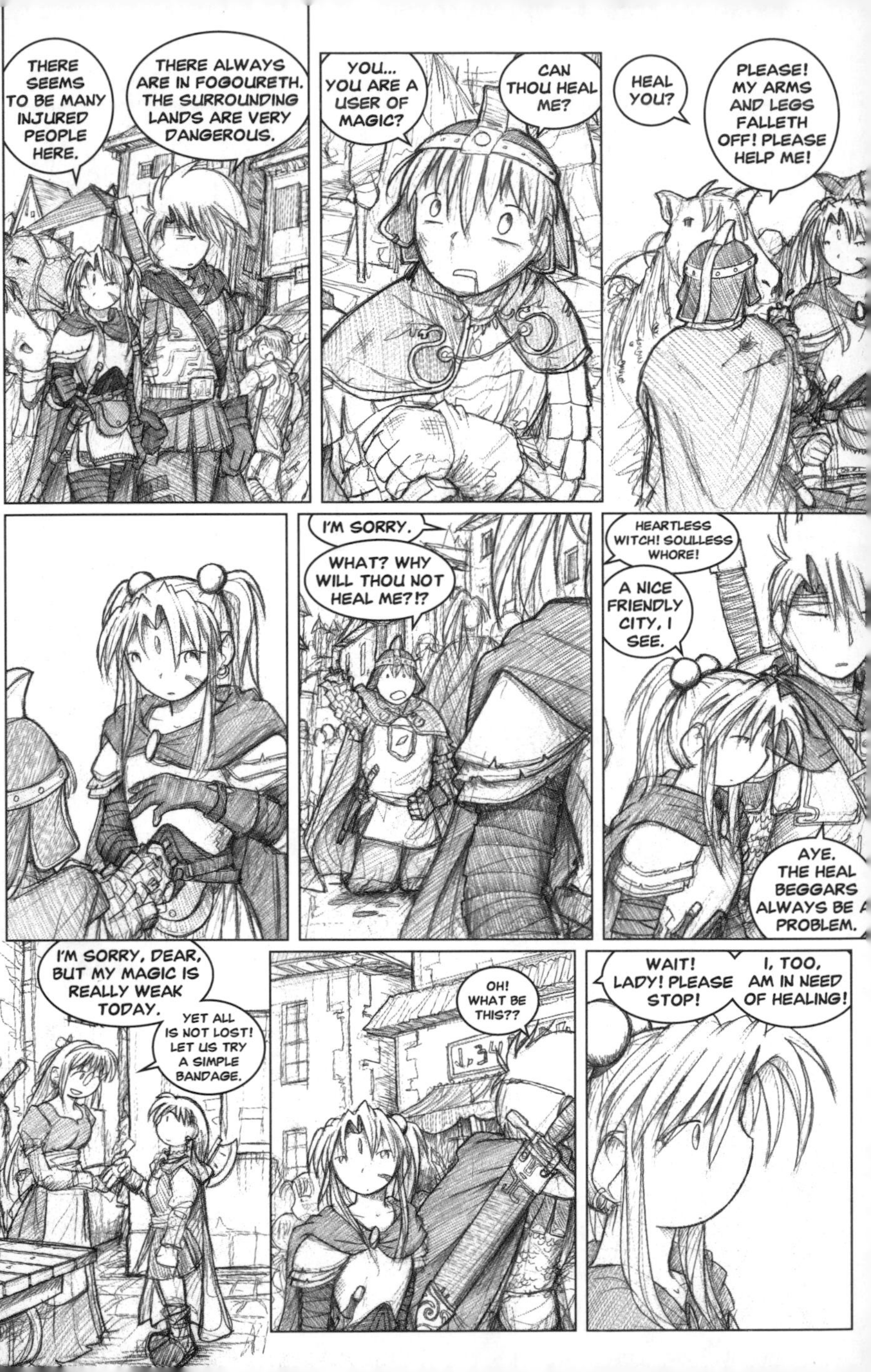
THERE SEEMS TO BE MANY INJURED PEOPLE HERE.
THERE ALWAYS ARE IN FOGOURETH. THE SURROUNDING LANDS ARE VERY DANGEROUS.
YOU... YOU ARE A USER OF MAGIC?
CAN THOU HEAL ME?
HEAL YOU?
PLEASE! MY ARMS AND LEGS FALLETH OFF! PLEASE HELP ME!
I'M SORRY.
WHAT? WHY WILL THOU NOT HEAL ME?!?
HEARTLESS WITCH! SOULLESS WHORE!
A NICE FRIENDLY CITY, I SEE.
AYE. THE HEAL BEGGARS ALWAYS BE A PROBLEM.
I'M SORRY, DEAR, BUT MY MAGIC IS REALLY WEAK TODAY.
YET ALL IS NOT LOST! LET US TRY A SIMPLE BANDAGE.
OH! WHAT BE THIS??
WAIT! LADY! PLEASE STOP!
I, TOO, AM IN NEED OF HEALING!

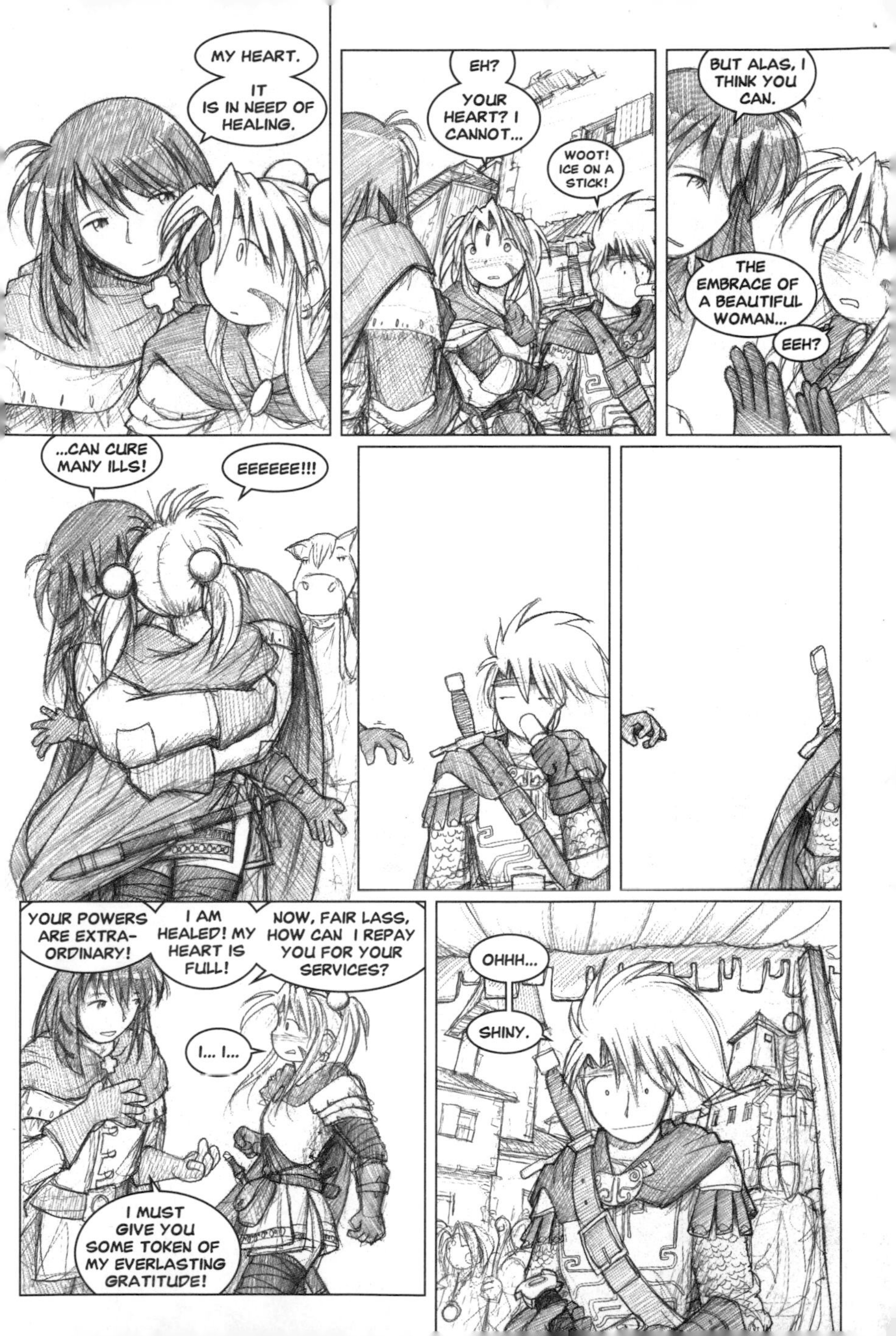
MY HEART.
IT IS IN NEED OF HEALING.
EH?
YOUR HEART? I CANNOT...
WOOT! ICE ON A STICK!
BUT ALAS, I THINK YOU CAN.
THE EMBRACE OF A BEAUTIFUL WOMAN...
EEH?
...CAN CURE MANY ILLS!
EEEEEE!!!
YOUR POWERS ARE EXTRA-ORDINARY!
I AM HEALED! MY HEART IS FULL!
NOW, FAIR LASS, HOW CAN I REPAY YOU FOR YOUR SERVICES?
I... I...
I MUST GIVE YOU SOME TOKEN OF MY EVERLASTING GRATITUDE!
OHHH...
SHINY.

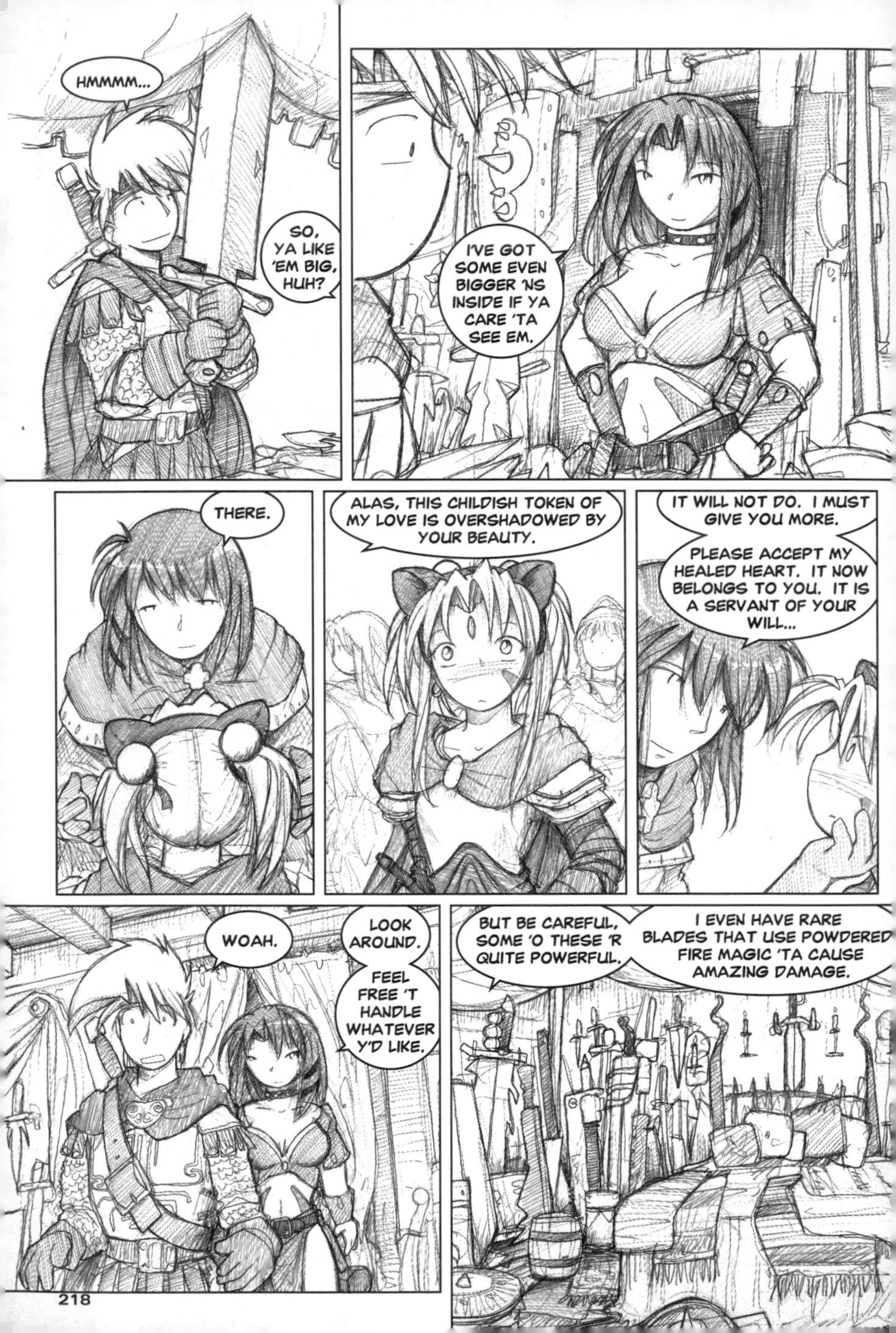
HMMMM...
SO, YA LIKE 'EM BIG, HUH?
I'VE GOT SOME EVEN BIGGER 'NS INSIDE IF YA CARE 'TA SEE EM.
THERE.
ALAS, THIS CHILDISH TOKEN OF MY LOVE IS OVERSHADOWED BY YOUR BEAUTY.
IT WILL NOT DO. I MUST GIVE YOU MORE.
PLEASE ACCEPT MY HEALED HEART. IT NOW BELONGS TO YOU. IT IS A SERVANT OF YOUR WILL...
WOAH.
LOOK AROUND.
FEEL FREE 'T HANDLE WHATEVER Y'D LIKE.
BUT BE CAREFUL, SOME 'O THESE 'R QUITE POWERFUL.
I EVEN HAVE RARE BLADES THAT USE POWDERED FIRE MAGIC 'TA CAUSE AMAZING DAMAGE.

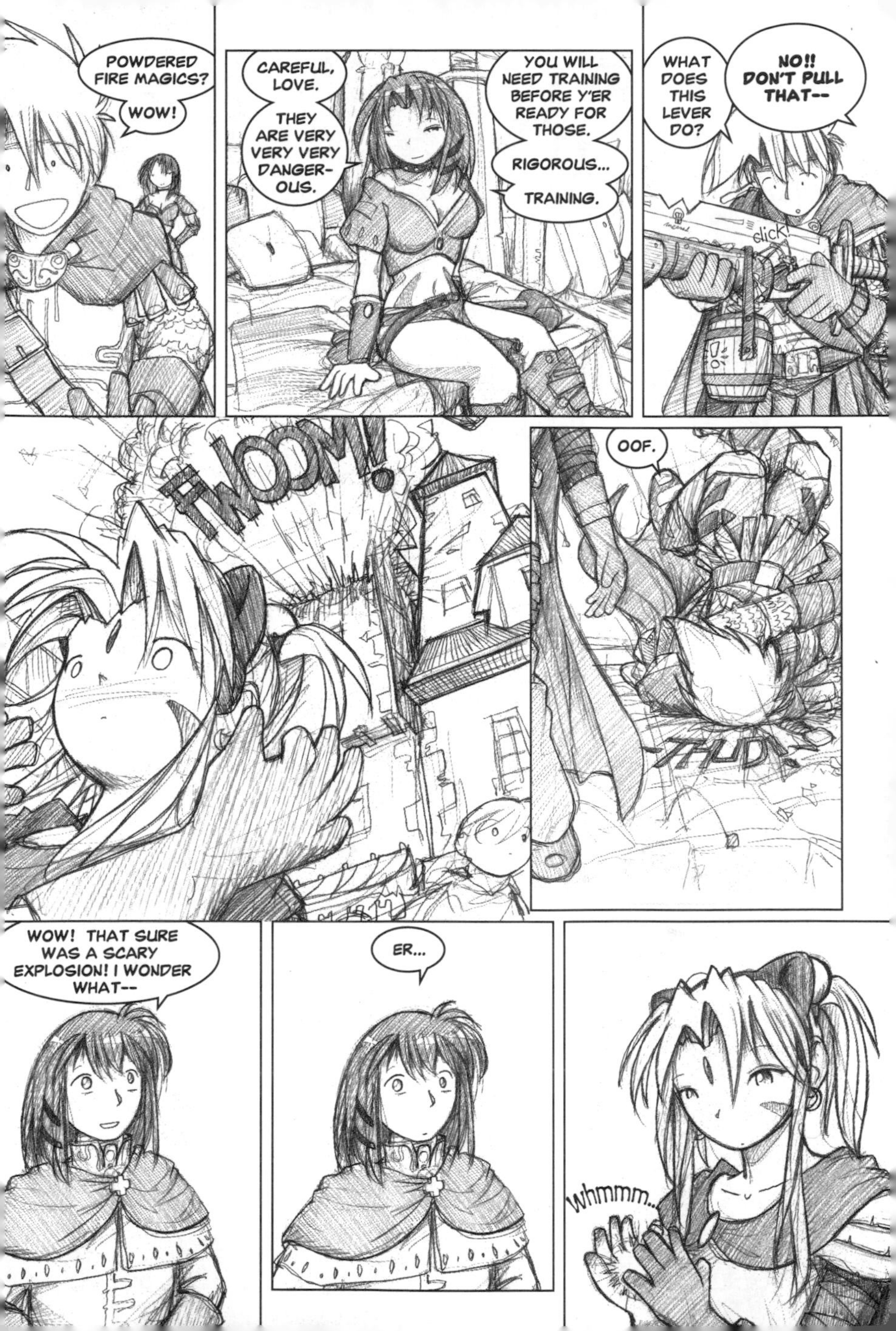
POWDERED FIRE MAGICS?
WOW!
CAREFUL, LOVE.
THEY ARE VERY VERY VERY DANGER-OUS.
YOU WILL NEED TRAINING BEFORE Y'ER READY FOR THOSE.
RIGOROUS...
TRAINING.
WHAT DOES THIS LEVER DO?
NO!! DON'T PULL THAT--
click!
FWOOM!!
OOF.
THUD
WOW! THAT SURE WAS A SCARY EXPLOSION! I WONDER WHAT--
ER...
whmmm...

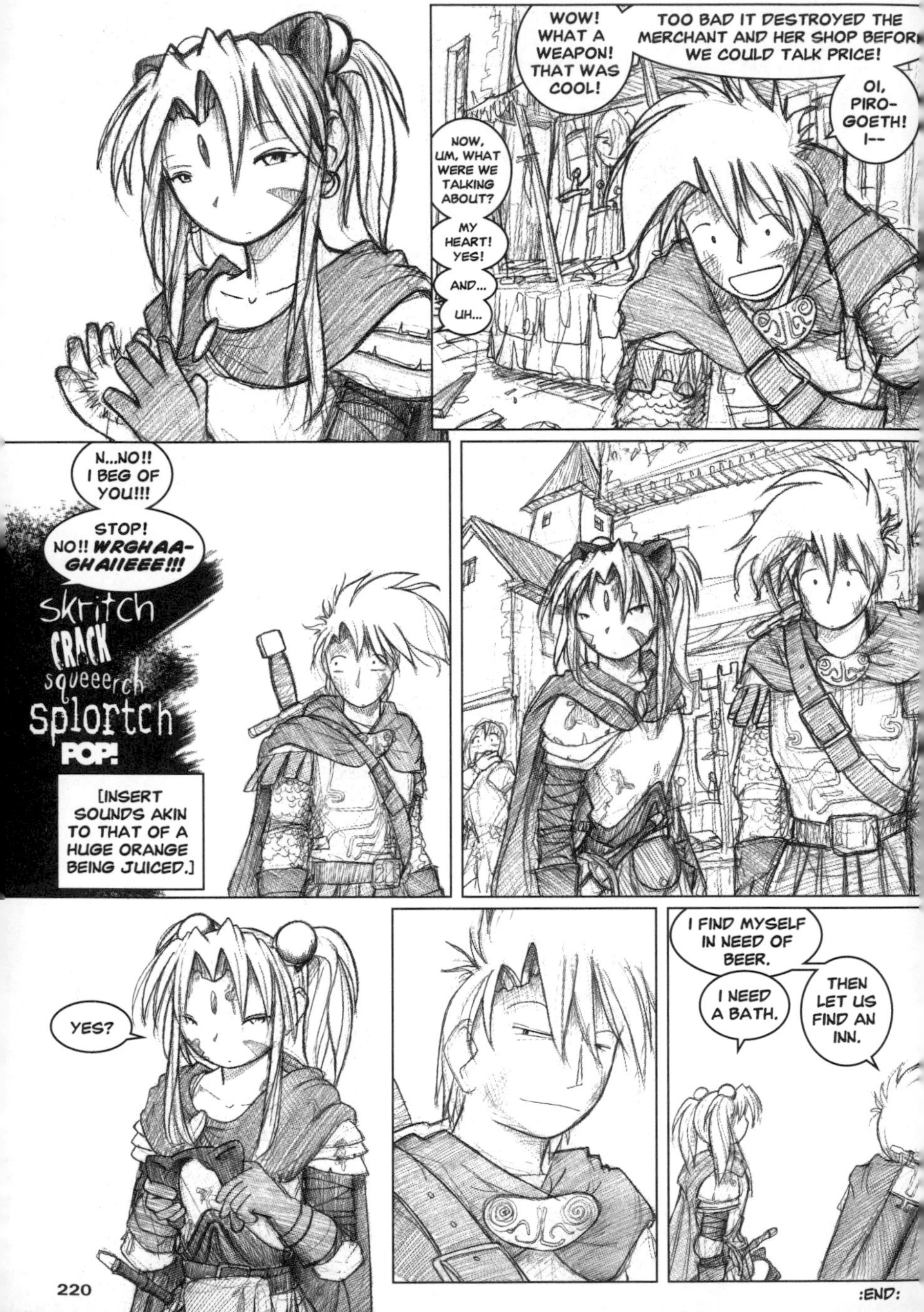
WOW! WHAT A WEAPON! THAT WAS COOL!
TOO BAD IT DESTROYED THE MERCHANT AND HER SHOP BEFORE WE COULD TALK PRICE!
OI, PIRO-GOETH! I--
NOW, UM, WHAT WERE WE TALKING ABOUT?
MY HEART! YES!
AND...
UH...
N...NO!! I BEG OF YOU!!!
STOP! NO!! WRGHAA-GHAIIEEE!!!
skritch
CRACK
squeeerch
splortch
POP!
[INSERT SOUNDS AKIN TO THAT OF A HUGE ORANGE BEING JUICED.]
YES?
I FIND MYSELF IN NEED OF BEER.
I NEED A BATH.
THEN LET US FIND AN INN.
:END:

Megatokyo - Volume 3 Index

This book contains strips from Chapters 3 and 4 and includes extra material produced between September 2002 and January 2004. For more information and more comics, visit www.megatokyo.com

Page No.	Strip Title	Date	Online Strip ID
	Chapter 03		
9	Am I Your Number One Fan?	2002-09-02	307
10	forgetting lots of things	2002-09-09	308
11	can you come hold my hair?	2002-09-13	310
12	your little fantasy	2002-09-17	311
13	multiplayer mode	2002-09-19	312
14	not as hot as coffee	2002-09-22	313
15	Camping the Sewer System	2002-09-25	314
16	a little too 3D for a 2D girl	2002-10-02	317
17	Damn Ninjas	2002-10-07	319
18	not enough to get deported.	2002-10-11	321
19	It's not safe here	2002-10-21	325
20	Tug and cup	2002-10-30	329
21	Careful, she s packing!	2002-11-01	330
22	numb to the devastation	2002-11-04	331
23	I know that stance	2002-11-06	332
24	Flowers and Chalk	2002-11-08	333
25	finally noticed	2002-11-11	334
26	Seraphim Fuku Check	2002-11-15	336
27	Today s Lesson	2002-11-20	338
28	blind and busted	2002-11-22	339
29	I will not teach NPCs	2002-11-25	340
30	the disappointment of reality	2002-11-27	341
31	student training	2002-11-29	342
32	damaged, as you are	2002-12-02	343
33	Super Moe-Moe Ball	2002-12-04	344
34	kisses of death	2002-12-06	345
35	oh look, more bombs.	2002-12-11	347
36	close range cruise	2002-12-13	348
37	just a little claw	2002-12-16	349
38	damaged in battle	2002-12-18	350
39	a few drawings and a little hype	2002-12-20	351
40	just... stuff	2002-12-27	353
41	Martians, actually	2002-12-30	354
42	unscheduled damage events	2003-01-03	355
43	pourtent	2003-01-06	356
44	falling and catching	2003-01-08	357
45	bottomless cup	2003-01-10	358
46	The Shame of the Gamera Family	2003-01-13	359
47	Real Player Characters	2003-01-15	360
48	this was nothin!	2003-01-20	362
49	now come along quietly!	2003-01-22	363
50	no wonder...	2003-01-24	364
51	small interruptions	2003-01-29	366
52	Boo, I have a plan	2003-02-01	367
53	Rejection Redux	2003-02-03	368
54	they re gonna change it	2003-02-05	369
55	crossed whiskers	2002-02-10	371
56	you already have fans!	2002-02-12	372
57	your first fan	2003-02-19	374
58	please, let me keep it	2003-02-21	375
59	That was very rude, Mr. Turtle!	2003-02-24	376
60	anime music is elevator music	2003-02-26	377
61	tossing turtles	2003-02-28	378
62	are you sad, mr. Piro-san?	2003-03-03	379
63	ping timeout	2003-03-05	380
04	Curiouser and Curiouser	2003-03-07	381
65	separate games	2003-03-10	382
66	reading into things	2003-03-14	384
67	the blissful ignorance of absentmindedness	2003-03-17	385
68	missing trains	2003-03-19	386
69	did you get her phone number?	2003-03-21	387
70	Battery Life	2003-03-26	389
71	A defensive breach	2003-03-28	390
72	ph34r m4 4ut|-|or1ty!	2003-04-02	392
73	A cornered beast is dangerous	2003-04-04	393
74	l33t 4g3n7 Largo	2003-04-08	394
75	please send more post-it notes	2003-04-11	395
76	hope for him yet	2003-04-14	396
77	just a little something	2003-04-16	397
78	Leave it to Seraphim! Julia Roberts Montage	2003-04-21	399
	Chapter 04		
79	Low Ping Rate	2003-04-23	402
80	Cereal Experiments Largo	2003-04-30	403
81	end user dress codes	2003-05-02	404
82	kuchun!	2003-05-05	405
83	a little more complicated	2003-05-07	406
84	can I get online, piro-san?	2003-05-12	408
85	someone to show me	2003-05-14	409
86	the smell of death is strong here	2003-05-21	412

Page No.	Strip Title	Date	Online Strip ID
87	dead batteries	2003-05-23	413
88	nothing at all	2003-05-26	414
89	Lead and Follow	2003-05-28	415
90	chomp!	2003-05-30	416
91	meanwhile... busy girl	2003-06-02	417
92	big trouble	2003-06-04	418
93	meanwhile... tug tug	2003-06-06	419
94	out of print	2003-06-09	420
95	avoided battles	2003-06-11	421
96	the helpless, damaged victim look	2003-06-13	422
97	an effective team	2003-06-16	423
98	where are they?	2003-06-20	425
99	after all these years	2003-06-23	426
100	a more recent vintage	2003-06-25	427
101	amusing little enigmas	2003-06-27	428
102	Klutzy is Cute	2003-06-30	429
103	equipment request	2003-07-02	430
104	mutual confusion	2003-07-07	432
105	suffering in silence	2003-07-08	433
106	mapping the real	2003-07-11	434
107	uneaten cake	2003-07-14	435
108	Threat Assessment	2003-07-16	436
109	Boo 2.0	2003-07-18	437
110	Just about done	2003-07-28	441
111	node for a social life	2003-07-30	442
112	Quite Real	2003-08-01	443
113	mirror, mirror...	2003-08-04	444
114	A nice friend	2003-08-06	445
115	Meanwhile... A little more sad	2003-08-11	447
116	dangerous things	2003-08-15	449
117	Meanwhile... pull here for cheer	2003-08-18	450
118	43 seconds	2003-08-20	451
119	Culture Shock	2003-08-27	454
120	posted anonymously	2003-08-29	455
121	a woman s voice	2003-09-03	456
122	intentions	2003-09-05	457
123	operational chatter	2003-09-08	458
124	tactical descent	2003-09-10	459
125	looming threats	2003-09-12	460
126	move those legs	2003-09-15	461
127	tragic deployments	2003-09-17	462
128	no less dangerous	2003-09-19	463
129	4659 7448	2003-09-22	464
130	a programed reaction	2003-09-24	465
131	not d34d yet	2003-09-26	466
132	Fly, you fool	2003-09-29	467
133	cheating	2003-10-01	468
134	data recovery	2003-10-06	470
135	feeling trust	2003-10-08	471
136	I will punish you most painfully!	2003-10-10	472
137	just a little something	2003-10-13	473
138	that trojan pony	2003-10-15	474
139	i liked yours better	2003-10-15	475
140	pl4yin it ruff	2003-10-20	476
141	he s gone	2003-10-22	477
142	hard hitting catnip	2003-10-27	479
143	dead grli3s	2003-11-07	482
144	falling off shelves	2003-11-12	484
145	extraordinarily massive	2003-11-14	485
146	credit limit	2003-11-17	486
147	proceeding with mission	2003-11-19	487
148	being decisive	2003-11-21	488
149	the ups and downs of hope	2003-11-24	489
150	make me!	2003-11-26	490
151	live video feed	2003-12-01	492
152	sneaking dangerously	2003-12-03	493
153	cellphone data	2003-12-10	496
154	he took a hamster in the face...	2003-12-12	497
155	falling down	2003-12-17	499
156	illusions of safety	2003-12-19	500
157	Reassess the situation	2003-12-22	501
158	arrested flight	2003-12-29	503
159	blown cover	2004-01-07	504
160	ph33r everything and everyone	2004-01-09	505
161	thanks	2004-01-12	506
162	pokapoka bento	2004-01-14	507
163	so unlike you	2004-01-23	511
164	juggling and balancing	2004-01-26	512
165	worth the effort?	2004-01-28	513
166	the convenience of impracticality	2004-01-30	514
167	Angel Eye for the Geek Guy	2004-02-02	515
168	Largo Kart Racing!	2002-10-04	318
169	NNM: Suicidal Rocket Tap	2003-07-25	440

Shirt Guy Dom Strips

171	SGD: Ninja vs. Schoolgirl	2002-10-28	328
172	SGD: Dom no kimyou na hatsuyume	2004-01-19	509
173	Pipe Cleaner Dom Theater	2002-10-09	320

Page No.	Strip Title	Date	Online Strip ID
	One-Shot (non-story) Episodes		
175	9-11-2002... just remembering...	2002-09-11	309
176	OSE: attack of the niece and nephew	2002-09-30	316
177	Piro & Seraphim: are you done yet?	2002-11-18	337
178	RL Piro and Seraphim - The Drama, Part 2	2003-06-18	424
179	OSE: I need publicity	2004-02-11	519
180	Otakon2003 highlights	2003-08-13	448
181	The few more days of Christmas...	2002-12-24	352
182	Valentines Day Doofus	2003-02-14	373
183	DPD: we got married :)	2004-02-16	521
	Grand Theft Colo		
185	Grand Theft Colo: Tokyo, Baby!	2003-04-18	398
186	ph34r d4 fr0	2003-04-23	400
187	GTC: My Poor Little Benelli	2004-02-04	516
188	GTC: Mechanical Enhancements	2004-02-06	517
189	GTC: Runaway Process	2004-02-09	518
190	GTC: more special, little pretty	2004-02-13	520
191	GTC: a hands on approach	2004-02-18	522
192	GTC: rro seeing the lines	2004-02-20	523
193	GTC: piro dead arting	2004-02-23	524
194	GTC: hard reboot	2004-02-24	525
	Dead Piro Art Days		
196	DPD: Fail Condition	2002-10-26	327
197	DPD: b4k4.md4	2003-03-12	383
198	DPD: Ping & Makoto	2003-05-07	407
199	DPD: l33t F0ld1ng skillz	2003-05-16	410
200	DPD: Megadustrial:r3m1x	2003-07-23	439
201	DPD: Motion Stopped	2003-08-08	446
202	DPD: Artifact no. 1	2003-10-03	469
203	DPD: take all the color away	2003-11-28	491
204	DPD: Miho timesinking	2003-12-15	498
205	DPD: Japan Invasion	2004-01-17	508
	In Search Of Lost Wings		
206-207	DPD: broken miho	2002-12-09	346
208	DPD: Grey Erika	2002-01-27	365
209	DPD: Kimiko	2003-02-07	370
210	DPD: small feathers	2003-04-25	401
211	DPD: glancing upwards	2003-07-04	431

STOP

This is the back of the book!

Uhm, *Megatokyo* was originally written in English, not Japanese you know. English reads left to right, remember? Duh. Stop being stupid, turn the book over and start from the other side.

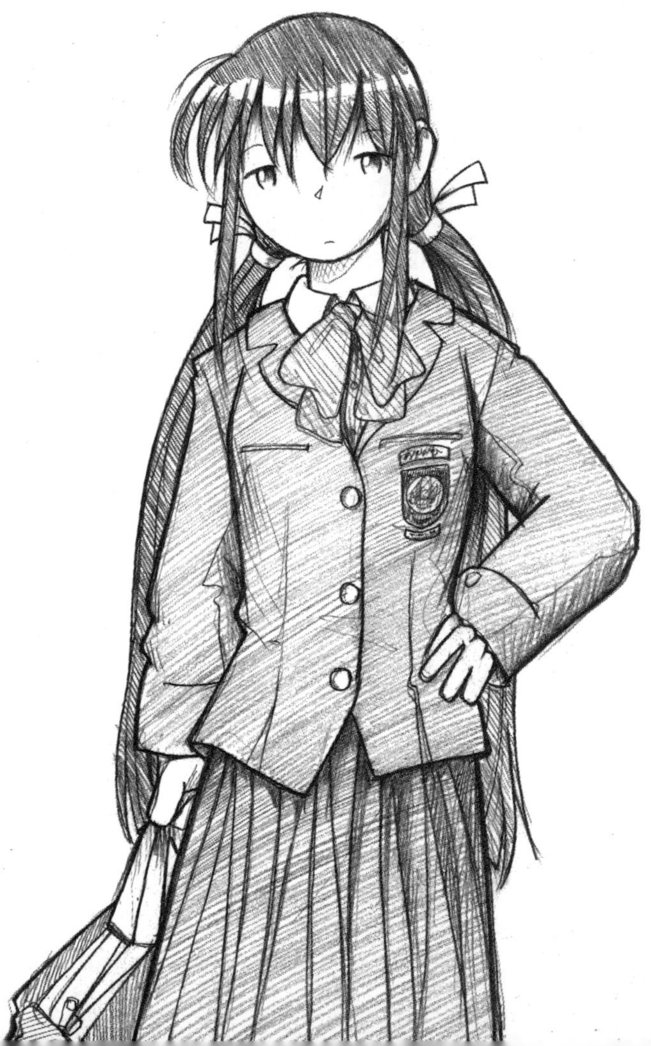